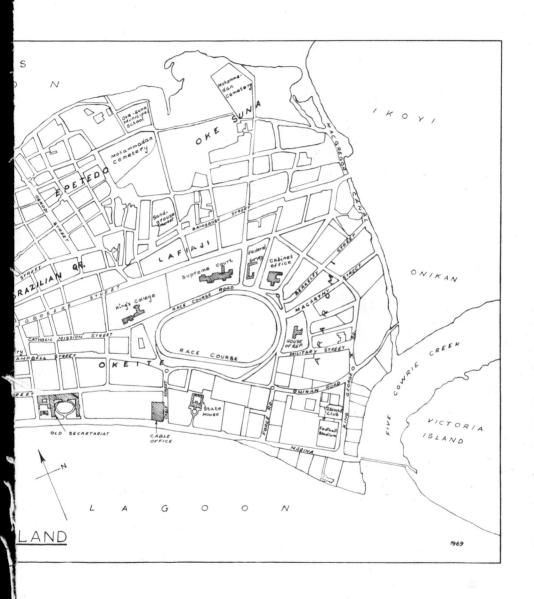

1969

Urbanization and Political Change

# URBANIZATION AND POLITICAL CHANGE

## The Politics of Lagos, 1917-1967

*by*
*Pauline H. Baker*

*University of California Press*
*Berkeley · Los Angeles · London*
1974

*University of California Press*
*Berkeley and Los Angeles, California*

*University of California Press, Ltd.*
*London, England*

*Copyright © 1974 by The Regents of the University of California*
*ISBN: 0–520–02066–9*
*Library of Congress Catalog Card Number: 70–162001*

*Printed in the United States of America*

To
Raymond

# Preface

In this study I examine the impact of urbanization on the politics of tropical Africa's largest city. The analysis focuses on three central concerns: the role of the African urban poor, the formation of a community power structure in a non-Western environment, and the dynamics of modernization in a developing city.

Nearly all my research was done while I was living in Lagos during the protracted crisis that began with the military coup d'etat of January 1966 and extended into the Nigerian Civil War. Although not directly concerned with the issues of the war, this study does probe the causes of conflicts that arise from the interaction between communal nationalism and modern socioeconomic aspirations. To the extent that such conflicts are fundamental to the urban problems of many modernizing societies, this work may have wide comparative relevance.

Many authors of books on Africa feel compelled to point out that their works are apt to be dated by the time they appear in print. Publications on urban politics are especially vulnerable to this defect, owing to the pace of events on the continent, and I am therefore no exception to this literary trend. Since the completion of this study, many dramatic changes have occurred in Lagos.

Among the most significant developments has been the continuing increase in the city's population. By 1972 Greater Lagos was estimated to contain 1.8 to 2 million people; by 1985 the city might grow to well over 4 million people. The increase was particularly noticeable after the end of the Nigerian Civil War, when the rate of migration seemed higher than ever before in the city's history. This urban population explosion has inevitably placed an unprecedented strain on the resources of the city government, which has been undergoing marked structural transformations during the period of military rule.

After the January 1966 coup d'etat, a civilian caretaker committee was appointed on the basis of functional representation by Colonel (now Brigadier) Mobolaji Johnson, the military governor of Lagos State. Spurred by strong public criticism of the city's administration, Governor Johnson set up a tribunal of inquiry in 1969, under the chairmanship of Chief J. S. O. Ogunnaike, to review the entire local government structure of the state. As a result of the tribunal's findings, a new caretaker committee for Lagos was appointed in 1972; it was based on the principle of geographical or ward representation employed by the old civilian regime. Colonel D. K. Sho-Silva, a Lagosian of Brazilian (or Amaro) descent, was installed as chairman of the council. This was the first and, at the time of this writing, the only instance of military rule reaching directly down to the local government level in Nigeria.

In another noteworthy development during the same year, Governor Johnson merged the Lagos Executive Development Board, formerly a federal statutory corporation, with the Ikeja Planning Authority and the Epe Planning Authority to form the Lagos State Development and Property Corporation. The new body has responsibility for the planning and development of commercial, industrial, and residential property and is accountable solely to the Lagos State government.

Lagos today continues to function as the nerve center of the most populous and prosperous country in sub-Saharan Africa. But it presents a disturbing picture of a community overwhelmed by urban problems encountered in both the developed and developing worlds. Like many Western cities, it is suffering from serious housing shortages, chronic traffic jams, an increase in the crime rate, inner city decay, pollution, weak financial resources, and a largely unstable urban population. These difficulties are compounded by uncontrolled expansion and growth, painfully poor social services, an inadequate administrative staff, unsanitary environmental conditions, corruption in official circles, and widespread unemployment, particularly among young school leavers who form the bulk of newly arrived immigrants.

The intervention of military rule in city government is indicative both of the importance that higher authorities attach to the capital and of the enormous complexities involved in the city's administration.

None of these transformations, however, alter the conclusions drawn in this study. Rather, they underscore the trends observed regarding the nature and the pace of urban change, and they place into sharper relief the social and political tensions stemming from rapid urbanization.

I am grateful to the people who aided me in this endeavor. Professor Richard L. Sklar, who in 1965 urged me to undertake the study, made valuable suggestions as to its preparation. Others who read all or parts of the manuscript and offered encouragement are Professors C. Sylvester Whitaker, Jr., Charles R. Nixon, Michael F. Lofchie, Robert R. Griffeth, and Gerald J. Bender. I am also indebted to Professors James S. Coleman and M. G. Smith for their stimulating teaching which greatly influenced my venture into African studies. Although they bear no responsibility for the interpretation of the material here, all have contributed in various ways to the production of this work.

Among the many Nigerians who provided generous assistance, I owe a special note of thanks to Oba Adeyinka Oyekan II, Chief H. O. Davies, Chief T. O. S. Benson, F. S. McEwen, Chief Adeniran Ogunsanya, Alhaji G. O. Dawodu, Alhaji Abdul F. Masha, N. A. Taiwo, Mrs. Elsie Femi-Pearse, Chief Joseph I. Talabi, Chief T. A. Doherty, Alhaji L. B. Agusto, Lateef Jakande, Mrs. Modupe Caxton-Martins, and Chief E. O. Dare.

Professor T. O. Elias, the chief justice of Nigeria, made the private papers of Herbert Macaulay available to me. Alhaji H. A. B. Fasinro, the town clerk of Lagos, granted me access to the files and records of the Lagos City Council; Mr. E. O. Abisogun was particularly helpful in guiding me through this voluminous material. I would also like to express my appreciation to all the former councilors who responded, despite the unsettled times, to the social survey I conducted in Lagos.

A. A. Adefalolu and S. A. Alase, two political science students at the University of Lagos, worked for me as research assistants during the summer of 1969. Akpan James tirelessly typed several drafts of this manuscript without complaint.

A one-term study leave granted by the University of Lagos relieved me of teaching responsibilities, thus giving me time to write major portions of this work.

Field research was partly financed by a National Defense Education Act Title IV Grant issued through the Political Science Department of the University of California, Los Angeles.

Finally, I owe my greatest debt of gratitude to my husband, Raymond, without whose constant moral support and unceasing drive this work would probably never have been completed. He shared my goals, helped me survive the rough trials of production, and acted as my sharpest critic. To Raymond, therefore, this work is lovingly dedicated.

P. H. B.

Lagos, Nigeria
September 1972

# Contents

Contents

Contents

PART I

*Perspective and Setting*

# CHAPTER I

# Introduction

## THE AFRICAN CITY

In recent years, students of newly developing societies have become increasingly aware of the strategic importance of urban areas for economic and political modernization. Lucy Mair, for one, has written that "it must be in the cities that the institutions of a large-scale African society will be built up."[1] Edward Shils has asserted that "modernization is concentrated in the population of a few large urban centers.... Cities are the centers of innovation, not just technological but political as well."[2] And Peter Gutkind has argued that "it is in the town that we witness the sharpest break with the past and see the major restructuring of African society taking place.... The urban areas of Africa bring home to us in concentrated form the task before the African people."[3]

Yet, compared with other areas of research, the study of African cities has been relatively neglected, particularly in the field of political science. Students of Africa have concentrated on country-wide or regional studies, on political movements such as nationalism or Pan-Africanism, or on major institutions such as the political party, the military, or the bureaucracy.[4] The few who have turned their attention to local politics usually focus on rural areas, either because of the scope of their studies or, more frequently, because they believe that the city is not part of the real Africa.

Obviously, a stronger emphasis on rural behavior is clearly justifiable in light of the predominantly agrarian nature of African society. But, unfortunately, some observers tend to portray urban and rural areas as mutually exclusive ideal types representing, respectively, modernity and tradition. The distinction between urban life and rural life has increasingly come to be used as a short-hand expression to convey differences between elite and mass, detribalized and tribalized, or westernized and African behavior. As a result, cities have been viewed as aberrations of African society, as "bastard and hybrid extensions of tribal societies, with urban residents cast as tribesmen in town."[5]

Only recently have these premises come under critical examination through empirical studies of urban Africa.[6] After World War II social anthropologists and, to a lesser extent, urban sociologists pioneered research in this direction. Cities were then utilized, however, as instruments through which social change (i. e., behavior that deviated from village life) was measured, or through which links to the rural hinterland were examined. The approach was to juxtapose the urban community against a rural backdrop in order to gain knowledge of untouched African life as it existed before colonial contact. So long as this approach prevailed, urban communities remained the stepchild of African studies, receiving cursory treatment and second-hand attention through theoretical constructions that did not fit. Historic cities like Timbuctoo were studied essentially as tribal societies on a larger scale, while new cities like Luanshya ("Coppertown") were examined as artificial creations of foreign import.[7]

Interest in African urban areas arose among political scientists in the 1950s when revolutionary political changes began to emanate from the cities prior to independence. During the nationalist period "national politics . . . [tended] to be primarily if not exclusively centered in urban areas; usually they . . . [were] a phenomenon of capital cities."[8] Instead of viewing African cities in anthropological terms as expanded tribal societies or alien imports, political scientists were inclined to see them as microcosms of larger societies or as pacesetters of national trends through which the pulse of African politics could be analyzed. Attention was focused on the role of political elites instead of on the rural masses, on the urban intelligentsia spearheading the revolt against colonial domination and traditional social structures: "In so far as the men and women of the urban elite do control the major social institutions which are involved in the modernization of their societies, they may be regarded as core members of a new political class."[9]

Not surprisingly, from this perspective, the process of urbanization has concomitantly been conceived as a variable of economic and political development in which "the degree of urbanization is . . . related to the existence of democracy."[10] In a similar vein, economic development has been correlated with the degree of political competitiveness in the new states, urbanization serving as one of the major indexes of economic growth.[11] Now "modernization is, in large part, measured by the growth of the city."[12]

Still, despite broad hypotheses about the significance of the city, relatively little is known about the internal dynamics and developmental role of the city in contemporary Africa. The paucity of existing knowledge makes it more difficult than is usually assumed to determine precisely how the city functions: ". . . it is clear, even from West African material, that there is no single model of 'the city'; and there are many mirrors through which it can be viewed. Not enough is known of urbanization in general to enable the student of a particular city to determine what is singular or otherwise."[13] The rapid pace of African urbanization has further complicated the issue. Although Africa is the world's least urbanized continent, with every country save South Africa and Egypt having less than 10 percent of its population living in cities, it has the highest rate of urban growth.[14] In the first half of the twentieth century the urban population living in cities of 100,000 or more increased by 629 percent. By 1960 more than 20 million people, or 8.1 percent of the total African population lived in cities of that size, whereas in 1960 the figure was a little more than 1 million, or 1.1 percent.

The meaning of this rapid urbanization in terms of other developmental processes is not certain. Are African cities centers of social upheaval, as some have postulated, or do such factors as the extended family system, the numerous voluntary associations, and the mobility of the population enhance urban stability? Are cities centers of elite domination, or are urban political structures dominated by nonelites who operate independently of national leaders? Are cities the vanguard of revolutionary change, or is there an inherent conservatism in the wage-earning population? Does the African city necessarily have a modernizing impact on its inhabitants, or does traditionalism survive in the urban environment?

3

Unanswered questions like these serve to underscore the extent to which urban Africa has been neglected as an area of research.

It is against such a background that this study is cast. My primary objective is to examine political processes in an urbanizing African community with a view toward determining how urbanization has affected the exercise and distribution of influence. Lagos, with its rich historical background, its rapid rate of growth, and its expanding economic and political importance, is particularly suitable for this kind of investigation.

Situated approximately 500 miles north of the equator in the far southwestern corner of Nigeria, Lagos is one of the few places along the West African seaboard where the Atlantic Ocean breaks through the coastline to form a natural harbor connecting with inland creeks and lagoons. Its origin dates back to the seventeenth century, when the town was founded and populated primarily by the Yoruba of southwestern Nigeria, Africa's most urbanized people.[15] Of the twenty-five or more Yoruba cities with more than 50,000 inhabitants which now exist in Nigeria, Lagos is the most highly advanced. It has blossomed into a "primate" city, characterized by heavier investment, a larger proportion of skilled manpower, and a higher consumption rate than any other community in Nigeria.[16] By 1963 it had become the largest city in tropical Africa, surpassing its nearest rival, Ibadan, just 90 miles to the north.[17] This study spans a fifty-year period of the city's growth, beginning in 1917 with the formation of a local town council and closing in 1967 with the creation of Lagos State as a constituent unit of the Federal Republic of Nigeria.

The question inevitably arises as to how my work fits into the tradition of research on comparative urbanization. At this point, two contradictory views of urbanization may be noted.[18] First, urbanization in the developing areas may be seen as a replay of what previously occurred in Europe and America:

> ... world-wide changes make it feasible to consider urbanization in the developing countries as an historical reiteration of the process followed some 150 years earlier by the west. ... If this assumption is valid, it means that the extensive body of data and knowledge accumulated about western cities can provide the standard to compare the process of urban development in newly moderniz-

4

ing countries elsewhere. . . . The important point . . . is that there is a set of social forces operative today, as they were in the west, which seems to be guiding the destinies of urbanization in the new nations.[19]

By contrast, the alternative position may be taken that urbanization in developing areas has distinct cultural attributes that differentiate the non-Western from the Western experience: ". . . what we learn of cities [in Africa] . . . can help us understand them elsewhere. Yet Africa presents distinctive features which accentuate the dominance of the cities. It is only on the threshold of urban development; its nations are new; its cities are few."[20]

The latter of these two views, for both substantive and methodological reasons, is endorsed here. Surely it would be premature at this early stage to take the position that African urbanization is a process that is exclusively or principally a product of technological development, as Western urbanization has been. While there may be similar forces at work, there is already sufficient evidence to suggest that African cities will not simply reproduce Western patterns of urban development, even with industrialization playing a larger role than ever before. The preindustrial origins of many towns, the absence of feudalism, the maintenance of rural ties, the communal ownership of land, the mobility of the urban population, the role of tradition, differences in social stratification, and so on—all are distinctive features in the African urban experience which should be given more intensive treatment before cross-cultural parallels are drawn. If African cities are to be studied objectively, they must not be judged in advance as late arrivals on a journey already completed by the West.

There is the risk, of course, of going to extremes in stressing the theme of cultural uniqueness, an error that can create an equally distorted image of urban Africa. Some observers have concluded not only that Western models are inadequate, but that rural Africa should be the only yardstick by which urbanization can be measured. The spirited debate over the degree of detribalization is indicative of this trend. As one observer has written,

When a research worker observes behavior in town with a background of rural patterns in mind he perceives the two types of

5

change in one context and it is difficult to separate one from the other. Many anthropologists working in towns thus tend to formulate their problems in terms of general theories of social change which are usually inappropriate. The clearest example of this type of approach is in those urban studies which formulate their problems in terms of "'detribalization" or "westernization" or simply "acculturation" in general.[21]

To avoid errors of this kind, urbanization is here conceived of as simply a demographic process of population growth in a delimited area. The view is taken that "an urban social institution is not a changed rural institution; it is a separate social phenomenon existing as part of a separate social system."[22] Lagos, as a developing city, is seen neither as a replica of a Western system nor as a variant of an African rural society; it is a distinct unit of analysis.

### CONTEMPORARY APPROACHES TO THE STUDY OF LOCAL POLITICS

Recent approaches to the empirical study of local politics have focused on the analysis of community power structure, and two major schools of thought have emerged. The stratification school teaches that most communities are ruled by an elite; the pluralist school holds that competing groups share in the effective exercise of power. The debate over the validity of these alternative models has come to rest in large part on the relative merits of the research techniques employed by each. In general, scholars in the stratification school have tended to adopt the reputational approach, whereas those in the pluralist school have inclined toward the decision-making or issue-area approach.[23]

Empirical studies spawned by this debate have concentrated mainly on analyses of American and European cities at fixed points in time. Three unique conditions set my work apart from most of the standard studies. First, the community being examined is a non-Western city.[24] Second, the scope of the analysis spans a period of fifty years, giving it a historical dimension rarely encountered in community power studies. Third, my essential concern is not simply to determine the nature of the power structure, but to ascertain the impact of one independent variable—urbanization—on the distribution and exercise of influence.

The stratification school begins with the assumption that political power is linked to wealth, prestige, and status. It posits the existence of a class of people who, by possessing these attributes, particularly economic resources, emerge as the "men of power." The object of empirical research is to discover who these men are and how they rank in influence. Pluralists challenge this basic premise, pointing out that a widespread belief in a power elite does not prove that it really exists. Instead of trying to identify the people who monopolize influence, the pluralists argue that an accurate picture of a power structure can emerge only through rigorous examination of a broad range of issues in which the actual influence of key individuals can be determined. Hence, the two schools differ at the outset in their basic points of departure. Stratification analysts view a community as a system of social action with competing socioeconomic classes, one of which is thought to be dominant, while pluralists insist that a community is a social aggregate of competing individuals, all presumed to be potential political actors. From this fundamental theoretical difference, divergent methodological approaches have been formulated.[25]

The technique most frequently employed by stratification adherents is intensive interviewing of ostensibly knowledgeable respondents selected from major institutional sectors of the community. Known as the reputational technique, this method relies on the "reputations" of power of community leaders as reported by reliable "judges." This approach was first applied to the study of Atlanta, Georgia:

> The men of power were located by finding persons in prominent positions in four groups that may be *assumed* to have power connections [italics mine]. These groups were identified with business, government, civic associations, and "society" activities. From the recognized, or nominal leaders of the groups mentioned, lists of persons presumed to have power in community affairs were obtained. Through a process of selection, utilizing a cross section of "judges" in determining leadership rank, and finally by a further process of self-selection, a rather long list of possible power leader-

ship candidates was cut down to manageable size for the specific purpose of this study. Forty persons in the top levels of power . . . were selected from more than 175 names.[26]

The power structure of the community was then pieced together by describing "where these persons are in relation to each other, and what they do in relation to each other so far as policy-making and policy-execution are concerned."[27]

Critics of this approach say that it measures reputed power instead of actual power, that it establishes the existence of a power elite by presuming it to be so (rather than by examining the roles of alternative groups in concrete political issues), and that it proceeds from the assumption that social stratification is based principally on the distribution of wealth. These and other methodological deficiences become even more apparent when evaluated in the context of a non-Western environment.

First of all, the pattern of social stratification in many non-Western areas is not identical with, or nearly so stable as, that of the West. Power and status do not rest principally on economic resources. Vertical class divisions are crosscut horizontally by ethnic, clan, kinship, and communal stratifications which are of enormous importance in social relations. It is premature to proceed from the assumption that class solidarity constitutes the primary or sole basis of social action, when these other factors have proved to be of equal or greater significance.

Second, it is likely that in many non-Western areas respondents selected as "judges" are themselves members of the local political elite or have intimate connections with those who are.[28] The reliability of such respondents in making unbiased evaluations of the men of power is therefore problematic. Furthermore, because of overlapping institutional affiliations among the elite, the distinction between leaders who are held in high esteem for social, religious, educational, hereditary, or other nonpolitical reasons, and those who are authentic political leaders, may not be discerned by their respective loyal followers. Even judges used as independent observers may identify certain men as leaders not because they *are* politically influential but because they *ought* to be.

For example, reputational scholars drawing up a list of community influentials typically ask respondents this question:

"Suppose a major project were before the community, one that required a decision by a group of leaders whom nearly everyone would accept. Which persons would you choose to make up this group—regardless of whether or not you know them personally?"[29] This question presumes that culturally homogeneous or socially integrated communities do have visible leaders whom nearly everyone would accept; that many prominent citizens are aware of the public decision-making process and salient political issues; that there is a high level of political consensus; and that functionally specific political roles are visible to the interested observer. These preconditions simply do not exist in communities, such as those in urban Africa, which have politically fragmented, socially unintegrated, and largely nonliterate migrant populations.

For these reasons, the cross-cultural application of the reputational approach may yield highly impressionistic findings. There are few objective tests a researcher might use to determine the level of communication between himself and his respondents or the degree of accuracy in his respondents' reports. Language difficulties also introduce problems. Dependence on native-born assistants does not simplify matters as a comparative study of Umuahia, Nigeria, and Nabale, Uganda, revealed:

> During our field research, several advanced secondary school students were tried out as research assistants for interviewing heterogeneous subsamples of respondents. We found that they could neither communicate with most selected respondents nor even tolerate them. When we interviewed these interviewers, they complained of the stupidity, the filth and the primitive state of the respondents. It seems that most students—and bureaucrats and party leaders—do not have the necessary link with ethnic groups other than their own—and sometimes not even with their own.[30]

The problem of weighing the testimony of prominent individuals from different institutional sectors, especially in communities composed of numerous subcultures with divergent levels of organization, integration, and development, also arises. To compensate for discrepancies, the researcher has to exercise personal judgment at several stages: in choosing a cross section of culturally relevant sectors from which respondents are to be interviewed, in evaluating the reliability and significance of responses, and in assessing respondents' ratings of the relative influence of community leaders. Conceivably, two scholars working independently could reach entirely different conclusions about the same community because of their highly subjective evaluations.

Finally, the reputational technique imposes a time limitation on generalizations about community power. One could, of course, following the Lynds' studies of Middletown,[31] conduct two or more separate studies of the same community over a period of time in a consecutive sequence of snapshot portraits. This procedure, however, detracts from the economy of the methodology and juxtaposes still-life pictures that compare the end products, not the process, of change. At best, both in this approach and in the issue-area approach, which suffers from the same limitation, one might measure or gauge political transformations but not trace how or why the transformations occurred.

Fewer difficulties arise in the issue-area approach, which tends to be associated with the pluralist school, but it, too, is not easily adaptable to a non-Western environment. Concentrating on a meticulous analysis of the participation of influentials in different policy areas, this approach was developed for the study of New Haven, Connecticut:

> From the reconstructed record of various decisions in different issue-areas, the author sought to determine which of the participants had most frequently initiated proposals that were later adopted as actual policy, or had successfully opposed proposals initiated by others. It was assumed that the actors who not only participated in the decisions but were most frequently successful according to those criteria were the most influential. The great advantage of the method is that it uses an operational test, however crude, for appraising the relative power of different participants in decisions, and thus it enables the observer to go behind mere office, reputation and activity. One disadvantage of the method is the time required to reconstruct decisions in sufficient detail; another is that operational definitions must sometimes be so crude as to lend themselves to serious criticism. For example, which man is the more powerful in a given issue-area: a man who initiates two proposals that are subsequently adopted without objections, a

second man who carries through one proposal over very strong initial objections, or a third who initiates 20 policy proposals but succeeds in securing the adoption of only one-third of them?[32]

Though more precise, the decision-making approach has been criticized because it concentrates only on controversial issues or decisions, because it offers no criteria of relevance for the selection of issues, and because it fails to identify what types of issues come before what types of participants. The first of these deficiencies has particular relevance for non-Western areas. By failing to treat issues that may be suppressed or withheld from public attention by leaders who fear political protest, the approach excludes political activities aimed at preventing controversies from arising, such as influence exercised for purposes of political repression. The quest for public office also lies beyond the purview of the decision-making approach. Such nondecisional or predecisional forces are significant because they may indicate important dimensions of uninstitutionalized influence or may suggest limits on the exercise of power which would normally escape the attention of researchers who restrict themselves to the analysis of public issues.[33]

Another difficulty in using this approach in non-Western areas relates to the problems of distinguishing between local and national politics and determining the degree of political autonomy exercised by community leaders. The issue-area approach makes the implicit assumption that community decisions reveal the nature of local politics, a reasonable premise that creates no real problem in Western societies with institutionalized political processes and a tradition of local self-government. But intense competition for national resources tends to be concentrated in the urban areas of developing nations where the boundary between local and national politics often is not clearly established. Therefore the analysis of local politics is complicated by the role of higher government authorities and by individuals operating at the local level who represent non-local interests. To what extent, for example, should federal civil servants or business managers posted to capital cities, wage earners with short-term residence, or nonresident officials of national political parties be legitimately regarded as influentials in the local community? These external interests may have an impact on the local

11

scene without ever exhibiting the public participation that would reveal their true significance. Although this approach has the advantage of going beyond mere office and reputation, it has the shortcoming of relying essentially on the manifest behavior of key individuals at the local level to detect patterns of influence.

Thus there are crucial practical weaknesses in the transfer of this approach to a non-Western enviroment. Unassertive individuals or groups with potentially powerful but as yet not fully exploited political resources would not be identified as relevant forces in a community's political process, even though they may in fact indirectly influence the formation of public policy. Moreover, the detailed evidence required by the issue-area approach might be spotty and highly subject to personal manipulation, depending largely on the researcher's contacts and his informants' cooperation. Issues may have to be selected on the basis of data accessibility rather than on the basis of objective relevance to the community's political life. Under these conditions, incomplete or unbalanced findings would distort conclusions regarding the actual power structure.

## A NEW APPROACH

Because of the flaws in conventional community power approaches, I am led to agree that the "research methods used by many investigators to cope with the special problems posed by cross-cultural research are primitive at best."[34] I have therefore designed an original approach for the study of local politics with three essential considerations in mind. First, the new scheme has to allow a cross-cultural analysis of local conditions without being so parochial or culture-bound as to lose relevance for comparative politics. Second, it needs a broad time dimension to encompass problems of change and continuity. Third, it has to provide for the overall view of the urban political process necessary for the examination of the impact of urbanization on political life.

These requirements have been met by the development of a relatively straightforward scheme of inquiry which proceeds from an initial identification of a basic set of political variables. These are: (1) the ruling strata—types of leaders inducted into public office and, where relevant, other leaders of political importance; (2) political resources—the means or inducements by which influence is exercised; (3) political behavior—patterns of partisanship and competition among contending sets of leaders, and patterns of public participation; and (4) the formal structure of government —functions, viability, and performance of authoritative local government and administrative institutions. These variables raise fundamental political questions in the context of urbanizaton: Who rules at which periods? What socioeconomic or political interest groups do the leaders represent? With what resources do these groups and leaders compete for influence? What is the structure of party organization at the urban level? To what extent does the urban electorate participate in the political process and what appeals do leaders and parties make to the electorate? How do local political institutions function under the pressure of rapid urban growth? What are the key determinants of political change at different stages, and to what extent is there continuity in urban political patterns? The list of related questions could, of course, go on. The point to be made here is simply that the selection of political variables followed the process of sorting out the basic questions to be answered and then incorporating them into a methodologically feasible scheme of inquiry.

The variables were supplemented by three detailed studies of political influence. The subjects selected for examination include an institution, an interest group, and an issue, all deemed to have been of durable or continuing importance to the community throughout most of the period covered in this work.[35] They are, respectively, chieftaincy, portraying the erosion of influence; market women, portraying unassertive influence; and the constitutional status of Lagos, portraying the interaction between external and internal influences.

Data were collected through three primary means. A sample survey of elected councilors yielded information on the changing socioeconomic backgrounds and political affiliations of local leaders. Documents, files, and memoranda of the Lagos City Council and of local branches of major political parties were extremely useful for several purposes. Extensive interviewing of community leaders, party officials, and local administrators provided a wide range of helpful information. These and other related methods of data collection afforded a degree of flexibility that permitted a wide scope of investigation and additional means of cross-checking conclusions, advantages that conventional community power approaches fail to offer.

The approach adopted here could be used for the study of urban politics in other areas. Some variables might need to be altered, depending upon the context of the study. In a military or authoritarian system in which parties are banned, for example, the variable of political behavior might be less relevant than, say, political mobilization. The types of subjects selected for detailed examination would, of course, also vary with the setting and the time period. Nevertheless, my basic approach—historical analysis of key political variables accompanied by case studies of influence—could be applied to any urban community during any stage of development. It satisfies the conditions of cross-cultural applicability, historical perspective, and comprehensiveness required for an analysis of the political correlates of urbanization. Hence it is especially suitable for comparative studies of urbanization and political change in modernizing societies.

# CHAPTER 2

*Growth of a City*

Lagos, 1861:

The site of the town, four miles from the entrance, is detest-able; unfortunately, there is no better within many a league. It occupies the western side of an islet about three miles and a half long from north-east to south-west, by one [mile] broad from north to south. . . . The first aspect is as if a hole had been hol-lowed out in the original mangrove forest that skirts the waters, where bush and dense jungle, garnished with many a spreading tree, tall palms, and matted mass of fetid verdure rise in terrible profusion. . . . [On] the 5th of August [1861] . . . a flag-ship was slipped and rigged near the British consulate, and Commander Bedingfield landed with his marines. A crowd of people and some chiefs were assembled at the palaver-house. The King, when civilly asked to sign away his kingdom, consented and refused, as the negro will, in the same breath. On the next day he affixed his mark, for of course he cannot write. . . . Without awaiting, however, the ceremony of signature, possession, nine-tenths of the law, was at once entered upon. The "Captain" read out the English proclamation, very intelligible to the natives, confirming "the cession of Lagos and its dependencies"—a pleasantly vague frontier. Then followed a touching scene. One Union Jack was hoisted in the town, another on the beach. "Prometheus Vinctus" saluted with twenty-one guns. The marines presented arms; three hundred fetish, or sanctified boys, as the convert people call them, sang a hymn, headed by their missionaries. . . . And as we English-men must celebrate every event with a dinner . . . forty-four Oy-ibos [sic], Europeans, and Africo-Europeans . . . sat down to meat...and added, as the phrase is, *éclat* to the great event. Thus, Lagos—rose.

—Sir Richard Burton

## Lagos, 1960:

Lagos was unlike anything I had seen before in Africa; it was more like an overcrowded city in India. It is on an island, with a lagoon between it and the mainland. Perhaps 400,000 people are jammed into this area, almost all of them selling something to someone. And most in evidence are the market women, for women are the small traders, buying on credit from any kind of concern, making their shilling on the pound profit, and buying again. Whole sections of the town are devoted to headscarves, and women walk nonchalantly down the street with two- or even three-foot piles of these scarves on their heads. One section concentrates on open-work sandals; another on notions. Down by the dock are shellfish and salted or fresh fish, while tied to the dock behind these stalls are what are called "canoes," heavy wooden boats which are rowed or poled and have flimsy sardine nets like great spider webs hanging triangularly from their tall masts. While women dominate the markets, both men and women have little shops, like boxes, with their wares lining the walls or on the floor at their feet.

All night [long] the city is alluring: candle flames flickering in small shops or on stalls by the road-side, green or pink electric light bulbs casting eerie shadows in beer parlors. Then I could not see so clearly either the open drains running in front of the markets and shops, or the people openly relieving themselves into them.

Always the city is intensely vital. All night long, people move up and down, never still.

—Gwendolyn Carter

### EARLY HISTORY

A comprehensive picture of the urbanization of Lagos is a prerequisite to the political analysis outlined in chapter 1. This chapter deals with the history, economic growth, and demographic patterns of the community as it evolved from the time of its founding as a small coastal village three centuries ago to its present-day status as the largest city in black Africa.

The first inhabitants of the area now known as Lagos were Aworis, a subgroup of the Yoruba people who are believed to have migrated early in the seventeenth century from their original home in Ile-Ife, the spiritual homeland of the Yoruba.[1] According to oral tradition, upon the death of an early traditional ruler in the town a dispute erupted between two brothers over succession to the throne. A diviner, after consultation with his oracle, ordained that the elder brother should leave the town with his supporters and follow the path of a basin placed in the Ogun River. His empire was to begin from the point at which the basin sank. At various places along the southern route the basin stopped, at Aro, Oke-Ata, and Iseri, where some of the wanderers remained, but it was not until the basin actually disappeared 100 miles downstream at a place called Idunmota, now at the foot of Carter Bridge linking Lagos Island with the mainland, that the people ended their migration and established the first known settlement in Lagos. The name "Awori" derives from the response to the question, "Where is the basin?" The answer is *awori* ("the basin has sunk").

The settlement was called Eko, probably from the Yoruba *oko* ("farm"), but it also could have been the name used by Benin conquerors in the mid-seventeenth century, *eko* meaning "war camp" in the Bini (Edo) language. Early Portuguese explorers referred to the town as Lagos, meaning lakes or lagoons, and it became the accepted English version, though most indigenes still use the traditional Eko.

The first settlement, located on the mainland in the area of Ebute Metta ("the three landing places"), was later moved to the island of Iddo ("a camp"). The Aworis were soon joined by peoples from neighboring provinces, particularly Ijebus and Egbas, who made Lagos their center of trade. Eventually, for greater protection from civil unrest in the interior, the settlers crossed over to the island that today constitutes the center of the city, establishing their village on the western corner, known as Isale-Eko ("lower Lagos"). The head of the original encampment, the Olofin, dis- tributed land among sixteen of his thirty-two sons, giving them white caps as insignia of their status, a tradition unique in Yoru- baland. This emblem still endures to designate the special class of headmen known as the Idejo or White Cap chiefs, symbolic

17

territorial owners of much of the land in and around the city. Descendants of the original Awori settlers form the heart of the traditional quarter of the city and the core of the slum-dwelling urban population.

Shortly after the Yoruba migration, several attempts were made by the kingdom of Benin, then one of the most powerful on the Guinea coast, to conquer the Olofin and his followers. After some failures, the oba (king) of Benin finally succeeded in capturing Lagos after the Olofin was allegedly betrayed by his wife, Ajaye. During the conflict one of the Bini war captains, said to have been the son of the oba of Benin, was killed in battle, and his body was brought home by a Yoruba chief named Ashipa. As a reward, Ashipa was appointed by the oba of Benin as the war chief and supreme ruler of Lagos, thus becoming progenitor of the royal dynasties from which future obas of Lagos were subsequently chosen.[2]

For two centuries Lagos paid tribute to the Benin empire, though over the years the observance came to be more of a ritual than an obligation. The population became a mixture of Yoruba and Edo with influences from other ethnic groups, including refugees from the western kingdom of Dahomey. Gradually the community of fishermen and farmers grew in size, especially after the Portuguese, who first reached the Bight of Benin in 1472, developed the slave trade for European markets.

By the early nineteenth century the slave trade had drastically changed the character of Lagos. From a small fishing village it burgeoned as the primary commercial center in West Africa for the purchase and sale of slaves. Prisoners of war captured during the Fulani jihad against the Oyo empire and the large-scale Yoruba conflicts added considerably to the human traffic. When ships had to be diverted from other harbors because of a British squadron, dispatched in 1807 to patrol West African waters and stop the transatlantic passage of slaves, Lagos trade intensified. As a newer port with channels and inlets well suited for easy evasion of British cruisers, Lagos became a natural alternative outlet to the diminishing availability of other suppliers.

The geographical advantages of Lagos for handling the slave trade were obvious: it commanded an entrance to the sea protected

18

from the rough surf by several swampy islands, and it afforded communication through a number of inland waterways and creeks to Badagry and Dahomey to the west and the Benin empire to the east. The 100-mile stretch of land reaching from Ouidah (Why-dah) in present-day Dahomey to Lagos came to be known as the Slave Coast. Kidnapped or captured slaves were marched or brought by canoe to Lagos, kept in special compounds on the beach called barracoons, and herded onto waiting slave ships. Natives of Lagos were themselves rarely victims of the trade, though many liberated slaves claimed Eko as their home, probably for reasons of economic gain and fear of being repatriated to the land where they had been captured. Lagosians acted as middlemen in the transactions, buying the slaves from the hinterland tribes and selling them to Europeans, who seldom ventured into the war-torn interior. The European goods used for barter included textiles, firearms, knives, cutlasses, hardware, bars of iron, copper and brass, spirits, and a variety of other provisions. Estimates of the total volume of human cargo from the 350-year-old practice, which reached its peak in Lagos at a time when other slave stations were dying, range between 15 and 20 million, these figures representing only those believed to have survived the voyages.

Efforts of the British naval patrols to suppress the slave trade with the assistance of consuls dispatched to the Gulf of Guinea after 1849, were frustrated along the Slave Coast where exports continued surreptitiously, owing to the skillful maneuvering of a group of suppliers led by Oba Kosoko. With the support of Portuguese slavers and interior allies based in Dahomey, Ijebu, and Oyo, Kosoko stiffly resisted measures designed to abolish the lucrative practice. Both English missionaries and European merchants who were trying to establish legitimate trade supported the British decision to intervene in the factional rivalry for the throne of Lagos, then raging between Kosoko and his uncle, Akitoye, who agreed to ban the slave trade if he was restored to office. In 1851 the British occupied Lagos, deposed Kosoko, enthroned Akitoye, and expelled the Portuguese.

The British paid little attention to the roots of the Akitoye-Kosoko dispute, which had arisen years earlier among competing royal lineages over the question of rightful possession of the throne

19

(see chap. 7 for details). Nor were the antislavery sentiments of Akitoye entirely genuine. They were predicated more on his desire to win British support than on any principled antagonism to the institution itself; he also had been subsidized by well-known slavers and, if the opportunity had arisen, would probably have participated in the slave trade himself. His only hope of regaining his throne, however, was to ally himself with a stronger power and appear as a friendly instrument of its ambitions. The desire of the British to abolish the slave trade was based as much on economic as on humanitarian motives, for by this time the palm-oil trade was growing steadily around the delta areas near Lagos. Since the town was relatively weak (though the first attack failed), military invasion seemed the most expedient way to check this trade, especially with cooperation from an indigenous ruler and the humanitarian rationalizations invoked by Christian missionaries.

Even after he was forced into exile, the deposed Kosoko was able to continue the slave trade by capturing up-country markets and diverting the distribution routes to Lekki and Palma, situated off the lagoon to the east. Neither Akitoye nor his ineffective successor, Docemo (Dosunmu), had the power or the authority to restrain Kosoko's activities in these areas. In addition, civil unrest continued within the Lagos community among those who regarded the Akitoye line as illegitimate. Threats of internal disorder, interrupted trade, and harassment from neighboring chiefs sympathetic to Kosoko's plight induced the British to seek a reconciliation a few years later. On the condition that he relinquish his claims to the throne of Lagos, Kosoko was recognized as ruler of the territories of Lekki and Palma, areas over which he already had de facto control. In 1863 he was allowed to return to Lagos, granted a pension, asked to give up his slaving activities, and, to the consternation of Egba traders, assured of continuing influence in the hinterland by the forcible appointment of two pro-Kosoko chiefs at Badagry.

All this maneuvering was to no avail, for the British were still unable to check those who were promoting the slave trade. Finally, the British Foreign Office issued instructions to its consul to annex the town in order "to secure forever the free population of Lagos from the slave-traders and kidnappers who formerly oppressed them; to protect and develop the important trade of which their town is the seat; and to exercise an influence on the surrounding tribes which may, it is hoped, be permanently beneficial to the African race."[3] Accordingly, on July 30, 1861, Oba Docemo was pressured into signing a treaty by which he agreed to relinquish all his royal prerogatives and cede Lagos to the British Crown, a step that formalized the authority of a government "which for 10 years had already been in the hands of the British."[4] At this point Lagos was officially designated as the Colony of Lagos and its inhabitants became British subjects, under British law, owing allegiance to the British sovereign.

### INCIPIENT URBANIZATION

Colonization ushered in a new era in Lagos, marked by the eventual suppression of the slave trade, the emergence of new forms of economic activity, and the gradual pacification of the interior. These conditions attracted increasingly large numbers of African and European immigrants to the town, swelling the population by as much as 60 percent by the turn of the century.

Among the most important immigrants who came to Lagos during the second half of the nineteenth century were a number of emancipated slaves who either were liberated by the British squadron while being shipped across the Atlantic or were self-emancipated slaves from Latin America who had earned their freedom while in captivity. Those freed by the British squadron were first resettled at Freetown, Sierra Leone, where they were cared for and educated by missionaries. The largest group among them were Yoruba-speaking peoples who came to be known as Akus[5] from their common greeting, a classification that has subsequently come to refer more narrowly to the Muslim descendants of liberated Yorubas. Their movement down the coast began early in 1839 when they first emigrated to their homes in Abeokuta and Badagry. After the British seizure of Lagos in 1851 the migration increased, and by the time of the cession of Lagos there were an estimated 2,500 Sierra Leonians in Lagos, representing about 10 percent of the town's inhabitants.[6] By 1865 they were estimated to be 20 percent of the town's population. Because of their European ways, their arrival was referred to as "the return of the daddies." They were occasionally identified by indigenous Lagosians as Oyinbos, the Yoruba term for white men, but more commonly they were known simply as Saros, a contraction of Sierra Leonian.

Self-emancipated slaves came from Brazil or Cuba where captives were allowed to accumulate independent incomes from their work and eventually to purchase their own redemption. Pooling their resources, the industrious *emancipados* made their way back across the Atlantic. Like the Saros, almost all Brazilian emigrants were of Yoruba descent, most of them being Egbas. In 1853 there were 130 Brazilian families living in Lagos; by 1857 they were as numerous as the Saros. Lagosians referred to this group as Amaros ("those who had been away from home") or Brazilians.

A third group of African settlers who migrated to Lagos during this period were Egba refugees expelled from Abeokuta in 1867 as part of a widespread Christian purge. The motives behind this event were more political than religious, since there had been long-standing disputes between Lagos and Abeokuta in matters of trade, boundary limitation, policing of the interior, and interference in Yoruba tribal affairs.[7] When the Egbas tried to levy duties on goods traveling on the Ogun River, the Lagos administration attempted to impose settlement of a boundary dispute. Instead of dealing with their opponents directly, the Egbas retaliated by expelling European missionaries and their converts whom the Lagos authorities were then obliged to resettle. The refugees were given tracts of land at Ebute Metta, the original mainland encampment of the Awori founders.

The European community in Lagos remained very small throughout the latter half of the nineteenth century, despite the growth of commercial trade and increasing administrative needs. Only 111 whites were registered in the census of 1881, as compared with 37,282 blacks and 59 mulattoes.[8] As late as 1901 only 308 Europeans lived in Lagos.[9]

Several reasons account for the small size of the European settlement. Initially it was due to the shifting status of the colony. Lagos was first under the jurisdiction of an administrator who was consul for the Bights of Benin and Biafra (1849–1853). When British activity increased, Lagos was given a full-time consul (1853–1861)

until a governor was appointed for the new Crown Colony (1861–
1866). Lagos, subsequently placed under the jurisdiction of the
governor of the Sierra Leone Settlement (1866–1874), was later
switched to the administrator of the Gold Coast Colony (1874–
1886). Finally, in 1886, Lagos achieved a degree of internal autonomy, with its own governor and central administration. For most
of the first twenty-five years of colonial rule, therefore, the town
was tied to other settlements and the official European community
was kept to a minimum.

The size of the expatriate community was also restricted by poor
health conditions. The ubiquitous malaria- and yellow fever-
carrying mosquito; customary local practices, such as burial of the
dead in shallow graves beneath the floors of family houses; and
congested living quarters subject to frequent flooding—all contributed to the unsanitary environment in the town. In the early
days of colonization the West African coast was known as the
"White Man's Grave"; Lagos in particular was said to claim "a
consul a year." In 1897 the European death rate in Lagos was more
than triple that in London.[10] Of those Europeans who were
attracted to Lagos, about half were merchants and missionaries
who came to the town after Kosoko's defeat in 1851. Many of the
traders were of French, German, or Italian descent, a small and
disunited group that competed bitterly for favors from the reigning obas. They acted independently of, sometimes even in opposition to, the colonial administration. One gets a sense of the extent
of their private influence in the town from the treaty that they, in
alliance with a few emigrant traders, negotiated with Docemo in
1859. In exchange for increased export duties paid in cowries,[11]
the oba agreed that no native would be permitted to build a house
" 'where the Merchants' stores are situated'; he [the oba] was to
give up trade himself; he was to see that, except for refusal to
pay duties, no merchant's trade was to be interfered with; he was
to collect debts from his people on behalf of the merchants and
to punish thefts; he was to allow traders to build their own houses
in any place they chose."[12]

The first missionary organizations in Lagos were the Church
Missionary Society and the Wesleyan mission, both established in
the early years of British occupation. In 1862 a Roman Catholic

mission followed. Missionaries found their most receptive adherents among the freed slaves who had previous exposure to Christianity, many of whom were given important ecclesiastical posts.

It was during the second half of the nineteenth century that, owing to changing economic and demographic patterns, Lagos began to emerge as a thriving community. By 1901 it was a heterogeneous town of more than 40,000 inhabitants—Aworis, Edos, Egbas, Saros, Amaros, other scattered ethnic groups, and Europeans—distributed disproportionately in relatively segregated districts; in fact, "by 1900, the face of Lagos had changed almost beyond recognition from what it was in 1850."[13] It was not only the place and the nature of immigration which gave the town a plural character; the emerging patterns of residence, social stratification, and contrasting life-styles in the community also added diversity. By the time Lagos was constituted a separate colony with its own administrative apparatus in 1886, it comprised four distinct subcommunities: the traditional Old Town of Isale Eko, Saro Town, the Amaro district (also known as the Brazilian or Portuguese area), and the European section.

### Old Town: Isale Eko

Isale Eko, on the northwest corner of the island, was larger than the other three districts put together. Estimated by the British consul in 1859 to measure 5 miles in circumference, it had 30,000 inhabitants. Despite their numbers, however, the influx of "strangers" posed a serious threat to the indigenes who lived in this area. After abolition of the slave trade cut off their prime source of income, they found that increasing scarcity of land and stiff competition in new forms of trade were squeezing them economically. The geographical and cultural separation of the indigenes compounded these social and economic disparities, stimulating an antagonism to settlers which was to remain a permanent feature of the town's social cleavages. Despite the imposition of colonial rule, Isale Eko remained a traditional Yoruba town, relatively untouched by the growing prosperity and commercialization introduced by legitimate trade.

Colonization had, however, deeply affected the politics of Old

Town; the dynastic dispute between the Kosoko and Akitoye factions remained a constant source of political turmoil. In order to win the cooperation of the indigenes for their respective economic, administrative, or evangelical objectives, most of the nonindigenous sections of the population were drawn into the political dispute. Tensions were exacerbated by the government's attempt to undermine traditional rulers by formally withdrawing powers from the oba of Lagos after the 1861 cession. While this policy considerably weakened the oba's authority, it also enhanced his personal popularity. But the oba depended for financial support on the benevolence of the colonial regime, which periodically suspended pensions or reduced export duties due the chiefs when their behavior conflicted with government policies. By contrast, members of the ousted Kosoko faction secured a direct source of income and substantial political influence by acting as unofficial intermediaries between the colonial administration and the indigenous population, both within and beyond the town. Because they proved to be more helpful in assisting the British in a smooth administration, Kosoko and his followers became the favored group among the official community, despite the fact that the former slave dealer, because of British intervention, represented the defeated and illegitimate line of traditional authority.

After Kosoko's death in 1864 his followers were led by a commoner, Chief Taiwo Olowo ("the rich gentleman"). An exceptionally wealthy trader of indigenous origin, Taiwo prospered from his position as middleman between groups jockeying for influence among the coastal population and hinterland tribes. Until his death in 1901, he was the most prominent Lagosian in town, exceeding the influence of the recognized chiefs not only because of his willingness to serve the colonial government, but also because of his leadership of a cohesive political faction and his links with interior tribes.

Meanwhile, Oba Docemo, who ceded Lagos to the British, made several unsuccessful attempts to reassert his authority when it became obvious that the government was taking direct control of his domain. Friction developed rapidly between the traditional ruler and colonial administrators, as indicated by Sir John Glover's remark that Docemo was "both a rogue and fool" who failed to

25

recognize that it was the British "who at his father's death took him out of a Fishing Canoe and made him King against the wishes of his Chiefs."[14] The discrepancy between the official status formally accorded the Akitoye-Docemo dynasty and the humiliating treatment members of the royal lineage suffered in practice created a deep sense of dissatisfaction which continued to be politically explosive for many years thereafter.

### Saro Town: Olowogbowo

Opposite Isale Eko, and occupying the southwestern corner of the island, was an area called Olowogbowo ("the maker has taken his things back") because of the frequent loss of goods from capsized canoes plying the strong currents in the offshore lagoon. The contraction to Ologbo became the common vernacular form, but the district also went simply by the name of Saro Town. Here burgeoned the first professional and intellectual elite of Lagos among a group of educated ex-slaves.

In 1853 Oba Akitoye granted the Olowogbowo district to "Daddy" William Akilade Savage, the head of the Saro community, and he in turn distributed allotments to individual Saro families on the understanding that, if the plots of land were not utilized, they would revert back to the oba. Nearly all Saro immigrants settled in Olowogbowo, creating a virtually autonomous quarter geographically separated from Isale Eko by swamps, creeks, and undeveloped land. A few years later the Sierra Leone Association was established with Akitoye's sanction; it was an organization that Glover described as having "in the days of Consul Campbell (c. 1853–1859) ruled both the King and Lagos."[15] The Saros— probably the most unified group in Lagos during the late nineteenth century—aided the Egbas, to whom many Saros were related, in resisting an invasion from Dahomey and in achieving peace with Lagos. They competed with European merchants in trade and commerce; they acted as interpreters and administrative assistants to colonial officialdom, eventually occupying positions of significant responsibility themselves; they served as arbitrators between the colonial government and local chiefs; and they became "native agents" of Christian missionaries. Saros "introduced European technology, institutions and beliefs, but not without participating in transforming some of them to suit African conditions and interests, and concomitantly, easing the adjustment of traditional ways to the innovations."[16]

Standing between the two worlds of European and African culture, the Saros were collectively distinguished from other Lagosians by their unique cultural background. They emulated English behavior and mannerisms, rejected native authority, and adopted Christianity; but most Saros were also fully conscious of their Yoruba origins, and some supported African practices of domestic slavery and polygamy and the maintenance of native churches within the missions. They held themselves socially aloof from the indigenous community and, in the eyes of the latter, seemed to be more related to the white man and more comfortable in his environment than in the traditional African setting. In fact, the Saros eventually lost the confidence of the indigenous community because of their frequent association with colonial policies and their close links with the European community.

Saro Town was internally self-sufficient, having its own schools, church, police force, jail, and courthouse. Like European traders, Saros built storehouses or "factories" along the Marina, a significant portion of which was located in the Ologbo district. Many became bulk distributors of imported goods and, as merchant princes, accumulated savings that substantially raised their standard of living. Saro children were sent to the United Kingdom for higher education, becoming on their return the first generation of African lawyers, doctors, surveyors, and journalists in Lagos. Most of them intermarried with other Saros, continuing the pattern of social exclusivity. They conspicuously displayed their wealth and culture, letting "it be known ... that they had been places, had seen sights, and had thus achieved a rank that no ordinary native in Lagos could hope to match."[17] Despite their humble background, Lagos Saros were soon regarded by Africans and Europeans alike as a sophisticated elite with wealth, status, and power.

### Brazilian Quarter

Just as the Saros had absorbed many of the cultural accouterments of their liberators, so the Amaro repatriates had absorbed

27

many of the cultural accouterments of their captors, particularly Portuguese names, the Portuguese language, and Catholicism. They established their district around Campos Square in the center of the island, a less advantageous, but more sanitary, part of the town. It became known as the Brazilian Quarter or Popo Aguda ("Portuguese Town").

Although as numerous as the Saros, the Amaros were less wealthy and less active politically; partly for these reasons, they were more acceptable to the indigenous elements. Most of the Amaros had exhausted their funds for self-repatriation, and upon their arrival in Lagos turned to the crafts they had learned in captivity—masonry, carpentry, cabinetmaking, tailoring, smithing and the like. They became the middle-class artisans of Lagos leaving their mark primarily in their architectural contributions which still decorate the town's streets.

The Amaros retained many elements of traditional African culture, somewhat transformed by Portuguese exposure. Many of them mixed their Catholicism with the worship of Sango, the Yoruba god of thunder. The Brazilian carreta masquerade with its colorful decorations was introduced in Lagos. Gay Latin-American songs and dances were preferred by Amaros, in contrast with the conservative Victorian tastes of the Saros. Having spent time in servitude and having gone to considerable effort and expense to return to Africa, the Amaros also tended to be industrious, thrifty, and submissive.

In behavior the Amaros contrasted sharply with the aggressive and ostentatious Saros, with whom the Brazilians had little in common. Because the Amaros were not so useful to the British as the Saros, and had more egalitarian values, they were not regarded by the indigenes with the same degree of antipathy:

> Brazilians as a group did not depart as far from native norms as did the Saros and so were not excluded as fully from social relations with natives. The Brazilian usually did not object to manual labor, nor did he possess a real or feigned formal education that the Sierra Leonian valued. Language barriers to social intercourse are usually associated with racial differences, but the experience of the immigrants who persisted in speaking their adopted tongue indicate that language differences in Lagos were

even more important than racial considerations. What was true of language differences was also true of differences in dress, customs, employment and homes. Environment rather than hereditary characteristics determined social groupings in Lagos.[18]

### European Community

The fourth major group in nineteenth-century Lagos was the heterogeneous European community, about half of whom were British administrators. Though representing less than 1 percent of the total population, at this stage they made perhaps the strongest impact on the town, establishing the physical foundations for the growth of the modern city. Government houses were built along the Marina and around the racecourse at the eastern end of the island. Later, in the twentieth century, Europeans tended to settle in the residential section of Ikoyi, on the eastern plains of the island, but throughout the earlier years of colonization they remained close to the native and emigrant quarters. Many traders lived above their warehouses along the Marina; missionaries lived among their congregations, either on the fringes or in the center of the African districts. These residence patterns reflected the divisions within the European community; unlike the indigene and emigrant groups, the Europeans did not cluster in a single cohesive community, but spread lineally from one end of the island to the other, principally in areas convenient to their work.

Largely from the efforts of Europeans, Lagos prospered economically. Exports varied from palm produce, representing more than three-quarters of the total, to rubber, timber, cotton, coffee, cocoa, and maize. Textiles, spirits, tobacco, building materials, salt, and other provisions were the major imported items.[19] By 1870 more than half a million pounds worth of goods passed through the port annually. Thanks to the active export-import trade, Lagos was "the ideal Colony from the Downing Street point of view, self-supporting and self-protecting. . . . So constant was the surplus of revenue over expenditure that in 1896, before it was necessary to raise money by loan for the large capital expenditure required for the bridges and the railway, there was a credit balance of over £50,000, invested in England."[20]

Much of this revenue was channeled back into the improvement of the town. During his administration (1866–1872), Sir John Glover extended the Marina and built the 60-foot-wide Broad Street (now Yakubu Gowon Street) through the heart of the town; these two arteries still provide the main routes in the city. Glover had street lamps constructed and proper wells dug; he encouraged the building of wharves and warehouses to cope with expanding commerce and sponsored the Glover settlement in Ebute Metta for Abeokutan refugees in 1868, the first attempt to apply the principles of town planning to Lagos. Each successive administrator, according to his personal predilections, introduced further improvements. Sir William Macgregor (1899–1904) carved a wide canal, running north to south through the island, which drained the swampy area between Lagos Island and Ikoyi.

Eventually the swamps and water holes were filled, and bridges were built to connect the island with the mainland. Telegraph links between Lagos and London were established in 1886; in the same year construction commenced on a railroad providing transportation to Ibadan, which was opened in 1900. By 1898, when much of Britain was still using gas or paraffin lamps, the streets of Lagos were lit by electricity. Understandably, Colonial Secretary George C. Denton predicted in 1890 that

> Lagos has a future of considerable importance before it. It is free from debt, has a trade of about 1¼ millions, and collects a revenue of between 70 and 75 thousand a year with the lowest customs tariff known. The expenses of administration compare very favorably with those of any other Colony, and it has great underdeveloped resources. With those conditions present it will indeed be strange if it does not long become one of the most valuable of Her Majesty's African possessions.[21]

His optimism proved to be well founded, for Lagos became the gateway to Britain's colonization of tropical Africa's most populous nation. As expansion into the interior progressed, Lagos continued to evolve into a dynamic urban community whose character contrasted sharply with the rest of the African landscape. Within its confines were retained the traditional Yoruba community of Isale Eko, resilient in the whirlwind growth of its surroundings; the sophisticated Saro community, providing Nigeria's first westernized elite; and the Amaro community, leaving an indelible mark on the face of the town. In time all these groups came to be referred to as "Lagosians," a term distinguishing them from the twentieth-century immigrants who, in coming to Lagos, further revolutionized its social and political structure.

The nineteenth-century foundations of Lagos continue to influence the contemporary city, not only in the old buildings and street names which testify to the rich history of the town, but in the social structure and political system, the roots of which predate the creation of Nigeria itself. The inequitable distribution of wealth and resources originating in this era, for example, assured the continued existence of the indigenous quarter as an urban ghetto; at the other extreme, it developed a privileged social elite which provided some of the nation's most prominent political leaders. Out of the nineteenth century also emerged the prolific voluntary associations, such as the Lagos Mutual Improvement Society, the Flower of Lagos Club, the Freemasons' Lodge, and the Templars, forerunners of the modern improvement or progressive unions and tribal associations which play a crucial integrative role in contemporary urban life.[22] Many of the old schools, mosques, churches, and markets of early Lagos still serve the community today, providing continuity with the past. And the dynastic split within Isale Eko and indigene-settler antagonisms continue to have relevance for the internal politics and social structure of the capital city, persisting throughout the urbanization and economic development of the twentieth century.

### THE MODERN CITY

Contemporary Lagos is situated on some 27 square miles of low terrain transversing three main islands, a slice of the mainland, and a stretch of undeveloped coastline. The heart of the city is located on the central island of Lagos, a sandy spit of land approximately 2 miles long by 1 mile wide on which a quarter of a million people live. Because of large-scale immigration, at least 40 percent of the urban population has been forced to settle in suburban areas. By 1963, 665,246 people lived in the city, but the entire metropolitan area, which covers some 40 square miles of territory, including Mushin, Ikeja, Somolu, Agege, and Ajegunle, was estimated at that time to contain at least 1.25 million people.

Although representing only a fraction of the nation's area and population, Lagos claims a disproportionately large share of its human and technological resources. By 1965, 36 percent (43 percent if Greater Lagos is included) of Nigeria's industries were located in the capital city.[23] The port of Lagos handles 70 percent of the nation's total imports and exports, and its manufacturing enterprises produce 42 percent of the national industrial output.[24] In 1962 Lagos claimed 38 percent of all motor licenses, 56 percent of all telephone calls, four out of twenty daily newspapers, and eighteen out of nineteen periodicals in Nigeria.[25] The capital has the heaviest concentration of skilled manpower in the country; the best communication, road, and harbor facilities; and the highest-paid workers. By objective standards of economic development, Lagos is unquestionably Nigeria's most advanced city.

The first decade of the twentieth century marked the beginning of modern urbanization, a process stimulated by the extension of the railway, the deepening of the harbor channel, the construction of the Lagos Steam Tramway, and the building of public facilities, including the General Post Office, the General Hospital, King's College, and the Old Secretariat. At the commencement of World War I, the pace of economic development slowed and the rate of immigration declined. Though there was no decrease in population, it was not until World War II that the city returned again to the frantic tempo of development and expansion which is still continuing.

Probably the single most important factor accounting for the modern economic growth of Lagos was the development of the port. Work commenced in 1906 on the construction of moles to break the strong ocean surf, on dredging the seabed to deepen the channel, and later on increasing the number of wharves and berths at Apapa. By 1912 the railway had also been extended 700 miles into the interior to reach Kano and points farther north, permitting more varied and valuable exports to flow in larger quantities. So fast had traffic expanded that by 1953 berthing facilities were found to be inadequate, and an additional £3.25 million was expended for reclamation of land and construction of piers, storage sheds, workshops, and other appurtenances. By 1962 Lagos was receiving nearly five times as much tonnage as it had in 1938.[26]

The increased capacity of Lagos as a port terminal spurred eco-

### TABLE 1

POPULATION GROWTH OF LAGOS, 1866–1963

| Year of census[a] | Total population | Intercensal increase or decrease | | Area covered by census[b] (in square miles) |
|---|---|---|---|---|
| | | Number | Percent | |
| 1866 | 25,083 | — — | — | [c] |
| 1871 | 28,518 | 3,435 | 14 | 1.55 |
| 1881 | 37,452 | 8,934 | 31 | 1.55 |
| 1891[d] | 32,508 | –4,944 | –13 | 1.55 |
| 1901 | 41,847 | 9,339 | 29 | [c] |
| 1911 | 73,788 | 31,919 | 76 | 18.00 |
| 1921 | 99,690 | 25,924 | 35 | 20.17 |
| 1931 | 126,108 | 26,318 | 27 | 25.59 |
| 1950[e] | 230,256 | 104,148 | 83 | 27.20 |
| 1952[f] | 267,407 | 37,151 | 16 | 27.20 |
| 1962 | 449,500 | 182,093 | 68 | 27.20 |
| 1963[g] | 665,246 | 215,746 | 48 | 27.20 |

[a] The first decennial census of Lagos was taken in 1871; the first enumeration for registration of births and deaths was taken in 1866.

[b] Before 1901, the census area included only that part of Lagos Island west of Macgregor Canal, i.e., all of Lagos Island except Ikoyi. In 1901 Ebute Metta was included. The total area covered by the 1901 census can be estimated at 3.85 square miles, the area of the island (1.55 sq. m.) plus Ebute Metta west of Denton Street (2.30 sq. m.).

In 1911 the boundaries of the town were defined according to the Sanitary District of Lagos, which nearly coincided with the town boundaries fixed in 1917. This township boundary was used for the 1921 census, but was expanded in 1927, bringing the 1931 census area to slightly more than 25 square miles.

By 1950 minor boundary changes had again been made; since then the area has remained at a total of 27.20 square miles.

[c] Not available (see note [b]).

[d] The 1891 census showed a decrease because it counted only those persons "ordinarily resident" in the houses visited, whereas the 1881 census had enumerated "all persons" in Lagos. Moreover, in 1881 enumerators were paid on a per entry basis, whereas in 1891 they were paid on a daily or job basis and hence might have been less assiduous in registering names.

[e] No census was taken in the 1940s because of the war, but one was needed in 1950 in order to compile voters' lists for Lagos Town Council election. The 1950 census covered Lagos only.

[f] Because Lagos was included in the Western Region count in the 1952 census, occasional discrepancies appear in the reported figures. Some sources put the city's population at 272,000 instead of 267,407, but the Federal Office of Statistics in Lagos has confirmed the lower figure.

[g] Because the 1962 national census was widely disputed, a new census was taken a year later. The 1963 census is believed to be more accurate, especially for Lagos.

SOURCES: P. A. Talbot, *The Peoples of Southern Nigeria* (London: Oxford University Press, 1926), Vol. IV; *Population Census of Lagos, 1931* (Lagos: Federal Office of Statistics, 1931); *Population Census of Lagos, 1950* (Lagos: Federal Office of Statistics, 1950); *Population Census of the Western Region of Nigeria, 1952* (Lagos: Government Statistician, 1953–54); *Population Census of Lagos, 1963* (Lagos: Federal Office of Statistics, 1963).

nomic development in other directions. Bulk goods imported into Nigeria were broken down for redistribution in Lagos and the interior, attracting numerous wholesalers, retailers, and commercial agents. Lagos itself grew as a market for imported consumer products, thanks to the high purchasing power of its wage-earning population. Improved port facilities stimulated development of the city's infrastructure, attracting private industry. Before 1951 industrial development was at a bare minimum, there being only fifteen major industrial establishments in Lagos, including public utilities. By 1959, 2,400 establishments in Lagos employed approxi-

TABLE 2

POPULATION DENSITY OF LAGOS MUNICIPALITY, 1911–1963

| Year | Density per square mile |
|------|-------------------------|
| 1911 | 4,098 |
| 1921 | 4,984 |
| 1931 | 4,850[a] |
| 1950 | 8,528 |
| 1952 | 9,903 |
| 1963 | 24,638 |

[a] The decline in 1931 is owing to the 1927 expansion of the municipal boundaries (see table 1, note *b*) and the high death rate caused by an outbreak of bubonic plague in Lagos in the 1920s.

SOURCES: *Population Census of Lagos, 1950* (Lagos: Federal Office of Statistics, 1950); *Population Census of Lagos, 1963* (Lagos: Federal Office of Statistics, 1963).

mately 40,000 workers, excluding factories located beyond municipal limits.[27]

The population of Lagos swelled from immigrants flocking to the city after the 1940s in search of jobs. Demobilization following World War II added to the heavy stream of job seekers, creating an unprecedented level of unemployment. In 1945, to cope with the problem, each employer of ten or more African workers was required by law to hire a number of veterans equal to 10 percent of his normal work force.[28] In addition, the labor exchange was closed to all inhabitants who could not establish six months' residence in Lagos. As intended, this restriction hit settlers from the provinces the hardest, but it did not successfully check immigration. As table 1[29] shows, by 1950 the population of Lagos was almost six times as large as it had been at the beginning of the century. By 1963 the density of population on Lagos Island had reached an incredible 125,000 persons per square mile, with about 100,000 daily commuters adding to the congestion. For the city itself, the average density in 1963 was almost 25,000 persons per square mile, equal to New York's Manhattan Island (see tables 2, 3, and 4). From

TABLE 3

POPULATION DENSITY OF LAGOS ISLAND, 1901–1963

| Year[a] | Density per square mile |
|---|---|
| 1901 | 25,000 |
| 1921 | 50,000 |
| 1931 | 58,000 |
| 1950 | 87,000 |
| 1963 | 125,000 |

[a] Figures for 1911 are not available.

SOURCE: *Population Census of Lagos, 1950* (Lagos: Federal Office of Statistics, 1950); *Population Census of Lagos, 1963* (Lagos: Federal Office of Statistics, 1963).

TABLE 4

INTERCENSAL INCREASE IN POPULATION IN LAGOS, BY DISTRICT, 1931–1963
(In percentages)

| District | 1931–1950 | 1950–1952 | 1952–1962 | 1962–1963 |
|---|---|---|---|---|
| Lagos Island | 50.4 | 12.0 | 14.4 | 46.0 |
| Ikoyi and Victoria Island | 187.3 | 16.2 | 121.7 | 44.4 |
| Mainland districts | 199.9 | 23.1 | 141.7 | 52.4 |
| All districts | 82.2 | 16.1 | 68.1 | 48.0 |

SOURCE: C. N. Ejiogu, "Survey of African Migration to the Main Migrant Areas of the Federal Territory of Lagos," paper read at First African Population Conference, University of Ibadan, Nigeria, January 1966, p. 2.

1952 until 1963, the average annual growth rate of the city had been a staggering 14 percent.

Geographically, Lagos has developed four functional zones: (1) the urban core located on Lagos Island, containing high-density housing and key commercial and administrative centers; (2) the mainland residential sections of Ebute Metta, Surulere, and Yaba, containing middle- to low-density housing and the university complex; (3) the residential areas of Ikoyi, Victoria Island, and parts of Apapa, containing low-density, high-priced housing;

and (4) the industrial, railway, and harbor areas situated at Apapa, Iddo, and the Marina side of Lagos Island.

It would be a mistake to infer that the impressive economic and social development of the past sixty or seventy years has transformed Lagos into a fragment of Europe in Africa. Although its economic development has been largely influenced by exogenous factors introduced from the West, the urban social structure is distinctly of African origin. The most pronounced and most consistent feature of the city's social structure, for example, is its large Yoruba population (see table 5). The Yoruba people are traditional urban dwellers who cluster in ethnically homogeneous, occupationally specialized, and politically centralized towns, with residential units based on lineage and kinship ties. Lagos is not one of the most

TABLE 5

PRINCIPAL ETHNIC GROUPS IN LAGOS AS PERCENTAGE
OF TOTAL POPULATION, 1911–1963

| Ethnic group | 1911 | 1921 | 1931 | 1950 | 1963 |
|---|---|---|---|---|---|
| Yoruba | 82 | 81 | 77 | 71 | 72 |
| Ibo | 0.5 | 2 | 4 | 11 | 15 |
| Hausa | 5 | 4 | 3 | 2 | 2 |
| Edo[a] | 0.5 | 2 | 3 | 4 | 3 |
| Other Nigerians[b] | 11 | 9 | 6 | 6 | 5 |
| Non-Nigerians | 1 | 2 | 7 | 6 | 3 |

[a] Edo included Kukuruku and Urhobo in 1931.

[b] Includes native foreigners, or Saros and Amaros. After 1931, these groups were included in one of the other major ethnic group classifications, principally Yoruba.

SOURCES: *Population Census of Lagos, 1950* (Lagos: Federal Office of Statistics, 1950); *Population Census of Lagos, 1963* (Lagos: Federal Office Statistics, 1963).

typical of Yoruba towns, but many features of Yoruba urbanism, particularly the pattern of ethnic homogeneity, have survived throughout the years of growth. Between 1911 and 1963 the city's population increased ninefold, but the proportion of Yoruba residents never fell below 70 percent of the total.

The majority of urban immigrants to Lagos, as well as the indigenes, have always been Yoruba. The first to come were repatriated slaves; the more recent and by far more numerous immigrants are job seekers, mostly from Abeokuta, Ijebu, and Oyo provinces. As table 6 shows, the Yorubas not only flocked to the city in larger numbers, but they also tended to stay for longer periods. In 1960, in

TABLE 6

LAGOS IMMIGRANTS BY ETHNIC ORIGIN AND LENGTH OF RESIDENCE, 1964
(In percentages)

| *Years resident* | *Yoruba* | *Ibo* | *Edo* | *Ibibio* | *Hausa* | *Other Nigerians* | *Other Africans* | *Total* |
|---|---|---|---|---|---|---|---|---|
| 0–4 | 33 | 46 | 31 | 52 | 80 | 53 | 51 | 40 |
| 5–9 | 22 | 23 | 25 | 22 | 11 | 28 | 17 | 22 |
| 10–14 | 15 | 13 | 13 | 3 | 3 | 9 | 10 | 13 |
| 15–19 | 9 | 9 | 14 | 6 | 3 | 6 | 7 | 9 |
| 20–24 | 8 | 7 | 9 | 4 | 3 | 3 | 2 | 7 |
| 25–29 | 4 | 3 | 2 | – | – | – | – | 3 |
| 30–34 | 4 | 0.5 | 3 | 0.6 | – | – | 2 | 3 |
| 35 and over | 5 | 0.5 | 2 | 1 | – | – | 10 | 3 |

SOURCE: C. N. Ejiogu, "Survey of African Migration to the Main Migrant Areas of the Federal Territory of Lagos," paper read at First African Population Conference, University of Ibadan, Nigeria, January 1966, p. 13.

TABLE 7

PERCENTAGE DISTRIBUTION OF PRINCIPAL ETHNIC GROUPS
IN LAGOS, BY WARD, 1960

| *Ward*[a] | *Population as percent of total* | *Yoruba* | *Ibo* | *Efik* | *Edo* | *Hausa* | *Non-Nigerian* |
|---|---|---|---|---|---|---|---|
| A | 13.9 | 92.0 | 2.1 | 0.7 | 0.3 | 0.7 | 1.6 |
| B | 14.9 | 92.0 | 1.4 | 0.6 | 0.2 | 1.6 | 0.5 |
| C (H) | 27.8 | 75.3 | 8.0 | 1.6 | 2.7 | 0.6 | 4.0 |
| D | 8.2 | 53.4 | 26.0 | 2.2 | 3.8 | 1.0 | 3.9 |
| E | 14.1 | 52.0 | 27.7 | 3.2 | 3.1 | 3.5 | 4.2 |
| F | 14.4 | 82.7 | 6.7 | 1.0 | 1.7 | 0.9 | 2.3 |
| G | 6.7 | 30.3 | 33.6 | 2.3 | 4.7 | 3.3 | 10.0 |
| All Wards | 100.0 | 74.5 | 11.9 | 1.6 | 2.1 | 1.4 | 3.3 |

[a] Wards A, B, C, and H are on Lagos Island (H was carved out of C in 1950, but they were treated as one unit in this survey); Wards D, E, and F are on the mainland; and Ward G is on Lagos and Victoria Island.

SOURCE: A. L. Mabogunje, "Lagos: A Study in Urban Geography" (Ph.D dissertation, University of London, 1961), p. 150.

all but one of the eight wards, a minimum of 50 percent of the residents were of Yoruba origin (see table 7). Ethnic homogeneity was highest in the inner city, where 75 percent of the island's population was Yoruba, and the oldest districts, like most traditional Yoruba towns, were more than 90 percent Yoruba.

This ethnic dominance has had a profound impact on the pattern of social integration in Lagos. Instead of the melting-pot model of urban assimilation, the process of urban acculturation in Lagos has been based on deference to, or conformity with, the customs and values of the dominant group. It has amounted to a "Yorubanization" of the city, for the Yoruba prevail not simply in numbers, but in the cultural life, the social institutions, and, as is shown later, the political structure of the town.

The non-Yoruba groups in Lagos, of which the Ibo-speaking people constitute the largest, come mostly from Nigeria's East-Central, South-Eastern, Rivers, and Mid-Western states. From 0.5 percent of the urban population in 1911 the Ibos rose to 15 percent in 1963 (table 5). Their migration to Lagos was as much a consequence of conditions that pushed them out of their homeland as it was a product of the pull of the city, for their movement to urban areas commenced in the 1920s, a time of relatively meager economic opportunity.

Pressured by severe overpopulation in the east and armed with newly acquired education and skills, the Ibos rapidly filled Nigeria's cities. They constituted 45 percent of the total non-Yoruba population of Lagos by 1950, the majority coming from Owerri Province, one of the most densely populated areas in tropical Africa. During the nationalist period the Ibos clashed with the Yorubas as competition between the two ethnic groups became intense, but gradually they came to represent a significant minority actively participating in local affairs. After the 1966 civil disturbances following two military coups d'etat, however, the number of Ibos remaining in noneastern cities dropped sharply; most of them rushed back to their homeland before the secession of the former Eastern Region and the outbreak of the Nigerian Civil War. No official statistics are available, but the number of Ibos in Lagos dropped from approximately 100,000 in 1963 to an estimated 17,000 to 38,000 by 1968.[30]

In 1963 the Yorubas and the Ibos together accounted for 87 percent of the total population of the city (table 5). The remaining population comprised a variety of other ethnic groups and nation-

38

alities; at least 23,000 were European expatriates.[31] The Edo, Hausa, Efik, and Ijaw communities represented the next largest groups, in that order, but at no time did any of them constitute more than 5 percent of the total, although, with one exception, their proportions steadily increased. That exception is the Hausa people, Nigeria's largest ethnic group from the far north, who have diminished in their proportion of the urban population over a fifty-year period, dropping from 5 percent in 1911 to 2 percent in 1963 (table 5).

The social heterogeneity of Lagos is reflected in the religious, age, occupational, and residential patterns far more than in its ethnic composition. The religious balance in the city shifted in favor of the Christians in 1950, whereas in the first half of the century the Muslim community had been dominant (see table 8).

TABLE 8

PRINCIPAL RELIGIOUS GROUPS IN LAGOS AS PERCENTAGE
OF TOTAL POPULATION, 1871–1963

| Religious group | 1871 | 1881 | 1891 | 1901 | 1911 | 1921 | 1931 | 1950 | 1963 |
|---|---|---|---|---|---|---|---|---|---|
| Muslim | 18 | 16 | 25 | 53 | 49 | 51 | 50 | 41 | 44 |
| Christian | 8 | 12 | 12 | 25 | 29 | 39 | 45 | 53 | 55 |
| Animist and others | 74 | 72 | 63 | 22 | 22 | 10 | 5 | 6 | 1 |

SOURCES: P. A. Talbot, *The Peoples of Southern Nigeria* (London: Oxford University Press, 1926), Vol. IV; *Population Census of Lagos, 1950* (Lagos: Federal Office of Statistics, 1950); *Population Census of Lagos, 1963* (Lagos: Federal Office of Statistics, 1963).

Islam was introduced into Lagos in the late eighteenth century by Hausa traders. It thrived among the local population even after the arrival of Christian missionaries in the early nineteenth century. By 1901 more than half the town was Muslim and a quarter of it was Christian. Not until the mid-twentieth century did the progress of Islam begin to level off, owing to the influx of Ibo and other eastern immigrants, most of whom were Catholic. Isale Eko now remains the largest and most solidly Islamic section of the city. In many respects the social cleavages that divide the city, though not necessarily religious in origin, are reinforced by this division, since Yoruba and Ibo, indigene and settler, and lower- and middle-class communities frequently coincide with the distinctions between Muslims and Christians. According to the 1963 census, Christians represented 55 percent, Muslims, 44 percent, and animists and others, only 1 percent of the population (table 8).

As might be expected, the urban population is becoming increasingly younger. By 1965, 42 percent of the city's inhabitants were fourteen years of age or less, compared with only 27 percent in 1931 (see table 9). Among young adults, the age structure has

TABLE 9

Age Groups in Lagos as Percentage of Total Population, 1921–1965

| Age group | 1931 | 1950 | 1963 | 1965[a] |
|---|---|---|---|---|
| 0–14 | 27 | 32 | 37 | 42 |
| 15–19 | 11 | 11 | 9 | 11 |
| 20–24 | 11 | 12 | 16 | 11 |
| 25–29 | 13 | 13 | 13 | 11 |
| 30–34 | 10 | 9 | 8 | 7 |
| 35 and over | 28 | 23 | 17 | 18 |

[a] Because the 1963 figures for the 15–19 and 20–24 age groups were believed inaccurate, owing to the tendency of young respondents to inflate their ages so as to be eligible to vote in the 1964–65 federal elections, the census office conducted a supplementary sample survey in Lagos in 1965, with the results shown here.

Sources: *Population Census of Lagos, 1950* (Lagos: Federal Office of Statistics, 1950); *Population Census of Lagos, 1963* (Lagos: Federal Office of Statistics, 1963); *Population Survey of Lagos, 1965* (Lagos: Federal Office of Statistics, 1965).

been fairly stable, with those between fifteen and twenty-nine consistently representing approximately 33 percent of the population. The age pattern reflects the continual influx over the years of youthful migrants, the primary source of unemployed workers in the city.

As determined by income and occupation, Lagos has a high degree of class stratification, although for those who are educated there is considerable occupational mobility. Of all the large towns in Nigeria, Lagos alone has no significant agricultural population, and with the exception of scattered fishing villages along the coastline, nearly the entire city depends upon commerce and industry.[32] At the top of the scale, representing less than 2.5 percent of the contemporary urban population, is a comparatively wealthy elite of high-ranking executives, including the directors of public corporations, business managers, and civil servants (see table 10), most of whom earn between £2,000 and £4,000 ($5,600 and

$11,200 at the pre-1971 conversion rate of N£1 = $2.80) a year, supplemented in many instances by other income. At the bottom of the social scale is a much larger class of minimally paid workers who earn from £120 to £400 ($330 to $1,100) a year. The disparity in income between upper and lower classes is vividly illustrated by the ratio of 20:1 between the salary of a permanent secretary, the highest career classification in the Nigerian civil

TABLE 10

OCCUPATIONAL GROUPS IN LAGOS, 1963

| Occupational group | Male | Female | Total | Percentage of total labor force |
|---|---|---|---|---|
| Professional, technical, and related[a] | 11,801 | 3,891 | 15,692 | 5.53 |
| Administrative, executive, and managerial[b] | 3,933 | 255 | 4,188 | 1.48 |
| Clerical | 37,054 | 4,757 | 41,811 | 14.74 |
| Sales workers (traders) | 24,631 | 49,149 | 73,780 | 26.01 |
| Farmers, fishermen, hunters, loggers, and related | 6,391 | 260 | 6,651 | 2.34 |
| Miners, quarrymen, and related | 228 | 7 | 235 | 0.08 |
| Transport and communications[c] | 18,749 | 611 | 19,360 | 6.82 |
| Craftsmen, production workers, and laborers | 87,825 | 4,758 | 92,583 | 32.63 |
| Service, sport, and recreation[d] | 21,218 | 5,414 | 26,632 | 9.39 |
| Unspecified or inadequately described | 2,545 | 228 | 2,773 | 0.98 |
| Total | 214,375 | 69,330 | 283,705 | 100.00 |

[a] Includes scientists, university lecturers, herbalists, artists, etc.
[b] Includes traditional chiefs, diplomats, directors, managers, working proprietors, etc.
[c] Includes engineers, canoemen, chauffeurs, transport managers, etc.
[d] Includes policemen, hotel managers, cooks, domestic servants, wardens, photographers, hospital workers, cleaners, etc.
SOURCE: *Population Census of Lagos, 1963* (Lagos: Federal Office of Statistics, 1963).

service, and the salary of a laborer in Lagos; the comparable ratio in London is 8:1.[33]

Even more significant indexes of the distribution of wealth in the community are the size of the lower-income groups and the degree of unemployment. In the sixties, the average annual income of an adult male wage earner in Lagos was approximately £216 ($600).[34] About 95 percent of all male workers employed in Lagos firms (with not less than ten workers) earned less than £570 ($1,600) a year, and 58 percent earned less than £210 ($580) a year.[35] Most of these wage earners are expected to support relatives away from Lagos as well as members of their extended families attached to their households. With these obligations and the high cost of living in Lagos, workers must frequently depend on other sources of revenue—loans, savings, rentals, gambling, and so on—for ordinary living expenses. A consumer survey conducted in Lagos in 1960 calculated that among the lower-income groups "a household would be 48.6 shillings per month in debt if other receipts were not received."[36] The lower-income groups—primarily artisans, production workers, traders, and laborers—constituted more than 70 percent of the total urban labor force in 1963 (see table 10).

TABLE 11

LABOR FORCE IN LAGOS BY AGE GROUP, 1963

| Age group | Number | Number working | Percent working | Percent of total labor force |
|---|---|---|---|---|
| 15–19 | 61,256 | 25,583 | 41.76 | 8.59 |
| 20–24 | 109,043 | 78,035 | 71.56 | 26.21 |
| 25–34 | 138,188 | 106,213 | 76.86 | 35.67 |
| 35–44 | 63,349 | 51,436 | 81.19 | 17.27 |
| 45–54 | 30,083 | 24,033 | 79.89 | 8.07 |
| 55–64 | 12,602 | 8,497 | 67.43 | 2.85 |
| 65–74 | 5,093 | 2,799 | 54.96 | 0.94 |
| 75 and over | 2,915 | 1,185 | 40.65 | 0.40 |
| Total | 422,529 | 297,781 | 70.48 | 100.00 |

SOURCE: *Population Census of Lagos, 1963* (Lagos: Federal Office of Statistics, 1963).

The most serious labor problem in Lagos is the large number of unemployed or unemployables, many of whom describe themselves professionally as "applicants," a designation suggesting a perpetual condition of unemployment. According to the 1963 census, 30 percent of the population fifteen years of age and over were without jobs (see table 11), but 41 percent of the population aged

twenty-one to thirty were found to be unemployed in a private survey of the same year, a figure that rose to 57 percent by 1966.[37]
Most of these jobless youths live with relatives or townsmen, often
remaining in the city for long periods in the vain hope of securing
positions; however, jobs simply do not exist in sufficient quantity.
During their stay the young people deplete the savings of the
wage earners to whose households they are attached and swell the
ranks of the expanding lower classes. Many unemployed youths
were absorbed by the army during the civil war, temporarily relieving the problem. But, as in the post–World War II period, eventual demobilization may flood the labor market with veterans, re-
surrecting the old problem on a larger scale than ever before.

The gap between the upper and lower classes in Lagos is bridged
by a relatively small middle class composed of some prosperous
traders, a few entrepreneurs, and middle-range managerial and
professional workers, who earn about £400–£800 ($1,100–$2,200)
a year. The expansion of the middle classes is limited both by the
meager employment opportunities in relation to the labor supply
and by the heavy financial burdens workers are expected to assume
once they achieve an income level that might otherwise permit
them to accumulate savings. The 1960 consumer survey of Lagos
revealed that, of all the expenditures of middle-income households,
"the most important item is the money spent on the maintenance
of relatives not living with the household. If considered together
with casual gifts to these persons, a total of 50.9 percent of monetary transactions is involved."[38] Thus, although the per capita income in Lagos is approximately 18 percent higher than the national
average,[39] this figure deceptively conceals the inequitable income
levels and the heavy financial obligations urban dwellers must
bear.

The urban class structure affects residence patterns in different
degrees, depending upon ethnicity, kinship, and time of settlement.
Class and ethnicity tend to be inversely proportional among higher-
income groups and directly proportional among lower-income
groups. Stated simply, the higher one's income, the less important
it is to reside with one's ethnic group; the lower one's income, the
more important it is to be with one's own ethnic or communal
group. This generalization applies to all but one significant section

43

of the urban community—the traditional quarter of the city. In sections of Lagos Island, where 75 percent of the residents are indigenous Lagosians, kinship is still an important criterion of residence, in many instances superseding class considerations.[40]

Yorubas are important in all areas of Lagos but are most heavily concentrated on Lagos Island and in Ebute Metta, the oldest districts of the city. The other mainland districts are populated chiefly by recent Yoruba immigrants whose settlement patterns depend primarily on their class positions; the more affluent among them usually locate in the newer districts in Surulere and Yaba.

Ibos have generally settled near their places of work, in Obalende, Ikoyi, Victoria Island (where many Ibos, employed as household staff, are commonly provided with housing on the compounds of their employers), Ojuelegba behind the railway compound, Apapa near the industrial plants, and in some sections of Yaba. Binis have established roots in Epetedo and Faji in the traditional districts of Lagos Island; the Urhobo, in Ereko; and the Efik, in Araromi and Ojuelegba.[41]

Nowhere in the city is ethnic segregation complete, however, and even in the traditional wards a scattered mixture of ethnic groups can usually be found. The pattern of separate stranger settlements common to many other Nigerian cities has not appeared in Lagos, although during the colonial period a settlement of this type was once contemplated for the Hausa community. The Hausas are still one of the most exclusive groups in Lagos, but since they constitute a very small proportion of the urban population they have not formed a closed residential community.

Two additional factors have inhibited the formation of separate stranger settlements in Lagos: the shortage of land and the high mobility of the population. It would be difficult for a segregated community to cut itself off in so tightly congested a city. Inevitably, with the scarcity of land and severe overcrowding, the community would be inundated by the constant flow of new immigrants. Also, the majority of immigrants to the city remain in Lagos for less than ten years, undermining the stability and solidarity of ethnic or communal enclaves. The breakdown by ethnicity of immigrants who settle for ten years or less is: Yoruba, 55 percent; Ibo, 69 percent; Hausa, 91 percent; Edo, 56 percent;

and Ibibio, 74 percent (see table 6).[42] Thus, although the city
is built around a permanent traditional community, the majority
of urban residents are transients in a perpetual state of resettlement.

In the heart of Lagos the phenomenon of the urban ghetto is
apparent, just as it is in many Western cities, but for exactly the
opposite reasons. In the United States, urban ghettos are a
consequence of a middle-class exodus and a lower-class influx. In
Lagos, the inner city is dominated by native-born inhabitants who
own land in the heart of the city, an area that has been the home of
their families for generations. These indigenous residents form in
effect a landed lower class, while the urban migrants who provide
most of the skilled labor for the commercial and industrial sectors
of the economy are forced to settle in the outskirts of the city.

The social divisions that exist in Lagos are therefore accentu-
ated by the spatial distribution of the separate social groups. The
least progressive, Muslim, indigenous, lower-class elements of
the population have the strongest claims as Lagosians, own the
most valuable land, and dominate the central business districts.
The more progressive, Christian, educated, middle- to upper-
class elements are the most mobile, constitute the largest proportion of the wage-earning labor force, and settle farthest from the
central business districts. The contemporary city is, in sum, a
community of basic contradictions: its modernity is built on a
strong base of tradition; its prosperity rests on pillars of poverty; its
cosmopolitanism cloaks a society of provincial groupings. Most
contradictory of all, the oldest and most solidified segment of the
urban community is, in essence, an "urban village" which still
retains the traditional characteristics of ethnic homogeneity,
communal land tenure, close kinship ties, and primary group
relationships.

# PART II

# Political Variables

# CHAPTER 3

# The Ruling Strata

The first, and perhaps the most crucial, variable in changing patterns of urban influence is the nature of the ruling strata, analyzed in terms of the social backgrounds and political connections of men inducted into local public office as well as of nonelected figures who exercise community influence. Since 1917, when a modern system of local government was introduced, Lagos has passed through four periods of political change in which a distinct social group can be identified as having wielded dominant influence in the city. Shifts in leadership occurred when the ruling stratum was displaced by another group rising from the lower ranks of the community. In the first stage (1917-1938) a handful of privileged African aristocrats monopolized leadership positions in the town; in the second (1938-1950), members of the nationalist elite predominated; in the third (1950-1959), middle-class Yoruba immigrants took control; and in the fourth (1959-1967), the indigenous elements seized the reins of power. The scope of political recruitment has thus progressively widened and the circulation of ruling groups has accelerated as urbanization, constitutional reforms, and economic development enabled new social forces to gain prominence.

### EMIGRANT ELITE

In the first part of the twentieth century Lagos was ruled by a colonial oligarchy consisting of British officialdom and an African urban elite. The latter was composed principally of liberated slaves who had acquired privileged positions of status and power in Lagos; they were English-speaking, Western-educated emigrants[1] or sons of emigrants with common socioeconomic backgrounds, cultural origins, and life-styles.

The first three men elected to the Lagos Town Council were typical representatives of this class. Adebesin Folarin, a barrister, was formerly Josiah Folarin Williams, the son of a prosperous merchant prince, Z. A. Williams. His colleague, R. A. Savage, a medical practitioner and editor of a Lagos weekly, the *Nigerian Spectator*, was a descendant of the original leader of the

TABLE 12

NATIVE FOREIGNERS IN LAGOS TOWNSHIP, 1911 AND 1921,
BY NATIONALITY AND COUNTRY OF EMIGRATION

| Nationality | Country of emigration | Number | |
|---|---|---|---|
| | | 1911 | 1921 |
| Belgian | Congo | — | 41 |
| British | Gambia | — | 8 |
| | Gold Coast [Ghana] | 634 | 1,192 |
| | Guiana | — | 9 |
| | Sierra Leone | 940 | 1,373 |
| | Saint Helena | — | 7 |
| | South Africa | 2 | 4 |
| | West Indies | 56 | 124 |
| | Total British | 1,632 | 2,717 |
| French | Cameroons | — | 175 |
| | Congo | — | 2 |
| | Dahomey | 1,493 | 1,857 |
| | Ivory Coast | — | 7 |
| | Senegal | — | 20 |
| | Togoland | — | 527 |
| | Total French | 1,493 | 2,588 |
| Cuban | Cuba | 24 | — |
| Liberian | Kru | 2,680 | 1,707 |
| Portuguese | Brazil | 327 | 193 |
| Spanish | Fernando Po | — | 18 |
| American | United States | 3[a] | — |
| Miscellaneous | | 197 | — |
| Total | | 6,356 | 7,264 |

[a] Negroes.

SOURCE: P. A. Talbot, *The Peoples of Southern Nigeria* (London: Oxford University Press, 1926), IV, 180.

Saro community in Lagos, "Daddy" William Savage. The third councilor, George D. Agbebi, a civil engineer, was the nephew of Majola Agbebi, an outstanding journalist, educator, and poet of early Lagos. These three councilors were second-generation Saros, the largest group in a distinct social stratum that came to be known as "native foreigners." As defined by the census of 1931, a native foreigner was "any person (not being a Native of Nigeria) whose parents were members of a tribe or tribes indigenous to some part of Africa and the descendants of such persons, and . . . any person, one of whose parents were members of such a tribe."[2]

There were 7,264 native foreigners in Lagos in 1921, representing 0.07 percent of the total urban population; a little more than a third of them originated in British territories (see table 12). Most of these retained the Anglo-Saxon names they had acquired in captivity or in Christian missions; most of them built elegant houses styled after English country homes, dressed in European clothes, sent their children abroad for schooling, and continued to worship in Anglican churches. A few combined Western manners with African patterns of behavior, such as mixing African and European names, practicing polygamy, or following a local African religion. But by and large it was Western, not African, culture that shaped their values, attitudes, and behavior. Many became doctors, lawyers, or prosperous traders who offered stiff competition to Europeans. By 1921, for example, there were twenty African as compared with four European lawyers and twelve African as compared with thirteen European doctors in Lagos. All the African professionals were native foreigners,[3] from whose ranks were drawn the first Africans recruited to the Nigerian Legislative Council, the Nigerian administrative service, and the Lagos Town Council (LTC).

When limited local representation was first contemplated in the 1920s, these emigrants were already an integral part of the colonial establishment. They had access to top-level administrators through formal institutional roles and through personal friendships or professional relationships. For most of them, the prospect of elective representation was not a major opportunity for personal political advancement.[4] In fact, most members of the African elite were apprehensive about the introduction of elections. Three leading native foreigners, Dr. Orisadipe Obasa, Sapara da Rocha, and R. A. Savage, requested postponement of the first election on the ground that the public was not well enough prepared for it.[5] Interest in the contest was so minimal that even the *Nigerian Pioneer*, a conservative Lagos newspaper, chastised the electorate for their failure to respond to the opportunity to choose their own representatives. On the eve of balloting the paper described "the vast majority of the populace, including a very large proportion of the educated class [as being] absolutely indifferent [to whether] . . . the polling would take place . . . at all."[6]

To the British, elective representation was a token gesture designed, in the wake of protests over introduction of a water rate, "to ease the burden of taxation."[7] It was therefore introduced with reserve. But despite the fact that only one-fourth of the council seats were elective, the social composition of the LTC during this period was significant for two reasons: it was the first local authority in British West Africa to have elected representatives, and it was the local government body charged with responsibilities in the country's administrative headquarters. The colonial regime permitted elections knowing that it was "safe" to do so; that is, educated native foreigners, having both the qualifications and the resources to win at the polls, would be the natural beneficiaries of the reform. It was the intention of the government that the elite be guided "along the same path as that of Europeans—increased participation in municipal affairs until they proved themselves fitted for the larger responsibilities of Government of their own communities."[8]

The socioeconomic composition of the LTC thus provides evidence of an Anglo-African power structure that dominated Lagos during most of the period of colonial rule. Between 1920 and 1938 the LTC consisted of a majority of European nominated officials, a small contingent of nominated African members, and three or four elected African members. All the African members, whether elected or nominated, were native foreigners. In this period the LTC was closed to indigenes, Muslims, traditional rulers, and middle and lower classes who constituted the majority of the population. Appendix I shows the ethnic, religious, and occupational composition of the small group of elected members who served from 1920 to 1950. All members elected before 1938 were of non-Nigerian origin, all were Christian, and all had high-income occupations.

Although native foreigners held positions of prestige and influence, they were still regarded by the British as aliens who would one day likely return to their own territories, that is, the countries of their liberation. Emigrants frequently moved between the coastal towns of West Africa for economic reasons, lending credence to the belief that they formed a political class having few ties to the Nigerian masses. They were in the somewhat paradoxical position of being a widely pursued but unrepresentative elite whom the colonial authorities eventually came to regard with suspicion and contempt, particularly when their political ambitions for national leadership came to light. By the time of the amalgamation of the northern and southern protectorates in 1914, the colonial government categorically imposed limitations on the extent to which the elite would be allowed to exercise their influence. Lord Lugard[9] stipulated that it was "a cardinal principle of British colonial policy that the interests of a large native population shall not be subject to the well-educated and Europeanized natives who have nothing in common with them and whose interests are often opposed to theirs."[10]

It is quite true that the gap between the educated native foreigners and the masses was exceptionally wide, but the skepticism of the colonial authorities toward the educated elite was based on a set of factors that had little to do with their concern for adequate representation. It was becoming evident that certain members of the elite were beginning to challenge authoritative decisions and, with increasing frequency, covertly to mobilize resistance to official policies. Although the emigrant community was politically divided into pro- and antigovernment factions, the dissatisfaction of colonial officials with selected members of the elite tended to be expressed indiscriminately against all the educated elements in Lagos.[11] The clandestine activities of a small segment of the emigrant elite also served to keep alive fears that the native foreigners could one day be saboteurs of the colonial establishment. Growing realization that few native foreigners had strong ties with Nigeria, that most had considerable talent and skill, and that many had access to the administrative complex made the colonial authorities wary of the potential threat to the security of the colony posed by this minority. Sir Hugh Clifford, governor of Nigeria from 1919 to 1925, affirmed Lord Lugard's earlier reservations about the growing ambitions of the elite:

> It can only be described as farcical to suppose that ... continental Nigeria can be represented by a handful of gentlemen drawn from a half-dozen coast towns—men born and bred in British administrative towns situated on the seashore who, in the safety of British protection have peacefully pursued their studies under British teachers, in British schools, in order to enable them to become ministers of the Christian religion or learned in the laws of England, whose eyes are fixed, not upon African native history or traditions or policy, nor upon their own tribal obligations and duties to their Natural Rulers which immemorial custom should impose on them, but upon political theories evolved by Europeans to fit a wholly different stage of circumstances, arising out of a wholly different environment, for the government of peoples who have arrived at a wholly different stage of civilization."[12]

Culturally, the native foreigners were marginal men standing between the two worlds of English and African society, yet not totally belonging to either one. To the Lagos masses, they were strangers, not *omo eko* ("sons of Lagos") or *omo ibile* ("sons of the soil"). Few were, or could establish that they were, descendants of royal families and therefore deserving of the special status they enjoyed. Many claimed origin in other lands or identified with other Yoruba subgroups, particularly the Egbas and the Ijebus. This heritage made them, as their name implied, "foreigners" in Lagos. The emigrants were resentfully viewed by indigenes as people "who had but recently left Lagos, mere nothings, and who now walked the streets as quasi-Europeans, learned men of the world."[13]

It was equally impossible for the emigrants to be socially accepted by the British, despite their emulation of Victorian manners and behavior. In the eyes of Englishmen, the native foreigners' attempts at linguistic eloquence often seemed bombastic, their formal dress ostentatious, and their pride in educational and occupational achievements overstressed. They were viewed as boastful, conceited, arrogant, and uppity, as amateurish imitators of the English upper class. Moreover, they invoked the "correct" social credentials for all the wrong reasons: they claimed they were born into fine old families by tracing their lineage, not to traditional royalty, but to ex-slaves; they claimed to be inheritors of large estates based, not on propertied wealth, but on earned income; they claimed they were cultured gentlemen, not by displaying the finer values of their own society, but by imitating the British. According to European norms, native foreigners were nouveau riche grasping for upward social mobility. However hard they tried, "black Englishmen" could not be recognized by their white mentors as social equals.

These social barriers and the constitutional limitations imposed by colonial rule prevented native foreigners from gaining unlimited domination over the town. Even with these restrictions, however, they continued to exert a formidable degree of influence, although not so much as in the late nineteenth century when the British maintained only a rudimentary administration and the European population was kept to a minimum. As a local aristocracy, the emigrant elite were destined to wield influence in excess of their numerical strength as long as there was little social change and as long as resources were concentrated in the hands of a few at the top. Their demise came when their number began to dwindle, when they lost exclusive control of the means of staying in power, and when they were unable to meet new challenges from rising classes. The chief reason for their decline was the spread of education, a resource that propelled a new nationalist elite to the forefront of urban politics.

### NATIONALIST ELITE

By the late 1930s, after recovery from the worldwide depression and the postwar slump in trade and after development of the port, a new labor force began to be attracted to Lagos. Economic activity stimulated by World War II further encouraged the trend. Drawn by job opportunities and the prospect of a better life, Nigerians flocked to the city by the thousands, swelling the population by 83 percent between 1931 and 1950 (see table 1, above).

55

Political Variables

From a staid, conservative town controlled by patrician Victorian aristocrats, Lagos became a dynamic city dominated by a new generation of educated nationalists who ushered in an era of political reform and, ultimately, of self-government.

Nationalism affected the patterns of urban political recruitment in three ways. First, it introduced sustained and organized competition for political office, replacing sporadic personal rivalry among well-placed notables. Second, it brought men who were not native foreigners or their descendants into position of leadership, adding new blood to what had been the domain of an exclusive social class. Third, and most important, it reshaped the political values and objectives of the African elite. Whereas the emigrants were aspiring members of the colonial power structure, the nationalists challenged the old social order and mobilized the masses into a countrywide movement for independence.

The majority of councilors elected to the LTC during the period 1938–1950 were still drawn primarily from the class of educated descendants of native foreigners (see app. II), but they were younger men who had a unique conception of their role in politics. They were fully conscious, as no earlier generation of Nigerians had been, of the injustice of colonial rule, and they were imbued with a racial consciousness lacking in the old elite. They were demanding eventual self-government, fuller participation, and immediate local government reforms. They exhibited militancy and a talent for organization, building their strength by mobilizing the masses for concerted and purposeful programs of action.

Whereas previous political competition had been largely limited to personal antagonisms between central figures, such as Herbert Macaulay versus Henry Carr, or Adeniji-Jones versus Kitoyi Ajasa (see chap. 4), the nationalist elite formed political alignments along new ideological lines. The Yoruba intelligentsia, assisted by immigrants from the west, established the Nigerian Youth Movement (NYM), while indigenous Yorubas in alliance with eastern emigrants supported the National Council of Nigeria and the Cameroons (NCNC), formed a few years later by Nnamdi Azikiwe, an Onitsha Ibo (see chap. 5). These parties had an impact on changing patterns of political mobilization and leadership. As a multitribal party embracing all elements of the new generation

56

of political leaders, the NYM campaigned on the theme that it alone could offer genuine Nigerian leadership, an allusion to the fact that its opposition was linked with the old-guard generation of native foreigners. The NCNC, whose membership was organizational, was the first party to mobilize successfully the urban masses indirectly through what was then the most effective political instrument—the numerous voluntary associations whose members were newly arrived settlers. Eventually, the NYM came to be regarded locally as an organ of the settler Yorubas who were rapidly becoming the largest group in the city. It is not surprising, therefore, that the Nigerian National Democratic Party (NNDP), which had dominated Lagos politics for the past two decades, allied itself with the NCNC, assuring continuity of leadership between two political generations in the city.

The transition of leadership from the old "black Victorians" to the new nationalist elite can best be illustrated by comparing two prominent councilors who held office during this period: Dr. C. C. Adeniji-Jones, an old-guard, antigovernment critic, and Dr. Akinola Maja, a younger, more militant nationalist. The two men had similar socioeconomic backgrounds. Dr. Adeniji-Jones was born in Sierra Leone, was educated in Freetown, and qualified as a physician at Durham University. He practiced medicine in England and Ireland before he came to Lagos in 1904 as a member of the West African Medical Service; thirteen years later he set up a private practice. Dr. Maja, born in Lagos to James and Elizabeth Pearse, received his early education at Methodist Ereko and Obun Eko schools in Lagos and took his medical training at Edinburgh University; in 1920 he returned to Lagos to join the government service as a medical officer. Both men were thus of Saro origin, Christian, highly educated, and of the same professional status.

Politically, Adeniji-Jones was an articulate but moderate reformer. He was a member of the Legislative Council and the Lagos Town Council (originally a nominated member, subsequently an elected member) and second president of the NNDP. Commonly regarded as Herbert Macaulay's chief deputy, Adeniji-Jones played the role of a one-man official opposition in the Legislative Council and became known for his incessant questioning, even harassment, of the government. It was his habit to force the government to make detailed defenses of its policy, as for example, in his call for a list of names, ranks, and departments of all the Africans appointed to administrative positions between 1927 and 1934; he openly challenged the motives and objectives of government decisions, as in his criticism of the income tax law introduced in 1927, which he unhesitatingly claimed "was not based on economic needs."[14] A master of oratory, Adeniji-Jones provoked heated controversy on a wide range of issues. But throughout it all he remained a man who worked well within established institutions. He never disputed the legitimacy of colonial rule, and he earned the respect of colonial administrators by his astute knowledge of, and respect for, parliamentary procedures. Unimpressed by the dramatic demands of the new nationalists, he became the only member of the NNDP to break with Macaulay over the latter's decision to ally with the NCNC in 1944.

Maja, on the other hand, was a radical who assiduously cultivated associational links outside the official community. During the course of his political career he was president of the Nigerian Youth Movement, president of the National Emergency Committee (a coalition of leading nationalists formed in response to the 1949 shooting at the Enugu colliery), president of the Egbe Omo Oduduwa (a Yoruba cultural association), chairman of the board of directors of the National Bank of Nigeria, an elected member of the LTC, a foundation member of the Action Group (political successor to the NYM), and a close confidant of Oba Adeniji Adele of Lagos who bestowed on him the title of "Baba Eko" ("Father of Lagos"). Whereas Adeniji-Jones criticized policies within the framework of ongoing debates, Maja invited direct confrontaton, breaking off the dialogue if necessary to make his point, as he did in his dramatic walkout from the LTC during his first term in office over the question of retrenchment of African employees. Although he had an elite background, Maja was unmistakably different from the older generation; while Adeniji-Jones was boycotting the NCNC in 1944, Maja was urging Azikiwe to demand immediate self-government.

The early fears of colonial officials that the educated elite might one day be saboteurs of the colonial regime were vindicated, but ironically the source of agitation was not, as had been expected, the generation that was well entrenched in the system. The threat came instead from a new breed of men—including native-born Nigerians like Azikiwe and sons of native foreigners like Maja who had had little or no previous association with the establishment— who had strong reactions against the servile uncle Tomism they perceived in their predecessors. As Azikiwe saw it, the task of the new nationalists was to avoid the mistakes of the past and achieve "mental emancipation" from the older generation in order to pursue the path of independence.[15]

### NONELITES

With the introduction of universal suffrage and a fully elective council in 1950, formerly disenfranchised classes burst into the forefront of Lagos politics. The decade preceding independence was thus characterized by the rapid emergence of nonelites, who were principally middle-class settlers of mixed religious, occupational, and ethnic backgrounds.

The first election held under democratic reforms became a fight between indigenous Lagosians and immigrants, the latter by that time constituting a majority of the electorate. Despite the fact that the 1950 election came at the height of the nationalist period, neither of the dominant political parties directly contested it. The newly formed National Emergency Committee (NEC), an umbrella nationalist organization, remained aloof for the sake of unity and urged member associations to do the same.[16] The NCNC and the NYM accordingly backed their respective local allies without fielding separate candidates of their own.

The NNDP—or Democratic Party as it came to be known— formed a "Triple Grand Alliance" with two local parties, the Nigerian Labour Congress and the Lagos Market Women's Guild, a tactic designed by the NCNC to gain the support of the settlers and of Macaulay's followers. Reflecting the heterogeneity of the immigrant population, the Democratic Party nominated sixteen Yoruba, six Ibo, and two Edo (Bini) candidates for the twenty-four seats on the council, a slate that also included women, wage earners, professionals, entrepreneurs, and Muslims.

Opposing the NNDP was a new grass-roots communal association, the Area Councils, formed by the recently appointed oba

of Lagos, Adeniji Adele II. Adele's organization consisted principally of Lagos aborigines concerned with defending themselves
against the overwhelming number of settlers in their midst. The
leaders of the Area Councils nominated only Yoruba (mainly Lagosian) candidates, with one exception—a European contesting a
seat in the expatriate residential area.[17] They had the backing of
the NYM, thanks to the mutual objective of opposing the NNDP-
NCNC alliance, but for the most part during this first popular
election the Area Councils remained an independent, locally
based communal organization which resisted all attempts at control by outside groups.

The contest was cast as a struggle between contractors, pensioners, traders, and shopkeepers against professionals and prosperous
businessmen, those with education, the men of "the wig and the
gown."[18] The Area Councils' candidates saw it as a competition
between indigenes and strangers, those "who had not been residing in their area or ward or [did not] understand . . . [the local]
language."[19] For the first time, ethnicity was introduced into local
politics. The characteristics of the newcomers which were most
resented were education and wealth, assets possessed in larger
proportions by the eastern ethnic groups, especially the Ibos who,
owing to circumstances in their homeland, came to Lagos better
equipped to compete in the urban labor market.[20] Oba Adele had
long harbored resentment against the NCNC because it earlier
opposed his nomination for the throne and advocated the exclusion of traditional authorities from local government. He therefore
enthusiastically mobilized the Area Councils to help prevent the
encroachment of non-Lagosian strangers in general and the ener-
getic Ibos in particular.

Election results revealed the depth of the split between the two
sections of the community. The Area Councils captured the two
traditional wards while the NNDP, with the support of the NCNC,
won sweeping victories in all other districts. The composition of
the new council, however, represented a milestone for both groups
in terms of representation: eighteen Yorubas, five of whom were
indigenes, and six Ibos were elected. Occupationally, the council
included barristers, pensioners, secretaries, a doctor, a printer, a

corporation director, and a tailor. The results affirmed that the days of elitism and aristocracy were over.

Between 1950 and 1959 the LTC continued to be penetrated by emergent groups in the community—the "new men" of urban Africa. These were not newly arrived youths who provided mass support for the nationalist movement, but older and well-established members of the urban middle class, usually between the ages of fifty and sixty-five, who had either been born in Lagos after their families resettled there during the interwar years or had migrated themselves as youths in search of employment. The majority were self-made men who had received at least a secon-

TABLE 13

AGE (IN 1967) OF LAGOS COUNCILORS, 1950–1966

| Age group | 1950–1959 | | 1959–1966 | |
|---|---|---|---|---|
| | Number | Percentage[a] of known | Number | Percentage[a] of known |
| 20–30 | — | — | 3 | 4 |
| 31–40 | 1 | 2 | 27 | 33 |
| 41–50 | 14 | 22 | 25 | 30 |
| 51–60 | 29 | 46 | 20 | 24 |
| 61 and over | 19 | 30 | 7 | 9 |
| Unknown | 28 | — | 14 | — |
| Total | 91 | 100 | 96 | 100 |

[a] Percentages rounded.

dary education and worked in salaried white-collar jobs. They were predominantly Christians who had lived in Lagos for a minimum of twenty-five years. More than 80 percent were Yoruba, but only a third were indigenous to Lagos. Of the nineteen councilors who were non-Yoruba, fourteen were Ibo. Urban leadership during the preindependence decade was therefore chiefly in the hands of the settler Yorubas who, after a number of years in the city, were turning to the fertile pastures of politics.

These leadership patterns were confirmed by a 1967 social survey of elected local officials who served between 1950 and 1966,[21] the results of which are reported fully in Appendix II. The socioeconomic and political characteristics of the local leaders are presented comparatively for two periods—1950–1959 and 1959–1966—in tables 13 through 22. The results reveal a characteristic dominance by a particular social group in nearly every classification.

TABLE 14

HOMETOWNS OF LAGOS COUNCILORS, 1950–1966

| Hometown | 1950–1959 | | 1959–1966 | |
| | Number | Percentage[a] of known | Number | Percentage[a] of known |
|---|---|---|---|---|
| Lagos | 37 | 50 | 42 | 50 |
| Outer Lagos | 5 | 7 | 5 | 6 |
| Ibadan | — | — | 4 | 5 |
| Abeokuta | 9 | 13 | 7 | 8 |
| Ijebu | 8 | 12 | 11 | 14 |
| Oyo | 1 | 1 | 4 | 5 |
| Ondo | 1 | 1 | — | — |
| Ilorin | — | — | 1 | 1 |
| Oshun | 1 | 1 | — | — |
| Ife | 1 | 1 | — | — |
| Ilesha | 1 | 1 | 2 | 2 |
| Ilashe | — | — | 1 | 1 |
| Ekiti | — | — | 3 | 4 |
| Benin | 2 | 3 | — | — |
| Warri | 1 | 1 | — | — |
| Asaba | 1 | 1 | — | — |
| Aro | 1 | 1 | — | — |
| Onitsha | 1 | 1 | — | — |
| Orlu | 3 | 4 | 2 | 2 |
| Abonema | 1 | 1 | 1 | 1 |
| Calabar | — | — | 1 | 1 |
| In Ghana | 1 | 1 | — | — |
| Unknown | 16 | — | 12 | — |
| Total | 91 | 100 | 96 | 100 |

[a] Percentages rounded.

Table 13 shows that more than three-fourths of the local leaders of known ages were fifty-one years of age or older in the period 1950–1959. Even allowing for the eight-year discrepancy between the end of the period and the date of the survey, most of the councilors still fell within this age group at the time they served in office; individual profiles in Appendix II give the ages of the councilors and the years in which they were elected to office.

Table 14 shows that of all the leaders who could be contacted, half who served in the earlier period identified Lagos as their hometown and 32 percent listed their hometowns in provinces close to Lagos—the colony provinces (outer Lagos), Abeokuta, and Ijebu. This measure of the breakdown between indigenous

TABLE 15

HOMETOWNS OF FATHERS OF LAGOS COUNCILORS, 1950–1966

| Hometown | 1950–1959 | | 1959–1966 | |
| --- | --- | --- | --- | --- |
| | Number | Percentage[a] of known | Number | Percentage[a] of known |
| Lagos | 30 | 41 | 37 | 45 |
| Outer Lagos | 5 | 7 | 4 | 5 |
| Ibadan | — | — | 3 | 4 |
| Abeokuta | 14 | 20 | 12 | 14 |
| Ijebu | 9 | 13 | 13 | 16 |
| Oyo | 1 | 1 | 4 | 5 |
| Ondo | 1 | 1 | 2 | 2 |
| Ilorin | — | — | 1 | 1 |
| Oshun | 1 | 1 | — | — |
| Ife | 1 | 1 | — | — |
| Ilesha | 1 | 1 | 2 | 2 |
| Ilashe | — | — | — | — |
| Ekiti | — | — | 1 | 1 |
| Benin | 2 | 3 | — | — |
| Warri | 1 | 1 | — | — |
| Asaba | 1 | 1 | — | — |
| Aro | 1 | 1 | — | — |
| Onitsha | 1 | 1 | — | — |
| Orlu | 3 | 4 | 2 | 2 |
| Abonema | 1 | 1 | 1 | 1 |
| In Ghana | 1 | 1 | — | — |
| In Sierra Leone | 1 | 1 | 1 | 1 |
| In Lebanon | — | — | 1 | 1 |
| Unknown | 16 | — | 12 | — |
| Total | 91 | 100 | 96 | 100 |

[a] Percentages rounded.

and immigrant leaders could be deceptive, however, for two reasons: first, nearly a fifth of the councilors' hometowns were not known (many of these were settlers who returned to their places of origin and would have been classified as immigrants); second, some of these councilors' fathers did not originate in Lagos (see table 15). Actually, indigenes of Lagos (i. e., those who listed Lagos as their hometown and their fathers' hometown) constituted less than 30 percent of the total number of councilors in the period 1950–1959. This low proportion of Lagosians is consistent with the figures on ethnicity in table 16, which show that of the over- whelming preponderance of Yorubas on the council, only 33 percent were indigenes. Forty-three percent of all elected leaders were non-Lagosian Yorubas who came from the Western Region. Collectively, settler Yorubas were the largest single group on the council, outnumbering Lagosians, Ibos, and other minority

TABLE 16

ETHNIC IDENTITY OF LAGOS COUNCILORS, 1950–1966,
WITH BREAKDOWNS FOR YORUBAS

| Ethnic identity | 1950–1959 | | 1959–1966 | |
|---|---|---|---|---|
| | Number | Percentage[*] of known | Number | Percentage[a] of known |
| Yoruba | 73 | 81 | 82 | 85 |
|   Indigenous Lagosians | 30 | 33 | 37 | 39 |
|   Lagos Muslims | 17 | 19 | 31 | 32 |
|   Lagos Christians | 13 | 14 | 6 | 7 |
|   Near Lagosians[b] | 5 | 5 | 4 | 4 |
|   Total indigenous Lagosians and Near Lagosians | 35 | 38 | 41 | 43 |
|   Non-Lagosian Yorubas | 38 | 43 | 41 | 42 |
| Ibo | 13 | 14 | 12 | 13 |
| Kalabari | 1 | 1 | — | — |
| Bini/Urhobo | 2 | 2 | — | — |
| Efik | 1 | 1 | 1 | 1 |
| Ijaw | — | — | 1 | 1 |
| Ghanaian[c] | 1 | 1 | — | — |
| Total | 91 | 100 | 96 | 100 |

[a] Percentages rounded.
[b] Residents of Outer Lagos.
[c] Ethnic identity unknown.

elements. The largest numbers came from Abeokuta and Ijebu provinces, and the majority had resided in Lagos for most of their lives, more than half since birth (see table 17).

The educational, religious, and occupational patterns (tables 18, 19, and 20) reveal the modern middle-class status of the ruling stratum. Of those councilors in the 1950–1959 period on whom information could be collected, 61 percent had completed second- ary or higher education, 68 percent were Christians, and 65 percent were in middle- to upper-income brackets, thoroughly assimilated into the urban economic structure. In the same period, only 17 percent served seven to nine years in office, and only four

TABLE 17

Length of Residence in Lagos of Councilors, 1950–1966

| Years resident | 1950–1959 | | 1959–1966 | |
|---|---|---|---|---|
| | Number | Percentage[a] of known | Number | Percentage[a] of known |
| 0–4 | — | — | — | — |
| 5–9 | — | — | — | — |
| 10–14 | — | — | 2 | 2 |
| 15–19 | — | — | 6 | 7 |
| 20–24 | 1 | 1 | 6 | 7 |
| 25 and over | 17 | 27 | 17 | 21 |
| Since birth | 45 | 72 | 50 | 63 |
| Unknown | 28 | — | 15 | — |
| Total | 91 | 100 | 96 | 100 |

[a] Percentages rounded.

TABLE 18

Education of Lagos Councilors, 1950–1966

| Educational level | 1950–1959 | | 1959–1966 | |
|---|---|---|---|---|
| | Number | Percentage[a] of known | Number | Percentage[a] of known |
| Attended primary school | 3 | 5 | 3 | 4 |
| Graduated primary school | 9 | 14 | 11 | 13 |
| Attended secondary or technical school | 13 | 20 | 33 | 41 |
| Graduated secondary or technical school | 22 | 36 | 20 | 24 |
| University education | 16 | 25 | 15 | 18 |
| Unknown | 28 | — | 14 | — |
| Total | 91 | 100 | 96 | 100 |

[a] Percentages rounded.

percent stayed on to serve ten years or more (table 21). The turnover rate was therefore fairly high, with 46 percent serving four to six years in office.

Nearly one-fourth of all the councilors elected between 1950 and 1959 were descendants of native foreigners, a minority that by this time was deeply split between the two major political parties in its political allegiances. As second- or third-generation descendants, many of them were now acceptable as "sons of the

TABLE 19

RELIGION OF LAGOS COUNCILORS, 1950–1966

| Religion | 1950–1959 | | 1959–1966 | |
|---|---|---|---|---|
| | *Number* | *Percentage[a] of known* | *Number* | *Percentage[a] of known* |
| Christian | 57 | 68 | 48 | 50 |
| Muslim | 27 | 32 | 48 | 50 |
| Unknown | 7 | – | – | – |
| Total | 91 | 100 | 96 | 100 |

[a] Percentages rounded.

TABLE 20

OCCUPATIONS OF LAGOS COUNCILORS, 1950–1966

| Occupation | 1950–1959 | | 1959–1966 | |
|---|---|---|---|---|
| | *Number* | *Percentage[a] of known* | *Number* | *Percentage[a] of known* |
| Professional, managerial, and executive | 24 | 27 | 21 | 22 |
| Salaried white-collar workers[b] | 33 | 38 | 27 | 29 |
| Self-employed[c] | 16 | 18 | 33 | 34 |
| Traders or merchants | 14 | 15 | 13 | 13 |
| Others[d] | 2 | 2 | 2 | 2 |
| Unknown | 2 | – | – | – |
| Total | 91 | 100 | 96 | 100 |

[a] Percentages rounded.
[b] Teachers, journalists, secretaries, clerks, etc.
[c] Entrepreneurs, artisans, and contractors.
[d] A Muslim religious leader and a jockey.

soil." The strangers in Lagos were no longer those with Saro or Amaro origins, but Nigerian immigrants who had poured into the city at an unprecedented rate since the interwar period and who had seized the reins of political power locally, just as the nineteenth-century emigrants had done before them. Both the descendants of native foreigners and the indigenes now made a common cause in unifying against this external threat; both in a political and in a social context, they had come to regard themselves, and to be viewed by others, collectively as Lagosians.

TABLE 21

NUMBER OF YEARS IN OFFICE OF LAGOS COUNCILORS, 1950–1966

| | 1950–1959 | | 1959–1966 | |
|---|---|---|---|---|
| *Number of years* | *Number* | *Percentage[a] of known* | *Number* | *Percentage[a] of known* |
| 3 or less | 30 | 33 | 56 | 59 |
| 4–6 | 41 | 46 | 23 | 24 |
| 7–9 | 16 | 17 | 11 | 11 |
| 10–13 | 3 | 3 | 5 | 5 |
| 14 or more | 1 | 1 | 1 | 1 |
| Total | 91 | 100 | 96 | 100 |

[a] Percentages rounded.

These nine years were thus marked by radical innovations in the patterns of political recruitment. Political participation was broadened to include those identified here as nonelites as well as grass-roots elements of the indigenous population. Concomitantly, ethnicity became a dominant feature of the political scene. Local political leaders, though still drawn from the ranks of the more successful elements of the urban population, were principally salaried white-collar workers belonging to the rising middle class who had displaced the educated or economic elites. Other interests were also represented on the council for the first time: minority ethnic groups, women, Muslims, and lower-income occupational groups such as traders and petty contractors, as well as members of less educated classes. Most significantly, however, the period was one of dominance by the Yoruba settlers, in which the seeds of intra-Yoruba factionalism in the city were just beginning to sprout.

INDIGENES

Two political parties, the Action Group and the NCNC, had come to dominate Lagos politics by the time of independence, but major patterns of political recruitment in the city could no longer be clearly seen from trends in party competition. The principal changes were occurring almost imperceptibly within the Yoruba community and within the party structures, partly because of the historic cleavage between settlers and indigenes which was now transcending ethnic boundaries, and partly because of the growing political consciousness of a group that had heretofore remained in the background—the indigenous Muslims. On the strength of their communal cohesion, Lagos Muslims steadily advanced in 'local politics. It was the socioeconomic characteristics of this group which were most clearly reflected in the composition of the council from 1959 to 1966.[22]

One of the most striking features of this period was the tendency for a more youthful council to be elected in each successive contest. Between 1959 and 1966 most councilors were between the ages of thirty-one and fifty. More than thirty-five percent were between thirty-one and forty when they served in office; a small percentage were between twenty and thirty. Symbolic of the change was the election in 1965 of a thirty-two-year-old chairman, Alhaji G. O. Dawodu, who first became a member of the council in 1957 at the unusually young age of twenty-four.

There was no significant shift in the geographical origin of councilors in the sixties. Fifty percent of those who served between 1959 and 1966 claimed Lagos as their hometown, as did the small percentage of councilors who served between 1950 and 1959 (see table 14). The later period marked a slight increase in the proportion of leaders from Ibadan (5 percent as compared with none), Ijebu (14 percent as compared with 12 percent), and Oyo (5 percent as compared with 1 percent), and a decrease in the proportion from Abeokuta (8 percent as compared with 13 percent). The findings about the hometowns of councilors' fathers were similar. Of 50 percent of the representatives who claimed Lagos as their hometown, 45 percent reported that Lagos was also the hometown of their fathers, a difference of 5 percent as compared with 9 percent in the former period (see tables 14 and 15).

The ethnic distribution of leaders affirmed that in 1959–1966 Lagos was still very much in the hands of the Yorubas. In fact, their proportion of the total membership on the council increased slightly, from 81 percent of all councilors between 1950 and 1959 to 85 percent between 1959 and 1966. Ibos dropped negligibly from 14 percent to 13 percent of the total, and other midwestern and eastern minority groups declined from an aggregate of 4 percent to 2 percent. Only one councilor, a Yoruba from Ilorin, was from the north. (See table 16.)

The most significant changes in the ruling strata of the two periods occurred within the Yoruba group (see table 16). Whereas between 1950 and 1959, 38 percent of all Yoruba councilors were

TABLE 22

SEATS HELD BY LAGOS MUSLIMS IN EACH COUNCIL, 1950–1966

| Years | Number[a] | Percentage[b] of total seats |
|---|---|---|
| 1950–1953 | 3 | 12 |
| 1953–1957 | 11 | 26 |
| 1957–1959 | 11 | 27 |
| 1959–1962 | 15 | 36 |
| 1962–1965 | 15 | 36 |
| 1965–1966 | 15 | 36 |

[a] Because this table refers to seats held by Lagos Muslims in each council, the figures here do not correspond to the figures for Lagos Muslims in table 16, which indicate the proportion of individual councilors in each period.

[b] Percentages rounded.

Lagosians and 43 percent were immigrants, between 1959 and 1966 these two groups had become exactly even. This equality in representation between indigenes and Yoruba immigrants came at a time when immigrants were still outstripping Lagosians in proportion to the city's total population.[23] The change in leadership represented only a slight variation in absolute numbers, but the fact that Lagosians did progress while the rate of immigration was rising is indicative of the dramatic and aggressive transformations that were occurring at lower levels of the indigenous community, particularly among the Lagos Muslims.

From less than a fifth of the council, Lagos Muslims rose to nearly a third between 1959 and 1966 (table 16). In terms of seats captured in each election, they had climbed steadily since 1950 (see table 22). Starting out with only 12 percent of the seats on the first fully representative council, they advanced to 36 percent in

1959, a level they maintained consistently thereafter. From 19 percent of the total Yoruba membership in the former period, Lagos Muslims rose to 32 percent in the latter. They advanced not at the expense of immigrants, as might have been expected, but at the expense of other Lagosians. Between 1959 and 1966 Lagos Muslims were more than five times as numerous as their Christian

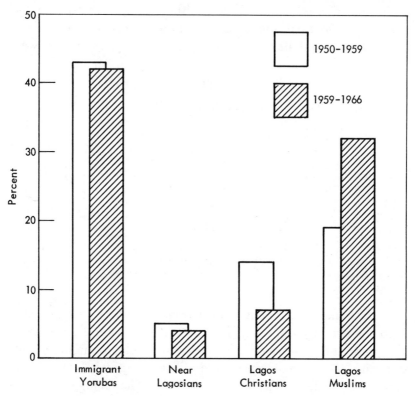

Fig. 1. Yoruba councilors as percentage of total councilors in Lagos, 1950–1959 and 1959–1966 (see table 16).

townsmen, whereas in the earlier period the difference between the two groups was only 5 percent (see table 16).

The growth in the proportion of Lagos Muslims, as compared with other Lagosians and immigrant Yorubas, is also shown in figure 1. Lagos Muslims, acting as a cohesive voting bloc, soon seized control of the majority party, thus achieving influence disproportionate to their minority representation. Capturing key committees and installing one of their own members as chairman of the municipal council in 1962, Lagos Muslims clearly exercised pivotal influence as the largest single corporate group on the council. It was they—not the Lagosians in general—who were responsible for balancing the distribution of councilors between indigene and immigrant Yorubas.

Other socioeconomic characteristics of the council reflect the rise of the Lagos Muslims and, to a lesser extent, the somewhat wider range of immigrant representation which appeared in the sixties. The length of urban residence of councilors was more varied, for example. Whereas only one councilor had resided in the city for less than twenty-five years before 1959, after that date 16 percent or fourteen councilors had lived in Lagos for less than twenty-five years and 2 percent for less than fifteen years; most of the representatives were born in Lagos or had lived there for twenty-five years or more, and none had lived in Lagos for less than ten years (table 17). Clearly, long-term residence was still an important criterion for political recruitment.

The educational, occupational, and religious characteristics of the councilors strongly reflected the lower-class origins of the Lagos Muslims. Only 42 percent of the representatives who served between 1959 and 1966 had completed secondary or higher education, as compared with 61 percent in the earlier period; 54 percent had primary or some secondary education, as compared with 34 percent in the 1950–1959 period (table 18). Occupational backgrounds revealed a preponderance of lower-income groups in 1959–1966; 47 percent of all councilors were self-employed contractors, artisans, small entrepreneurs, traders, or merchants, as compared with 33 percent in that category before 1959 (table 20). The religious distribution shows a sharp rise in Muslim representation, from less than a third of all councilors in 1950–1959 to exactly half in 1959–1966 (table 19), an increase due not only to the increase in indigenous representation but also to the increase in Muslim immigration from the west. The turnover rate of councilors was higher than ever, with 59 percent of the total number in 1959–1966 having served for three years or less (table 21). This rapid turnover rate is consistent with the rise of new interests in local politics and the progressive youthfulness of the council in each successive election.

71

The changing face of the council was seen by many councilors as a revolutionary breakthrough for the lower classes. One respondent said that before 1962 the LTC consisted of councilors who were the elites of society—businessmen and highly placed people —but that 1962 brought a revolution for the common man. Beginning in that year, clerks, petty contractors, traders, and lawyers were elected to the council.[24]

The "common man" had, indeed, come to dominate the council. In fact, his influence had begun to be felt as early as 1959. It was associated not simply with a change in the class composition of the council, but with a general political renaissance among the indigenous elements of the community. Not only recruitment patterns, but other factors, such as the dissociation of the oba of Lagos from the Action Group, the growing demands for a Lagos state, and controversies over allocation of land by the Lagos Executive Development Board, indicated the growing divisions between indigene and immigrant Yorubas. Although still relatively weak in terms of numbers, wealth, or education, the indigenes experienced a growing sense of political consciousness which propelled them to prominence after independence.

As a consequence, after 1959 the common man was represented on the council in larger numbers than ever before, with eighteen clerks, fifteen contractors, and thirteen traders. The typical councilor was no longer a professional doctor, lawyer, or journalist, or a comfortable member of the urban middle class; he was a native of Lagos or a long-term resident who lived in the old quarter of town, in Isale Eko or its environs, areas regarded by most immigrants as the slums of the city. He was better educated and more prosperous than the average Nigerian living in the countryside, but in terms of the urban status structure he was still considered a member of the lower class, receiving few of the rewards of modern urban development. Deprived of direct influence in the town from the first colonial contact, he had finally carved a position of political power in his own community.

The circulation of different types of political leaders after 1917 indicates how the criteria of political recruitment changed in a fifty-year period of modern local government. Contrary to the familiar sequence of political development, in which the variables of political change are transformed from traditional to modern attributes, precisely the reverse occurred in Lagos. From 1917 to 1938 modern attributes of wealth and education, possessed by a small class of non-Nigerian Africans, were the determinants of political recruitment. Between 1938 and 1950 wealth was separated from education and a new intelligentsia of educated nationalists was prominent, including native-born Nigerians of mixed ethnic background. From 1950 to 1959, when the nationalists gave way to the new middle class consisting principally of Yoruba immigrants, the major criterion of recruitment came to be ethnicity. Finally, from 1959 to 1966, origin became the foremost determinant of political recruitment and indigenous Lagosians—particularly the Lagos Muslims—captured control of the council. Recruitment criteria had therefore changed from wealth and education to ethnicity and origin; as determined by the nature of the ruling strata, the urban political structure had traveled the route from an aristocracy to a nationalist oligarchy, to domination by an ethnically homogenous middle class, to communal home rule.

CHAPTER 4
*Political Resources*

The second variable in this study of urban political influence is the use of political resources. Although political influence is normally regarded as a function of the use and distribution of political resources, the two may be so closely interrelated as to be virtually inseparable. Wealth, for example, may be viewed as an economic means to achieve influence or as a sign of political achievement itself. Other resources may likewise be conceived of either as instruments for the pursuit of influence or as rewards accruing to those who have already attained positions of power.

Some of the key political resources examined here reflect this duality. They were selected for their importance at different stages of the city's development and for the range of different types of influence they illustrate. No one group or interest has monopolized all key resources, nor has any single resource been of fixed or permanent importance in the community. The significance of each has varied in effectiveness in response to a number of factors.

Wealth and education were important in the early colonial years, for they brought office, status, and position to a small elite who monopolized public life; but these resources have lost effectiveness as they gradually became accessible to wider elements of the population, and today they are no longer guarantees of political influence. Another resource is charisma. During the colonial period and in the first stages of the nationalist period, Lagos politics was dominated by a colorful leader who never held public office, a man who used his charismatic appeal as a resource to sway large segments of the disenfranchised urban population. Land is a political resource that has long been the focus of friction between indigenous and nonindigenous forces, and group solidarity has

74

accounted for the political ascendancy of the indigenes in recent times.

Other resources relevant to political action are numbers, the right to vote, legitimacy, legality, and so forth. The predominant position of the middle-class Yoruba settlers in the fifties, for example, was an outcome of their combined resources of numbers and the right to vote. While not all significant resources can be covered in this study, those selected for closer examination are among the most important in explaining how various segments of the local population managed to acquire or exercise influence at crucial stages in the history of Lagos.

### WEALTH AND EDUCATION

The small Anglo-African elite that dominated Lagos in the early years comprised notables whose positions of influence were attributable almost entirely to their monopoly of wealth and education. These assets enabled them to capture both nominated and elective office, to command associated resources, such as control over information, and to build up private fortunes and personal status to a level other Africans could not hope to attain. By the first quarter of the twentieth century they could boast of three generations of university education, of elaborate Edwardian homes, and of a genteel way of life imitative of that of the English upper class. Many native foreigners were able to accumulate savings by pursuing two or three careers simultaneously, combining a profession in law or medicine, for example, with journalism, business, or an administrative position. They were able to live at a standard equal to, and sometimes above that, of Europeans. The resident of the colony, Henry Carr, was a Saro who drew an annual salary of £1,200 ($3,360) plus duty pay of £524 ($1,467), in addition to rent and vehicle allowances.[1] By contrast, young European apprentices attached to trading companies at the time earned only £80–£120 ($224–$336) a year plus maintenance.[2]

The degree of concentration of wealth in Lagos can be seen in the income tax figures for the 1928–29 fiscal year, when this revenue was first collected. Table 23 indicates, from the average tax paid, that the income of African professionals was above that of European nonofficials and about equal to that of Syrians, most of whom were prosperous traders. The average tax paid by a European official was £5.18.0 (about $16); by an African professional £4.10.0 (about $12); and by a general African, only 5s. (about 70¢).[3] Of the 16,618 persons classified as general Africans, about half (8,817) were government employees such as clerks and office staff. According to an official occupational roll, the rest were mostly

TABLE 23

INCOME TAX PAID IN THE COLONY OF LAGOS, 1928–1929

| Taxable population | Amount collected (in pounds) | Number of persons taxed | Average tax per person (in pounds) |
|---|---|---|---|
| *Within municipal area* | | | |
| European officials | 2,858. 1.0 | 508 | 5.18.0 |
| European nonofficials | 1,096.10.0 | 281 | 3.18.0 |
| Syrians | 261. 0.0 | 58 | 4.10.0 |
| Indians | 8.10.0 | 7 | 1. 6.0 |
| African professionals[a] | 260.16.0 | 56 | 4.10.0 |
| General Africans | 8,404. 4.0 | 16,618 | 0. 5.0 |
| Total | 12,889. 1.0 | 17,528 | 0.14.0 |
| *Within colony provinces* | 23,182. 3.0 | 53,335 | 0. 8.0 |
| Penalties | 32.16.0 | — | — |
| Grand total | 36,104. 0.0 | 70,863 | 0.18.0 |

[a] Lawyers and doctors only.

SOURCE: *Annual Colonial Report: Nigeria*, 1928, App. II, p. 15.

carriers, salesmen, laborers, artisans, and other low-paid semi-skilled or unskilled workers.[4]

The educational inequities in the community were also extreme. In 1921 only about 10 percent of the population was classified by the census as educated (able to read and write), 20 percent as imperfectly educated (able to read only), and the rest as illiterate.[5] Since schools were controlled primarily by missionaries, Christian emigrant families were the first and, in the early years, virtually the only ones to benefit from modern education; most Muslims preferred to keep their children out of school rather than risk religious conversion by sending them to Christian establishments. The Anglican and Wesleyan missions accounted for thirty of the forty-seven schools in Lagos in 1921 and served more than half of the 9,805 pupils enrolled. There was one Baptist school, and the eight Roman Catholic schools were patronized mainly by Brazilian emigrants. Of the indigenous African churches, only the United Native African Church provided education; it established two schools, but student attendance was relatively small. The government supported one secondary school, King's College. In the early 1920s Alhaji L. B. Agusto, West Africa's first Muslim lawyer, attempted to set up in his home a Muslim primary school to teach modern subjects, but lack of funds, a dearth of qualified staff, and insufficient public interest brought failure, and Lagos Muslims fell far behind Christians in educational opportunities.

Lacking modern skills, the indigenes steadily lost influence after the abolition of the slave trade. Riches that had formerly accrued to the Kosokos of Lagos from that endeavor now lined the pockets of Europeans and native foreigners engaged in legitimate trade and commerce, wage labor, or professional occupations. Without the resources of wealth and skills, it was virtually impossible for indigenes to exert meaningful political influence. Emigrants were the only non-Europeans qualified to enter the administrative class and participate in the activities of central decision-making bodies. The policy of direct rule and the restricted franchise in the colony legally barred the majority of the population from taking an active part in political affairs. Even the oba of Lagos was stripped of all political authority and became financially and constitutionally dependent on the colonial government.

Inevitably, native foreigners emerged as intermediaries or political brokers between the masses and the colonial authorities. Trading on their elite status, they created a network of influence that extended beyond the township itself. For example, African lawyers permitted to appear before the Supreme Court, which had sole and original jurisdiction in the colony, represented villagers living in the colony provinces in return for payments in the form of favors or rights, special prerogatives equivalent, in most instances, to conferment of the status of an overlord. These privileges were exercised freely in such matters as trade disputes, dealings with other Yoruba kingdoms, chieftaincy succession, and relations with Lagos. In this way there developed an informal clientage system in the colony which increased the formal influence of the elite. Naturally, in order to maintain their influence, African members of the Legislative Council and other native foreigners opposed the establishment of native courts in the colony provinces, a plan they successfully resisted until 1938. But when native courts were established in the provinces, heads of rural communities continued to defer to those who were thought to be in positions of influence in the capital.[6]

Having monopolized the administrative positions open to non-Europeans, dominated the electoral process, and gained supremacy over the less privileged elements in the colony, educated Africans used their resources to capture control of what was perhaps one of the most significant instruments of influence—the press. As no other segment of the community had either the means or the inclination to indulge in this enterprise, the emigrants enjoyed a clear monopoly of the newspaper industry.

The first newspapers, like the first educational institutions, were started by missionaries, but by the 1920s a number of independent publications were in circulation. Nearly all were deeply embroiled in Lagos politics and could be identified with particular members or factions of the emigrant community. Among the most prominent were John Payne Jackson's *Lagos Weekly Record*, Alfred Williams' *Lagos Standard*, and James Bright Davies' *Nigerian Times*; all were liberal, antigovernment publications. The *Nigerian Pioneer*, a conservative progovernment paper, was run by Kitoyi Ajasa, a close friend of Lord Lugard's. Two newspapers came to be of primary influence in the early 1930s: the *Lagos Daily News*, the first local daily, published by Herbert Macaulay in order to further the interests of his newly formed Nigerian National Democratic Party; and the Nigerian *Daily Times*, founded in 1926 with the backing of European interests represented in the Lagos Chamber of Commerce and run by the dean of Lagos journalists, Ernest Ikoli. The *Daily News* was openly propagandistic and promoted those issues closest to its editor's heart; the *Daily Times* was far less partisan and of superior professional quality. Sir Adeyemo Alakija, the first chairman of the latter's board of directors, and Ikoli were both fierce opponents of Macaulay. They were disdainful of his pompous oratory typical of many black Victorians, critical of his tight personal control over the paper, and contemptuous of his sensationalistic editorial policy which was clearly popular with the masses. On the other hand, Chief Obafemi Awolowo, a former political journalist, described the contrast between the newspapers from the popular point of view:

> The *Nigerian Daily Times* was technically the best paper then in circulation; but it was, on strictly professional assessment, an unpardonably dull journalistic and literary product: a veritable stagnant pool of stale, colourless news; and a musty reservoir of articles which lacked animation, pungency and nationalist flavor. In content and style the...*Lagos Daily News* [was]...the very antithesis of the *Nigerian Daily Times*, and therefore much better.... [But it] had ceased in 1934 to answer to the name of a daily newspaper. It published only when Herbert Macaulay... could afford to buy newsprint and ink and persuade his irregularly paid and half-starved compositors to work. [But] whenever this paper made its appearance it sold like hot cakes.[7]

Since most newspapers were owned and operated by the same person, they became personal political instruments of the town's most prominent citizens. With a few rare exceptions, none of the proprietor-editors were professional journalists, but doctors, lawyers, teachers, or administrators.[8] Macaulay was originally a civil engineer; John Payne Jackson, a merchant; James Bright Davies, a civil servant; and Ernest Ikoli, a teacher. To the comment that "newspaper writing was confined almost exclusively to the local 'aristocracy' of intelligence,"[9] one might add, significantly, that the same people also formed the exclusive aristocracy of wealth. The appearance of the *West African Pilot*, the *Service*, and the *Comet* in the 1940s symbolized the arrival of a new political generation of uncompromising nationalists. Competition forced the *Daily News* to close down in 1936, a move that presaged the first electoral defeat of the NNDP two years later.

Nnamdi Azikiwe replaced the *Daily News* with the *West African Pilot*, which became the most popular nationalist organ in Lagos. Educated in the United States, Azikiwe changed the format of the press to stress social equality and human interest in feature articles, popularizing the news for mass consumption: "For the first time the smiling face of the third-class clerk in the government or commercial houses appeared side by side with that of a lawyer or politician. Gone, clearly, was the day when newspaper publicity was the prerogative of only those at the top of society."[10]

Azikiwe's journalism was both good business and good politics. The *Pilot* achieved the widest circulation ever reached by a newspaper at that time, sales hitting the 20,000 figure by the mid-1940s. The *Pilot's* success spawned a chain of publications known as the Zik Group of papers, which included the *Eastern Nigeria Guardian*, the *Nigerian Spokesman*, the *Southern Nigeria Defender*, and the *Comet*. Azikiwe gained political capital from his enterprises, using them not only as instruments of mass communication but as weapons of political opposition through which the rights of Nigerians were asserted. Victimization of the *Pilot*, either by direct government attacks or by a less conspicuous lack of cooperation, was presented as evidence of colonial exploitation.[11] "Freedom of the press" became a watchword of the nationalist movement and journalism an integral part of the struggle against colonialism.

Gradually the number of newspapers multiplied, the coverage and scope of stories broadened, and technical quality improved. The *Daily Times*, an enterprise that combined expatriate capital with Nigerian management, grew considerably in the 1950s. By the time of independence it was outselling all other dailies in the country. The vernacular and religious press, professional journals, and magazines joined the market at an accelerated rate. Government-supported papers captured the reading public in particular areas and were associated with particular regions: the *Morning Post* in Lagos, the *Daily Sketch* in the west, the *Nigerian Outlook* in the east, the *New Nigerian* in the north, and, somewhat later, the *Observer* in the mid-west. In all, Nigeria has given birth to more than 168 separate publications, including magazines and trade journals, over 60 percent of which have emanated from Lagos. Yet after World War II very few Nigerian publications could be said to be any longer concerned exclusively with Lagos affairs.[12] The proliferation of newspapers was indicative of the spread of wealth and education and the consequent decline of the privileges of native foreigners.

Wealth and education declined in importance after World War II partly because they became more widely accessible and partly because other resources, such as the right to vote and the size of the immigrant population, became more significant. In contrast with the 10 percent literacy rate in 1921, for example, Lagos boasted a 48 percent literacy rate by 1950, and more than half of the children aged five to nine were attending school.[13] Native foreigners, constituting only a small proportion of the educated

TABLE 24

LITERACY OF LAGOS RESIDENTS, AGED 5 OR MORE, BY ETHNIC GROUP, 1950
(In thousands)

| Ethnic group | Total | Literate | Illiterate | Not stated | Percentage literate[a] |
|---|---|---|---|---|---|
| Yoruba | 143 | 67 | 76 | [b] | 46 |
| Ibo | 22 | 13 | 9 | [b] | 57 |
| Edo, Kukuruku, Urhobo | 9 | 4 | 5 | [b] | 47 |
| Hausa | 4 | 1 | 3 | [b] | 18 |
| Others | 9 | 5 | 4 | [b] | 56 |
| Not stated | 4 | — | — | 4 | — |
| Total | 191 | 90 | 97 | 4 | 47 |

[a] Percentages rounded.
[b] Less than 500.
SOURCE: *Population Census of Lagos, 1950* (Lagos: Federal Office of Statistics, 1950), p. 15.

elite by mid-century, were greatly outnumbered on the Lagos Town Council by a new middle class rising from the lower ranks of the community.

Instead of being linked with particular class privileges, wealth and education now came to be associated with ethnic privileges. Owing to extensive penetration of the Eastern Region by Catholic missions, Ibos tended to be better educated than other groups, and the impression grew that they were therefore beginning to dominate the town. The impression was reinforced by the rate of Ibo migration into Nigerian cities. By 1952 Lagos had the largest concentration of Ibos outside the east, representing a total of 45 percent of all non-Yoruba peoples.[14]

Tables 24 and 25 compare the educational achievements of ethnic groups in Lagos during the period of heaviest immigration. In 1950, 57 percent of all Ibos in Lagos were literate, a rate 10 percent higher than the urban average.[15] In a 1964 survey of immi-

TABLE 25

DISTRIBUTION OF EDUCATION AMONG LAGOS IMMIGRANTS, BY ETHNIC GROUP, 1964

(In percentages)

| Educational level | Yoruba | Ibo | Edo | Ibibio-Efik | Hausa | Other Nigerians | Non-Nigerians | Total |
|---|---|---|---|---|---|---|---|---|
| No education | 16.9 | 14.1 | 21.2 | 7.7 | 36.3 | 13.9 | 18.9 | 16.3 |
| Primary education | 56.3 | 62.1 | 53.9 | 62.2 | 49.9 | 55.5 | 58.5 | 57.6 |
| Secondary education | 21.7 | 16.9 | 21.2 | 24.5 | 10.8 | 22.2 | 16.9 | 20.7 |
| Training college | 3.4 | 4.2 | 2.0 | 3.6 | 2.1 | 5.6 | 5.7 | 4.8 |
| University | 1.7 | 2.7 | 1.6 | 2.0 | 0.8 | 2.8 | — | 1.9 |

SOURCE: C. N. Ejiogu, "Survey of African Migration to the Main Migrant Areas of the Federal Territory of Lagos," paper read at First African Population Conference, University of Ibadan, Nigeria, January 1966, table 16(ii).

grants in Lagos, eastern minority groups—Ibo and Ibibio-Efik—likewise proved to be the most widely educated.[16] These achievements were viewed by the Yorubas as an unfair advantage in the competition for employment. Their attitude was reinforced by the conspicuous presence of Ibos in federal offices and by a social network of voluntary associations which encompassed nearly all Ibo immigrants. The Ibo State Union in Lagos functioned, in effect, as an ethnic employment bureau. Most members also had affiliations with other clan and town associations, providing further contacts that would lead a new immigrant to a job or, at the very least, to relatives or townsmen who could help him get settled until he found suitable work.[17]

Such linkages convinced other groups that the Ibos were collectively designing to rob them of employment. Other minorities had formed similar organizations as a defense against Yoruba domination, but the Ibos, as the largest group of all, were the prime targets of resentment.[18] By the 1960s, therefore, they were believed to have captured substantial control of the city. However widespread this belief, the Ibos, despite their educational achievements, did not in fact exercise as much influence in Lagos as was commonly thought. They had not translated their national prominence into local control, in either political or economic matters.[19] All available evidence points to the opposite conclusion: in areas of the most intensive competition, such as control of the city council, the labor market, retail trade, and ownership of property, the Yorubas easily remained in control.

By 1963 nearly 100,000 Ibos were living in Lagos, representing some 15 percent of the municipal population.[20] The percentage of Ibo seats on the Lagos City Council (the LTC became the LCC on October 1, 1963) did not exceed the Ibo proportion of the population in either of the two periods examined earlier; and in some instances the Ibos were underrepresented. Of 187 councilors elected after 1950 only 20, or about 11 percent of the total, were Ibos. Even the party linked with Ibo interests in the Eastern Region, the NCNC, was run mainly by Yorubas in Lagos. Federal institutions with substantial decision-making control in the city, particularly the Ministry of Lagos Affairs and the Lagos Executive Development Board, were likewise manned chiefly by non-Ibos; incumbents were usually northerners or Yoruba allies of the nationally

## TABLE 26

### Gainfully Occupied Nigerian Males in Lagos, by Ethnic Group and Occupation, 1950

| Occupational group | Yoruba | Ibo | Edo[a] | Hausa | Others | Total |
|---|---|---|---|---|---|---|
| Professional, technical, and related | 2,068 | 300 | 100 | 103 | 265 | 2,836 |
| Managerial and administrative | 1,070 | 238 | 84 | 18 | 150 | 1,560 |
| Clerical and related | 6,889 | 1,698 | 515 | 31 | 820 | 9,953 |
| Sales workers | 5,704 | 341 | 129 | 359 | 145 | 6,678 |
| Farmers and fishermen | 1,556 | 31 | 29 | 40 | 132 | 1,788 |
| Transport workers | 2,240 | 468 | 224 | 29 | 365 | 3,326 |
| Craftsmen and production workers | 18,444 | 2,200 | 736 | 281 | 744 | 22,405 |
| Laborers | 6,814 | 2,007 | 717 | 293 | 614 | 10,445 |
| Protective service workers | 409 | 773 | 175 | 244 | 309 | 1,910 |
| Domestic and personal service workers | 3,372 | 3,110 | 949 | 291 | 1,011 | 8,733 |
| Unidentifiable | 156 | 39 | 24 | 2 | 2,638 | 2,859 |
| Total | 48,722 | 11,205 | 3,682 | 1,691 | 7,193 | 72,493 |

[a] Includes Kukuruku and Urhobo.

Source: *Population Census of Lagos 1950* (Lagos: Federal Office of Statistics, 1950), p. 21.

dominant Northern Peoples' Congress. Clearly the Ibos were not politically dominant in the authoritative governmental institutions in the city.

The same generalization applies to the Ibos with respect to economic affairs. Their low rate of unemployment concealed their rather high degree of class stratification. The total number of gainfully occupied male Ibos in Lagos in 1950 was slightly more than 11,000, about 15 percent of the labor force. Although the largest percentage of all Yoruba male workers were in the middle-income groups, the largest percentage of all Ibo male workers were in the lower-income groups (see table 26). Yorubas were predominant among clerical staff, craftsmen, and production workers, while Ibos were predominant only among domestic and personal service workers. Thus the Ibos did not claim a disproportionately large share of the labor market or of salaried jobs, for which there was keen competition among immigrants. In fact, a great many Ibos were at the base of the occupational pyramid because of their willingness to take low-status jobs as laborers and servants.

In retail trade and property ownership, sensitive areas that affected both indigenes and immigrants, the Ibos were likewise of secondary importance. Only 3 percent of the gainfully occupied Ibo males in 1950 were traders (listed in the census as "sales workers"), as compared with 12 percent of the Yoruba males (table 26). (Had figures for women been included there would be an even more striking disproportion in favor of the Yorubas, since Yoruba women traditionally dominated trade in the city.)[21] Ibo traders rarely operated on so large a scale as did Yoruba traders, and for the most part they dealt in wholesale transactions, specializing in commodities related to the region of origin, such as yams, rice, or gari from the east, which were preferred by the Ibo market (see chap. 8 for Lagos markets). The low participation of Ibos in retail trade is also suggested by a comparison of rents collected on Lagos market stalls immediately before and after the 1966 crisis which provoked an Ibo exodus from noneastern cities. Figures from the LCC indicate that there was only a slight decrease in stallage fees after the Ibos returned to the east.[22]

As a whole, Ibos owned surprisingly little property in Lagos. Some members of the Ibo upper class did receive valuable plots

## TABLE 27
### ETHNIC ORIGINS OF LANDLORDS IN LAGOS RESIDENTIAL AREAS, 1960
(In percentages)

| Residential area | Lagosian | Egba | Ijebu | Other Yoruba | Total Yoruba | Ibo | Other Nigerian | Non-Nigerian |
|---|---|---|---|---|---|---|---|---|
| Idumagbo | 75 | – | 15 | 10 | 100 | – | – | – |
| Ebute-Ero | 63 | 25 | – | 12 | 100 | – | – | – |
| Idunshagbe | 73 | 18 | 9 | – | 100 | – | – | – |
| Oke Awo | 18 | 11 | 35 | 18 | 82 | – | – | 18(D) |
| Isalegangan-Aroloya | 46 | 29 | 17 | 8 | 100 | – | – | – |
| Idunmota-Alakaro | 60 | 10 | 10 | 20 | 100 | – | – | – |
| Offin-Itolo | 40 | 20 | 10 | 30 | 100 | – | – | – |
| Olowogbowo | 56 | 11 | 11 | 22 | 100 | – | – | – |
| Ereko-Agarawa | 29 | 57 | – | 14 | 100 | – | – | – |
| Okepopo | 42 | 16 | 16 | 24 | 98 | – | – | 2(T) |
| Epetedo. | 86 | 7 | – | – | 93 | – | 4(B) | 3(G) |
| Faji | 47 | 16 | 5 | 16 | 84 | – | 5(I) | 11(D) |
| Brazilian Quarter | 56 | 33 | – | – | 89 | – | – | 11(T) |
| Lafiaji | – | 66 | – | 31 | 100 | – | – | 11(T) |
| Okesuna | 11 | 25 | 39 | 12 | 88 | – | – | 12(G) |
| Araromi | – | 18 | 55 | 27 | 100 | – | – | – |
| Obalende | 9 | 6 | 13 | 23 | 52 | 13 | 3(H) | 33(TG) |
| Ebute Metta East | – | 35 | 18 | 47 | 100 | – | – | – |
| Yaba | – | 48 | 25 | 25 | 98 | 2 | – | – |
| Ebute Metta West | – | 37 | 36 | 27 | 100 | – | – | – |
| Ojuelegba | – | 21 | 42 | 17 | 80 | 8 | 4(E) | 8(T) |
| Yaba East | 16 | 34 | 34 | 16 | 100 | – | – | – |
| Mushin | 11 | 36 | 17 | 28 | 92 | 4 | 4 | – |
| Shomolu | – | 18 | 35 | 39 | 92 | 8 | – | – |
| Surulere | – | 31 | 23 | 19 | 93 | 23 | 4(E) | – |

KEY:  B – Bini    D – Dahomian    E – Efik    G – Ghanaian    H – Hausa    I – Itsekiri    T – Togolese
SOURCE: A. L. Mabogunje, "Lagos: A Study in Urban Geography" (Ph.D. dissertation, London University, 1961), p. 144.

of land during the civilian regime as patronage distributed to federal officials and other well-placed notables of mixed ethnic backgrounds. But figures on the ethnic origins of landlords in Lagos, gathered in a 1960 sample survey,[23] show that after the Lagosians, the two most important property-owning groups in the city were the Egba and the Ijebu, although numerically each represented a smaller proportion of the urban population than the Ibo. (see table 27).

In sum, even though the federal capital had the largest concentration of Ibos of any city outside the Eastern Region, the myth of Ibo domination in local affairs had little basis in reality.[24] This point needs to be underscored because of the degree to which Ibos were believed to be in control; such beliefs were partly responsible for the secession and the civil war in Nigeria, and they indicate the extent to which urban political competition had come to be seen in terms of particular group affiliations based on ethnicity and origin.

Even had the Ibos attempted to convert their aggregate resources into instruments of political influence, it is doubtful that their wealth and education would have been decisive assets. By the 1950s these resources had come to be among the least relevant determinants of office. Lower- and middle-class workers had regularly been displacing local elites. Less than 17 percent of the councilors who served between 1950 and 1966 had a university education, and the overall educational level of the council had been steadily dropping. Nor did business leaders—economic notables such as J. Ade Tuyo of the De Facto Bakery, T. A. Braithwaite of the African Alliance Insurance Company, S. B. Bakare of S. B. Bakare and Brothers, O. Ojukwu of Ojukwu Transport, and a number of other prominent Lagos-based businessmen—exercise significant influence in local affairs. This picture is contrary to many English and American models of community power, in which wealthy businessmen are presumed to be of key importance in city politics.[25] In Lagos, the political goals of these wealthy businessmen—as of the Ibos—were realized at the federal level.

During the 1960s Lagos politics was fast becoming an arena for the common man, for whom wealth could hardly be an element crucial to political success. Money could, of course, be used, legitimately or illegitimately, to mobilize voters and finance campaigns. There have, however, been comparatively few allegations of bribery in Lagos elections; most irregularities were concerned with attempts at impersonation or misrepresentation. Given the humble backgrounds of so many leaders, there is little reason to believe that private wealth was used to buy political office; most candidates, in fact, had to rely wholly on their parties to relieve the burden of campaign expenses. Even party wealth has not been a requisite of electoral victory in Lagos; the Action Group had its most spectacular successes in 1962 and 1965 when, owing to national party crises, its top leaders were imprisoned and its assets were frozen. From being vital resources used to gain power, wealth and education had now come to be regarded as vital objectives rather than as preconditions of power.

CHARISMA

Charisma[26] is a transitory and unstable resource, but in Lagos it largely accounted for the reign of an astute member of the urban aristocratic elite who became the legendary Father of Nigerian Nationalism, namely, Herbert Samuel Heelas Macaulay. Still warmly remembered by old Lagosians, Macaulay, thanks to his popularity with the indigenous community, held a position of unsurpassed influence for approximately forty years. He was the classic example of an informal political actor who wielded extensive power without ever holding public office.[27]

Unlike other charismatic leaders in Nigeria, such as Adegoke Adelabu of Ibadan,[28] Macaulay was for, but not of, the common people whom he led. He was by origin a Saro aristrocrat, by training a civil engineer, and by inclination a celebrity and politician. Born in Lagos on November 14, 1864, he was the son of the Reverend Thomas Babington Macaulay, founder of the Church Missionary Society Grammar School, and grandson of the Right Reverend Samuel Crowther, the first African bishop of Niger Territory. Like most Saros, he received his early education in Lagos, then spent some years in England where he pursued advanced studies in engineering. Upon his return to Lagos in 1895 he became surveyor of crown lands and launched a private practice as an architect. He soon developed a reputation as a man of many talents—journalist, orator, publicist, violinist, horseman, and historian. His home, "Kirsten Hall," was a popular salon for the Victorian elite, and it is said that he was the first Nigerian to own and operate a motor car. Status-conscious and formalistic, he was the model of the "black Englishman" par excellence, right down to his handlebar moustache, his starched white suit, and his wide bow tie.

It would have been impossible for Macaulay to have wielded as much influence in the town as he did without the solid backing of large segments of the indigenous community. However committed he was in principle to the goals for which he fought, Macaulay designed a shrewd political strategy, always keeping in mind the practical necessities for maintaining influence. Essentially, his strategy rested on four fundamental elements.

First, Macaulay took up causes of particular factions within the traditional community, rather than defending the rights of Africans in general. In so doing, he deepened existing communal cleavages, capitalizing on the large followings that leaders of rival groups could swing in his direction. This tactic also provided identifiable and exploitable issues without necessitating an attack on the legitimacy of colonial rule. Thus, Macaulay allied himself with the House of Docemo, the dominant royal lineage, and with the Jam'at Congregation, a breakaway Muslim sect.[29] It was from these two groups and from the market women that he derived his strongest and most numerous supporters.

Secondly, Macaulay's politics were laced with a series of local issues that were related to one another by no overriding objective or ideology, not even by a commitment to anticolonialism. Macaulay never wavered in his loyalty to the Crown and was eminently proud of the fact that he was a product of British civilization.[30] Each protest, each demonstration, each campaign, was directed, not against the political structure, but against particular policies, such as the proposal to impose a water rate, the passing of an offensive ordinance, or the banishment of a chief. Macaulay's missions were to redress grievances and to demonstrate to his faithful followers that they would ultimately be rewarded for their fealty.[31] It is not surprising that the peak of Macaulay's popularity coincided with the occasions on which he achieved concrete victories on the issues that mattered most to the community: when Chief Oluwa won compensation for his appropriated land from the Privy Council in 1921,[32] when the Jam'at Congregation gained control of the Central Mosque in 1924,[33] and when the Eleko was reinstated as head of the House of Docemo in 1931 after a six-year exile.[34]

The third element in Macaulay's strategy was his vigorous pursuit of the organizational requisites of power: finances, publicity, and a working organization. Among his most ardent supporters were the tight-knit and well-organized market women who maintained control of the town's retail trade and contributed the bulk of Macaulay's financial resources. Publicity was gained by Macaulay through the sensationalistic *Lagos Daily News*. His lieutenants were brought into the fold of the Nigerian National Democratic Party, formed in 1922 for the purpose of contesting elections to the Lagos Town Council and the Nigerian Legislative Council. Party members were handpicked by Macaulay from the elite group of native foreigners; the party was narrowly concerned only with the politics of Lagos; it operated on the authoritarian command of its founder; and it lacked both ideology and platform. The NNDP was, in essence, a club of the community's political elite built around Macaulay who personally selected all the party's nominees, directed their campaigns, and dictated their policies after they had been elected to office.

Finally, Macaulay's strategy rested on the careful cultivation of an inner circle of allies and associates from whom he could expect undivided allegiance. These cohorts were drawn from both the elite and indigenous communities. C. C. Adeniji-Jones, J. E. Egerton-Shyngle, T. A. Doherty, Eric Moore, and S. H. Pearse were among Macaulay's top aides. Lemomu Braimah and Alhaji Ishawu from the Muslim population, Chiefs Ojora and Oluwa from the order of White Cap chiefs, Eshugbayi Eleko from the House of Docemo, and Madam Alimotu Pelewura, the *alaga* of Ereko Market, provided Macaulay's links with the major interest groups among the indigenous population. By defending the causes of these leaders, Macaulay alienated their respective rivals, leaving behind a string of political enemies. For this reason he was often regarded, particularly by the colonial authorities, as an unscrupulous opportunist who would shrewdly exploit any disturbance for his own political gain.

However prejudiced the colonial government may have been, its evaluation of the charismatic leader contained at least a kernel of truth, for Macaulay was known to go to extraordinary lengths to maintain his influence.[35] Time and again the responsibility for conflict in the town was laid at Macaulay's doorstep. The chiefs who refused to recognize the head of the House of Docemo installed by the British were said to be "patrons of the Democratic Party," and the rebellious Jam'at Congregation was reported to be "influenced by the leaders of the Democratic Party [who] . . . put political considerations before those of religion."[36] Lord Hailey voiced the opinion that "since the date of the decision in the Apapa case the claim made by the White Cap chiefs had had political rather than juridicial significance, being one of the contentions advanced against the Government (though based on unsubstantial arguments) by the clique known as the National Democratic Party."[37]

Many of Macaulay's contemporaries in the elite community shared the same views. Macaulay callously vilified the character, qualification, and integrity of his opponets, leaving many of them bitterly hostile and vengeful. His strongest adversaries were Sir Adeyemo Alakija, Sir Kitoyi Ajasa, and Henry Carr—all conservative members of the colonial establishment. For example, Macaulay called for the resignation of Carr, resident of the colony, denouncing him for being "the Fifth Wheel of the Nigerian Administrative Coach," a man who was "popularly known to have imbibed foreign or western ideas and mode of thinking and action."[38] Eventually, as Macaulay's targets multiplied even his own disciples began to abandon him. His chief deputy, C. C. Adeniji-Jones, refused to endorse his decision to ally with the NCNC in 1944. Another former associate revealed privately that the split within the ranks of the Democratic Party, primarily as a result of Macaulay's autocratic methods, was evident long before then.[39] But whatever the reason, it was evident that Macaulay's ruthlessness caused deep divisions within the community and, in later years, even within his personal entourage.

As nationalist activity expanded at the beginning of World War

II, Macaulay was forced to share the political limelight with younger nationalists and to seek an acceptable accomodation with the new generation. The foremost nationalist of the 1940s, Nnamdi Azikiwe, commanded the support of the Ibo population in Lagos, then numbering 10,000, and was the source of inspiration for the Yoruba middle class. In 1944, therefore, Macaulay joined forces with Azikiwe, forming an alliance between the indigenous Lagosians and the non-Yoruba immigrants.

Azikiwe deferred to the elder statesman, crowning him president of the NCNC and accepting the somewhat misleading designation of Macaulay's "political son." There was, of course, little chance that Azikiwe would ever inherit Macaulay's political values or his political empire.[40] It was impossible for Macaulay to designate an heir; his popularity was wholly personal, a phenomenon that could be neither routinized nor transferred. The brief association of the two leaders, however, eased Lagos through a difficult transition from colonial rule to an era of modern political activity.

Ethnic solidarity was obviously of little importance to Macaulay at any point in his career. In fact, he deliberately shunned the Yoruba leadership rising in the west because of the mutual antagonism between himself and Obafemi Awolowo, then secretary of the Nigerian Motor Transport Union. Awolowo was contemptuous of Lagos politics, with its petty rivalry, its lack of discipline, and its opportunism.[41] Early in their relationship Macaulay spurned Awolowo's budding nationalist efforts to organize a strike of transportation workers because Awolowo had also asked Sir Adeyemo Alakija, one of Macaulay's strongest opponents, to lend assistance.[42] After that incident the two men avoided any form of political collaboration. It was only after Macaulay's death, and even then with some hesitation, that Awolowo began to extend his political organization to the Lagos masses.

Macaulay died at the age of eighty-two on May 7, 1946, while on a nationwide tour with leaders of the NCNC. His last requests were to "tell the National Council delegates to halt wherever they are for four days for Macaulay and then carry on," and to "tell Oged[43] to keep the flag flying."[44] Macaulay's funeral was attended by more than 100,000 people in Lagos. Women mourned him by closing the markets for two days. Nnamdi Azikiwe delivered the funeral oration, praising the dead leader for his "imperishable legacy, the struggle for the attainment of social equality, economic security, religious tolerance and political freedom."[45] Macaulay's death marked the end of a historic chapter in Lagos politics.

Whatever one may think of his methods or motives, there is no denying that Macaulay played a crucial role in the politics of Lagos and contributed significantly to the political development of the town. He laid a foundation of political protest for future leaders to follow; he mobilized the lower classes for political action through modern institutions; and he encouraged the African masses to defend their rights and their heritage. Concomitantly, he built a reservoir of local power which no one since has been able to match. In a sense, he resembled the old ward politicians of American cities, although there were significant differences between the two types of leaders. For one thing, Macaulay did not operate an urban machine. On the contrary, he had no bureaucracy to speak of, and he was careful to see that loyalty was directed to himself personally rather than to his party. For this reason the NNDP expired with Macaulay, whereas New York's Tammany Hall outlived men like Boss Tweed and George Washington Plunkett.[46] Moreover, American ward politicians gained their influence by mobilizing large immigrant communities which had the vote; Macaulay's supporters were the disenfranchised indigenous population. Most of the ward politicians had humble social origins and rose to power by outmaneuvering the local gentry; Macaulay and his associates were themselves the local gentry—all members of an aristocratic elite functioning in a colonial situation.

These differences notwithstanding, the two types of leaders were remarkably alike in their historic roles as marginal figures who bridged the gap between two unintegrated political communities. The ward politicians provided a link between the worlds of Europe and America in the slums of New York or Boston; Macaulay provided a link between the worlds of England and Africa in the slums of Lagos. In both instances the urban masses had the same traditional concept of politics as a personal affair in which government was vested in a powerful local ruler. Macaulay combined the prestige and status of the local elite with the authority of a local chieftain, in whom indigenes found a replica of the kind of sovereign they had respected before colonial rule. This duality was the source of the charisma through which he became a local hero, both promising and delivering more to his constituents than any other leader of his time.

LAND

Ordinarily, land would be regarded as part of the resource of wealth, especially in a city like Lagos where property is in exceedingly high demand and in desperately short supply. In Africa, however, land has a special significance rooted in values that transcend immediate economic considerations. Although traditional attitudes toward land among Lagos Yorubas have undergone some transformation over the years, in the older sections of the city, where land has been in the hands of indigenous descent groups for centuries, communal ownership of property has profound sentimental and social values as an expression of group cohesion.

Rights to Lagos land were originally vested in the sons of the Olofin who were designated as Idejo or White Cap chiefs. The exact number of Idejo chiefs, the property they hold, and the nature of their proprietary rights have since become subjects of considerable controversy and litigation. Oged Macaulay listed twelve original Idejo chiefs; Dr. T. O. Elias argued that there were only four; and G. B. A. Coker, affirming the legendary number, claims that there were sixteen.[47]

Even more confusion surrounds the question of the precise holdings of Idejo chiefs. Because the original allocations were made for the purpose of distributing farmlands among a small population according to need, no definite frontiers or boundaries were delineated.[48] Moreover, private title to and sale of land were unknown in traditional Yoruba society.[49] Customary law provided that land belonged to the patrilineal heads of occupying families, remaining with them and their descendants for as long as there were members who still needed it. Lineage heads could grant usufruct rights to settlers or strangers, usually in return for a proportion of its yield, but neither an original inhabitant nor his descendant could individually alienate his entitlement unless his family collectively sanctioned the transaction. Land was handed down to succesive offspring of the family through the eldest male descendants, but all branches of the lineage had equal rights with regard to the use of, income from, and disposition of property.[50] The Idejo chiefs in Yorubaland had limited rights in this system. Although they were literally known as "landowners," they acted essentially as executive trustees of communal estates, and neither they nor the oba of Lagos had the sole authority to alienate family property or claim it as personal property.

Confusion was first introduced when Oba Akitoye began to parcel out sections of the town to Saro and Brazilian emigrants, ostensbily in conformity with the custom of allowing settlement without actually granting ownership rights. Plots were let to emigrants for residences, commercial activities, and the building of warehouses. Docemo continued the practice, but went one step further by granting written concessions on the assumption that the seeming sale of land to educated Africans might deter further British encroachment in Lagos, a belief widely encouraged by ambitious emigrants who appreciated the growing economic value of property. When the slave trade was cut off by the British, income from these rents or "sales" of land became an alternative source of revenue to the oba and the traditional chiefs, whose economic position was becoming increasingly insecure. Thus, more than 100 years ago, property came to be regarded as a private, moneymaking enterprise in Lagos.

The concept of individual ownership of land was extended by a system of land grants introduced by the colonial government. Disbursement of property by the government was justified on the ground that the Treaty of Cession forfeited native claims to land after 1861.[51] Private titles known as crown grants were therefore disbursed in disregard of customary law. Some Idejo chiefs tried to legalize their claims to land in this way, acquiring proprietary rights to which they were not normally entitled under Yoruba law; Oba Docemo took several crown grants himself. To make matters worse, another ordinance was passed entitling persons who had occupied land for three years, but who had not paid rent or tribute, to claim private titles from the government. This ruling meant that land could be granted to squatters or strangers, an opportunity enthusiastically welcomed by the emigrants whose proprietary rights had not theretofore been established. Allotments made by the oba of Lagos dating as far back as 1853 were formally designated as private holdings. By 1908 approximately 4,000 crown grants had been issued for the colony, 75 percent of them on Lagos Island alone.[52]

This system of individual holdings deprived many families of property that was rightfully theirs. Among the worst exploiters were Idejo chiefs and other lineage heads who selfishly used the English system to increase their own power and wealth. As sole legal owners, they could now sell or mortgage at their own discretion family property with which they were entrusted, retaining the profits themselves. Occasionally, land was also used as collateral by the family heads or "owners" to establish credit for the purchase of European goods. As foreclosures and sales increased, communal lands became fragmented or lost. Between 1908 and 1912, the Lagos Lands Office recorded 1,493 sales and 442 mortgages. Uncontrolled partition of family property continued unabated until the early part of the twentieth century, when the average crown grant amounted to little more than one-eighth of an acre, a plot so small that it could reportedly be purchased for "a bag of cowries and a case of gin."[53]

The famous Apapa land case of 1921 marked the beginning of a trend toward reversing the process. It arose over resistance to the government's compulsory acquisition of land in Apapa which had been occupied by persons who were paying tribute to Amodu Tijani, head of the Oluwa family.[54] Tijani claimed that, as an Idejo chief, he was entitled to financial compensation. With the help of Herbert Macaulay he brought his case before the Judicial Committee of the Privy Council and in the final judgment was awarded £22,500 ($63,000). The Privy Council held that the Treaty of Cession did not constitute a valid transfer of property rights to the British sovereign, as the colonial government had contended, because the oba of Lagos did not have the authority to pass proprietary rights to the Crown, and the Idejo chiefs were in no way subject to the oba's control with regard to the disposition of family property.[55]

While the ruling in the Apapa land case put a stop to government encroachment on communal land, the confusion that had built up over the years by the dual systems of land tenure remained unresolved. In fact, the system is still a source of considerable controversy and litigation. Much communal land now held by customary tenure is not registered, and commercial firms wishing to obtain or lease property frequently have difficulty in tracing the rightful owner. Even major government buildings and installations in Lagos may have no record of legal tenancy, possession being held presumably by virtue of the length of occupancy. In fact, there is evidence "to justify the inference that Chiefs Onisiwo, Oluwa, Olotu, Oniru, Onikoyi and Aromire are Idejos and do own land,"[56] but as yet no comprehensive survey of family-held property has been made in Lagos. In the words of a 1957 report, "conveyancing in Lagos today . . . is often a matter of taking a deep breath, boldly reciting a fee simple and then 'touching wood.' "[57]

The judgment in the Apapa land case also failed to define precisely the rights of Idejo chiefs who had often abused their privileges. Their rights were not clarified until a series of ordinances were passed in 1947 after an intensive investigation by Sir Mervin Tew.[58] The cumulative impact of these ordinances was to reassign communal land to families whose claims could be reasonably validated.

The institution of family property has thus remained very strong in Lagos, even down to recent times, although residence and land-use patterns have changed considerably. Large areas of Iddo, Ijora, Apapa, and Lagos Island have been converted to industrial and commercial use. Overcrowding and high rents have dispersed family units in Isale Eko, but one may still find a number of old family houses there, many of them occupied by original lineages; a 1961 study of central Lagos reveals that nine-tenths of the resident owners in Isale Eko were born in Lagos, more than half of them in the houses they were still occupying.[59] Members of extended families who cannot be housed in one dwelling usually find lodgings near the family compounds: "It is nothing uncommon, in central Lagos, to meet twenty of your kinsfolk in the course of an ordinary day."[60] Despite narrow lanes, dilapidated houses, and malodorous markets which give the impression of an impoverished

97

and depressed slum, Isale Eko has remained a vibrant, bustling, animated neighborhood whose residents own some of the most valuable property in the city, control the lion's share of trade in the local markets, and exhibit a unique sense of organic unity unmatched by any other urban grouping. The touchstone of their community pride and solidarity is land, a resource to which the indigenes attach deep significance and for which they have a sentimental feeling.

Increasingly, property ownership has come to be regarded not only as an instrument of group cohesion but as a means of achieving group influence. Part of the fear of domination by the Ibo population in Lagos was based on the erroneous belief that the Ibos were accumulating large blocks of property; similar allegations were made against political parties and federal politicians. In 1962, for example, an Action Group supporter asserted that crown land allocation was based on two principles: party affiliation and regional origin.[61] Party and regional influence in land matters has been exercised mainly through public projects sponsored by federally controlled institutions, particularly projects initiated by the Lagos Executive Development Board (LEDB), a statutory corporation which was responsible for land development and town planning in Lagos. Legally responsible to the federal government (until the creation of Lagos State in 1967), politically obligated to the parties in power, and functionally oriented toward satisfying the needs of urban residents, the LEDB was the focus of intense counterpressures from all conflicting interests in the competition for land.

Of all the LEDB projects, the one that best illustrates the use of land for political purposes is the Central Lagos Slum Clearance Scheme, a project conceived in 1951 to provide for the clearance of a 70-acre triangular block of land in the densely populated commercial district of Lagos Island, where approximately 30,000 indigenous Lagosians resided.[62] Under the plan the LEDB was to purchase the designated area, redevelop it with open spaces, wider streets, and new plot layouts, and then, at 120 percent of the acquisition cost, sell it back to the original owners, who were expected to rebuild according to modern standards. The LEDB's objectives were to provide better health conditions, stimulate the construction of improved housing, relieve traffic jams, and modernize the city so that the nation could be proud of its capital.

Owing to the anticipated increase in the value of the property, it was expected that the original owners would scramble to repurchase their plots, but the indigenes who owned most of them did not share the board's enthusiasm. When work began in 1956, police had to be sent in to protect the laborers who began the demolition.[63] Once the project was under way the violence subsided, but the Lagosians uniformly continued to express opposition to the project. To mollify their grievances and alleviate the suffering of displaced persons, the LEDB indemnified affected individuals by settling them in a rehousing estate at Surulere, some 5 miles away, until they could repurchase their land. The LEDB also provided a fund of £200,000 to compensate individuals who endured unusual financial hardship owing to loss of trade or rents as a consequence of the scheme.

However well intentioned the project may have been at the outset, unanticipated problems resulted in unjust land distribution, which was felt most deeply by the indigenous community. Foremost among the difficulties was the inability of the original landowners to repurchase their property. The displaced persons had to pay 20 percent more for their land than the amount they had received in compensation, and they needed additional funds to modernize their houses. Most indigenes simply could not raise the neccessary money. Even the compensation price could not always be collected once it had been distributed among all the members of the lineage, as required by tradition. The money was either spent before it could be reinvested, or the family could not come to an agreement about repurchasing the property. Moreover, it was impossible after widening the streets and creating open spaces to redistribute plots to all the claimants; of the original 70 acres, only 43 were available for reallocation. To increase the supply, the LEDB began to carve up plots into irregular strips with a frontage of 25–30 feet and a depth of 80–100 feet. This solution, of course, defeated one of the purposes of slum clearance, for it made inevitable the same old pattern of narrow, congested construction. It also further dampened the hopes of the indigenes that they might profit from the scheme; the prospect of investing more money in a smaller plot confirmed their belief that the project was neither well planned nor well executed.

Four years after commencement of the project, £1,368,690 had been paid in compensation, £90,000 had been awarded for hardship cases, and 6,000 people had been moved, but no headway had been made in redevelopment. Faced with growing dissent from the indigenes, the LEDB decided in 1958 to launch a supplementary scheme to reclaim at a cost of £750,000 a low-lying swampy area between Ikoyi and Lagos known as Southwest Ikoyi. The major portion of this land was to be sold as freehold property to persons affected by slum clearance; the remainder was to be leased to civil servants and the general public. Upon completion of the scheme in 1961, however, the Ministry of Lagos Affairs abruptly withdrew the LEDB's authority to allocate the plots in Southwest Ikoyi. In a letter to the board, the permanent secretary wrote that "the Prime Minister has directed that those plots in the Southwest Ikoyi Layout allocated for distribution to central Lagos landowners by the Board are forthwith withdrawn. . . . It is proposed that the lay-out of plots in question be redesignated and allocated directly by Government—primarily to senior civil servants."[64]

In 1963 the federal government further decided that displaced persons who lost income as a result of slum clearance could be more meaningfully compensated by shop allocations instead of by the direct monetary payments they had been receiving. The Ex-gratia Compensation Committee was specially created by the Ministry of Lagos Affairs to supervise the erection and allocation of 756 temporary shops in the slum clearance district. The LEDB opposed the decision on the grounds that the occupants of temporary shops would not willingly move once they were settled, and that the project would drain off resources needed for more important jobs. The minister overruled these objections and ordered construction of the shops to proceed. There resulted a splitting of functions in what was essentially still one project: the

LEDB was responsible for demolition and resettlement; the federal government allocated land and shops.

The slum clearance plan deprived the indigenes of their land and fell far short of its stated goals. At the time of this writing, only 25 of the 70 acres of land have actually been acquired by the LEDB. Of these 25 acres, only 3.60 have been redeveloped. The rest of the land stands idle as undeveloped or partly paid-for allotments, used as improvised playgrounds, parking lots, garbage dumps, comfort stations, or markets for itinerant traders. The area gives the impression of having been "re-slummed."[65] Ironically, most of the materials in the new installations, officially regarded as temporary, are of poorer quality than those of the demolished dwellings. Sanitary conditions continue to be just as bad as ever, traffic is equally congested, competition for space has intensified, and land values have been inflated. Moreover, the LEDB incurred substantial debts in trying to implement the scheme. In 1966 arrears of rent on acquired property amounted to £32,030.2.7; an additional £38,649.3.6 was still outstanding in the reconveyance of a number of plots. These were the largest uncollected revenues for any of the board's capital projects. The *UN Report* estimated that it would cost at least another £5 million to complete the urban renewal originally envisioned by the LEDB.

The political costs generated by the slum clearance project have cut just as deeply into the community. Altogether, 11,170 persons (about two-thirds of them tenants) have been displaced and only 179 plots in central Lagos have been made available for repurchase. Temporary shops built for Lagosian traders have, for the most part, been given to persons not affected by the scheme. Under the open-door policy adopted by the Ex-gratia Compensation Committee, any trader who wanted a shop in central Lagos was eligible for allocation.[66] The shops were dispersed to friends, relatives, and well-connected individuals who had influence with the federal authorities. The same abuses marred the distribution of plots in Southwest Ikoyi which were intended for persons displaced by slum clearance. In the final distribution, 238 plots, representing nearly the total number available, were sold to prominent politicians, civil servants, armed forces officers, and other notables, friends, and relatives.[67] Only twenty-four houses, four years after their completion, were released for sale to displaced persons.

The military governor of Lagos State, Colonel Mobolaji Johnson, attempted to rectify the abuses in land distribution shortly after the establishment of a military regime. To reduce favoritism, temporary shops in Lagos were to be divided into two categories: 60 percent were to be reserved for traders displaced by slum clearance, and 40 percent were to be reserved for all other applicants. State land, including the remaining plots in central Lagos, were henceforth to be allocated by ballot, excluding persons who had already received land, either by assigment or by transfer. A "one man, one plot" principle was to apply. Little progress has been made in redistribution, however, since the new policies were laid down in 1966.[68]

To Lagosians, the lessons of the slum clearance scheme are clear. They have been forcibly removed from their homes and places of work for an uncompleted project that, without improving conditions in the area, has brought severe financial losses to all parties concerned. Even more disturbing, however, is the fact that land and shops have been granted to settlers who, in the eyes of Lagosians, have no legitimate claim to the property. More than any other public project, this scheme has crystallized the social conflict between indigenous landlords and traders who want to protect their birthright and their livelihood, and nonindigenous interests—real estate speculators, merchants, and government officials—whose concerns lie in development of land for economic profit and national pride. However much control the indigenes might gain locally, they are likely to remain in a weak position with regard to land, which comes under the jurisdiction of higher authorities.

Still, in light of the degree of urbanization in Lagos over the past fifty years, it is remarkable that traditional forms of land tenure have been retained for so long in the heart of the city. As competition has increased, Lagosians have stiffened in their determination not to surrender the property remaining in their possession; initial steps have already been taken to mobilize landowners who seek to protect their traditional rights.[69] Just how effective these efforts will be in the future depends on the nature of the accommodation to be made between the forces of continuity and change. As in the past, the control of urban land will reflect to a great extent the balance of power between local and higher authorities, between lower and middle classes, and between indigenous and nonindigenous interest groups in the country.

GROUP SOLIDARITY

Group solidarity means the consciousness of a common identity or interest among a given set of individuals. This collective sentiment has been tapped by skillful leaders to mobilize public opinion and generate citizen participation, principally among groups based on origin, religion, ethnicity, or class.

The group that has emerged with the strongest and most sustained sense of solidarity is an aggregate known as the Lagos Muslims. The term "Lagos Muslims" has occasionally been used to refer loosely to all Lagosians, whether or not they are Muslim. In the strict, and correct, sense of the term as used here, Lagos Muslims are defined as indigenous Islamic inhabitants who regard Lagos as their place of origin (i.e., their hometown and their father's hometown).

In 1911, indigenes accounted for 80 percent of Lagos inhabitants, but by 1950 the proportion had dropped sharply, to only 37 percent of the urban population and 17 percent of the metropolitan population.[70] By 1963 the number of indigenes had dwindled to slightly more than a quarter of the total urban population (see table 28). Nevertheless, Lagos Muslims, who account for the largest share of the indigenous population, have exhibited a strong sense of communal cohesion, deriving from their common history, origin, and ethnicity; from centuries of residence on land that is owned by the dominant lineages; and from the existence of durable patterns of internal social organization within the heart of Isale Eko. Although urbanization has made traditional life difficult to maintain intact, many aspects of the past have survived in the original form.

Physically, Old Town has changed very little; it has simply

grown more congested and has expanded its boundaries into the neighboring areas of the island. Nearly all the dwellings, except for some houses built after slum clearance, are old one-story structures crowded into narrow, winding streets. Some lanes are barely broad enough to accommodate the open sewers, single-file pedestrian traffic, and scores of stalls from which petty traders sell their wares.

TABLE 28

INDIGENOUS AND IMMIGRANT POPULATIONS IN LAGOS, 1911–1963

| Year | Total population of Lagos | Immigrants as percent of total population | Indigenes as percent of total population |
|---|---|---|---|
| 1911 | 73,766 | 20 | 80 |
| 1921 | 99,690 | 23 | 77 |
| 1931 | 126,108 | 59 | 41 |
| 1950 | 230,256 | 63 | 37 |
| 1963 | 665,246 | 73 | 27 |

SOURCES: Figures for 1911, 1921, 1931, and 1950 from A. L. Mabogunje, "Lagos: A Study in Urban Geography" (Ph.D. dissertation, University of London, 1961), who used the population censuses of Lagos, and P. A. Talbot, *The Peoples of Southern Nigeria* (London: Oxford University Press, 1926), Vol. IV. I calculated the percentages for 1963 from statistics on the distribution of population by ward given in *Population Census of Lagos, 1963* (Lagos: Federal Office of Statistics, 1963).

This "higgledy-piggledy mass of Yoruba slum houses"[71] forms the city's most run-down area with the worst housing and sanitary conditions of any urban ghetto.

Family relationships which cement the community together have not deteriorated in this environment. Descent groups are the basic units governing social and political relations. Having outgrown the family compound, households now tend to live apart, but brothers, sisters, and children of most Lagos families in this district typically settle within walking distance of one another. Family elders are recognized as senior authorities who represent the collective interests and lineages in community affairs. Intimate kinship relations and daily face-to-face visits are a normal part of the communal culture.[72] Kinship ties are also formalized in periodic meetings of descent groups. Of the various ethnic groups holding regular, formal meetings in Lagos, "the proportion is highest for those born in Lagos: 69 had regular meetings at least once every month. . . . Some were small councils of parents and children, but more commonly there would be a dozen to thirty present, occasionally over a hundred."[73] Kinship ties are further reinforced by adherence to traditional marriage practices. In a 1964 survey of marriage and family growth in Lagos, polygamy, an institution upheld by religious and cultural norms, was found to be still very much in evidence.[74]

Remnants of the ancient Yoruba political structure based on the authority of lineage heads and titled chiefs also have survived in Isale Eko, although the functional significance of chieftaincy institutions has undergone some transformation (see chap. 7). Like the English monarch, however, the oba of Lagos today symbolizes the unity of his people, and a considerable degree of prestige and status is attached to his office as to all hereditary chiefs in Lagos. It is through the maintenance of traditional structures such as these that the Lagos Muslims have retained their sense of corporate existence. Islam has reinforced communal identity, but the religion has not always been a unifying force, particularly when the major Islamic sects were first being established in Lagos. Introduced in the eighteenth century by Hausa traders, Islam was first permitted to be openly practiced by Oba Kosoko in 1841. Through conversions, the original congregation expanded rapidly. In 1864, at the edge of the traditional quarter on what is now Nnamdi Azikiwe Street, its members built the Central Mosque, which remains to this day the most popular Muslim house of worship in the city.[75]

The first breach in the orthodox congregation occurred in 1876 when a breakaway faction called the Al-Koranic or Shakiti people protested the importation of books other than the Koran by the Hausa imam (priest). Led by a Nupe preacher from Ilorin, the Al-Koranic faction separated from the main body and constructed a second mosque in Aroloya; they have continued to reject the use of commentaries and insist on the sufficiency of the Koran for theological guidance. In 1919 the Al-Koranic congregation itself split over choosing a successor to their first imam, and the dissident faction established a third branch of Lagos Muhammadanism centered in the Okepopo Mosque.

Meanwhile, dissatisfaction was growing in the original Central Mosque over the orthodoxy of the chief imam, Lemomu Braimah, who had been installed in 1901. He had come under severe personal attack for his views on a constitution for Muslim religious organizations, his handling of finances, and his exclusive rules for the use of the mosque. Lagos Yorubas wanted to expel the Hausa leaders in the Central Mosque and establish local control. In 1916 a rebel faction that went by the name of Jam'at precipitated the "Muhammadan Unrest," a struggle for power which shook the entire community. In 1924, after a stormy series of violent clashes and lockouts and a court appeal to the Privy Council, the Jam'at finally wrested control of the Central Mosque from the parent body. The conservative faction, which came to be known after its leader as the Lemomu party, was driven out of the congregation and established the fourth rival mosque nearby with the aid of Alli Balogun, a wealthy Muslim trader.

A fifth major branch of Lagos Muhammadanism, the Ahmadiya, was introduced into Lagos in 1916; it was the first Muslim group to be invited in by the local inhabitants. The Ahmadiya was originally founded in India by one Mirza Ghulam Ahmad (d. 1908) who claimed to be the messianic successor to Muhammad; this view was heretical, for orthodox Islam holds that Muhammad was the last true prophet. The Ahmadiya was radical in other respects as well: it argued that the jihad was meant to be fought with words, not swords; that the education of Muslim children should include modern subjects like arithmetic, science, and English; and that there was no harm in incorporating quotations from the Bible into the Muslim liturgy. Some local Muslims attracted to the modern features of Ahmadiya, particularly its views on education, invited the Indian missionary, Abd-ur-Rahman Nayyar, to come to Lagos in 1921. A small group including Prince Adeniji Adele II, then a civil servant, and Alhaji L. B. Agusto, a Muslim of Brazilian descent, founded the Lagos branch. Initially the Ahmadis attempted to affiliate with one of the established sects. Too liberal in ritual for the Lemomu faction and too loyal in politics for the Jam'at, they were warmly received by the Al-Koranic people, with whom they shared a mosque. After a four-year absence in England during which he studied law, Agusto returned to Lagos in 1924 to find that the Ahmadis had come too much under the influence of the Indian missionary whom he had originally invited to Lagos. Agusto and his followers then left the Ahmadiya and established a separate body known as the Islamic Society in Nigeria, or the Jam'at Islammiya.

The Ahmadiya subsequently experienced further fragmentation. Expelled from the Aroloya Mosque in 1934 by non-Ahmadi Koranic worshipers, it split in 1937 over the question of foreign control. The loyal Ahmadiya faction, led by Nayya's successor, F. R. Hakim, favored continued Indian leadership, while the Independents, led by K. R. Ajose, one of the original founders of Ahmadiya, led a movement for complete Africanization. In 1939 these factions separated into two autonomous societies: the Ahmadiya Movement in Islam comprised the Independents, who won legal control over all Ahmadiya property; and the Sadr Anjuman Ahmadiya included the Loyalists, who continued to maintain close connections with their Indian counterparts. In 1959, on the initiative of L. B. Agusto, an attempt was made to unify these disparate Muslim groups into the All-Nigerian Muslim Council, a federation of Muslim societies. Each member group was given equal representation on the governing board, except that the Central Mosque, in deference to the outstanding size of its congregation, had twice as many representatives as each of the other groups. In 1963 another rival organization, the Nigerian Muslim Council, was formed under the leadership of the chief imam of the Central Mosque.

Rather than appeal to the group solidarity of the indigenous community as a whole during these early years of intrafaith rivalry, political leaders exploited the solidarity of particular Muslim factions. The key group aiding Macaulay's rise to fame, for example, was the Jam'at Congregation, whose theological rebellion was fully in concert with Macaulay's political agitation; like Macaulay, the congregation defied the government in 1916 by openly resisting the introduction of a water rate. Three years later, the internal dispute within the Muslim community reached a climax, at one point necessitating the intervention of the fire brigade to quell fighting that broke out inside the mosque.[76] In the subsequent struggle Macaulay became a close adviser to the Jam'at, using every weapon at his disposal to defend its position. It was under his influence that Eshugbayi Eleko destooled one of Lemomu's strongest supporters, Alli Balogun, and appointed a member of the Jam'at, Sani Shitta, to the prestigious position of Seriki Muslimi of the Lagos Muhammadans. Eshugbayi, though not a Muslim, took it upon himself to announce the appointment of the Jam'at candidate, Ligali ibn-Nalla, as chief imam of the Central Mosque, a move that precipitated his own eventual deportation by the government. A reconciliation meeting of the two parties to the Muslim dispute was held in 1924 at the home of Alli Balogun, with Macaulay and Egerton-Shyngle in attendance. It collapsed when the Jam'at stubbornly insisted on the appointment of its own candidate as the only solution to the conflict, but it is likely that the two outsiders were partly responsible for "the unyielding position adopted by the Jam'at."[77]

Macaulay remained a close collaborator of the Jam'at throughout the court proceedings for control of the Central Mosque, a prize that would virtually guarantee the future status and growth of the ruling sect. The successful outcome of the Jam'at's petition brought him as much adulation among the Muslim community as success in the Oluwa land case had brought him among the White Cap chiefs. In the fight for the mosque, Macaulay secured his political future by capturing the most rapidly expanding religious group in Lagos. The Jam'at's fiercely independent stand against northern influence, its control of the most prestigious mosque in town, and its close ties with Eshugbayi Eleko and Macaulay made it soar in popularity. By the late 1930s, forty-eight of the fifty-eight mosques in Lagos belonged to the Jam'at, and half the town was solidly Muslim, including most of the well-organized and prosperous market women who formed the bedrock membership of the Democratic Party.

Predictably, Macaulay's support of the Jam'at drove his opponents to the opposite corner. Lemomu Braimah had the support of most of Macaulay's antagonists, including a number of conservative but highly respected members of the urban elite—Dr. John Randle, Sir Kitoyi Ajasa, Sir Adeyemo Alakija, Henry Carr— and a handful of prominent indigenes, including Chief Obanikoro, the senior White Cap chief, and Alli Balogun. But these forces lacked the unity, resources, and prestige of the Jam'at Congregation.

From these early religious conflicts three broad traditions of Muhammadanism have evolved in Lagos, each appealing to a different class of citizens.[78] First, the traditionalists or fundamentalists consist of the Lemomu and Al-Koranic sects. Oriented toward Ilorin, their local Mecca, and influenced predominantly by the Islamic north, they are firmly committed to upholding the strict letter and law of Islamic doctrine and are intolerant of compromises with African religion. This is the Islam that appeals to the elders, the orthodox, and most of the non-Yoruba Muslims who see Muhammadanism as an exclusive civilization transcending tribal or racial distinctions. The fundamentalists have close ties with Hausa leaders, many of whom have been imans, are strongly legalistic in their interpretations of the Koran, conduct their liturgy in Arabic, and dutifully observe the rites and religious hierarchies of Islam without ever really having adapted it to the local environment. This Islam has been aptly described as a "semi-integrated intrusion," one that has not penetrated into the hearts or the souls of the majority of the community.

The second tradition may be described as an Africanized Islam centered in the Jam'at Congregation, the largest in Lagos. The Jam'at has indigenized the faith to suit the needs of local inhabitants, mixing local Yoruba beliefs and superstitions with basic Islamic doctrine. It rejects foreign control, tolerates animist influences, and stresses the communal solidarity of Islamic worshipers. This is unquestionably the Islam of the masses, the type of religion with which the average Yoruba can easily identify without having to sacrifice his traditional culture.[79]

Finally, there is a secular Islam that appeals to the urban elite, the neo-Muslim townsmen who, while rejecting Christianity, still feel that there are serious deficiencies in Islam as it exists in either of the other forms. The several Ahmadiya sects and the Ansar-ud-Deen Society, a quasi-religious and quasi-educational organization, have become the focus of attention for these reformers. Regarded as deviationists or revisionists by more conservative sects, neo-Muslims tend to be attracted to Islam individually, rather than through family or group conversion. They conduct their liturgy and distribute propaganda in English, they allow women to enter mosques, they encourage them to educate their children in modern subjects, and they have led the way in translating the Koran into African languages. Whereas traditionalists refuse to compromise with customary animistic practices in order to preserve the purity of Islam, neo-Muslims refuse to compromise with the pagan practices in order to preserve the progressiveness of Islam. The Ansar-ud-Deen Society, which has spread out from Lagos into the interior, has established well over 200 primary and secondary schools in the country.[80] With the continuing spread of education, secular Islam is likely to become more popular among the expanding urban proletariat.

The fact that Islam has always prospered in towns may account for the rapid advances it has made among urbanized Yoruba.[81] In Lagos, Islam spread most rapidly among the urban poor and has evolved simultaneously into a territorial, ethnic, and class religion. It is associated with the local inhabitants as opposed to the minorities, and with the common man as opposed to the elite.[82] Although many Yoruba immigrants are also Muslims, Islam in Lagos has come to be primarily an indigenous faith in which social ethics and communal solidarity are given more emphasis than ritual obedience and spiritual dogma. Islam does not cause social disintegration or challenge traditional institutions; yet it is flexible enough to accomodate innovations that arise from local demand. Whereas dissension and conflict among Muslims once weakened their solidarity, the various Muslim sects in Lagos now give the religion a strength and vitality that allow it to survive in the midst of rapid urbanization. For these reasons, Islam has become a means of communal identity, a label by which the indigenous Lagosian can determine where in the complex environment he really belongs.[83]

Christianity, by comparison, holds little appeal for the traditional community. It stresses individualism against kinship and communal values; it rejects polygamy and worship of traditional deities despite strong attachment to these customary practices; and it is associated principally with upper- and middle-class immigrants who are often the objects of resentment and scorn. As Christianity grew, becoming the majority religion in Lagos by 1950, thanks to immigration, the solidarity of Lagos Muslims intensified. Internal disputes were minimized and political activity became more extensive. In 1953, the United Muslim Party, a local political organization opposed to the incursions of both Yoruba and non-Yoruba immigrants, was formed. During the 1950s a number of Muslim voluntary associations sprang up, and local Muslim leaders began to take an active role in politics—men like Jibril Martins, member of the Ahmadiya Movement and founding member of the Nigerian Youth Movement; Oba Adeniji Adele II, an Ahmadi with his own political organization; and Dr. I. Olorun-Nimbe, a Lagos Muslim who was elected the first mayor of Lagos.

This surge of activity was far more than a religious awakening; it was a reshaping of the political consciousness of the indigenous community as a whole. By the late 1950s, Muslim interests were clearly identified with indigenous interests. Associations exclusively concerned with native-born Lagosians proliferated: the Lagos Aborigines Society, the Egbe Omo Oba (Society of the Sons of Obas), the Lagos Royalists, and the Egbe Omo Ibile Eko (Society of Descendants of Lagos Aborigines). Leading the political renaissance was a new generation of educated Muslims linked with the Ahmadiya and Ansar-ud-Deen societies. However unconventional their religious beliefs and behavior, they commanded the support of the indigenous community to an extent that the Christians could not even begin to match. Throughout the city, the influence of Lagos Muslims began to be felt. Within the Action Group they carved out a position of central control; by the 1960s, when the Action Group captured control of the council, Lagosian candidates were appointed to senior posts whenever possible. "By and large the candidates did not [even] need to lobby, for their origins were their strength and those with strong Lagos connections were certain of being favored in the absence of competition from others of the same background."[84]

The group solidarity of Lagos Muslims has vastly overshadowed that of other groups based on ethnic or class loyalties. Immigrant Yorubas in Lagos, who have maintained their customary loyalties to their towns of origin, are therefore divided into various subgroups based on traditional territorial ties. Egbas and Ijebus constitute the largest Yoruba groups after the Lagosians; but they and other Yorubas support a string of communal associations which

111

undercut efforts toward unity. Similar divisions fragment the Ibo population in Lagos, among whom village or clan organizations are popular. The pressure to belong to these particularistic organizations is quite strong in the urban environment, not only because of the material benefits that individual immigrants feel they might derive from membership in the societies, but also because failure to belong means that one is likely to be ostracized by others of his village or ethnic group.[85]

Ethnic solidarity is also undermined by the tendency of some immigrants to redefine their status in the urban community in order to associate themselves with groups that are more influential or socially acceptable in the city. An immigrant, for example, finding few people in the town from his village or clan, may redefine his identity in terms of geographically or linguistically related aggregates in order to improve his social standing. Minority groups are partcularly prone to this kind of affiliation, since they are often familiar with the language and culture of the dominant group in their home region, assets that make the transition more credible. "Rivers people" or "easterners" may be adopted in preference to the specific categories of Ijaw or Ibo. Sometimes an ethnic identity is attached to a particular occupational or territorial group; in Lagos, for example, nightwatchmen and northerners are frequently regarded indiscriminately as "Hausamen."[86]

The fluidity of social identity in the urban setting shows how nontraditional roles may be interpreted in terms of neotraditional values. Social redefinition usually favors dominant or influential groups, which set the standards for others to emulate. But whatever particular categorization may result, the important point is that this type of social change contributes neither to intergroup ethnic assimilation nor to intragroup unity. Rather, the major social groups in competition for influence and status tend to be singled out more clearly than ever before. Overriding emphasis therefore has been placed on Ibo-Yoruba rivalry in Lagos as the most intense ethnic competition in the city. In fact there have been equally strong rivalries within these groups, particularly among the Yoruba.[87] It is at this subethnic or intraethnic level that Lagos Muslims have proved to be the most effective.

Of all the major social groups in the city, however, those based on class or economic cohesion have proved to be the weakest. The early Lagos elite may perhaps be regarded as the only exception to this pattern, but they represented a distinct cultural group, united as much by origin as by common socioeconomic background. Labor unions have not been effective instruments either in gaining improved conditions for the working class or in generating sustained political activity. In fact, in terms of class influence at the local level, the urban proletariat has been singularly apolitical. Self-employed entrepreneurs, contractors, traders, and white-collar workers have been much more aggressive politically, as data on the social composition of the council confirm. Neither of the major political parties has a labor wing, and organized unions played only a secondary and temporary role in mobilizing the masses during the nationalist period.

There are basically two reasons for the lack of class solidarity in the urban community: the social composition of the working class and the structure of the labor movement. The majority of the urban working class is a heterogeneous collection of wage-earning immigrants whose economic concerns are limited to personal and immediate material gains. Their organizational energies are directed toward groups that offer meaningful emotional satisfaction. Unless the occupational group has ethnic or territorial ties, the effective gratifications derived from tribal or communal unions nearly always command precedence over the impersonal rewards of membership in economic or occupational unions.[88] Most members of the urban working class are also aware of their comparative social position in the larger society; against the urban unemployed and the rural peasants, the urban wage earner is relatively well off. Difficult as it may be for some workers to make ends meet, owing to the high cost of living and heavy family obligations, they still do not experience the sense of rootlessness and despair felt by their jobless brothers and cousins. By and large, the trade unions are unsympathetic to the plight of the unemployed, for they

> view the large pool of unemployed as a constant threat to their bargaining position. Small-scale employers in the construction industry, for example, are ever ready to hire the unemployed at wages well below the statutory minimum.... The trade union movement is committed to protecting the privileges of their

113

(working) membership. When men lose their jobs the trade unions show little interest in them.[89]

Nor is the structure of the labor movement conducive to unity; in 1967 there were five central organizations and hundreds of shop unions.[90] Most labor unions function as special interest agencies aimed at resisting incursions from competing labor groups in particular small-scale industries. Unions also suffer from weak leadership, poor financial resources, and minimal interest among the rank and file.[91]

The Lagos Muslims are truly unique, having a degree of spontaneous accord and organic social consciousness unmatched by any other group. They represent, in the most fundamental sense, a *Gemeinschaft*-type community as conceived by Ferdinand Tonnies.[92] United by blood, locality, land, origin, ethnicity, religion, and class, the Lagos Muslims share a plurality of identities which have not created conflicts of loyalty as in other social groups, but rather have reinforced the natural harmony of overlapping interests that collectively constitute their most valuable political resource.

CHAPTER 5
*Political Behavior*

The preceding analysis of the urban power structure has depicted
four successive types of ruling strata dominant in Lagos over a
period of fifty years and the key political resources they employed
to gain influence. The focus now shifts from the power structure
to political behavior, discussed in this chapter under three head-
ings: (1) origin and growth of the urban party system; (2) internal
structure of major parties and their sources of popular support; (3)
response of the public as determined through ward electoral patterns. The most striking feature revealed by the data is the gradual
rise of the indigenous community, an achievement made possible
through the conversion of a party of social integration into a party
of community control, through consistent political solidarity, and
through superior electoral tactics.

ORIGIN AND GROWTH OF THE PARTY SYSTEM

Early political associations in Lagos functioned more as pressure
groups than as actual political parties. The first of these was the
People's Union, formed in 1908 by two physicians, John Randle
and Orisadipe Obasa, to protest the imposition of a water rate. In
1911 the Lagos auxiliary of the Anti-Slavery and Aborigines Protection Society was established by some of the outstanding civic
leaders, including Herbert Macaulay, Sapara Williams, S. H.
Pearse, J. P. Jackson, C. J. da Rocha, and O. Alakija. In the 1920s
the Reform Club, whose functions were more social than political,
and the Lagos chapter of the National Congress of British West
Africa, initially sponsored by Dr. Akinwande Savage, were established. All these groups were active in sporadic protests against

115

specific measures imposed by the colonial regime, but they did not challenge the legitimacy of colonial rule or enter into contests for public office.[1]

## Major Parties

The party system in Lagos began with the organization of the Nigerian National Democratic Party in 1923. Founded by Herbert Macaulay, the NNDP—or the Democratic Party, as it came to be known—had a monopoly of all elected seats on the Lagos Town Council and the Nigerian Legislative Council from its beginning until 1938.[2] During the 1920s and 1930s the party was involved, directly or indirectly, in nearly every public controversy in the community.[3] Its elite composition, the absence of an ideological framework or a hierarchical organization, and its limited objectives made the NNDP a protoparty not far removed from the political associations that predated it. Essentially the organization was a circle of aristocratic gentlemen who, in announcing their allegiance to the NNDP, were in effect pledging support to Macaulay.

Informal membership in the NNDP was claimed to be about 10,000, a figure probably derived from the estimated size of the crowds Macaulay drew at public rallies; his audiences were more an indication of his personal popularity than actual party mobilization. Formal party membership amounted to only two or three dozen people, a cadre of workers from whom Macaulay demanded unflinching loyalty. Those who received the party's nomination were required to take an oath pledging complete allegiance both to the party and to the Crown.[4] Measured against the political spectrum of later Nigerian parties, the NNDP was quite conservative, particularly in its professed loyalty to the British Government. Among the objectives listed in the constitution, for instance, were the following:

> ... to secure the safety and welfare of the people of the Colony and Protectorate of Nigeria as an integral part of the British Imperial Commonwealth, ... to maintain an attitude of unswerving loyalty to the throne and person of His Majesty's King Emperor [*sic*] by being strictly constitutional in the adoption of its methods and general procedure, ... to endorse and approve the truism that

cooperation of the governed with the governing body is the shortest cut to administrative success, . . . [and] to endorse the ideal of the British Empire as a Commonwealth of free nations linked by a common sentiment of loyalty to the King Emperor.[5]

The party that first challenged the hegemony of the Democratic Party was the Nigerian Youth Movement (originally the Lagos Youth Movement), a nationalist organization formed in 1934 as an outgrowth of the controversy over a new educational program at Yaba Higher College (now Yaba College of Technology).[6] The chairman of the Lagos branch of the NYM was Chief H. O. Davies, a Lagos barrister who eventually left the party because he disagreed with the plan to merge Lagos with the west.[7] The vice-chairman of the NYM was Chief Bode Thomas, a Yoruba lawyer from Oyo who became deputy leader of the Action Group before his early death at the age of thirty-four. Two prominent Lagosians, Dr. Akinola Maja and Jibril Martins were also leading NYM activists. In 1938 the NYM won the Legislative Council elections and the LTC elections, dealing the NNDP its first electoral defeat.

The Democratic Party attempted to check its opposition in 1944 by allying with the newly emergent National Council of Nigeria and the Cameroons, an organization formed that year by Nnamdi Azikiwe. But in terms of ideology and membership, the NCNC was quite unlike its ally; committed to an egalitarian philosophy, it was socially heterogeneous and solicited mass support through indirect membership.[8] Despite the prestige accorded Macaulay as the Father of Nigerian Nationalism and as president of the NCNC, it was clear that the enthusiasm generated among the bulk of the Lagos electorate was for Azikiwe, who found his supporters among the new immigrants of Lagos, particularly easterners who between 1911 and 1950 increased their numbers fivefold.[9]

From 1938 to 1950, contesting elections independently, the NNDP captured only one LTC seat, from Ward C. In the Legislative Council it was a different story: the NNDP-NCNC alliance won all the seats after 1945 with the exception of one independent. By the time of the 1950 LTC election, the popularity of the coalition was so great that the newly enfranchised electorate returned eighteen of the alliance's twenty-four candidates. In the Western Region election of 1951, in which Lagos was to elect five candidates to the House of Assembly, the NNDP-NCNC candidates swept the polls. After Macaulay's death in 1946, however, the NNDP began to recede into the background, outpaced by its more vigorous and progressive partner. As a radical, predominately Christian, and nationalistic organization, the NCNC had little to offer to the particularistic Lagos Muslims who had followed Macaulay's lead out of sheer personal devotion. Macaulay's charismatic appeal, his tactical willingness to champion the individual causes of local factions, and the political conservatism of his party enabled him to achieve a fusion of traditional and modern interests in Lagos which the NCNC could not possibly duplicate. Azikiwe[10] had no special appeal for the indigenes, and he and his party were ideologically opposed to the Victorian constitutionalism of the old-guard elite represented by Macaulay. Thus, in the new politics of the nationalist era, the indigenes were suddenly faced with the reality that without Macaulay, they had no political home.

The vacuum was filled by a grass-roots neotraditionalist party called the Area Councils, formed in 1950 by the oba of Lagos, Adeniji Adele II, to contest the first election for a fully representative council.[11] The most striking feature of the Area Councils was its communal appeal to the indigenes, who were becoming increasingly restive and fearful over the alleged domination of their town by strangers. The precise origin of the Area Councils is somewhat obscure, but apparently the organization was first conceived of as the basis for a system of local government rather than as a political party per se. In a speech celebrating the first anniversary of the beginning of his reign, Adele recalled that

> in 1948, a Memorandum was submitted to the Government that the revision of the LTC constitution should follow the lines of the Area Councils.... Again, on the 21st of February, 1949, another Memorandum signed by all the Lagos chiefs ... was submitted praying for the creation of the Area Councils and a central council for Lagos.... As apparently our requests were being brushed aside, copies ... were forwarded to all the Members of the Legis-

lative Council, the three Chief Commissioners and the Commissioners of the Colony on the 17th March, 1949. . . . [The] three
Lagos members did nothing and in consequence of this, the Chiefs
refused to meet them on their return to Lagos after the session.
On . . . 22nd March, 1949, the *West African Pilot* [declared its
support for the Area Councils]. . . . All this happened while Oba
Falolu was on the throne. Thus the foundation of the Area Councils was laid while I was still a Government servant, serving in
Kano some 700 miles away.[12]

Adele's detailed explanation of the origin of the Area Councils
was a defense against the NCNC's allegation that the councils
were client associations loyal to Adele and that they were acting
as agents of the Crown. Replying to these charges, Dr. J. Akanni
Doherty, a leading member of the NYM, confirmed that the Area
Councils had been formed when the government asked the people
to prepare a new constitution for local government. The Democratic Party and the NYM, he explained, submitted a proposal that
the oba be made mayor of Lagos. At that time Oba Falolu and his
chiefs also asked that the Area Councils be formed, and Doherty
stated (contradicting Adele) that this request was supported by
the three Legislative Council members.[13]

Many prominent nationalists, including Jibril Martins, Chief
Bode Thomas, and F. Rotimi Williams, were nominated on the
Area Councils ticket for the 1950 LTC election, along with notables in the traditional Lagos community. In hopes of capturing
the mayoralty, Oba Adele headed the list of candidates. Although
backed by the NYM, the Area Councils were, at least at the outset,
fiercely independent. They spurned appeals for unity from the
National Emergency Committee (NEC), a federation of nationalist associations which wanted to participate in the selection of
nominees. One spokesman for the Area Councils asserted that the
selection of candidates would remain the exclusive perogative of
the party's members, "who would not defer to any central
organization." Moreover, he declared that they would see to it
that nobody with a "strange" tongue ever got a chance to subvert
the organization. "If it means anything," the *Daily Times* editorial-
ized, "the reply . . . bears nothing other than the symptom of a
new awakening on the part of Lagos. . . . But while welcoming

it, we must warn the city fathers against the tribal instincts gradually making themselves manifest at the moment."[14]

Azikiwe likewise refused to cooperate with the NEC for the Lagos election, confident that the NCNC was then in a stronger position than any other party. Yet both he and Prince Adeyinka Oyekan, a patron of the NCNC and a contender for the throne of Lagos, were forced to withdraw from the election. Zik was disqualified because of a technicality;[15] Oyekan was withdrawn by the party because the election was shaping up as a popularity contest between himself and Oba Adele, a situation that gave the incumbent a decided advantage. Under a triple alliance composed of the Democratic Party, the Nigerian Labour Congress, and the Lagos Market Women's Guild, the NCNC-NNDP fielded some of its best-known members. When all six seats in the traditional quarter were won by the Area Councils and the remaining ones went to the NCNC, the foundation stones of the urban two-party system were firmly laid in place.

The 1950 election was a turning point in the party system of Lagos not only because it indicated the future direction of party growth, but also because it stimulated unprecedented political participation, with more than 26,000 urban residents going to the polls. A number of new local parties which nominated candidates in selected wards also emerged: the F Ward Ratepayers' Association, the Nigerian Women's Party, and the A Ward Voters' Association.[16] Although none of these associations constituted a real electoral threat to the major parties, they indicated the depth of political consciousness that existed among the formerly disenfranchised population. The Nigerian Labour Congress and the Lagos Market Women's Guild, which joined the NCNC-NNDP alliance, were not in themselves political parties, but corporate members of the NCNC which allowed the leaders of the parent body to control the nomination and electioneering procedures of the triple alliance.

The 1950 election was also significant in that it exposed the fragility of nationalist unity. The NCNC's success in the election made local collaboration with any other organization superfluous. Although the NYM was reluctant to plunge directly into the contest, it too openly endorsed one of the local parties, the Area

Councils, to which it "lent" some of its members for needed "guidance."[17] All the while, however, the NYM properly kept its distance, at least nominally, so as not to alienate the sensitivities of the indegenes who were intensely jealous of their autonomy.

Finally, the extreme polarization of the electorate was incontrovertibly confirmed by the returns in the 1950 election. Oba Adele received the highest number of votes of any single candidate (2,572) but, more importantly, his Area Councils carried only the wards dominated by Lagosians. Despite the Yoruba majority in all other wards, there was not a single deviation from the pattern of NCNC success in immigrant-dominated constituencies. It is also noteworthy that in all but one of the six multimember wards carried by the NCNC, at least one Ibo candidate was on the winning ticket. (Six of the eighteen NCNC councilors elected in 1950 were Ibos.) Although ethnic conflict was apparent at this stage, it was ostensibly of secondary importance to the immigrant voter as compared with the strength of nationalist appeals.

Over the next three years the party system in Lagos was affected by two important developments: a split in the ranks of the NNDP-NCNC alliance and the formal inauguration of the Action Group. In September 1951 Azikiwe submitted a report to the NCNC convention held in Kano, Northern Nigeria, in which among other things he objected strenuously to the impending incorporation of Lagos with the Western Region under the Macpherson Constitution.[18] As part of the west, he argued, Lagos would have to be represented in the House of Representatives through the Western House of Assembly. A regional legislature dominated by one party could block the passage of a popular Lagos candidate to the central legislature, as well as control all legislation for the city, then Azikiwe's base of operations. His prophetic warnings were vindicated months later when he was prevented from entering the federal House of Representatives, an event that precipitated a schism in his party.

In the Western Region election of 1951, five NCNC representatives from Lagos were popularly elected to the Western House of Assembly: Nnamdi Azikiwe, Adeleke Adedoyin, Dr. I. Olorun-Nimbe, H. P. Adebola, and T. O. S. Benson. Two of these candidates were to be indirectly elected by the regional legislature to the federal House of Representatives; the NCNC expected that Nnamdi Azikiwe would be among those chosen. The Action Group, however, bypassed Azikiwe and chose Olorun-Nimbe and Adeleke Adedoyin, who polled first and third, respectively, in the popular election.[19] Olorun-Nimbe, who had by then been made mayor of Lagos, was asked by the party to resign in favor of Adedoyin, also a Lagos town councilor. According to the NCNC's plan, Adedoyin would then decline the nomination for the central legislature in favor of Azikiwe. Olorun-Nimbe shocked the party not only by refusing to comply with the request, but by publicly condemning the venture, alleging that "there is organized corruption among the Lagos Town Councilors."[20]

Alternatively, the National Executive of the NCNC offered Adedoyin the post of town clerk of Lagos, a highly remunerative and prestigious position, in exchange for his withdrawal from the competition for the federal House of Representatives. Adedoyin accepted, and in an emergency meeting presided over by the deputy mayor and attended only by NCNC members, the Lagos Town Council approved his appointment. Outraged at being overridden, Olorun-Nimbe asserted before the council that this action "confirmed his allegation of organized conspiracy and corruption . . . [and that] the procedure adopted in the appointment was crude, irregular, suspicious, corrupt and a stupendous joke."[21] But Adedoyin's appointment had to be ratified by the Western Region governor-in-council before it could be finalized. The acting town clerk, D. M. O. Akinbiyi, who was sympathetic to the Action Group, provided evidence of improper recruitment procedures, allowing the west to block the plan to get Zik to the center.

The Adedoyin affair had deep repercussions on the Lagos NCNC. In retaliation for Olorun-Nimbe's defiance, the NCNC members of the council rescinded their decision to pay the mayor a stipend of £2,500 for the duration of his term of office.[22] E. A. Oluyele Bright was elected mayor in October 1952, and Olorun-Nimbe was expelled from the party.[23] As standard-bearer for the NNDP faction, Olorun-Nimbe was the NCNC's chief link with the indigenous community. When the breach between him and the party first occurred, the Executive Committee of the NNDP passed a vote of no confidence in the councilors for their "disrespectful behaviour to the Mayor."[24] Then followed a resolution from the Isale Eko Area Youths to the Western Region government, dated March 10, 1952, requesting the governor to set up a committee of inquiry into the affairs of the LTC. By expelling Olorun-Nimbe, the NCNC was clearly shedding its base of support among those Lagosians who had remained faithful to the memory of Macaulay.

The Adedoyin affair also led to centralization of the local NCNC organization. National leaders began to direct party affairs in order to minimize the risk of local factionalism and indiscipline. The in-fighting connected with the Adedoyin episode also discredited the party's image during the crucial years when Nigeria's first experiment in local self-government was being closely watched, and it provided Zik's opponent, Obafemi Awolowo,[25] then minister for local government in the Western Region, with the ammunition needed to dissolve the council and institute local government reforms that were unfavorable to the NCNC.[26] In vain did the NCNC protest, threatening that the new legislative proposals "would seriously interfere with the peaceful conditions prevailing in [the] Municipality."[27]

It is possible that the difficulties in the NNDP-NCNC camp and the new local government reforms convinced Action Group leaders that the time was propitious for them to play a more direct role in the internal affairs of the city. In 1950 when the party was launched nationally, by Awolowo, it was by no means certain that a branch would be opened in Lagos. Awolowo had a traditional abhorrence of Lagos politics, dating back to the time when Macaulay rebuffed him early in his career because he had solicited the support of one of Macaulay's rivals (see chap. 4). Now Azikiwe's hold on Lagos deepened Awolowo's hostility toward his NCNC opponent[28] and toward the "intrigue, petty bickering, and confusion"[29] he felt was characteristic of the seacoast town. Moreover, Awolowo recognized that he had to cultivate a regional power base in order to make headway in national politics. His headquarters was therefore located in Ibadan, in the Yoruba heartland, not in Lagos, which had been the choice of all previous parties.[30]

After the successful disruption of the NCNC in Lagos, however, and in an attempt to forge a united Yoruba front, the Lagos branch of the Action Group was formed on May 5, 1951. The party was an amalgamation of two preexisting and fundamentally dissimilar organizations—the NYM and the Area Councils. Under the banner of the Area Councils–Action Group alliance, the party linked the particularistic orientations of the indigenes with the Pan-Yoruba nationalist ambitions of the Yoruba middle class and intellectuals.[31] In local politics, this was an unbeatable formula for electoral success.

From a minority party, the Action Group rapidly rose to command a significant following in the 1950s and to be the majority party in the 1960s. The strength of the party rested on a superior organizational structure reaching down to the precinct levels of the community, on a natural identification with the Yoruba majority, and, for the first few years of its existence when it was establishing itself, on the support of the oba of Lagos who, in conjunction with other Muslim and local leaders, delivered the indigenous and Islamic votes. Within the Yoruba community the party bridged the gap between indigenes and immigrants, between Muslims and Christians, and between the masses and the elite. It made no attempt whatsoever to appeal to minority groups, recognizing that such recruitment might alienate some of the Yoruba elements whose support was more valuable. The participation of progressive Ahmadiya Muslims, including Adele, was particularly helpful in healing divisions based on origin, religion, and class. Within a few years the NCNC was reduced to a position in which it could count only on the support of minority elements in selected constituencies.

The NCNC's strategy was directed toward exploiting the weaknesses of its rival rather than toward building a foundation of support for itself. So thorough was the Action Group's offensive that by 1957 the NCNC realized that it could win a local election and still not control the council, for traditional members of the council who were sympathetic to the Action Group could tip the voting balance in the latter's favor. The distribution of seats was also at this time imbalanced in favor of the Action Group; Wards D and E, with large immigrant populations from the east, were underrepresented, whereas Ward A was overrepresented (see section on urban electoral patterns, below).

The NCNC also concentrated on eliminating fraudulent practices, as opposed to the AG which was bent on increasing the number of its votes. Before the 1957 election, for example, the NCNC made a house-to-house check to verify the identity of people on the voters' list in order to prevent impersonation.[32] A total of £4,700 to finance this effort was to be raised from branch members and regional and federal party organs.[33] At the same time the AG was exerting its efforts more effectively toward increasing the voter turnout and augmenting its popularity in key sections of the community, particularly among market women, small businessmen, youths, and wage earners.

The NCNC likewise mobilized the ethnic minorities ignored by the AG, but this activity merely nourished factionalism within the party. Although dominated by Yorubas, the Lagos NCNC included a number of Ibos, such as F. M. Moronu, S. O. Maduike, G. Oparah, and Fred Anyiam, as well as members of other minorities, such as E. A. Manuel (Kalabari), J. U. Isuman (Bini), N. A. Cole (Urhobo), and Malam Ibrahim Dan Sekondi, representing the affiliated Northern Elements Progressive Union. By contrast all AG candidates, without exception, were Yoruba. Fears of Yoruba domination within the NCNC were common among minority elements, particularly the Ibos. They regarded the NCNC's support of a Lagos state, for example, as an attempt by the NCNC Yorubas to maintain a Yoruba government in the city.[34] NCNC women complained they were not getting as much patronage as other groups. In 1964 Adeniran Ogunsanya, president of the Lagos NCNC, warned the Ibo State Union and top officials of the national NCNC that there existed within the branch organization a serious "cleavage between Ibo NCNC'ers on the one hand and Yoruba NCNC'ers on the other."[35] So sensitive was the NCNC to its external image in a Yoruba city, however, that it decided at one point that a Yoruba name must be found for the Lagos NCNC branch "to counteract AG propaganda that it was an Ibo organization."[36]

Thus, while the Action Group was launching a clearly defined bridge-building strategy aimed at solidifying the Yorubas, the NCNC was picking up the fringe groups of the electorate, a disparate collection of people whose only common goal was to displace the Action Group. Together with the weak organizational structure of the NCNC, this policy served to increase party fragmentation between youths and elders, Ibos and Yorubas, indigenes and immigrants, and professionals and wage earners. The NCNC's approach could have been more successful had its heterogeneous appeal been more effectively backed up by vigorous organization, particularly after 1959 when it briefly regained control of the council. Just before the election, Oba Adele withdrew support from the AG because he disagreed with it as to the number of traditional chiefs to be appointed to the council. Consistent with its policy of "divide and rule," the NCNC opportunistically backed up Adele's demands (see chap. 4). His subsequent defection and the high voter turnout in the preindependence election brought the NCNC its first electoral victory after the inception of the AG in Lagos. To assure Adele's continued support, the NCNC, in cooperation with the federal government, rewarded him handsomely. During the next three years his stipend was raised to £1,800, his title was officially upgraded from head of the House of Ado to oba of Lagos, his Iga, described as the "Buckingham Palace" of Lagos, was exempted from payment of rates, and the LTC added £20,000 to the £50,000 allocated by the federal government for renovation of his palace.

Confident that it had, at last, crumbled the base of Action Group support in Lagos, the NCNC fully expected to win the 1962 election with a minimum of effort. Moreover, by that time the AG was deep in the throes of a national crisis involving a treason charge against Awolowo and an inquiry into the party's financial assets. Divided, broke, and humiliated, the Action Group seemed destined for defeat. Instead, the electorate swept the party to its biggest victory yet, a result of Yoruba sympathy for the Action Group, of the efficient organization and dedication of local party members, and, most important, of the rise of Lagos Muslims within the party's inner ranks. In spite of Adele's defection, the Action Group retained the support of the bulk of the indigenous community and was, indeed, becoming a vehicle for their growing ambitions. Whether by design or by circumstance, the reorientation of the AG toward the indigenous community proved to be one of its greatest strengths. It brought the party into line with the interests of the common man and provided it with a ready cadre of workers whose motivations for electoral success depended upon more than immediate material gain. The party accomplished this turnabout without sacrificing its basic appeal as a Yoruba party and without endangering its well-established organizational structure. Just at the time when the NCNC had relaxed its efforts owing to a false sense of confidence, the AG had regrouped for a stunning come-back. Similarly, in the 1965 election the AG captured all but seven seats on the council. The NCNC had been reduced to an ineffec-tive organ for the political outs of Lagos, having come full circle in fifteen years, from being the majority party enthusiastically re-turned to power with three-fourths of the seats to becoming a minority party that could barely salvage one-sixth of the seats.

The poor showing of the NCNC is even more striking in light of the fact that the two major local parties had just formed an im-portant alliance at the national level. Because of its own difficulties with its senior partner in the national government, for the 1964–65 federal election the NCNC joined the AG in the United Pro-gressive Grand Alliance (UPGA). The new coalition was pitted against the Nigerian National Alliance (NNA), consisting of the Northern Peoples' Congress and a splinter group of the AG, the new NNDP. The UPGA was conceived, however, by high-ranking party leaders for national purposes. The unworkability of the alli-ance locally was vividly demonstrated when the respective branch organizations failed to agree on a common slate; Lagos was the only area in the country in which the UPGA broke down and the two partners fielded separate candidates. Even after the AG won overwhelmingly, the basic tension between the two parties contin-ued to be reflected in the selection of the new council chairman. Initially, Alhaji A. F. Masha was certain of reelection; but he had held, in conformity with national party directives, that the 1965 election was a friendly contest and he had promised that the AG would work in the spirit of the UPGA. In a surprising upset, Alhaji G. O. Dawodu, a Lagos Muslim who, as organizing secretary of the Lagos AG, was probably the individual most responsible for its spectacular success, was elected council chairman instead. Dawodu was among those members of the Action Group who re-sisted the demands of the NCNC to share the slate of UPGA seats equally and who urged the AG to "go it alone."

*Political Variables*

Dawodu's election as council chairman, and the overwhelming victory of the AG in 1965, were both symbolic of the dominant trends that had come to characterize politics in Lagos. First, against the greatest odds, the AG had grown from a minority party which originally was reluctant to function in Lagos to a majority party which had gained genuine grass-roots popularity through mass membership and effective organization reaching down to the lower ward and precinct levels of the community. Secondly, and perhaps even more significantly, the AG had undergone deep internal changes which transformed its character. By penetrating the inner ranks of the city's most popular political organization, Lagos Muslims had achieved central control of the authoritative institutions of local government, becoming the single most influential communal group in local politics.

*Minor Parties*

Since 1950 several minor parties have been significant on the local scene. The United Muslim Party (UMP) was founded in 1953 as an outgrowth of the Society for Promoting Muslim Knowledge (an educational association created in 1947) and the Muslim Welfare Association (a cultural group formed in 1950). The patron of the UMP was Adam Idris Animashaun, Seriki Musilimi of Lagos and general secretary of the Jam'at Congregation; the founder and president was Muhammad Raji Bakrin Ottun, an Ahmadi Muslim and a journalist associated with the *West African Pilot*. In 1959 the UMP unsuccessfully contested one seat, from Lagos Central, for the federal legislature. For the most part it operated as a pressure group leading the anti-Adele and anti-AG forces of the traditional community. Its most significant activities were part of its lobbying for the interests of the indigenous Lagosians; it made the first formal demand for the creation of a Lagos state in 1956 and, in the following year, protested the raising of rates, the council's expenditure of funds, and the recruitment policies of the town clerk. In a 1958 petition submitted in conjunction with the NCNC Market Women's Association, the UMP called for an investigation into the council's administration of market women's affairs. As a result, a commission of inquiry was

128

appointed whose findings discredited the AG prior to its 1959 defeat in the local elections.[37]

The Nigerian Labour Party founded in 1956 with Michael Imoudu, "Nigeria's No. 1 Labour Leader," as president, never captured any seats or gained much popularity. The Socialist Workers' and Farmers' Party (SWAFP), a Marxist-Leninist party launched in 1964 and led by Dr. Tunji Otegbeye, a radical leftist, was equally unsuccessful. Imoudu, Otegbeye, and another trade-union leader, Wahab Goodluck, president of the Nigerian Trade Union Congress, all ran in the 1964–65 federal election and were badly defeated. The Lagos electorate was unfailingly indifferent to appeals for class solidarity, even in the local election of 1965 in which the SWAFP contested several seats.

Parties based in the Northern Region also attracted little support in Lagos. In light of the city's small Hausa population it is not surprising that the country's most powerful party, the Northern Peoples' Congress, remained aloof from Lagos politics. The NPC Lagos branch, led by Alhaji A. I. Laguda, president, and P. Young Brimah, general secretary, was closed down in 1965 on instructions from party headquarters in Kaduna, Northern Nigeria, ostensibly for financial reasons.[38] The Northern Elements Progressive Union opposed to the NPC, was affiliated with the NCNC in Lagos.

The recently inaugurated Nigerian National Democratic Party was of somewhat more importance than other minor parties. Launched in Lagos in 1963, the NNDP attracted the disaffected members of the Action Group, principally those who were followers of S. L. Akintola, Awolowo's former deputy with whom he clashed in 1962, as well as some former members of the NCNC. It was a potentially bigger threat to the established parties in Lagos because it had the blessing of the Northern Peoples' Congress, which controlled the federal government, because it was a predominantly Yoruba party, and because it was led in Lagos by well-known national leaders: Chief S. T. Hunponu-Wusu, a senator and zonal leader; Chief H. O. Davies, branch chairman and leader; Chief O. A. Fagbenro-Beyioku, member of the Branch Executive; and T. O. S. Benson, NNDP member of the federal legislature from Lagos. The NNDP also included notables, such as Dr. J. Akanni Doherty, former president of the Lagos AG; Oged

Macaulay, son of Herbert Macaulay; A. J. Ojikutu, the Balogun (field marshal) of Lagos Muslims; and Mrs. Modupe Caxton-Martins, the alaga of Tejuoso Market. The 1964 LCC election was the first local election contested by the NNDP. Although nominating candidates for all forty-two seats, five days before polling day it dramatically announced its withdrawal in favor of an alternative undisclosed master plan to capture Lagos and the Lagos City Council.[39] Essentially, the master plan consisted of a pervasive infiltration of local government institutions through nonelectoral means with the aid of the NPC-controlled federal government. As first articulated privately by a high party official (whose grand strategy is here quoted in full), it portrays the kind of party influence that could be exerted behind the scenes:

> Since it is clear that the NNDP is not in control of the Lagos City Council, efforts should be made to see that the NNDP has an effective say and an opportunity to help its members and all the functionaries of the LCC through the influence of the NPC which appears to be a friend of the party thus:—
>
> LMTS [Lagos Municipal Transport Service]:
> It was published in the Daily Times sometime ago that the present LMTS Board headed by Mr. F. S. McEwen had been dissolved by the Ministry of Lagos Affairs and that the new Bill which established the Board as a statutory corporation empowers the Minister to appoint a Chairman and 6 members of the Board, while the LCC will appoint 5 members. Furthermore, the LCC has decided to recommend Councillor Odeku as Chairman and the names of 5 LCC nominees had been decided. I will suggest that the NNDP should use immediately all its influence to see that the Minister rejects the LCC nomination and appoints an NNDP man as Chairman, and that of the 6 members to be nominated by the Minister, the NNDP should have 4, for as a result of this the NNDP will be in control of the Board and therefore use it to its own advantage.
>
> *LEDB* [Lagos Executive Development Board]:
> Top officials of the Board should be bought over by the NNDP so that they can cooperate with the party in its aim to check the desire of the Ibos to own as much landed property in Lagos as

possible. The NNDP should also use its influence with the Minister to make the Minister accept its nominee to replace any member who has completed his own term of office.

*LCC—Education Committee:*

This is another Committee of the LCC which is important to the public because it is responsible for all Primary Schools in Lagos. At present Hon. Ogunsanya is the Chairman of the Committee and uses his influence to favor NCNC men when contracts in the Committee are being awarded; this, I understand is another Statutory Board under the Minister for Lagos Affairs and . . . the present members of the Board have almost completed their tenure of office. I also suggest that the Minister for Lagos Affairs should also be approached in respect of this matter.

*National Motors, Gaiser and Other Western Region Government Agencies in Lagos:*

While we examine the possible ways of wading our influence into some Boards of the LCC through the influence of the Minister for Lagos Affairs, we must not overlook the other agencies of Western Region Government based in Lagos and Ikeja. I suggest that the Lagos Branch of the NNDP should recommend to the Leaders in the West that it is only members that stay in Lagos that should be considered for Board appointments in all Government agencies situated in Lagos and Ikeja. This arrangement will enable us to help out party supporters in Lagos and will also make them feel they are part and parcel of the Western Region. Whilst I believe that the Party in Power must have influence in all these agencies, I strongly suggest that the agencies be run in a way that will bring credit to the Government of the day, e.g., less party interference in the day to day running of such agencies and much emphasis . . . placed on making more profit by the agencies.

*NPC/NNDP:*

In order to make the points I raised earlier realizable then we must reach certain understandings with the NPC. For instance, some of the NPC members (Yoruba) in Lagos still believe that they should remain as they are. One of them even told me that Alhaji Ribadu [then minister of defense and a high-ranking member of the NPC] advised them to remain as they are and

131

they will be given their own share of Board appointments when occasions arise. This method, if true, will amount to unnecessary dissipation of energy in various directions. We should make the leaders of the NPC ask their followers in Lagos to team up with us as it was in the West, and that when Board appointments are available each member will be rewarded according to his service in the Party. It is also necessary at this stage for an understanding with the NPC to be struck, for this will enable our members who are contractors and are registered in Lagos to win contracts and thereby be of use to the Party in Lagos.

## Unemployment and the NNDP:

[The] majority of our people today are looking for jobs. The question of fetching jobs for party supporters had been the greatest headache felt by parties in Lagos and the West. I will suggest that in order to reduce the burden of the situation on our party direct instructions should be given to party members who serve in Boards and Corporations to see to it that party boys are given jobs. Instructions should also be given to Party contractors when they win any contract to employ Party Boys as this method will keep them on some temporary jobs till they are able to get permanent ones.

## Forthcoming Federal and LTC Elections:

As we are all aware, the next Federal Election can take place any time this year. This election will give the NNDP the opportunity to assess its strength of followship [*sic*] and as such I am suggesting that the setting up of an election committee be recommended forthwith. This Committee will make programmes and examine all means of winning seats for the NNDP in Lagos during the forthcoming Federal Elections. As this is a big task, I humbly suggest that this Planning Committee be constituted into an Election Committee to plan ways whereby the NNDP may win any seat in the forthcoming Federal Election as enumerated above.

At the same time, we must also remember that it is important that we plan well our programmes for the Federal Elections because whatever might be our achievements at that election will affect the MORALE of our supporters during the LTC election which follows in a year's time.

The NNDP's strategy for capturing control of Lagos amply illustrates how institutional loopholes and backdoor maneuvering could permit political parties to wield influence within the city without a mandate from the people. But it also illustrates, more fundamentally, the extent to which the urban political system had, for all practical purposes, become closed to minor parties, driving them into impossible positions in which their only hope of gaining influence was through nonelectoral means. This situation was not due to any collusion or monolithic control by a power elite drawn from the major parties. To the contrary, some leaders of the NCNC feared that the NNDP and the AG, as Yoruba parties, were conspiring collectively to drive the NCNC from Lagos. This electoral insecurity was indicative of the degree to which the city had evolved into a stable one-party-dominant system. By the 1960s minor parties had little, if any, chance to survive at the polls. They were regarded by major AG leaders as unfortunate distractions which neither threatened to displace the AG's well-established position nor split its electorate in borderline districts. Invariably, minor parties either never got off the ground or, once launched, followed one of three courses: they were absorbed into the major parties; they withered with time into oblivion; or, if surviving at all, they became narrow interest associations expressing the demands of particularistic factions, but offering no real alternative leadership.

### INTERNAL STRUCTURE OF MAJOR PARTIES

The internal structure of the major political parties has been shaped by three principal factors: (1) the goals and political styles of the dominant party leaders; (2) the resources at a party's command (solidarity, leadership, mass support, finances); and (3) the degree to which a party has been able to maintain functional relevance for the dominant groups in the community. Such factors as ideology or doctrine, national party directives, or the type of electoral system have been of comparatively little importance to internal party machinery. In illustration, four parties are discussed here: the old NNDP, the NCNC, the Area Councils, and the AG.

## Nigerian National Democratic Party

As observed earlier, the first party to emerge on the Lagos scene was a protoparty with a minimum degree of organization and a maximum degree of centralization. Superficially, Macaulay's Nigerian National Democratic Party had the trappings of a modern party organization: a constitution, a loyal band of party officials, and a rudimentary concept of party membership. But these were misleading indications of the party's actual structure. The constitution was not a guide to its internal organization, but an ambitious statement of unfulfilled goals;[40] the officials did not constitute an established administrative staff, but a core group of personal followers of Macaulay with no fixed terms of office and no defined spheres of responsibility; the members of the party were not card-carrying, dues-paying subscribers, but unidentified individuals who attended mass rallies. Structurally, the NNDP fitted the type of organizational model that was based on charismatic authority—one that was foreign to everyday routine. It consisted of a restricted circle of notables grouped around the party's central personality, a man who exercised autocratic and personal leadership throughout his lifetime. For this reason the NNDP never developed a stable, rationalized, or hierarchical structure.[41]

The small group of notables who constituted Macaulay's disciples were drawn from the traditional and elite communities on the basis of personal loyalty and the extent of their political following. None of the traditional leaders, such as Eshugbayi Eleko, Chief Oluwa, or Madam Pelewura, had any official status in the party; they constituted a second-echelon level of auxiliary supporters through whom Macaulay reached the masses in a meaningful, if indirect, way. The NNDP was immensely popular, especially during the 1920s and early 1930s when it had no opposition. This kind of elite party was related to its public essentially as a patron is related to his client: "Elite parties . . . consist essentially of a nucleus of persons enjoying status and authority within the existing social order—an elite of chiefs, religious leaders, or wealthy bourgeois—and depend largely upon established ties of obligation and loyalty between the 'elite' and the 'people.' "[42]

The NNDP, lacking subsidiary units either outside Lagos or at lower levels of the community, had no formal channels of communication with the public. It was financed by irregular donations from market women, community leaders, and members of the aristocratic elite. Discipline was closely controlled by Macaulay, who regarded deviants as personal rivals; nominations were made by Macaulay in the privacy of his home. The NNDP was thus an association of the faithful structured on one essential principle—the absolute authority of Macaulay. It survived as long as Lagos existed as a highly stratified, relatively unchanging community dominated by Anglo-African elites. The party reflected the interests of the local notables, was essentially committed to the maintenance of the status quo, and was held together by the charismatic qualities of its leader. There was no successor to Macaulay and no stable administrative staff to sustain his legacy. The NNDP, like Macaulay, was a product of a particular age, destined to wither away with changing times.

### National Convention of Nigerian Citizens

By way of contrast, one of the most outstanding features of the National Convention of Nigerian Citizens was that its nationalist origins continued to be reflected in its structure throughout the period of its existence in Lagos. From the time of its inception in 1944 it was based on a congress-type structure: it had broad nationalist goals and a loose organization; it emphasized the idea of representing all the people; and it attempted to unite with preexisting organizations.[43] The NCNC was established as an agglomerate of functional associations grouped around a core of decision-making leaders headed by Nnamdi Azikiwe. Because of the broad scope of its membership, it was plagued with internal fission and indiscipline even after direct membership was introduced in 1952.[44]

Administratively, the Lagos NCNC had the status of a zone or region, theoretically headed by the Lagos Working Committee, a broad collegial body composed of all NCNC federal ministers, NCNC senators from Lagos, NCNC members representing Lagos in the federal House of Representatives, the leader of the NCNC in the council, twenty-one members elected by the Lagos parliamentary constituencies, and 168 representatives elected from each of the forty-two subwards. In practice, the party was run by the Central Executive Committee, consisting of the top officials of the branch organization (chairman, vice-chairman, secretary, treasurer, publicity secretary, financial secretary, legal adviser, auditor, and senior executive secretary), two representatives from each of the eight wards, and two representatives from the NCNC Youth Association, the Zikist National Vanguard, and the NCNC Women's Association.[45]

Decision making and control of the party were highly concentrated in the hands of national party leaders, as the composition of branch organs suggests. Seven of the nine officers of the Branch Executive were members of the NCNC National Executive Committee, and the chief local leaders in Lagos were Adeniran Ogunsanya and F. S. McEwen. Ogunsanya was chairman or zonal leader of the Lagos NCNC, president of the NCNC Youth Association, chairman of the Federal Loans Board, Lagos councilor for eight years, and federal minister of housing and surveys. In 1967 he became the attorney general of Lagos State. In his capacity as zonal leader he had primary responsibility for, and supreme authority over, local party affairs, including nominations, the distribution of patronage, and the formation of party policy in the council. F. S. McEwen was national secretary of the NCNC, general manager of the *West African Pilot*, general manager of the African Continental Bank, and Lagos councilor for fourteen years, in three of which he was chairman. Other prominent national leaders included T. O. S. Benson (minister of information; national financial secretary of the NCNC), A. K. Blankson (editor of the *West African Pilot*; national auditor for the NCNC), Chief Kolawole Balogun (federal minister of research and information; NCNC national secretary), Chief O. A. Fagbenro-Beyioku, and Chief H. O. Davies.

Under the NCNC Branch Executive were three federal executive constituency committees with jurisdiction in parliamentary electoral districts; each committee had fifteen members and was active only at the time of federal elections. At the primary level there were party units in the eight major wards, each of which had a chairman and a secretary.[46] After 1963 delegates or agents of the NCNC were appointed for each of the forty-two subwards or precincts of Lagos, but they were not integrated formally into the party structure. There was, in fact, no formal party organization in these lower precinct or electoral districts. The regional headquarters of the NCNC was located at Campbell Street on Lagos Island, but the bulk of party business was conducted through the national secretariat, situated at Yaba Roundabout, the crossroads of suburban Lagos.

The Lagos NCNC had a number of affiliated groups, including the Northern Elements' Progressive Union,[47] the NNDP,[48] the Ibo Union, the NCNC Youth Association, the Zikist National Vanguard, the Lagos Market Women's Guild (inherited from Macaulay), the NCNC Women's Association (organized in 1958), the House of Docemo (also inherited from Macaulay), some labor unions (through the affiliation of H. P. Adebola and O. A. Fagbenro-Beyioku), and a host of small ethnic associations. Some of these affiliates challenged the formal structure and authority of the party. For example, the NNDP defied party leadership in 1951, the Youth Association and the Zikist National Vanguard were militant rivals of the branch organization led by party elders, and the Ibo Union was jealous of Yoruba predominance in the party.

After the defeat of the NCNC in the 1962 election, an investigation into the conduct of the election and the structure of the branch organization was conducted by the NCNC Reorganization Committee for Lagos, appointed by the Central Working Committee of the national headquarters, with Dr. K. O. Mbadiwe, minister of aviation, as chairman.[49] Mbadiwe emphasized that the reorganization of the Lagos branch was aimed at the rank-and-file membership in the wards and was meant to achieve a stable party no longer "run by a handful of men—but a party which derives its existence by the support of the masses."[50]

As a result, a new NCNC Lagos bylaw, passed in 1963, delineated a modified structure aimed at the precinct or subward level. Each of these forty-two electoral districts was to have an NCNC executive committee modeled on the Branch Executive, except for the absence of a legal adviser. Moreover, Mbadiwe set forth new proposals for the nomination of candidates, a particularly sensitive point of contention among the lower ranks of the party, who resented the concentration of authority in the hands of top officials.[51] The normal practice was to have nominations forwarded from the wards to the Branch Executive where the party slate was fixed, but many nominations originated from the Central Working Committee, with the result that locally unpopular candidates were often chosen. It was proposed that this function now be granted exclusively to the ward organizations.[52]

Unfortunately the plan to reorganize the party never took hold, owing to the absorption of party leaders in national and regional concerns and the understandable lack of enthusiasm for the changes on the part of the Branch Executive. Consequently, as the fortunes of the Lagos NCNC declined, intraparty disputes increased. Several different ad hoc committees burgeoned, all competing for dominance in the party. The Lagos branch of the Youth Organization, for instance, began a campaign to take over the organization of elections from the Branch Executive. It decided to cooperate with the national organization only when a deadline was given for reorganization.

A more serious local dispute between Fagbenro-Beyioku and Mbadiwe reached national party headquarters. Fagbenro-Beyioku, styling himself "Leader of the NCNC in Lagos," began campaigning on the slogan, "Lagos for the Lagosians." Mbadiwe complained to Michael Okpara, premier of the Eastern Region and national president of the NCNC, about Fagbenro-Beyioku's stream of letters to the premier regarding Lagos affairs. Fagbenro-Beyioku, when accused of playing a "subversive role"[53] in the party and of being "tribalistic," replied that he was merely stressing the needs of the indigenes and argued that the Action Group, "with entirely the natives and Yoruba votes, . . . can always win elections in Lagos." More pointedly, he wrote: "The greatest propaganda the AG had used against our party in Lagos is that it is an Ibo party and that was the sentiment they whipped up in the last LTC elections. With you now aspiring to become the Chairman of the Lagos Working Committee, what do you want to make of the Party in Lagos?"[54] This exchange between Fagbenro-Beyioku, a Yoruba trade unionist from Ikorodu, and Mbadiwe, an Ibo businessman from Orlu, was characteristic of the ethnic, occupational, and authority conflicts endemic to the party throughout most of its existence in Lagos.

The financial resources of the Lagos NCNC were derived from a number of sources: membership subscriptions (6 pence per month), levies on elected officials, donations, entertainment, voluntary contributions, sales of membership cards, buttons, and flags, and so forth. The African Continental Bank was the prescribed bank of the party. In the 1965 local election, the party spent £6,600 for campaign expenses, of which £5,000 was withdrawn from the bank, £1,350 was collected from councilors, and £250 was donated.[55] Other funds were occasionally received from the beneficiaries of patronage, part of whose profits flowed back into party coffers. For example, the Commercial and Industrial Transport Services, a newly formed company given a large conservancy contract by the council when the NCNC was in control, deposited £200 a month into the party's treasury out of its estimated £2,500 monthly profit.[56]

Probably the weakest feature of the NCNC was its inability to broaden the image, formed at the time of its origin, of a Christian, professional, and predominately Ibo party. While flexible in its administrative procedures, the Lagos NCNC was inflexible in its membership and decision-making procedures. It is true that the party was progressively dominated by Yorubas, particularly after Azikiwe had become premier of the Eastern Region and with major Ibo leaders such as Nduka Eze, Mbonu Ojike, Fred Anyiam, and others concentrating on regional and federal politics. But the party was still predominantly Christian[57] and, at its top reaches, was still being run by professional or upper-level occupational types. Of the forty-three Lagos Muslims who served on the Council, only four were members of the NCNC. Obviously, there had been little identification of the NCNC as an indigenous or local party, even though it supported the drive for a Lagos state. Furthermore, no attempt was made until 1963 to democratize the organization by giving more authority to the lower units and widening the nomination process. Even then the effort to reform the party was an externally induced disciplinary move from the top. Although it was aimed at overcoming basic defects, the reform movement had relatively little impact. The NCNC therefore remained what it was at the start—an agglomerate of associated groups ruled by a central clique of prominent political figures.

## Area Councils

To understand the organization of the Area Councils it is necessary to understand the traditional authority structure on which it was based. The traditional political system that prevailed in Isale Eko centered on the paramount chief or oba, a constitutional monarch selected by the kingmakers from one of the royal families of Lagos. The oba shared executive authority for local affairs with four classes of graded chiefs ranked by function: the Akarigbere chiefs (kingmakers), the Idejo chiefs (landowners), the Ogalede chiefs (priests), and the Abagbon chiefs (warriors). Seniority within each class was determined by the order in which the *iwuye* or installation ceremony was performed, the final act in the appointment process in which, traditionally, a cap, a staff, and a chair were given to the chief to affirm his title. These senior chiefs constituted the oba's council of state. An inner circle of the most trusted chiefs was known as the Ilu Committee. This committee, together with a cross section of elders, family heads, and leaders of important interest groups, such as Muslims and market women, formed the Egbe Ilu, which was, in effect, a town council of community representatives. Members of the Egbe Ilu had collaborated with Macaulay, but they were not officially integrated into the NNDP.

Inspired by the oba of Lagos, Adeniji Adele II, the Area Councils were modeled on this traditional system. At least one area council was set up in each of the city's electoral wards, with individual branches in subwards that were coterminous with traditional neighborhoods, especially those on Lagos Island. For example, the Okepopo Area Council, the Olowogbowo Area Council, and the Alakoro Area Council each comprised community leaders who, in the older districts, would probably be members of the Egbe Ilu. Each area council elected two delegates to serve on the Central Advisory Council, whose members chose from among themselves the officers of the party. Oba Adele was president. The secretary, N. A. Taiwo, was a Christian sawmiller whose home in Isale Eko became the party's working headquarters.

The Area Councils functioned as a modernized version of the

Egbe Ilu. Its separate chapters were self-governing units, but all were responsible to the Central Advisory Council which, like the Ilu Committee, was an inner circle of party chieftains. As in the traditional system, the oba was the supreme authority who acted after consultation with his advisers. Essentially, therefore, the Area Councils formed a particularistic party appealing primarily to the Lagosians. For tactical reasons, however, it included a number of non-Lagosian Yorubas recruited from the Nigerian Youth Movement, the most notable among them being F. Rotimi Williams, general secretary, and Chief Bode Thomas, vice-president. With the exception of R. C. Irving, an Englishman who was secretary of the Lagos Chamber of Commerce and who ran on the Area Councils ticket in a district with a large non-Nigerian population, no other non-Yorubas were members of the party. Oba Adele, an African chief who acted as an effective bridge linking the traditional community to modern politics, was the prime motive force behind the Area Councils.

In opposition to the Christian-dominated political organizations that had prevailed during the nationalist period, the Area Councils had the support of prominent Ahmadiya Muslims including Chief Imam Alhaji Y. P. Sodeinde, Alhaji Jibril Martins, and the oba himself. The Area Councils likewise appealed to elements in the traditional community who were opponents of the dominant House of Docemo. Adele, as the first duly selected oba after the cession of Lagos who was not a descendant of Docemo, revived traditional political loyalties of royal lineages that were rivals of the House of Docemo and transformed them into a modern electoral asset. But the Area Councils were too parochial and too poor to survive alone. The party contested only one election independently, in 1950, and captured only the traditional wards. It was then faced with the dilemma of remaining a permanent dwarf party or of joining forces with another, larger organization. It chose the latter solution and, with the NYM, was absorbed into the Action Group in 1951. In deference to Adele, the new association was named the Area Councils–Action Group Alliance. In actuality, however, the joining together was a merger, not a coalition, and the Area Councils became a party within a party, a nucleus within a larger body from which the indigenes continued to exercise influence in the community.

## Action Group

The Action Group, the best-organized political party in the city, experienced the greatest internal transformation. When first established in 1951, the Lagos Action Group was a party with a dual character. From the NYM it inherited a leadership structure of predominantly Christian elites, including professionals, businessmen, and intellectuals. From the Area Councils it inherited a mass base of support consisting of predominantly lower-class Muslims of indigenous origin. This dual personality, which could have split the party, actually became a major electoral asset, allowing the AG to appeal to the two major elements in the dominant Yoruba community. Latent tensions between these two factions were kept under control through a superior organizational structure and through the party's ability to accept orderly internal change.

Structurally, the Lagos AG was a four-tier organization reaching down to the lowest levels of the political community.[58] In theory, the highest body within the party was the Divisional Conference, consisting of the chairman or leader of the opposition in the municipal council, all AG representatives in the federal legislature, all AG councilors, members of the Divisional Executive, members of the constituency committees, two representatives from each electoral district, five representatives of the Women's Wing, and five representatives of the Youth Association. In practice, the central policy-making body was the Divisional Executive, originally composed of five officers, two traditional chiefs, the organizing secretary, all AG councilors, and one unofficial member, Alhaji Jibril Martins. The first divisional chairman, who had primary responsibility for all party matters in the city, was Chief Dr. J. Akanni Doherty, a Christian physician who was the party's federal vice-president. After 1962, when the organization of the AG was streamlined and new local leaders began coming to the fore, the divisional chairman was Alhaji A. F. Masha, a Lagos Muslim who was chairman of the council (1962–1965). In 1964 the Divisional Executive was reconstituted to have more broadly based membership, including eleven officers, the chairmen and secretaries of the eight major wards, the constituency secretaries, the party's representatives in the federal legislature, the chairman or leader of the opposition in the council, and ten unofficial members.

The second tier of the AG was the Constituency Organization, headed by an executive committee composed of seven officers, fifteen unofficial members, and the representatives of the three constituencies in the federal legislature. The general membership of the constituency unit included all members of the Executive Committee, all councilors in the constituency, and four representatives from each ward in the constituency. The unit was primarily active during federal elections but also had a continuing functional significance in the Divisional Conference. The chairmen of the three constituencies were all vice-chairmen of the Divisional Executive.

At the next lower level was the Area Organization, one for each of the eight major wards of the city. The Area or Ward Organization was the highest unit composed only of local members—all councilors in the area and members of the area Executive Committee. Each Area Executive consisted of seven officers, twelve unofficial members and all councilors within the ward. Members of the Area Executive could be elected only from among the members entitled to attend the area meeting.[59]

Finally, the primary units of the party were executive committees, one in each of the forty-two electoral districts or precincts. Each committee had seven officers and eight unofficial members. These precinct units were the basic cells of the party in which rank-and-file members exercised control. Most of the executive precinct leaders were respected community leaders; the precinct organization included all the party members in the district.

Officers of the party were supposed to be elected annually by representative members of subsidiary units; in the precincts officers were to be elected at large in a general meeting of party members. At higher party levels, elections were not held regularly; between 1959 and 1966 only two elections for the Divisional Executive took place. Only at the precinct level did officers change regularly according to standard procedures.

The social composition of the party leadership was similar to the social composition of the AG faction on the council. Of the official list of 106 local party leaders, including the chairmen and secretaries of all party units in 1958 and all candidates elected to the LTC in 1957, all but two were Yoruba.[60] All ninety-six AG councilors elected after 1950 were Yorubas, fifty-four of them Muslims and thirty-nine Lagos Muslims.

The nomination system of the Lagos AG was based on direct participation by individual members of the party. Candidates were nominated by the constituency, ward, or precinct executives in their respective districts and were presented for "primary election" at a meeting of rank-and-file members. The candidates thus selected had to be confirmed by the Divisional Executive; if the latter did not ratify a nominee, the lower party unit had to nominate another candidate. Since nominations did not originate from the top, most candidates were popular "local boys" or "native sons" whose vote-getting capacities had already been tested in the primaries.[61] Coming up through the ranks in this way, Lagosians—particularly Lagos Muslims—began to penetrate the inner party machinery, especially after 1959. Of the sixty-three council seats held by the AG after 1959, more than half, or thirty-three, were filled by Lagos Muslims.

The AG councilors and a number of selected officials of the branch were members of the Parliamentary Committee, which met monthly with the Divisional Executive. During the years when the AG had majority control of the council, the chairman was "elected" by the Divisional Executive and his appointment was formally confirmed by the council. The divisional chairman and the council chairman were the two primary officials of the party. Before 1959 the AG chairmen of the council were Egba Yorubas: Chief F. Rotimi Williams (1953–1954) and A. O. Lawson (1954–1959), both of whom were Christian lawyers. After 1959 the AG chairmen of the council were Lagos Muslims: Alhaji A. F. Masha (1962–1965), a merchant, and Alhaji G. O. Dawodu (1965–66), the political organizing secretary of the Lagos branch.

At the national level, the Lagos AG was regarded as part of the Western Region party structure. The chairman of the Lagos AG plus ten members elected by the Divisional Conference were permitted to attend the Regional Conference in the west. The party's constitution also stipulated that, for representation on the executive committees of the Regional Conference, "Lagos is [to be regarded as] a division [of the west] and each federal constituency in Lagos shall be counted as two regional constituencies."[62]

In financial matters, the Western Region treasury was regarded as the regional treasury for Lagos.

Before 1959 the oba's Iga served as the local party office. Subsequently, the Lagos Action Group headquarters was located in the Olowogbowo area of Lagos in "Elephant House," an old Brazilian-style building that once belonged to S. H. Pearse, a prominent Saro and a supporter of Herbert Macaulay.

The Lagos AG also had a number of affiliated groups and wings attached to the branch organization. The Area Councils, officially an allied organization, in actuality was well integrated into the inner workings of the party. The Lagos branch of the Egbe Omo Oduduwa, a theoretically nonpartisan Yoruba cultural organization led by J. A. Ajao, was a fraternity of the city's professional and intellectual Yoruba elite, most of whom were members of the AG. Women and youth wings of the party were organized at the divisional level, rather than as separate and potentially rival arms of the party. Before 1959 the oba of Lagos and nearly all the chiefs of Lagos were solid AG supporters; even after Adele's official declaration of neutrality, many chiefs continued to adhere to the party. Religious leaders, particularly from the Jam'at and Ahmadiya congregations were strong supporters of the AG.

Of all the associated groups the AG cultivated, the market women were by far the most important. They were treated as a separate local public whose support was assiduously cultivated. The branch secretariat maintained a staff of market supervisors assigned to the major urban markets; they helped resolve disputes, coordinate the women's activities, and solicit their financial contributions and votes. Formal market wings of the party were set up in each of the major markets in the mid-fifties, and by 1964 there was a party chapter in every market in the city. Each chapter worked parallel to, and in cooperation with, the precinct units of the party.

The key figure responsible for the victories of the AG in the elections of 1962 and 1965, and the one who used the party machinery to best advantage, was the political organizing secretary, Alhaji G. O. Dawodu. First joining the council in 1957, he subsequently became a full-time worker in the divisional and regional executives of the AG. His annual salary—he was the only paid

executive officer in the branch—was £1,160. Dawodu accomplished his most remarkable work, however, when the finances of the
party were frozen and he was no longer receiving a regular
salary.[63] In addition to activating the established party units, for
electoral purposes Dawodu selected volunteer street leaders in
each ward who led teams of workers in house-to-house canvasses
so they could get to know the people, determine the status of the
party, and report back to the divisional committee. From this
reconnaissance operation, electoral strategy was developed to
concentrate on the borderline wards. Constant efforts were made
to get AG voters out to the polls; just before the 1965 election, in
fact, party workers could be seen at night canvassing the neighborhoods of Lagos. Mainland villagers and wage earners in large
corporations were mobilized by the party as well, mainly through
direct contact by teams of party workers. Never in the history of
the city's politics had so much been gained with so little.

This type of organization was not unusual for the Action Group,
which was noted for the efficiency and quality of its staff and for
its generous support of a cadre of loyal party workers. In 1958 the
Federal Executive, for example, appropriated nearly £5,500 for
local staff expenses in Lagos and £2,500 for cars, motorcycles,
and bicycles. It was standard practice for election supervisors to
be appointed for each contest at the ward level. But the remarkable fact of the party's organization was that it improved at a time
when the party had no funds and when there was a ban on political meetings in the city. As the chairman of the AG Youth
Association put it, "it was our darkest hour, [yet] . . . the Action
Group emerged resoundingly triumphant."[64]

Before 1962 the Lagos AG was thought to have been better
financed than any other party in the city. Its financial connections
included the National Bank of Nigeria, incorporated in 1933 by
Dr. Akinola Maja, Dr. J. A. Doherty, and H. A. Subair, founding
members of the NYM and high-ranking leaders of the AG. Dr.
Maja, "Baba Eko" of Lagos, vice-president of the Lagos AG, and
"father of the party," was formerly chairman of the bank's board of
directors, and Dr. J. A. Doherty was general manager. Two
smaller banks were likewise associated with the party: the Agbon-
Magbe Bank, whose manager, Chief M. A. Okupe, was a divisional

leader of the Action Group in Lagos, and the Merchant Bank. Other resources were available to the Lagos AG through its control of the council. Distribution of patronage was just as important to the party's strength as financial resources. Alhaji Masha, emphasizing this fact, explained how contracts were awarded in the council on the basis of political needs:

> As for petty contractors we had about 42 elected members and about 4 traditional members and that makes 46. Most of these contractors are our supporters in one way or another. I must explain that. These contractors approach councillors so that their names could be considered by the City Engineer when an advertisement is out for tenderers to tender for these petty contracts [*sic*]. Sometimes we receive more than 300 applications and, at a time, we would probably want only one hundred contractors out of the three hundred for all these specific items. So you know what happens. The three hundred would want their names to come in, and therefore they approach this councillor and that councillor. So at the meetings of the Tenders Committee councillors would bring the names of their supporters which may be, say, two or three or more and it is left to the Committee to say, well, we have to appoint only this person and that person; probably one from you, one from me, and so on.[65]

The AG's ability to change and to adapt to new social forces was perhaps its greatest strength. Its dual personality eventually matured into a distinct indigenous character. This development came about through normal procedures, not through an intraparty coup or a revolt against existing party leadership. Evidence of the growing influence of indigenous members could be seen in the offices they held in the party, the increasing number of seats they captured on the council, and the policies the party adopted. The AG, for example, favored the slum clearance scheme in the fifties which the indigenes strongly opposed. By the 1960s the party was split between the indigenes who favored the creation of a Lagos state and the immigrants who, in conformity with Western Region policy, were in favor of closer ties between the west and Lagos. Finally, in 1965, when the AG and the NCNC were supposed to be maintaining the United Progressive Grand Alliance, Lagos

Muslims refused to honor higher party directives and ran their own slate of candidates.[66]

By this time the Lagos Muslims had clearly taken control of the Action Group. They did not do so, however, by making the party any more particularistic in its appeal. It was still a Yoruba organization, including immigrants, Christians, professionals, and intellectuals. But these groups were not in command, as they had been in the past, and the party machine had been retooled to serve the interests of local people. In both composition and organization, the Lagos AG had become the direct opposite of the Lagos NCNC: the latter's weaknesses were the former's strengths. Whereas the Lagos NCNC was a highly centralized, weakly articulated, and ethnically heterogeneous party run by an individualistic Christian elite with close ties to the national party headquarters, the Lagos AG was a decentralized, well-organized, and ethnically homogeneous party run by a cohesive group of Lagos Muslims with few ties to its national executive. The functional role of the AG in Lagos was changing to suit the needs of the dominant corporate group in the community. The tremendous local successes in the 1960s, when the AG was undergoing its severest tests nationally, show how a party of urban social integration could be transformed into a party of urban community control.

### URBAN ELECTORAL PATTERNS

On May 29, 1920, in the first election in British West Africa, approximately 350 residents of Lagos selected three men from a nonpartisan slate of seven candidates to represent them on the Lagos Town Council. The franchise was extended to every male property owner over the age of twenty-one who occupied a tenement in Lagos assessed at a capital value of at least £225 or having an annual rental value of at least £15.[67] The Eleko's bell ringers or town criers had made the public proclamation of the election, which was conducted in a quiet, orderly way, with no public campaign. Voters placed an X next to a candidate's name, and provision was made for illiterates to vote orally with the election officers marking the ballots. Polling took place at the old

Glover Hall where each elector cast one vote for a single member running in his ward. For the next fifteen years, three representatives to the municipal council were chosen triennially in this fashion.

In 1923 quinquennial contests were introduced to select three members from Lagos for the Nigerian Legislative Council. Ten candidates were nominated, and separate electoral lists based on somewhat different voting qualifications were drawn up. Eligible voters were males twenty-one years of age or older who were British subjects or natives of the Protectorate of Nigeria and who earned an annual income of at least £100. In these contests, plural voting was allowed. All Lagos was treated as one constituency and each elector was entitled to cast ballots for three candidates. A total of 1,601 people voted in the first Legislative Council election.

Until 1938, both municipal and legislative elections were dominated by the Nigerian National Democratic Party. As in all one-party systems, the nominating process determined the election outcome and the actual polling evolved into a mere formality. So strong was Macaulay's hold on the town that by 1929 many seats ceased being contested at all. Two of the three NNDP candidates in 1929 and all the candidates in the 1932 and 1935 LTC elections were returned unopposed. In Legislative Council elections, competition tended to be somewhat keener, but it was not until the emergence of organized opposition that elections in Lagos became effective contests in which the outcome was not predetermined.

In 1935 the number of elected representatives to the Lagos Town Council was increased to four, and one ward on the mainland (Ebute Metta) was added to the three island wards. Yaba and Surulere, outside the Lagos assessment area, were not yet included in the balloting.[68] The municipal franchise was extended in 1941 to tenants who paid an annual rent of at least £18 and who had resided in Lagos for three months.[69] Registration procedures were slightly relaxed so that property owners needed to make only one claim to have their names kept on the voters' lists. Tenants, however, were still required to reregister for each election, as landlords had done in the past. In 1947 the number of elected members on the Lagos Town Council was increased to five, the annual requirement for voter qualification in Legislative Council elections was lowered from £100 to £50, and the residency requirement was fixed at twelve months.

Before 1950 voting was a privilege of the wealthy classes, and relatively few nonliterates participated. The largest number of voters taking part in municipal elections during the first thirty years was 1,649 in 1923. Usually voters numbered only a few hundred, despite the fact that thousands of residents were legally eligible. The turnout was higher for elections to the Legislative Council, since it was the forum for debate in which members ostensibly had more influence. In 1947, for example, 3,935 of 5,379 registered voters, or 73.15 percent, turned out for the Legislative Council contest.

The reasons for the comparatively mild interest in municipal elections is not difficult to discern. First, until 1941 a resident had to pay rates to be eligible to vote and most property owners preferred to remain disenfranchised rather than reveal their holdings to the tax authorities. Second, the franchise was not a device by which the electorate could influence policy. As one African councilor noted, the electorate knew their representatives could always be outvoted by an official majority of nominated members.[70] Third, the LTC was regarded as a colonial institution to provide services aimed at satisfying European needs. In matters such as sanitation, trading, traffic, and building and housing regulations, the council acted as a regulatory or prohibitive body restricting normal practices of the African community. Finally, electoral competition was confined to members of the non-Nigerian elite of native foreigners who monopolized positions on the council. Even after the rise of the Nigerian Youth Movement in 1938, the masses were not assimilated into the electoral process; in the eyes of the indigenes, contests were simply converted into competitions between two sets of countervailing elites. Cumulatively, these conditions accounted for the low turnout of voters in pre-1950 contests; the cause was not the intrinsic indifference or apathy of the electorate, an explanation usually put forward by the colonial authorities.[71]

With the introduction of a universal franchise in 1950, voter participation increased substantially, although since then the town has experimented with several different types of electoral systems which have probably affected voter turnout. For the 1950 election the city was divided into eight multimember wards of unequal population. Wards A and B, for example, with approximately 18,000 inhabitants each, were given the same number of representatives as Wards D and G, with 9,000 and 7,000 inhabitants, respectively. Ward C, which contained more than 30,000 inhabitants and covered the entire eastern half of Lagos Island, was divided into two, so that the newly constituted Ward C contained approximately 15,000 and Ward H contained 17,000 inhabitants.[72] Since three representatives were elected from each ward, the twenty-four-member council was unequally apportioned in terms of population. According to the electoral system adopted for the 1950 election, in each ward the councilor with the lowest number of votes retired after one year, the councilor with the next lowest number of votes retired after two years, and the councilor with the highest number of votes served a full three years. Through staggered elections, one-third of the council would rotate yearly. In the same election the franchise was extended for the first time to women and the residence requirement was reduced to six months.

This system survived for only two years. In 1952 the elected council was dissolved by the Western Region government and a caretaker committee was appointed in its place. In 1953 multimember districts were abolished and existing polling units were divided into single-member districts with an average of 2,835 voters in each, except for E6 (867 registered voters), E5 (1,887 registered voters), and G3 (1,449 registered voters). The new council elected under this system was the first to include traditional members, who were chosen separately from among themselves for six-year terms. A minimum of forty-one single-member districts was fixed in order to assure that the traditional members (then numbering eight) should not exceed one-fifth of the elected members.[73] Annual elections for one-third of the council were replaced in 1953 by triennial elections for the whole council.[74]

Although Lagos was separated from the Western Region in 1954, the 1953 local government law setting down these electoral regulations remained in force until a bill that placed the LTC under the control of the governor-in-council was passed in the federal House of Representatives in 1956. Municipal elections scheduled for October 1956 were postponed to January 1957 so that the electoral system could again be reviewed. At the urging of the NCNC, the federal government reduced the number of traditional members in the council from eight to four, increased the number of seats on the council from forty-one to forty-two (one additional seat in Ward E), raised the residency requirement for electors from six to twelve months, and reintroduced multimember districts and plural voting. The town was divided into fourteen constituencies, with varying numbers of seats in each ward.[75] Voters were permitted to cast as many ballots as there were councilors to be elected in each constituency.

The cumulative confusions caused by these electoral experiments came to a head in the 1957 election, giving rise to administrative difficulties. The returning officer reported that the voters' list used contained so many errors that it had become obsolete.[76] The errors were understandable: the 1957 list was based on the 1954 federal election list, which had been based on the 1950 municipal election list, which had been compiled from the 1950 census enumeration. Technically, the revision of the voters' list depended exclusively upon submission of claims and objections by individual voters; in practice, however, submissions came in bulk from political parties and were therefore less reliable. Decisions on claims and objections rested entirely on the personal discretion of the revising officer, who rarely had the time or the means to investigate the charges properly. The deficiencies in the voters' list were compounded by delays and complications arising from plural voting. The process of checking for duplicate votes was long and arduous and provided many opportunities for fraud and error. Moreover, although each voter might have as many as four votes to cast in his ward, many people, failing to understand the system, cast ballots for only one candidate.

For these reasons, the electoral system was once again revised in 1959. Single-member districts were reintroduced to conform to the pattern prevailing in the rest of the country. A new voters' list was compiled, and representatives were reapportioned on the basis of recent population changes: Ward A was reduced from six to four seats because people had been displaced by the slum clearance scheme; Ward D was increased from three to four seats as a result of the development of Apapa and parts of Surulere; and Ward E was increased from seven to eight seats because its population had been increased by new immigrants. Each constituency was delineated so that a councilor represented approximately 10,000 inhabitants.

The system of eight major wards subdivided into forty-two single-member constituencies was used in municipal elections from 1959 to 1966. In 1965 the town clerk proposed that the LCC

TABLE 29

Voting Population and Voter Turnout in Lagos, 1950–1965

| Year | Number of eligible voters | Number who voted | Percentage turnout | Percentage increase in voting population | Percentage increase or decrease in voter turnout |
|------|---------------------------|------------------|--------------------|------------------------------------------|--------------------------------------------------|
| 1950 | 114,700[a] | 26,000[a] | 22 | — | — |
| 1953 | 115,106 | 28,958 | 25 | 0.4 | +12 |
| 1957 | 170,041 | 54,728 | 32 | 48 | +89 |
| 1959 | 174,000[b] | 101,648 | 58 | 2 | +85 |
| 1962 | 177,173 | 84,367 | 47 | 1 | -17 |
| 1965 | 269,463 | 101,840 | 36 | 57 | +20 |

[a] Figures are rounded because exact data are unavailable. The 1950 election was conducted by the federal government.

[b] For the 1959 election, also conducted by the federal government, the only exact figure given was the number who voted. Therefore the number of eligible voters is an estimate, placed roughly halfway between the numbers for 1957 and 1962.

Source: Lagos City Council files.

be enlarged to forty-five members so as to reflect demographic changes in the city, with apportionment on the basis of one councilor to every 15,000 inhabitants.[77] It was proposed that Ward A lose one member since some population had been displaced by the building of the second mainland bridge; that Wards D and E gain one and two members, respectively, because of population growth in these rapidly developing areas; and that Ward G gain one member because of new settlements on reclaimed land in Southwest Ikoyi and Victoria Island. Although a fresh voters' list was drawn up for the 1965 contest, the redistricting laws were not passed by the federal legislature until October 1965, too late for the municipal elections of that year. The 1965 list was to be used in 1968, but no election took place that year because of the military take-over of Nigeria in 1966.

The rates of voter turnout after the introduction of universal suffrage varied irregularly. Perhaps the most significant conclusion to emerge from the data (see table 29) is that voter turnout did not increase proportionately with the voting population in the period 1950–1965. The periods of fastest growth in the number of eligible voters were 1953–1957 and 1962–1965. In the first period, voter turnout increased by 89 percent, nearly double the percentage increase in the voting population. In the latter period, voter turnout rose by less than one-third of the percentage increase in the voting population. A similar divergence was apparent between the 1959 and 1962 elections, when comparative stability in voting population was accompanied by a sharp drop of 17 percent in voter turnout, representing a decrease of some 17,000 in the number of voters. It is likewise significant that although the number of qualified voters increased by nearly 100,000 between 1959 and 1965, the number of those who cast ballots increased by less than 200.

These patterns provide insight into the role of residence as a factor conditioning urban political participation. It has been hypothesized that residence is a key variable among the determinants of voting patterns: "Even when demographic and socioeconomic differences are taken into account, the longer the length of residence in the community, the greater the likelihood of voting.... Therefore: the more rapidly a community grows, the lower the turnout in that community is likely to be."[78] The aggregate figures for voting population and voter turnout in Lagos between 1950 and 1965 (table 29), and the constituency breakdowns for the 1962 and 1965 elections from data in the City Council files, suggest that this proposition does not hold for the capital city. At the aggregate level, the periods of most rapid growth (1953–1957 and 1962–1965) were not the periods of lowest voter turnout. It may be concluded, therefore, that immigrants who came to Lagos during these years did exercise their voting rights. Conversely, the periods of comparatively lower rates of population growth (1950–1953 and 1957–1962) do not coincide with the periods of larger voter turnout. Rather, the rate of change in voter turnout gradually increased until the peak year of 1959, then declined in 1962, and started upward again in 1965, while the number of eligible voters varied unevenly, with no discernible pattern. Even at the lower constituency levels, changes in voting population and voter turnout do not correlate. The data show a relatively small increase in voter population and a low voter turnout in some constituencies (B5, C1, C4, E2, E8, F1, F2) and a large increase in voter population and a high voter turnout in others (A1, B2, E4, E6).[79] Ward F

TABLE 30

VOTER TURNOUT BY WARD IN ELECTIONS OF 1962 AND 1965
(In percentages)

| Ward | 1962 | 1965 |
|------|------|------|
| A | 55 | 43 |
| B | 55 | 44 |
| C | 54 | 40 |
| D | 42 | 26 |
| E | 43 | 30 |
| F | 40 | 33 |
| G | 37 | 33 |
| H | 58 | 43 |
| Average | 47 | 36 |

SOURCE: Lagos City Council files.

is a good example. The highest turnout in 1962 was in F1, a developing district situated near the University of Lagos and comprising 3,957 electors. At the other extreme, the lowest voter turnout was in F6, one of the oldest districts in the city which then had 4,249 electors. In the 1965 election, the population growth in both districts was nearly equal, an increase of 1,713 in F1 and of 1,594 in F6. Yet the turnout dropped drastically from 46 percent to 32 percent in F1 and rose sharply from 25 percent to 39 percent in F6.

These figures do not totally invalidate the thesis that residence longevity is linked to political participation. Indeed, there is some evidence to confirm the premise that the longer a person resides in a community, the more inclined he is to become politically active. No councilor, for example, lived in Lagos for less than ten years, and the vast majority of councilors were resident for more than twenty-five years or spent all their lives in the capital. The data on voter participation in 1962 and 1965 by wards (see table 30) also suggest that, on the whole, the older neighborhoods tend to have higher voter turnouts than more rapidly growing areas. There was a noticeable difference between Lagos Island and mainland wards in 1962 and 1965: in the wards with the highest rates of voter turnout, A, B, C, and H, the rates were higher than the municipal average, while in wards D, E, F, and G, on the mainland and the surrounding residential islands, the rates of voter turnout

TABLE 31

NUMBER OF COUNCIL SEATS WON, BY PARTY AND WARD, 1950–1965

| Party | A | B | C | D | Ward E | F | G | H | Total |
|-------|---|---|---|---|--------|---|---|---|-------|
| *1950* | | | | | | | | | |
| Area Councils | 3 | 3 | – | – | – | – | – | – | 6 |
| NCNC/NNDP | – | – | 3 | 3 | 3 | 3 | 3 | 3 | 18 |
| *1951* | | | | | | | | | |
| Area Councils | 1 | 1 | – | – | – | – | – | – | 2 |
| NCNC | – | – | 1 | 1 | 1 | 1 | 1 | 1 | 6 |
| *1953* | | | | | | | | | |
| AG | 6 | 6 | 2 | – | 2 | 4 | 1 | 4 | 25 |
| NCNC | – | – | 3 | 3 | 4 | 2 | 2 | 2 | 16 |
| *1957* | | | | | | | | | |
| AG | 6 | 6 | – | – | – | 6 | – | 5 | 23 |
| NCNC | – | – | 5 | 3 | 7 | – | 3 | 1 | 19 |
| *1959* | | | | | | | | | |
| AG | 4 | 6 | 1 | – | – | 5 | – | 4 | 20 |
| NCNC | – | – | 4 | 4 | 8 | 1 | 3 | 2 | 22 |
| *1962* | | | | | | | | | |
| AG | 4 | 6 | 2 | 1 | 3 | 6 | – | 6 | 28 |
| NCNC | – | – | 3 | 3 | 5 | – | 3 | – | 14 |
| *1965* | | | | | | | | | |
| AG | 4 | 6 | 5 | 3 | 3 | 6 | 2 | 6 | 35 |
| NCNC | – | – | – | 1 | 5 | – | 1 | – | 7 |

SOURCE: Lagos City Council files.

were lower than the municipal average. These figures relate to comparisons between immigrant and indigene behavior, however, whereas overall growth in voter population refers mainly to immigrants. In general, it is reasonable to conclude that residence is not an important variable for voter turnout among immigrants, but that indigenes, by virtue of their natural vested interests in the town, exhibit a consistently higher rate of political participation.

A ward-by-ward analysis of electoral patterns from 1950 to 1965 yields on overall profile of the socioeconomic determinants of voting behavior. To clarify the analysis that follows, a summary of the results of each election by party totals is given in table 31.

### Wards A and B

The most stable and densely populated districts in Lagos are Wards A and B, situated on the western half of Lagos Island and comprising the traditional quarter where most of the Lagos Muslims reside. According to the 1963 census, these wards collectively contained about 19 percent of the municipal population. Ward A, with four councilors, has been proportionately declining in size owing to urban renewal projects that have displaced several thousand residents. Ward B, the larger of the two districts, with six representatives, is the heart of the indigenous community. Well over 90 percent of the population in both wards is Yoruba, and the great majority of residents are Lagosians. Economically, the inhabitants range from lower- to lower middle-class workers who are mostly traders, merchants, craftsmen, clerks, or property owners living off rents from family land. These two wards, without exception, exhibited consistent and usually overwhelming support of the Action Group or its affiliate, the Area Councils, and tallied good voter turnouts.[80] The electorate constituted a virtual bloc vote for the AG which the NCNC had been unable to penetrate.

### Wards C and H

The other two wards on Lagos Island reflect a mixture of new and old Lagos. Sections of Ward H, the island's "waist," have deep historical roots, particularly in the Brazilian Quarter. Parts of Ward C, the eastern wing of the island, rank among the most prestigious areas of the city; with government buildings, ministries, State House, the federal legislature, the Supreme Court, and so forth located there, Ward C is the nerve center of the administrative complex and was formerly the colonial headquarters. With about 8 percent of the total population, Ward C maintained a fairly stable growth rate and was allocated five seats on the council. Before 1966 about three-fourths of its inhabitants were Yoruba and one-fourth were Ibo. The district is about evenly divided between Christians and Muslims. Occupationally, it contains white-collar workers, traders, small businessmen, and pensioners.

*Political Variables*

Because of its heterogeneous population, Ward C is the only island ward where the NCNC was able to gain a foothold. The AG began making inroads in 1959 and finally captured all five seats in 1965. Like the other island districts, Ward C exhibited relatively high voter turnouts in 1962 and 1965. Ward H, on the other hand, with 11 percent of the population and six seats on the council, more closely resembles the traditional wards socially and politically. Dominated largely by Yorubas and Muslims, it contains many traders and merchants (except for the Brazilian Quarter where, customarily, clerical workers and artisans reside); it exhibited a decided preference for the Action Group and enjoyed a high voter turnout.

## Ward D

The mainland wards, where the bulk of the immigrants settle, are the most competitive and, by far, the fastest-growing districts in the city. Although containing more than 60 percent of the municipal population in 1963, they collectively controlled only half the seats on the council, a situation that the 1965 reapportionment proposals were designed to correct. Geographically, Ward D is the largest in the city, occupying nearly the entire western half of the mainland. It includes the major industrial centers of Apapa, Ijora, and Iganmu, the port and harbor facilities, the railway compound, developing areas in Surulere, and some coastal strips of land up to Light House Creek. Before 1966 Ward D contained 16 percent of the total urban population, slightly more than half of whom were Yoruba, about a quarter were Ibo, and the rest were minority and non-Nigerian inhabitants. The majority of residents are Christians and are employed as clerical or technical workers, stevedores, factory workers, or other skilled laborers. There is also a high-rent, low-density residential area in Apapa for top-level executive and professional staff attached to the railway, port, and industrial operations, many of whom are Europeans. In 1959 council representation for Ward D was raised from three to four seats, a number still inadequate for a district of that size and importance. It had traditionally been an NCNC stronghold, but the Action Group captured one seat in 1962 and three seats in 1965. Voter turnout was below average. Ward D had the lowest rate of voter turnout in the city in 1965 when only 26 percent of the electorate went to the polls.

## Ward E

The electoral district with the largest number of seats in the city is Ward E, where at least 24 percent of the total number of the urban population resides. Ward E is also the fastest-growing area of Lagos. In 1953 it had six seats on the council; in 1957 the number was raised to seven and in 1959 to eight, intended to be expanded in 1965 to ten. The ward, stretching across the northern frontier of the city from Lagos Lagoon on the east to Surulere on the west, forms a buffer zone between central Lagos and the suburbs lying beyond the municipal boundaries. Here are located many of the city's major educational and medical institutions: the University of Lagos, Yaba College of Technology, the Medical Research Institute, Queen's College, West African Examinations Council, Lagos University Teaching Hospital, and numerous missionary schools.

The residential sections of Ward E range from middle-class areas in Surulere to upper-class districts in Yaba. Before 1966 slightly more than 50 percent of the inhabitants were Yoruba and about 27 percent were Ibo; the rest were Efik, Edo, Hausa, and non-Nigerian. There is a heavy concentration of Christians and a disproportionate number of white-collar workers, professionals, teachers, and related workers. The NCNC, the traditional favorite, consistently captured the district. It still held the majority of seats in 1965, when its foundations in all other areas had eroded. Voter turnout in Ward E was always well below average.

## Ward F

Wedged between the indigenous and immigrant sections of Lagos is Ward F, one of the oldest areas in the city. Originally settled in the nineteenth century by Christian refugees from Abeokuta, it is now the site of pivotal road junctions. It includes Iddo Island, Ebute Metta, and a bulge of the mainland projecting into Lagos Lagoon. Ward F is the most stable mainland electoral district. Its six councilors represent 14 percent of the municipal population. After the traditional island districts, it has the next highest concentration of Yorubas in the city. More than 80 percent of the population is of Yoruba stock, and most of these Yorubas are Christians. Occupationally, they are traders, clerks, or small entrepreneurs. With two exceptions, Ward F was consistently loyal to the Action Group, following the island pattern, but it exhibited lower than average voter turnout, following the mainland pattern.

## Ward G

Until recently, Ward G was the smallest electoral district in Lagos, but it has been growing rapidly because of extensive land reclamation and property development. In 1965, with 8 percent of the population, Ward G was supposed to be given four seats instead of three. Consisting of Ikoyi and Victoria Island, it is the elite section of Lagos where the largest European, diplomatic, and upper-class Nigerian residencies are concentrated. It also includes Obalende, a middle-class residential area, and parts of the undeveloped coastline reaching down to Light House Beach, the southernmost point of Lagos. Ward G is the only ward lacking a Yoruba majority. In 1960 a third of the population was Ibo, approximately 30 percent were Yoruba, and 10 percent were non-Nigerians (table 7). Although separated from the mainland by Lagos Island, Ward G exhibited the same political characteristics as the mainland wards. Until 1965 it was firmly in the NCNC camp and voter turnout was lower than the municipal average.

## Conclusion

The Action Group was strongest in districts with the largest Yoruba, Muslim, and lower-class populations, while the NCNC was strongest in the heterogeneous wards, with Ibo and other minority populations, Christians, and middle- to upper-income groups. The noticeable correlation between wards with low voter turnout and NCNC party preference suggests that had the NCNC organized its campaigns more effectively and got more of its supporters to the polls it would have probably fared better in local elections, particularly in the later years. The low voter turnout in NCNC wards was due not only to poor organization, but also to voter

apathy among immigrants. This weakness could have been overcome. The Action Group, for example, through its able political
organizing secretary, Alhaji G. O. Dawodu, picked up borderline
wards by conducting house-to-house canvasses extending into the
night, rallying the market women, and playing on the theme of
Yoruba solidarity to draw immigrants to the polls.

TABLE 32

WARD REPRESENTATION IN LCC, SHOWING MALAPPORTIONMENT,
PROPOSED REAPPORTIONMENT IN 1965, AND NEEDED REAPPORTIONMENT
BASED ON 1963 CENSUS FIGURES

| Ward | Population in 1963 | Percentage of total city population | Number of seats allotted | Proposed reapportionment, 1965 | Needed reapportionment[a] |
|---|---|---|---|---|---|
| A | 47,551 | 7 | 4 | 3 | 3 |
| B | 79,841 | 12 | 6 | 6 | 5 |
| C | 53,450 | 8 | 5 | 5 | 4 |
| D | 104,037 | 16 | 4 | 5 | 7 |
| E | 158,932 | 24 | 8 | 10 | 11 |
| F | 95,542 | 14 | 6 | 6 | 6 |
| G | 50,732 | 8 | 3 | 4 | 4[b] |
| H | 71,703 | 11 | 6 | 6 | 5 |
| General | 3,437 | — | – | – | – |
| Total | 665,246 | 100% | 42 | 45 | 45 |

[a] Based on one councilor for each 15,000 inhabitants.
[b] Ward G, which technically should be allotted three seats, is given four because,
like Ward C, it has 8 percent of the population and because it is one of the most
rapidly developing areas in the city. The argument against raising Ward G's representation from three to four is that a large number of non-Nigerians reside in the
ward.
[c] Persons not resident in Lagos but counted in census.

Malapportionment in the city's electoral districts also tended
to favor the AG, because the areas with the highest growth rates
were inclined to be NCNC-dominated wards. All things being
equal, the high population growth rate between 1962 and 1965
would have been expected to favor the NCNC, since Ibo immigration was increasing and the traditional NCNC strongholds were
swelling in population. Although it was by no means the most
important factor accounting for the NCNC's fate, low apportionment in the fastest-growing wards undoubtedly played a part in
the party's poor showing in the 1962 and 1965 elections. Even the

reapportionment worked out in 1965 by the town clerk would not have corrected all the imbalances that existed. Table 32 compares the proposed apportionment in 1965 with needed reapportionment as strictly calculated on the basis of one councilor per 15,000 inhabitants. Cumulatively, it shows that the NCNC-dominant wards (D, E, and G) should have been raised from a total of fifteen to twenty-two seats, and the AG-dominant wards (A, B, F, and H) should have been lowered from a total of twenty-two to nineteen seats.

Finally, it might be noted that despite the expansion of the electorate and the increase in voter turnout, urbanization did not consistently result in changes in voting behavior. In fact, one of the most interesting patterns revealed by these data is the degree of political continuity, particularly in the traditional wards which solidly backed the Action Group and consistently had a higher voter turnout than the mainland wards. The solidarity of the Lagos Muslims evident in voting patterns had significance beyond the boundaries of their own constituencies. The electoral process was influenced not only by their bloc vote, but by their manipulation of the majority party as well. Thus, despite the fact that modern Lagos has been continuously swelling with immigrants, electoral returns increasingly favored the *omo ibile* ("sons of the soil").

CHAPTER 6
*Formal Structure of Government*


Both the power structure and political behavior are affected by
the authoritative institutions through which community influence
is channeled. The discussion of the fourth variable of the framework outlined earlier—the functions, viability, and performance
of the formal structure of government—should begin with a brief
review of the factors that lend importance to authoritative institutions in an urbanizing city such as Lagos.

First, in a developing community of this type, informal interest-
group leaders do not play so important a role in the political process as do similar leaders in the West.[1] Their relative ineffectiveness may be attributed to three sources of weakness: they speak
for a mixed public thus diluting the strength of their appeals; they
make diffuse demands instead of concrete policy proposals; and
they lack independent resources to make a meaningful political
impact on their own. Consequently, in order to acquire a significant degree of influence, they must concentrate on shaping the
formal decision-making process directly, either by swaying public
officials or by seeking personal control of authoritative institutions.
In Lagos, meaningful political influence generally has not been
exercised by informal interest-group leaders without ultimate
reference to formal authority structures.

Another factor that tends to emphasize the importance of the
formal governmental machinery is the position of the city nationally. Because of the size and significance of Lagos, considerable
decision-making control has been vested in federal or regional
institutions. Depending upon the configuration of political forces,
this diffusion of authority has provided opportunities for external

groups to wield influence in local affairs and for local groups to achieve wider influence through higher governmental institutions. Some examples are provided in the discussion of political parties (chap. 5), and another is treated in more detail in the case study on the constitutional status of Lagos (chap. 9). Data in this chapter show how interest-group competition and jurisdictional conflict are created by a fragmented local government structure.

The final factor to bear in mind is the relatively recent and alien origin of local government institutions in Lagos. Because of the weaknesses inherent in the process of institutional transfer from a Western to a non-Western environment, decision-making powers vested in authoritative institutions have often shifted to other centers of power such as the political parties in control of the institutions or higher governmental authorities at regional and federal levels. Thus, these three elements—the ineffectiveness of informal leaders, the national importance of the city, and the foreign origin of local government institutions—draw attention to the variable role that authoritative structures may play in the exercise of community influence.

#### THE COUNCIL AND THE POLICY PROCESS

Although a town council was not formally established in Lagos until 1917, the institutions responsible for municipal administration before that date may properly be described as embryonic units of local government. The first such unit, created in 1899, was the General Sanitary Board, an advisory council whose nine members were appointed by the governor of Nigeria. The board had no separate staff of its own and no powers to raise or allocate funds. In 1904, when the board became defunct, the central government assumed all developmental and administrative functions in the town. The board was revived in 1909 under a new name, the Lagos Municipal Board of Health, and with new membership. It included three Africans (S. H. Pearse, Sir Kitoyi Ajasa, and Sapara Williams), three technical officers (the medical officer of health, the municipal engineer, and the municipal secretary). and three members representing European commercial interests. Like its forerunner. the Lagos Municipal Board of Health had no staff or funds of its own and subsisted on an annual government grant.

The Lagos Town Council created in 1917 was simply an up-graded version of the sanitation authority. The ordinance estab-lishing the council authorized *changing the title* of the local authority from [the] Lagos Municipal Board of Health to the Lagos Town Council [italics mine]."[2] The ordinance also revised the composition of the council, which was to have not more than twelve and not less than six members, all appointed by the governor of Nigeria. The first LTC included the administrator of the Colony of Lagos (designated as president), the secretary of the southern provinces, the principal medical officer, the legal adviser, the commissioner of lands, the assistant treasurer, and five other nominated members, three of whom were Africans—S. H. Pearse, Eric Moore, and S. J. Sawyer. Financially, the LTC oper-ated as a continuation of the Board of Health. The administrator of the colony traced the revenue of the council back to 1915 (when technically the LTC did not exist); at that time the board's budget was £7,919 ($22,000), as compared with the £18,107 ($50,500) allocated to the council at the time of its official inauguration.[3]

Eric Moore argued before the Legislative Council that the government should have gone one step further and introduced elective representation, a proposal that initially met with uniform disapproval from the colonial authorities, who were reluctant to enfranchise people unwilling to pay their rates. It was soon real-ized, however, that even restricted representation might induce the populace to accede to the government's tax plans. In 1920, therefore, the first election was held for three seats on a franchise specifically extended to rate-paying property owners who, as beneficiaries of council, would presumably be attracted to the new measure. But the right to vote did not excite indigenes suffici-ently to make them want to pay for the privilege, at least not for a council with limited authority and three-fourths of whose mem-bers were Europeans nominated by the governor.[4] Consequently, only native foreigners, who were already paying taxes and had already gained access to the colonial bureaucracy, profited from the new measure.

Both as a representative and as an administrative body, the LTC was a static and effete institution for the first twenty years of its life. In 1932, when the council's makeup and operation came under review, the administrator of the colony urged reorganization so that a substantive executive head could be designated. "At present," he noted in a memorandum, "there is no real head and it is therefore extremely difficult to make the various branches of the Town Council keep in full touch with each other and the Departments of Government and the local firms and institutions outside the Council."[5] The administrator recommended that the composition of the council be broadened and that his position as its figurehead president be changed so as to give him real executive powers. T. A. Doherty, an elected member, agreed that these proposals constituted a step in the right direction, but he argued "that the time has arrived when the affairs of the Council should be handed lock, stock, and barrel to the Africans."[6] The government agreed in principle to reconstitute the council by replacing the solicitor general, the deputy director of health services, and the district officer of the colony with two more elected members and one nominated member, all of whom could be Africans. Since the council would then have an equal number of Africans and Europeans, it was hoped that its image as a solely government body would be somewhat reduced.

Implementation of this plan was considerably delayed. Although when eventually implemented, the plan was slightly modified, the impetus for equal representation of the races and for increased autonomy of the council had been provided. An additional elected member was added to the council in 1935. In 1937 more authority was granted for planning and construction of streets and sewage installations. Financial independence was achieved in 1938 when the government agreed to replace its annual grant with a fixed sum in lieu of rates on its property. Three years later, European and African membership was balanced by the addition of nominated African members, one to represent market women and one to represent unenfranchised classes. In 1947 the elected membership was raised to five, and a nominated member to represent the oba and the chiefs of Lagos was included. On the eve of the introduction of a fully elective council, the LTC's membership of fourteen comprised four European officials, five unofficial members (two Europeans representing commercial interests and three Africans representing, respectively, Lagos chiefs, unenfranchised classes, and market women), and five elected African members.[7]

For most of the period of colonial rule, the council remained a care and maintenance institution closely controlled by the central government. Its powers were specifically limited to vehicle licensing, provision of public health facilities, rudimentary market maintenance, control of the sale of native liquor, direction of motor traffic, and regulation of pawnbrokers, cinemas, and public halls. According to the colony's annual report for 1932,

> It is worthy of note that the departments of [the central] government carry out in Lagos a number of functions usually exercised by the Town Councils themselves in the municipalities of the U. K. Water and electricity supply is provided by the P.W.D. [Public Works Department]; the Police Department maintains order and provides the Fire Brigade; the Medical Department provides Hospitals and supplements the health services rendered by the Town Council; the L.E.D.B. [Lagos Executive Development Board] is in sole control of Town Planning and Slum Clearance.[8]

All "political affairs" were beyond the jurisdiction of the council and were placed solely "in the hands of the Commissioner of the Colony" who was directly responsible to the governor.[9]

Urban social services were administered on an ad hoc basis as the need arose, with little forethought or planning. A number of competing institutions were launched as interim organizations to meet particular problems. The first and most powerful of these was the Lagos Executive Development Board, created in 1928 after an outbreak of the bubonic plague. Charged with the responsibility for town planning and slum clearance, the LEDB soon became a rival of the LTC. For many years it had no prescribed representation from the council, and even when the president of the LTC was made an ex officio member of the LEDB in 1936, the board was still not obligated to follow the council's advice or to keep the council informed of its impending projects.

Lack of coordination was further exacerbated by the formation of several other autonomous agencies: Lagos Port Advisory Board (1936), Lagos Drainage and Swamp Reclamation Board (1939), Lagos Housing Committee (1942), Mosquito Control Board (1945), and Government Offices Sitting Commitee (1945). Following the nineteenth-century pattern of English local government, urban administration in Lagos had become a confusing maze of interim committees appointed to deal with specific needs. By 1946, "in practically every branch of activity within Lagos Township, there ... [was] no concerted action; each party, whether it be a board or a committee or department ... [carried] out its functions unrelated to the functions of others, though sometimes they ... [were] very similar."[10]

This anachronistic system was overhauled in 1950 as a result of the innovations in colonial policy introduced by the British Labour Party after it was returned to power in 1946. The secretary of state for the colonies, Arthur Creech Jones, in his famous dispatch of 1947 formulated a fresh approach aimed at the creation of "efficient, democratic and local government," stressing that "the term local government must not be interpreted narrowly; it covers political questions, ... judicial questions, ... and economic questions."[11] While the primary target of these reforms was the native authority system prevailing in rural areas, the new policy had a far-reaching impact on urban government as well.

The dispatch brought about sweeping changes in 1950; the introduction of a fully elected council, of universal suffrage, and of responsible local government immediately made urban government truly democratic and local. Administratively, however, the LTC still left much to be desired. Standards of efficiency plummeted with democratization, for elected councilors tended to use their official powers for personal or party gain. In the face of public opposition, for example, the council voted an annual remuneration of £2,500 ($7,000) for the mayor, which the federal government was forced to veto. Allegations that councilors were demanding a "tax" on goods from market women who were not supporters of the party in power were common. Contracts and employment were distributed by councilors on the criterion of party allegiance. Finally, after the Storey Commission, which was appointed to investigate the council's administrative conduct, had confirmed, among other things, that the post of town clerk was improperly filled, the council was dissolved and a caretaker committee was appointed in its place. Only two years after its adoption, Nigeria's first experiment in local self-government collapsed as a dismal failure.[12]

Obviously, abrupt institutional change and the councilors' lack of experience accounted in large degree for the breakdown. Before 1950, elected representatives had made up only one-quarter of the total membership of the council. Of the twenty-four representatives elected in 1950, only two—Dr. I. Olorun-Nimbe and Adeleke Adedoyin—had had prior experience on the council. But two other factors probably had even more influence on the course of events in the early 1950s. The first was the naïve assumption by colonial authorities that local government could become overnight a bastion of political liberty and a training ground for democratic leadership. As one observer put it, the expectation of the government was that "through local authorities on their own doorsteps, peasant and herdsman, schoolmaster and trader were to learn the arts of democratic initiative and control which they would soon apply to parliamentary government at the center. And when independence came, the local authorities would stand guardians of local and individual liberty against the hand of absolutism at the top."[13] Second, by failing to take into account the different ways in which English and African local government systems had evolved, the colonial authorities miscalculated the impact of the reforms on urban politics. Whereas local government in the United Kingdom was a product of centuries of rule by a civic-minded, landowning local gentry which had little need for, or concern with, the remunerative compensations of public office, in Lagos local self-government was the product of a sudden reformist policy which directed that a set of alien institutions be imposed on a community ruled by nationalist elites in quest of power. Concerned with pragmatic political needs, the nationalists were far less committed to standards of democracy and efficiency set down by colonial overlords than with winning popular support.

The constitutional structure under which the reforms were introduced further encouraged the sacrifice of administrative integrity in the interest of political gain. As part of the pattern of allocating additional political responsibility to Nigerians, the 1951 Macpherson Constitution assigned local government to the control of regional authorities. Lagos was thus placed under the jurisdiction of the Western Region, an action leading to conflict between the Action Group, in control at the regional level, and the NCNC, in control at the local level. The 1952 dissolution of the LTC was as much a politically inspired maneuver designed to wipe out Action Group opposition as it was a repudiation of irregularities within the council. Moreover, having achieved control of Lagos, the Western Region was not about to give it up easily. Shortly after the merger of Lagos with the west, the NCNC began to press for the separation of Lagos and its creation as a federal territory. The Western Region resisted, threatening to secede, if necessary, to retain Lagos. In this way the politics of the capital became subject to the clashes of regional and party competition, just at the time when stability and order were most needed.

Over the objections of the Action Group, Lagos was separated from the Western Region in 1954, without the latter's secession. During the short period when that region was in control of the capital, however, the basic structure of modern local government had been established. Guided by the English Local Government Act of 1933, the Lagos Local Government Law of 1953 set up a system of administrative units modeled on the English county borough.[14] Although there have been subsequent amendments, basically this system remains in operation to this day.

The 1953 law gave extensive powers and duties to the LTC, even though the council was not financially or administratively equipped to exercise them fully at that stage of its development. Among its most important functions were provision of new housing after slum clearance; public health (control of food stores, keeping of animals, supervision of businesses endangering public health, and other services relating to health); welfare for the aged and the destitute; roads (maintenance of streets and sewers and provision of public lighting); traffic (licensing of vehicles and control of traffic flow); provision and maintenance of markets and control of street trading; provision, with federal government approval, of public transportation; municipal trading; licensing of vehicles, cinemas, theaters, tradesmen, and professionals; sewage disposal and sanitation; provision and maintenance of parks and other public areas (cemeteries, swimming pools, libraries, museums, etc.); and primary education.[15] The council was also empowered to raise funds, to acquire and dispose of land, to levy rates, and to pass bylaws and regulations. Also in accordance with the 1953 law, a fixed number of traditional members were brought into the council for the first time, and the oba of Lagos was made ex officio president in place of the mayor, whose office was abolished. The law expanded the council's membership to forty-one, revised the electoral system, and created single-member electoral districts in all the urban wards.

After 1953 the LTC expanded rapidly, steadily advancing in its ability to fulfill the ambitious goals laid down for it. In nearly all the duties listed above, the council gradually took on increased responsibilites, whereas prevously it had been inactive or only mildly concerned. In 1958 the LTC initiated a municipal bus service by purchasing the assets of J. & A. Zarpas. In the face of competition from numerous commercial lines and mammy wagons, it expanded its original fleet of 43 buses to some 250. In 1959 the LTC assumed its powers over primary education from the federal government, and went on to establish five elementary schools: Okesuna Primary, Okesuna Infants, Ijero Municipal, Obele-Odan Primary, and Yaba (Igbobi) Primary. Obviously, the public demand is far too heavy for these five schools, and the overwhelming majority of children still attend private or missionary schools. But municipal education is at least available now, as it was not before, to lower-class families who for reasons of religious conviction or poverty could not make use of existing educational facilities.

The LTC also expanded its activities in the area of public health, a responsibility it shared with the federal Ministry of Health. Areas of jurisdiction were divided roughly into curative medicine, controlled by the federal government, and preventive medicine, handled by the council's Public Health Department, a distinction that has not always been entirely satisfactory. The LTC is concerned with maternal and child health, including domiciliary midwifery and school care; immunization; health education; and environmental services such as food inspection, overcrowding, control of insects and domestic animals, and inspection of work-shops and trades. On April 1, 1967, in accordance with the recommendation of the *Saville Tribunal Report*, which reviewed the council's operations, market administration, one of the most significant areas of responsibility, was transferred to the Public Health Department from the Town Clerk's Office. Other notable council achievments include the construction of new markets and of new public recreational centers, libraries, and swimming pools, road improvements, and the provision of school meals.

Only three significant laws after 1953 altered the local govern-ment structure before the military take-over in 1966. In 1956 the LTC was placed under the supervision of the governor-in-council instead of the Western Region government, a measure that was two years overdue. At that time traditional members were reduced from eight to four. After a special inquiry into the relationship of the LTC with the federal government, the Lagos Local Government Law of 1959 was passed; it strengthened federal powers to suspend the LTC if it was not performing satisfactorily, standardized electoral procedures for federal and local elections, and gave traditional members the right to vote in the council.[16] Finally, the Lagos Local Government (Amendment) Act of 1963 further empowered the minister of Lagos affairs to give directives to the LTC, a right that was tantamount to a veto of council de-cisions. Lagos was given city status on October 1, 1963, when Nigeria became a republic, and the Lagos Town Council was thereafter known as the Lagos City Council. In 1967 an ultramodern city hall was completed at a cost of £1,213,935 (about $3 million), a fitting monument to an institution that fifty years before had become simply an upgraded sanitation board.

The LCC was dissolved on April 20, 1966, four months after the first military coup d'etat in Nigeria.[17] The caretaker committee appointed in its place consisted of representatives from major institutional bodies and interest groups: Lagos Chamber of Com-merce and Industry; Nigerian Union of Teachers; Nigerian Ports Authority; Ikeja Area Planning Authority; Lagos Executive

Development Board; federal ministries of Finance, Establishment, Works and Housing, and Economic Development; armed forces; Nigeria Police; traditional chiefs; market women; Muslims; Lagos Merchandise Traders' Association; Nigerian Tenants' Association; Lagos Territory and Environs House Owners' Association; director of prisons; and heads of departments of the LCC. In the absence of elections, the caretaker committee continued to function as the municipal authority throughout the course of the Nigerian Civil War. (In 1971, after the end of the civil war, this caretaker committee was dissolved, along with other Lagos State local government councils, when a tribunal of inquiry advised reform of the local government structure.[18] A new caretaker committee was appointed in April 1972, with a military officer, Colonel D. K. Sho-Silva, as chairman.)

Although the council came close to imitating the structural features of the English county borough, it had less success in matching its English counterpart in decision-making processes. In theory, the same policy procedures applied in Lagos as in the United Kingdom. Council business was supposed to be conducted through a series of specialized committees which decided, after consultation with officials, what recommendations to forward to the full council for ratification. When the council approved committee proposals, they were sent to the appropriate administrative departments for implementation. In practice, however, this simple three-step procedure from committee to council to department operated quite differently in Lagos.

The LCC had nine standing committees: education; estates and general purposes; highways, roads, and drains; establishment; markets, parks, and cemeteries; public health; finance; library; and tenders. Committee members did not usually regard themselves as councilors assigned to special duties, but as councilors who attended meetings in which the discussion was confined to one specific topic. Any number of councilors could attend committee meetings, thereby undermining any sense of corporate existence or responsibility which a committee might develop. Nonmembers who opposed a committee's recommendation could not vote, but they could have the measure overruled at the next plenary meeting. To avoid such a stalemate, all views were usually taken into account in the preliminary stages. The basic objectives of the committee system—to expedite council business and to create specialized spheres of competence—were therefore lost. A councilor's account of how the Tenders Committee had operated in the past amply illustrates the point. As he explained it, all councilors, after obtaining a list of registered petty contractors from the Town Clerk's Office, would normally attend the Tenders Committee meeting where council contracts were awarded. Each councilor would push his preferred candidates until all the jobs were distributed:

> Whenever we were in the Tenders Committee about three or four councillors would be the headmasters because they would be directing the affairs. They know everybody must submit the names of their favourites to them. For example, what Councillor [X] did at the last Tenders Committee. . . . He prepared a list, jumped from his own seat to the Chairman and gave the list. Everybody was embarrassed. . . . They were disgusted. . . . Councillors turned the Committee House into a market place by submitting their lists and jumping from one place to another. The Chairman was shouting, "Order, order."[19]

As required by a standing order,[20] committee recommendations were submitted to the council at its monthly meetings, accompanied by voluminous and detailed reports on such items as swimming pool attendance; interments classified by religion, type of grave, and grave site; specifications and blueprints of drains, latrines, and sewers; and lists of books purchased for public libraries. Each report was dutifully considered paragraph by paragraph, at full council meetings. Substantive questioning could take place only if members submitted their queries in writing to the chairman. All voting on policy matters was done by a show of hands, and any five members could request that the vote be recorded in the minutes. Rigid as these rules may seem to have been, the standing orders conveniently provided that any regulation could be suspended at a council meeting by a majority vote of those present.

Council meetings fluctuated between the extremes of boredom[21] and disorder; either they were full sessions devoted to the minutiae of urban administration and made tedious by excessive paperwork, or they sank to the level of rancorous debates between party factions. Resolution of crucial issues was nearly always predetermined in advance of council meetings by party caucus. Voting patterns, as recorded in the minutes, nearly always conformed to party alignments. The composition of committees was likewise subject to party control. A selection committee, comprising members whose party affiliation reflected the political complexion of the council as a whole, allocated individual assignments. Every councilor was constitutionally required to serve on at least one committee. Inevitably, key chairmanships were held by leaders of the majority party, the choice positions being on the Finance, Tenders, and Establishment committees, from which party patronage could be most readily dispensed.

Two examples reveal the extent to which party discipline dominated council proceedings. First, at the LTC meeting of June 3, 1958, Chiefs Obanikoro and Eletu Odibo, both traditional members, proposed on behalf of the oba and the chiefs of Lagos that traditional membership be increased from four to twenty-one. In support of the motion, the chiefs complained that their opinions were often disregarded by elected councilors and that they were never given committee chairmanships. Speaking for the NCNC, Councilor F. M. Moronu announced that he was "resolutely opposed" to the motion. Councilor Ogunsanya, leader of the Lagos NCNC, added that since the four chiefs on the council represented the four classes of natural rulers, the number was adequate. The Action Group, angered because the chiefs had refused to accept its original offer to increase the number to eight, also opposed the motion. "It was inconceivable," the LTC chairman stated, "that the number of traditional members . . . should be increased to such an extent that they would be able to hold the balance of power to the council."[22]

Seizing the opportunity to drive the AG and the chiefs apart, Ogunsanya suddenly, without benefit of caucus, shifted his stand and announced that his "party had changed its mind . . . and would now recommend that the number of traditional members be either 4 as he had first suggested or 21 as proposed by the traditional members."[23] Ogunsanya forced the motion to a vote and

on the strength of party allegiance carried all the NCNC councilors present with him. Among them were two members of the
ad hoc committee who had formerly opposed the motion; for that
reason they were disqualified by the chairman. Had it not been
for this maneuver, the proposal would certainly have passed.
Choosing between the alternatives of raising traditional membership to either eight or twenty-one, the council split evenly,
eighteen members voting each way; the tie was broken by the
chairman, an AG councilor, who followed his party's line.

In the second incident, party competition entirely disrupted
the business before the council. At the meeting of October 3, 1963,
the AG chairman of the LCC, Alhaji A. F. Masha, rebuked
Ogunsanya, then a member of the federal legislature, for
supporting the 1963 bill that empowered the federal government
to issue directives to the council. Masha alleged that it was Ogunsanya's accusations of AG malpractices which induced the
federal government to assert stronger supervisory control. The
NCNC demanded the right to reply, but Masha ruled that
communications from the chair were not open to debate and
deferred to the town clerk to advise on the matter. According to
the minutes, the latter

> made several attempts to speak but was prevented by shouts from
> councillors, shouting "we do not hear the Town Clerk's advice" or
> words to similar effect. When eventually he spoke he advised that
> the Chairman's address could be debated. The Chairman agreed
> to allow debate but only after other items on the agenda were con-
> sidered. The majority of members agreed and the Chairman ruled
> accordingly. At this stage some councillors moved towards the
> Chairman's table, addressing him in loud voices and in a rude and
> objectionable manner. Councillor ... [X] seized the official files
> on the table and the Town Clerk immediately ordered some of his
> officers present to recover the files from him. As feelings were
> running high, police had to be called in.[24]

### THE MUNICIPAL BUREAUCRACY

In the execution of policy there were also significant departures
from the English model. In standard administrative structures of

this type, the number of departments usually corresponds to the number of standing committees. The Lagos council, however, had six departments and nine committees. Each department was headed by a senior executive officer—treasurer, public health officer, education officer, personnel officer, city engineer, and town (or city) clerk. Understaffed and underfinanced, the municipal administration was also hampered by misallocation of functions among some of its departments. The treasurer, for example, supervised traffic police, dispensed hackney carriage (taxi) licenses, and was responsible for storekeeping, but he was not given full jurisdiction over all cash receipts. The collection of market women's fees was the responsibility of the Town Clerk's Department, but is presently handled by the Public Health Department.

A more fundamental difficulty, however, concerns the relationship between the administrative and legislative arms of local government. While department heads and committee chairmen were expected to work closely, they were, in theory, also supposed to have separate spheres of responsibility. In practice councilors often acted as though officials were personal staff members to whom they could unilaterally issue instructions. They frequently overstepped their authority and attempted to use personal influence to direct administrative procedures, particularly in matters concerning staff appointments, prosecution of individuals for infringement of bylaws, and allocation of market stalls. Middle-level officials who depended upon councilors' recommendations for promotion and rank were not always unwilling to cater to the demands of elected leaders who might later prove to be valuable to their careers.

At higher levels the distinction between policy-making and policy-execution functions is even more seriously blurred by party influence.[25] The clearest illustration is found in the history of the office of town clerk. Of all the officers in the municipal bureaucracy, the town clerk is the most important; for in his position are combined the roles of secretary, legal adviser, chief administrator, and chief electoral officer. He is primus inter pares among department heads, but is vested with a disproportionate share of executive authority. Specifically, as modeled after his

British counterpart, the town clerk of Lagos has the responsibility for convening, setting the agenda for, and preparing minutes and reports for all council meetings; for advising the council as to its legal powers; for communicating with the public; for collecting rates and other charges; for serving as returning officer in elections; for taking custody of charters, deeds, records, and documents; for advising the president and the chairman of the council of their duties and responsibilities; for signing checks with the municipal treasurer; for approving construction plans with the city engineer; and for seeing that all policies determined by the council are efficiently and lawfully executed. No office in any other Nigerian bureaucracy can compare in sheer scope of operations and multiplicity of functions with that of the town clerk. He is the pivot on which the entire local government machinery turns. Because of this concentration of power, the position of town clerk has been subject to intense political rivalry.

When the LTC was first instituted, the municipal bureaucracy was tied to the central government; Lagos was unique in this respect and consequently it has the only local government bureaucracy whose civil servants operate in conformity with national standards.[26] But until the council was given an African majority and made to face the urgent problems of urbanization, there was no demand for an autonomous administrative staff. Only in the late 1940s were steps taken to develop the local bureaucracy. An Englishman, C. Martin, was the first town clerk of Lagos, serving from the mid-1940s to 1949. His assistant was M. A. Sho-Silva, a Nigerian who joined the council's staff in 1913 as a third-class clerk earning £18 a year and had, thirty-three years later, worked up to the position of deputy town clerk at a salary of £730 a year. Upon Martin's retirement, Sho-Silva was appointed acting town clerk and was slated to take Martin's place. At that point, however, the introduction of representative government politicized the council and with it, the municipal administration. Sho-Silva was unceremoniously forced into retirement,[27] and the post was offered instead to Adeleke Adedoyin, an Ijebu barrister who was then also an NCNC councilor and a member of the Western Region House of Assembly. Adedoyin's nomination as town clerk was part of an NCNC plan to get Nnamdi Azikiwe into the central legislature (see chap. 5). According to the electoral college system operating at the time, the Western Region legislature was to elect two of its five Lagos delegates in the regional assembly to the federal House of Representatives. The plan was that Azikiwe, having been turned down on the first ballot, would replace Adedoyin when a suitable position could be found for the latter. But the Action Group blocked the move with the aid of D. M. O. Akinbiyi, the assistant town clerk, who coveted the post of town clerk himself. Akinbiyi provided the Western Region government, which had to confirm the appointment, with evidence showing that the post had not been properly advertised, that the candidate Adedoyin had not been properly interviewed, and that his qualifications had not been taken into consideration. Akinbiyi was rewarded in 1953 when the Action Group gained control of both the council and the regional government; he became, at the age of twenty-nine and with only one year's experience, the first African town clerk of Lagos.[28]

Shortly thereafter Akinbiyi came under serious criticism for his tendency to centralize all administrative responsibilities in his own hands. At the demand of the LTC Workers' Union, a commission was appointed by the federal government to inquire into the council's staff relations. While noting that Akinbiyi was an able officer, the commission's *Dosunmu-Stapleton Report* condemned him for "reluctance to delegate his authority," warning that "relations with his Heads of Departments and senior officers have deteriorated to a degree that is already reducing the efficiency of the organization and could, if not checked, end in its breakdown."[29] When the NCNC came to power in 1959, Akinbiyi was further blamed for malpractices in the collection of market women's fees during the AG's administration (see chap. 8). Akinbiyi's powers were then slowly whittled away. In 1959 the federal government reassigned the town clerk's duties as chief returning officer to the permanent secretary of the federal Ministry of Lagos Affairs. Check-signing powers and the authority to approve building plans were also taken away from the town clerk on the ground that his participation caused too much delay. Finally, Akinbiyi was dismissed from office for inefficiency and disloyalty, and S. J. Mayaki, a Mid-Westerner backed by the NCNC, was confirmed in his place in 1961. The electoral duties that had been taken away from Akinbiyi were restored to Mayaki.

Predictably, the new town clerk faced the opposition of the Action Group when it returned to power in 1962. A tribunal of inquiry appointed in 1966 found that Mayaki had abused the privileges of his office during his tenure and had been guilty of favoritism, mismanagement, dishonesty, and incompetence.[30] Dismissed by the federal government in 1967, he was succeeded by Alhaji H. A. B. Fasinro, the former deputy town clerk and the first Lagos Muslim to become chief administrative officer in the municipal beauraucracy.

Fasinro's appointment was bitterly contested. In fact, his closeness to the top of the administrative hierarchy had created resentment long before the post of town clerk had become vacant. Mayaki had bypassed Fasinro whenever possible in favor of the senior assistant town clerk, S. D. A. Ogunbiyi, a Western Region Yoruba who was also in line for appointment as town clerk. Michael Ani, former permanent secretary of the federal Ministry of Establishments, after investigating the council's administrative organization, proposed that the office of town clerk be split into two divisions; he recommended that the town clerk should be a person with administrative experience, not a legal practitioner. This recommendation was widely interpreted by Lagos Muslims as an attempt by nonindigenous elements to prevent Fasinro's appointment.[31] In fact, the proposal favored Ogunbiyi, who had poorer legal qualifications, over Fasinro. Accordingly, Ogunbiyi issued false statements to the press announcing that the proposed reorganization was already under way, and he actively lobbied for the amendment. Finally, after the creation of Lagos State, Fasinro was confirmed as town clerk and plans to reorganize the bureaucracy were shelved.

Despite party politics and ingroup fighting over bureaucratic jobs, the local civil service kept pace fairly well with the rate of urbanization. In 1944 the council had a permanent establishment of 358 and a daily-paid staff (laborers, carpenters, mechanics, etc.) of 3,000;[32] by 1966 it had a permanent establishment of 2,354 and a daily-paid staff of 3,537, the largest number of daily-paid employees on the payroll of any institution in the nation.[33] In 1941 only two trade unions, the LTC Workers' Union and the LTC African Staff Union, dealt with municipal labor problems. By 1967 there were five recognized unions: Municipal and Local Authorities Workers' Union, Nigerian Motor Drivers' Union, Lagos City Personnel and Staff Union, Association of LCC Senior Service Officers, and Nigerian Union of Nurses.

Staff appointments and promotions were regulated by different authorities, depending upon the grade of employment. All senior positions with annual salaries of £900 or more ( £800 before 1964) required the prior approval of the minister of Lagos affairs. This function has now been transferred to the Lagos State government.[34] Intermediate grade appointments are most susceptible to political influence, since the council controls recruitment at that level. There has been no independent service agency as existed, for example, in the former Western, Mid-Western, and Eastern Regions. In 1959 Sir John Imrie suggested that one be created, and a municipal service commission was authorized by the 1963 Lagos Local Government (Amendment) Act. But it never was established because of the stiff resistance of the council. A council subcommittee argued that such a commission would not be insulated from party politics as intended because its recommendations would have to be approved by the chairman, that it would cause considerable delay, and that it would require unnecessary expenditures.[35] The real reason for the council's resistance, however, was its disinclination to surrender a primary instrument of influence. To elected councilors, staff recruitment is a source of party patronage; to professional administrators, it is a guarantee of administrative autonomy.[36] Nevertheless, in 1968, the Lagos State government indicated its intention of establishing a service commission with powers to appoint, promote, and discipline senior staff in all local government councils in the state.[37]

The performance record of the municipal staff is mixed. After making his study, Michael Ani concluded that the local bureaucracy lacked direction, purpose, and principles as "a result of abject ignorance of the council's regulations and . . . the effect of totally subordinating the personnel department to the Town Clerk's Office."[38] On the other hand, earlier reports noted that the administrative staff provided the city with adequate social services and initiated many new programs under difficult circumstances.[39] Indeed, administrators were the primary source of inspiration for community development projects, while councilors, aware of the risks involved in unpopular schemes, tended to be conservative. Staff initiative has been particularly noticeable in the short period of council operation under a military regime. Heads of departments have been conscientious and zealous administrators, filling the vacuum created by the absence of elected councilors.

OTHER GOVERNMENTAL AGENCIES

## Lagos Executive Development Board

The growth of a number of local administrative organizations, arising in response to specific needs, has made Lagos a battlefield of competing institutions, each jealous of the others' privileges and prerogatives. The results have been fragmentation of authority, competition for scarce resources, duplication of efforts, and opportunities for the exercise of undue political influence. Probably the most powerful of these auxiliary bodies was the Lagos Executive Development Board, a federal statutory organization formed in 1928 after the bubonic plague caused an alarming number of deaths. (In 1972 the LEDB was combined with two other planning authorities in neighboring districts to form the Lagos State Development and Property Corporation.) Intended as a temporary authority to clear slums and improve housing conditions, the LEDB started with an initial grant of £200,000 ($560,000). Soon after its inauguration, the question of "overlapping [functions] of the LEDB and the Town Council"[40] was raised by the administrator of the colony, who suggested merger of the two bodies. The LEDB, he was told, was conceived of as a planning authority like those in India and Malaya, where "the principle is accepted that the municipal body is not . . . a suitable organization for controlling the development . . . of a town, especially so where the expenditure of government grants is involved."[41] The proposal for merger was denied and the board continued as an independent body.

At first the LEDB was run by a secretary, a town planning officer, and a city engineer, aided by a dozen clerical and technical workers. In 1936 the president of the LTC was made an ex officio member. In 1944 the commissioner of lands was made chairman, and a deputy financial secretary, a deputy director of health services, and one representative from the LTC were added. The early achievments of the board, which included clearing some of the most congested areas in the Idumagbo area of Lagos Island, were popular and effective. Unlike later slum clearance schemes, which ran into substantial local opposition because of exorbitant rates charged for repurchase of plots, the LEDB permitted owners to buy back cleared land at 80 percent of its original value. By increasing the value of land and bearing the costs of development, the LEDB "was looked upon as the layer of the golden egg."[42] By 1946, 54 acres of slums had been cleared at a cost of £740 ($2,000) an acre.[43] The total cost of land purchases, compensation for buildings, and engineering works was £167, 651 ($468,000).

The board gradually came under a great deal of criticism by higher authorities for its unprofitability, its failure to coordinate with the LTC, and its ambivalent status as a quasi-local government institution. The *Hoskyns-Abrahall Report* (1946), reviewing plans for the future development of Greater Lagos, emphasized that the LEDB should eventually be absorbed into the LTC, particularly after the council became a fully representative body. Not only would it be politically inadvisable to split important local government functions between two authorities, it was argued, but the merger of the two would engender more civic spirit. If the merger occurred, LEDB land would not be the property of the Crown but of the municipality. "The ownership of the land by the municipality is in fact far nearer traditional Yoruba land tenure— the family head holding the land on behalf of the family—than any individual freehold ownership could be."[44]

These arguments went unheeded by colonial authorities as the two institutions continued to grow in stature. In 1949 their ambiguous relationship was again questioned with regard to the ability of one to countermand the decisions of the other. The town engineer clarified the functional specializations of the board and the council. It was the board's responsibility, he asserted, to see that proposed construction did not clash with town planning schemes and was suitable for its site, while the LTC was to see that the buildings complied with municipal bylaws. "It meant in effect that the LEDB dealt with sites and the LTC with the structures . . . and Council's approval must be obtained before the building began."[45]

When a representative council was elected in 1950, agitation for closer links between the two organizations resumed, but the government was unresponsive to suggestions of increased councilor representation on the board, although the town engineer, the medical officer, and the municipal treasurer were invited to serve on appropriate board committees. In response to the council's argument that it was always intended that the LTC should take over the LEDB, the governor replied that he agreed in principle, but added that the "time was not yet ripe."[46] Meanwhile, the LEDB was embarking upon its most ambitious and controversial project, the Central Lagos Slum Clearance Scheme (see chap. 4). Responding to protests from the electorate, the LTC vigorously opposed the scheme, arguing that it should be carried out only after consultation with the people through their elected representatives.[47] The LTC found itself powerless to effect any change in policy, and from that time onward clashes between these parallel agencies became a recurring feature of the administrative process in Lagos.

In its latter-day form the LEDB functioned in opposition to many of its original objectives. Although theoretically delegated with the responsibility for town planning, it illustrated more than any other local institution the anomalies of unplanned growth; incorporated as an interim agency with limited functions, it became an ostensibly permanent structure with sweeping powers; conceived as an urban renewal body to serve the public, it evolved into an instrument serving higher authorities. Both in form and in function, the LEDB little resembled in the sixties the unobtrusive slum clearance agency it was meant to be when it was formed four decades earlier.

The most recent enabling law under which the board operated was the Lagos Town Planning Act of 1958, which superseded the 1928 legislation creating the board.[48] As defined by the 1958 law, the LEDB's powers included zoning, demolition, rehousing, redistribution of property (private or public, buildings or roads), payment of compensation, and compulsory acquisition and disposal (through lease or sale) of land. The LEDB also had the power, though it had never been exercised, to demand that the council raise revenues for town planning.[49] The board had a minimum of ten members—senior medical officer, city engineer harbor master, town clerk, two city councilors (nominated by the LCC), one person nominated by the Lagos Chamber of Commerce, and three members appointed by the Lagos State government (previously by the federal minister of Lagos affairs)— plus any additional persons appointed by the Lagos State government at its own discretion. The Lagos State government was given unlimited power, formerly exercised by the federal government, to reduce or augment the size of the board, including the power to appoint the chairman and deputy chairman. In 1965 the board's membership numbered seventeen persons, including eight ex officio members.

No master plan has ever guided the LEDB's operations. Projects have been formulated and executed piecemeal, usually without the participation of the LCC.[50] The extent of the board's operations may be seen in the proposed capital expenditures for the 1962–1968 development plan: a staggering £15 million, about four times the budget of the LCC. Two-thirds of this money was to be derived from the board's own resources. Recurrent annual expenditures of the LEDB on social services amounted to £60,000 or £70,000 ($168,000 or $196,000).

The internal structure of the LEDB gave an extraordinary degree of power to the office of chairman. For the first eight years after independence, the chairman was Sir Kofo Abayomi, a physician who was former president of the Nigerian Youth Movement, a former member of the Legislative Council, and head of the LTC caretaker committee appointed in 1953. Altogether, Abayomi served on the board for a total of twenty years. As chairman he was the source of all institutional authority: "Sir Kofo was the LEDB and the LEDB was Sir Kofo."[51] Only he and two other members were needed for a quorum; all plans had to receive his personal approval; only he could authorize evictions or issue notices requiring individuals to forfeit property; only he could call meetings. Although not authorized to do so, he handpicked all chairmen of the LEDB's comittees. With unlimited tenure, wide powers, and the "personal magnetic ego"[52] he attributed to himself, Sir Kofo, checked only by the Ministry of Lagos Affairs, ran the LEDB as a private fiefdom.[53]

Other officers of the board, except for ex officio members, were usually appointees of the federal government. As seen by indigenous Lagosians, the composition of the board was symbolic of the intrusion of higher authorities into the internal affairs of the city. Chief Gilbert B. A. Akinyede, former board member and counsel for the Association of Land Owners and Residents of Central Lagos, vividly revealed the depth of this feeling in testimony before the Sagoe Tribunal, which provides insight into the relationship between local government institutions and socioeconomic tensions in the city:

> It will be seen that the Constitution of the Board is very elastic and the Minister has, in the past, used the powers vested in him to appoint additional members or vary the constitution of the Board. Immediately before Independence the powers were used so well that several distinguished and very enlightened and articulate members of the community were appointed to the Board and these elites adorned the Board for about four years. . . . most of these members came on the Action Group ticket. Later, . . . members of [the] NCNC were appointed into the Board and the standard was still high. The standard fell however when practically all these men were sacked and replaced with more humble members of the community. . . .
>
> The reason for the poor standard of members was due to the fact that the Nigerian Peoples' Congress decided to fill the vacancies, created by the sack of the eminent members, with their supporters in Lagos and they had very poor material to choose from. Therefore, barring the exception of the Chairman, Sir Kofo Abayomi, and one or two others, the Board and its members were more objects of pity and contempt than of admiration or of honor in and outside the Board's offices. It was a great relief, therefore, to all who had the interest of a well planned and better developed Lagos at heart to see the motley crowd that answered the name LEDB, towards the end of the First Republic, swept away following the fateful events of the 16th day of January, 1966.[54]

The local resentments caused by the narrow composition of the board were compounded by administrative defects. The artificial division of authority between the LEDB and the LCC repeatedly caused inaction, inconvenience, or loss of property or income by landlords and real estate investors. For example, the board made decisions regarding zoning, but the council actually approved the building plans of private developers and the plans to acquire and develop public land. The board often designated an area as a public space when the council lacked sufficient funds for development. In such instances, plots lay undeveloped while the owners were deprived of the use of their property, possibly for years. To eliminate such wastefulness, the board decided in the late 1950s that owners could, on their own initiative, reclaim property not acquired by the LTC within three years of its acquisition for development. In the meantime, of course, the property owner would not have been compensated and would also have to bear the legal expenses necessary to get the plot rezoned. Owing to poor planning, the LEDB sometimes invested capital to purchase plots, only to discover afterward that it lacked reserve capital for development. On occasion, compensation was not paid on properties that had been transferred to the LEDB more than six years earlier.[55] There was no legal requirement that the board had to compensate owners within a certain period of time, although it was free to acquire property compulsorily at notice.

The Lagos City Council bore the brunt of public criticism for this confused state of affairs. Misallocation of plots and favoritism in the award of housing contracts (see discussion of the Central Lagos Slum Clearance Scheme in chap. 4) caused deep public grievances, especially among indigenes who suffered most from LEDB property acquisition. Since most of the members appointed to the board by the federal government in the past were NCNC or NPC supporters, the indigenes had little opportunity to influence LEDB policies. Frustrated and embittered, they blamed their councilors for inadequate representation of their interests. In this sense, then, the early warnings of some of the colonial authorities that the division between the LEDB and the council would be unworkable were vindicated, for the two institutions came to function as rival bodies, responsible to different authorities and representing entirely different interests.

## Lagos City Transport Service

The Lagos City Transport Service (formerly the Lagos Municipal Transport Service) is a quasi-autonomous division of the council having no separate legal status. It was established in 1958 when the council bought the assets of J. & A. Zarpas for half a million pounds ($1.5 million approximately). In 1964 a management board with six members, five of them from the LCC and one an experienced businessman, was appointed by the federal government. Three ex officio members—town clerk, city treasurer, and general manager—were also named. Between 1958 and 1964 the transit service operated essentially as a committee of the council; since 1964 it has functioned as a commercial enterprise accountable to the council.

The administrative difficulties of the LCTS stem primarily from the problems inherent in municipalization of a private concern. The new agency had to restructure a family business into a large-scale, government-owned organization. Large overheads, stiff competition, labor problems, and management difficulties have plagued the service since it started and profit margins have been dwindling yearly. Probably its severest handicap is the competition from four or five private bus lines and a variety of independent commercial vehicles, such as unmetered taxis, mammy wagons, vans, truck or lorries, and minibuses. Hundreds of these vehicles ply the city streets without permits or with licenses issued for suburban routes only. The LCTS has always intended to enlarge its fleet so that it could buy out competitors, prohibit "pirate" transporters, and function as a monopoly in the manner of other public utilities. But population has grown faster than the ability of the LCTS to expand. It is estimated that illegal operators provide at least half of the urban passenger transport. The quasi-commercial and quasi-governmental status of LCTS tends to limit its effectiveness. For the LCC, the LCTS is a key source of revenue since it contributes at least £100,000 annually. Unlike the LEDB, which competes with the council, the LCTS is a subsidiary totally controlled by the local government.

## Lagos Education Committee

The provision of school facilities in Lagos was originally based on the traditional British concept of private education for the privileged few who could afford it. Consequently a superior but very small educated elite was created in conformity with the British pattern. Only in the past two decades has mass public education been accepted as an objective. The introduction of free primary education in Lagos in 1957 caused school attendance to soar; it jumped from 38,072 in 1956 to 63,064 in 1958. By the late 1960s more than 113,000, or 90 percent, of eligible children of school age in Lagos were enrolled in 126 elementary schools run by individual proprietors, missionaries, or municipal authorities.

The chief executive agency supervising these schools is the Lagos Education Committee, appointed and controlled by the federal government until 1967 when the Lagos State government took over the responsibility. In 1957 the LTC had officially been designated the local education authority. Before the creation of states, however, the federal government provided up to 70 percent of the funds for education in the city. For all practical purposes, therefore, the LEC has operated as a committee of the federal (or, more recently, the state) Ministry of Education. It is the supreme educational authority in Lagos. Of its fifteen members, eight represent the council and seven represent various missionary bodies–the Roman Catholic Mission, the Christian Council of Nigeria, the Council of Muslim School Proprietors—and the Nigerian Union of Teachers. The LEC functions through two specialized subcommittees: the Tenders Subcommittee, which oversees expenditures for school supplies, and the Establishment of New Schools and Discipline of Teachers Subcommittee, which is primarily concerned with staff and management matters. The LEC has complete decision-making power over elementary schools and may dictate curricula, school calendars, and standards for recruitment of teachers. Even the council handles the five municipal schools through the LEC. This arrangement has been criticized on the grounds that it compromises the council's delegated powers and causes unnecessary complications. In the past the federal government appointed members to the LEC after each municipal election and appropriated the funds necessary for the council to maintain its schools. Moreover, the chief education officer of the council has acted more or less as an agent of the federal or state government to which he is responsible, rather than as an official of the council. The LEC therefore shares many of the problems of the LEDB, but it is a more representative body because the majority of its membership is drawn from the council.

## Health Services

Public health has also encountered serious difficulties in keeping pace with urbanization. Rising demands for services are compounded by the absence of a coordinating agency to integrate the activities of the federal government and the LCC. Three bodies provide health facilities in Lagos: (1) the federal Ministry of Health offers in- and outpatient hospitals and dispensaries, laboratory and X-ray facilities, and special services such as port health and malaria and tuberculosis treatment; (2) the Lagos City Council provides health services for care and child welfare, is responsible for environmental sanitation, including roads, open spaces, markets, abattoirs, food inspection, and so on, and sponsors health education through locally elected ward health associations; and (3) the federal Ministry of Labour runs family welfare services, youth councils, and juvenile reform homes. Some of the services provided by the federal government have been transferred to the Lagos State Ministry of Health. Since each institutional division operates in its own watertight compartment, there is considerable overlapping of functions in some areas and, in others, serious deficiencies. A bill to create a comprehensive Lagos health service council was proposed in 1963. This council would have provided health services in the same way the Lagos Education Committee provides educational services. The measure was unacceptable to the council, however, because only two of the eighteen members would have been councilors and because the federal government would have been able to requisition any of the council's property, staff, or equipment for public health purposes. The bill was eventually withdrawn.

As a consequence, although Lagos does have the best medical services in Nigeria, by international standards urban health conditions are still appallingly poor. Infant mortality in 1965 was 42.6 percent of total live births, and 20.1 percent of all babies delivered were stillborn.[56] In 1960, 54.5 percent of all deaths in the city occurred among youngsters aged five or under.[57] Poor housing, overcrowding, and inadequate sewage are the root causes of diseases that take the largest proportion of young lives. Environmental controls would make headway against the five leading killers: pneumonia, bronchitis, malaria, dysentery, and diarrhea.[58] Until more funds and better organization are forthcoming, the situation is unlikely to improve. In fact, at the present rate of urbanization, health facilities may be so overtaxed that standards could decline. In densely populated wards, such as A and B, where health conditions are poorest, there are no environmental control units operating at all. The five child welfare clinics run by the council deal with only 40 percent of the infants in the city.[59]

Political competition has thus far precluded effective reorganization of health administration, and responsibility is still shared by the council and higher government authorities. In 1962 Dr. O. Adeniji-Jones, medical health officer, said he had long "argued and planned for the gradual expansion of Council's Health Services in keeping with the proposed increase in status of the Council. It is with regret that I am forced to realize that the provisions of the Constitution and the existing political climate which has insisted on the perpetuation of a Ministry for Lagos Affairs, precludes the realization of any such development."[60]

### ROLE OF THE FEDERAL GOVERNMENT

As the seat of the central government, Lagos has been subject to strong control by higher authorities ever since the territory was first colonized by the British. Lagos was selected as the capital for obvious reasons: its excellent harbor facilitated trade and communications; it was a prosperous community well situated to provide access to the interior; and it had an educated elite which collaborated with the British in the colonial bureaucracy. Yet, despite these advantages, Nigeria's first governor, Sir Frederick Lugard, did not want to keep Lagos as the capital indefinitely. He detested the town, which he regarded as the unreal Africa, and deplored the problems it created for his administration.[61]

Lugard intended to move the capital to Kaduna, some 550 miles away, when the Northern and Southern Provinces were amalgamated; to place Lagos under the administration of the Southern Provinces; and to shift the southern headquarters from Lagos to Yaba, a mainland suburb about 4 miles from the island but now fully integrated into the municipality.[62] The Colonial Office rejected the first proposal because of practical difficulties. Of Lugard's other attempts to reduce the status of Lagos, only the second was partly fulfilled. The lieutenant governor of the Southern Provinces assumed the duties of administrator of the colony, as Lugard had wished, from 1916 to 1927, but the change was little more than a reshuffling of titles.

The question of the status of Lagos recurred several times thereafter, particularly in the constitutional conferences of the 1950s, but by then Lagos had grown into a thriving commercial center, a political nucleus of African nationalism, and an economic lifeline. Expatriate firms and the colonial government had made heavy investments in Lagos, and to shift the capital at that point would have entailed substantial financial losses and political risks. As a result, the issue turned not on the question of whether Lagos should remain the capital, but rather on what the intergovernmental policies should be for a capital city of this type (for political implications, see chap. 9).

During the early colonial period the relationship between local and central authorities was determined by direct rule, a policy that, as defined by C. L. Temple, lieutenant governor of the Northern Provinces, "places the government of the country entirely in the hands of European officials, minor posts only, such as clerkships, being filled by natives, while the policing of the country is entrusted to European officers, with coloured subordinates in Government employ wearing Government uniforms. This system necessarily entails . . . replacing the Native Leader by the European official, with his native staff."[63] In practice, the policy was only partly applied in Lagos, for the African elite was encouraged to occupy significant administrative posts at levels much higher than clerkships. Direct rule was not aimed at excluding all Africans from the administrative machinery, but simply at excluding natural rulers from political responsibility. In fact, direct rule in Lagos was, both in theory and in practice, much like the policy of direct rule adopted in French West Africa, which encouraged the emergence of a westernized African elite as intermediary rulers.[64] As in the French territories, the precedent of centralization established by this policy in Lagos influenced the evolution of political institutions long after the achievement of self-government.

The administrator of the colony was the key man in the town's colonial structure: he was ex officio chairman of the LTC, the chief tax collector, and the supreme authority on land matters. Because he was "the link between [the Council] . . . and the Central Government,"[65] he had to assume, as one observer put it, "a somewhat Jekyll-and-Hyde personality."[66] Major services— water, electricity, police, fire protection, the judiciary—were wholly administered by the government, while health and medical services were partly subsidized and administered from the center. The department heads in the municipal bureaucracy were all officers in government service. Little wonder that the council was regarded essentially as a colonial institution that failed to inspire political interest or civic pride.

After the introduction of a fully representative council in 1950, the powers delegated to higher authorities continued to follow the earlier pattern of tight centralization. The specific role of higher authorities with respect to an elected council was not defined until the Lagos Local Government Law of 1953 was passed. The regional authority, then acting as the superior authority, was given the prerogative to hold inquiries, appoint local government inspectors, ratify senior appointments, disapprove budgetary expenditures, prevent the council from levying rates, review bylaws, regulate the acquisition and disposal of land, and dissolve the council if it failed to discharge its functions properly. After Lagos was separated from the Western Region and made a federal territory, all these powers were transferred to the federal government. The Constitutional Conference of 1957 decided that they would be exercised through the new Ministry of Lagos Affairs, which was part of the Ministry of Mines and Power from 1957 until 1959. Oba Adele quaintly described Lagos at this time as an "orphan child [who] has now gained a father."[67]

The Ministry of Lagos Affairs had four divisions. The Administrative Division assumed responsibility for the council, the LEDB, and the Nigerian Building Society,[68] for the allocation of government houses, and for other general matters; the Land Division dealt with all state lands in the federal territory; the Registry Division controlled registration of titles to land in Lagos;[69] and the Valuation Division evaluated property for rate assessment. It is worthy of note that all divisions, in one way or another, had something to do with land, three of them exclusively.

In August 1963 a bill was passed empowering the minister of Lagos affairs to give directives to the council when necessary. By then, party cleavages had strained relations between the ministry and the council. This measure made them worse and further dampened the council's initiative. "Alhaji Masha and Alhaji Dawodu both admitted . . . that this constant fear that the Council would be dissolved [by the federal government] acted as a strong deterrent against any outward bids by the Council to assert an independence"[70] that might bring punitive action. In February 1966, after the first military coup d'etat, the Ministry of Lagos Affairs was dissolved and its powers were divided between two other federal ministries. Municipal matters went to the Ministry of Internal Affairs, while responsibility for the LEDB, town planning, and land tenure was handed to the Ministry of Works and Housing. When Lagos State was created in 1967, it was given responsibility for all local government councils in its territory. Although complete formal arrangements had not yet been worked out at the time of this writing, it is likely that the Lagos State government will inherit many of the powers previously exercised by the federal government; it had already begun to supervise health and education. Whatever powers are delegated to the state government, however, as long as Lagos remains the federal capital it will inevitably be subject in some degree to control by federal authorities.[71]

LOCAL GOVERNMENT FINANCE

However much autonomy may be formally granted to the municipal council, its dependency status is ultimately tied to the "power of the purse." When first inaugurated the Town Council was heavily subsidized by grants-in-aid, which varied according to annual requirements. In 1917 the LTC's public revenue amounted to £43,310, more than half of it coming from the central government.[72] In 1929 the subsidy reached a peak of £62,500. In successive years, however, the grants were reduced in an effort to economize until they were set at a fixed sum of £20,000 in 1936. The balance was made up from the council's own revenues, mostly from property rates. The net effect of the reductions was to restrict municipal spending; the amount disbursed by the LTC in 1929 was about £120,000, as compared with approximately £80,000 in 1935. During these years the council was also required to refund any unused surplus to the federal government, a measure that forced it to live solely off its capital. Finally, in 1938, the system of fluctuating grants-in-aid was abandoned in favor of a more stable arrangement; the government then agreed to pay a fixed sum in lieu of rates on government-occupied buildings, plus a 50 percent contribution toward the costs of providing health services and a 60 percent contribution toward the costs of maintaining trunk roads.

Despite heavy reliance on government support, twenty-five years after the council was established it had acquired fixed assets of some value, including roads, pumping stations, markets, abattoirs, offices, staff quarters, cemeteries, and vehicles. Some of these items were provided at government expense, while others were turned over to the council for maintenance; the LTC purchased some properties out of its own funds or through loans, while land was procured from crown grants transferred to the council with the permission of the commissioner of lands. In 1941 the council was empowered to levy rates.[73] Even so, it still needed substantial support from the central government.

Municipal expenditures rose sharply when postwar immigration swelled the city's population. In 1950 the budget was approximately £350,000; by 1958 it had reached £1,098,000. New responsibilities were steadily being turned over to the council, yet there was little improvement in its financial situation. Not until 1958 was a comprehensive review of the financial relationship between the federal government and the council commissioned. The *Imrie Report* recommended that existing arrangements be supplemented by additional government contributions on a percentage of cost basis for each new service transferred to the council (the system used in the United Kingdom). The increments consisted of a contribution of 70 percent toward the cost of primary education and a revised scale of contributions ranging from 50 percent to 100 percent toward the cost of road maintenance. By 1959 government payments in lieu of rates amounted to about £175,000 a year.

When the Ministry of Lagos Affairs was created in 1957 it was given, among other things, power to supervise local government expenditures. Estimates could be altered by the ministry; if there was a delay in approval of the budget, the council was permitted to make expenditures only for recurrent items that had been approved the year before. Ordinarily, estimates were circulated to the ministries of Education, Works and Housing, Health, and Finance before they were sent to the Ministry of Lagos Affairs for confirmation. Whereas during early colonial years the council's funds had been subject to control by only one central authority, now they were scrutinized by an array of federal departments; as a result, bureaucratic delay and political backbiting hampered the budgetary process.

Municipal expenditures skyrocketed after independence. Intent on improving the condition of the capital city, as befitted its status, the federal government expressed growing impatience with the council's inability to keep pace with urban needs. On the other side, F. C. O. Coker, former city treasurer, reported to the Saville Tribunal that the federal government "definitely slowed down the growth of services by refusing to pay grants due in accordance with the [1959] Ordinance and by refusing to allow an increase in rate poundage whilst at the same time failing to undertake the statutory [property] revaluations which would expand the basis upon which the Council raises revenue."[74] In the decade 1957–1967, municipal expenditures far outstripped revenues. The amount spent in 1966–67 ( £4,996,620) was approximately five times larger than the amount spent in 1957–58 (£911,000) and double that spent in 1964 ( £2,091,100). The federal government refused to allow rates to be raised commensurately. In 1957–58 more than 70 percent of the council's expenses were met from rates, whereas in 1966–67 that source of income accounted for only about 40 percent of revenue. Government contributions did not make up the shortfall. Payments in lieu of rates were fixed at the 1961 level, even though the number of government buildings, embassies, and diplomatic residences had increased considerably. In addition, the percentages of service grants were cut in 1964 when the government realized that it had not allowed adequate funds for these outlays in its estimates. Since contributions of the federal government were not mandatory, the council had no authority to contest the government's decision to withhold revenues. As of March 31, 1966, therefore, the federal government owed the Lagos City Council more than three-quarters of a million pounds ($1,500,000).[75]

Basically, the financial system of the LCC has not changed since 1959. Property rates account for about 45 percent, and government contributions for about 40 percent, of total revenues. The council has increasingly turned for supplementary funds to its income-earning assets, particularly the LCTS, which contributes at least £100,000 annually from profits, and markets, which yield about the same amount. Rate income increased substantially after 1960, but rate arrears have increased even faster. Formidable administrative problems, created by the constant change in the number and composition of buildings, a highly mobile population, and a shortage of qualified staff, complicate tax collection in Lagos.

In the wake of the civil war and the creation of states, whose financial needs will most certainly have priority in government estimates, it is unlikely that government contributions for urban expenses will be substantially increased. The council will therefore either have to bleed its own income-earning assets even more, raise the rates, or retrench its services just at the time when the needs of urban areas are reaching a new high.

# PART III

*Studies in Influence*

CHAPTER 7

*Chieftancy: The Erosion of Influence*


In the period 1917–1967 urban political change moved progressively toward democratization and localization, with political influence passing steadily from national or external interests to resident groups. The chief beneficiaries of these reforms in modern times were the Lagos indigenes, an underprivileged group of slum dwellers having less education, wealth, and prestige than competing groups. On the sheer strength of communal nationalism, the Lagosians gradually rose to power at the peak years of urban development, becoming the pivotal group in control of the majority party and the local council after Nigeria gained independence.

In Part III of this study these developments are further explored through three case studies concerning, respectively, an institution, an interest group, and an issue, all of them deemed to be of continuing importance to the community. As indicated earlier, the criterion of enduring significance was determined in each instance by the recurrence of controversy or by the judgment of community or party leaders as confirmed by public records and evaluations by leading citizens. A second factor that guided selection was type of influence: chieftaincy illustrates the erosion of influence, market women exhibit what is here termed unassertive influence, while the constitutional status of Lagos demonstrates the interaction beween internal and external influences. The final consideration was the importance of the subjects to the interests of the Lagos indigenes. Though consistently gaining in power, Lagosians had varying degrees of success in achieving their goals on particular issues, depending upon time and circumstance. In the discussion on land, for example, it is shown (see chap. 4) that during the fifties indigenes were virtually powerless against the encroachment of higher government authorities. Yet ten years later, as recounted in the section dealing with the office of town clerk, the indigenes were victorious in capturing a post considered to be of special importance in the administration of local affairs. The three case studies examined in Part III probe deeper into the complexities of urban politics, showing the decline of traditional chieftaincy in a modernizing community, the erratic influence of the potentially powerful market women, and the triumph of the indigenes in their struggle against external forces for political autonomy. Together they reveal political transformations in Lagos by analyzing major trends through specific studies of influence.

The first case study concerns a political institution that has undergone profound change over the past few decades. While attachment to traditional authorities in the capital still exists among indigenous Lagosians who regard loyalty to chiefs as part of their allegiance to their town of origin, the influence of traditional authorities has eroded considerably with the imposition of colonial rule, the emergence of new forms of economic activity, and the introduction of representative government. As local notables, chiefs still enjoy a large measure of status and prestige, and they are occasionally important in intracommunal politics, particularly when the question of royal succession arises or when parties seek their endorsement for local elections. But compared with the position they once claimed, Lagos chiefs are mere shadows of their former selves, remnants of an ancient kingdom that now functions principally as a source of cultural pride and communal patriotism for traditional elements.

## CHIEFS IN TRADITIONAL SOCIETY

Of all the Yoruba kingdoms, Lagos has always been the most remote from the mainstream of traditional Yoruba culture. Lagosians consider themselves to have a unique legendary origin, a distinct corporate identity, and a separate development, all of which are reflected in the evolution of the institution of chieftaincy. The first formal chieftaincy position in the town was created in the seventeenth century by the oba of Benin in gratitude to an Awori warrior named Ashipa, who had brought home the body of the oba's son, a war captain killed in battle while conquering the area in and around Lagos.[1] Ashipa was given the title of Oloriogun or head war chief of Lagos, a status symbolized by the bestowal of an *abere* sword and a *gbedu* drum used only by hereditary rulers. Although Ashipa never assumed the title of oba or king himself, all his successors have been accorded that honor.

The first ruler properly installed as oba of Lagos was Ashipa's son, Ado, who continued to serve as emissary of Benin. Ado exacted tribute for his overlord from the island of Iddo, across from Isale Eko where the Olofin, the original founder of Lagos, resided with his followers. Ado's successor, Gabaro, merged the two settlements and set up his capital at Idungaran, the Olofin's meeting place which thereafter became the oba's residence and administrative headquarters.

It was during the reign of Gabaro (c. 1666–1704) that the first class of subsidiary chiefs is said to have been officially created.[2] In deference to the Olofin who had earlier divided Lagos land among his sons, Gabaro established the order of Idejo or landowning chiefs. Under Ologun-Kutere (c. 1749–1775), the fourth oba of Lagos, other classes of functionally specialized chieftaincies were created: the Akarigbere chiefs (kingmakers), drawn from the delegation of Bini officials stationed in Lagos; the Ogalede chiefs (diviners or priests); and the Abagbon chiefs (warriors).[3] These authorities collectively constituted the king's court or Council of State. The most important members served on the Ilu Committee, an inner circle of advisers, or chief ministers, constituting the oba's "cabinet." As in other Yoruba chiefdoms, the oba was expected to consult with these and other community leaders in governing the town.

By the late eighteenth century Lagos began to throw off Benin suzerainty. Ologun-Kutere was the last oba to be buried at Benin and Idewu Ojulari (c. 1819–1834) was the last to pay tribute to to Benin. Until the imposition of British rule, however, Lagos chiefs continued to be crowned at Benin in ritual observance of their historical connections. But as Lagos became more autonomous, traditional authorities became less able to depend upon the use, or the threat of the use, of external force to secure their tenure of office. Competition for the stool correspondingly intensified, particularly after increased trade added further economic incentives for political domination. By the first half of the nineteenth century, chieftaincy was coveted by dynastic factions anxious to profit from the resources that naturally accrued to the ruling strata.

The slave trade profoundly affected both the foreign and the domestic influence of the Lagos chiefs. Oba Akinshemoyin (c. 1704–1749) first invited the Portuguese to Lagos and laid the foundations for a flourishing trade; Lagosians received valuable goods such as guns, ammunition, tobacco, and spirits in exchange for slaves passing through their harbor. Thereafter, the ruling houses maintained a virtual monopoly, with slavers receiving handsome royalties, customs, and valuable gifts which made them the object of widespread envy and esteem.[4] Their sphere of political influence with neighboring communities expanded considerably, particularly in the Egba and Ijebu areas contiguous to Lagos and in weaker settlements, such as Badagry, which gradually came to pay homage to Lagos and to depend upon Lagosians for defense. The degree of influence and wealth accumulated by the oba of Lagos was apparent by the time of the reign of Olugun-Kutere, who sent the king of Dahomey a hundred slaves, a hundred kegs of gunpowder, a hundred pieces of cloth, a hundred bags of cowries, a hundred demijohns of rum, and a hundred rolls of tobacco to dissuade him from attacking Badagry.[5] For continued access to this kind of wealth, the oba and his ruling chiefs had to ensure a steady supply of slaves from the interior. As a result, they often became embroiled in the affairs of the Yoruba hinterland. Oba Kosoko, for one, acquired important allies in Dahomey, Porto Novo, Ijebu, and Oyo. With this network of supporters, he was able to maintain himself on the throne of Lagos, to harass the British administration, and to continue the slave trade despite the British squadron patrolling the West African coast. Eventually even the British were forced to come to terms with Kosoko, who managed to keep the influence he had built up during his reign long after he lost possession of the throne in 1851, when the British occupied Lagos.[6]

The oba of Lagos held supreme, though not absolute, power

in the town. He was partly limited by the constant threat of sub-version or disloyalty from rival candidates for the stool, by the necessity to share authority with subsidiary chiefs, and by the influence of the Ilu Committee, but he had considerable latitude in exercising his royal prerogatives if he proved to be a popular and effective leader. His most extensive "constitutional" powers emanated from his judicial functions: he could levy fines, sentence a defendant to imprisonment, sell him into slavery, or, in serious cases, inflict capital punishment. Persons who came to Lagos from the interior could also be brought before him for criminal offenses, and even after the emigrant population began to establish their own courts, the oba retained final jurisdiction in disputes involving indigenous Lagosians.[7] In addition, the oba could grant trading concessions and protection to merchants, usually in return for ma-terial compensation. Having authority over land use, he awarded valuable plots to traders, emigrants, and commercial establish-ments. He formulated the town's policy in such crucial matters as overseas trade, the activities of missionaries, and the town's relationship with other Yoruba states. As paramount chief he was ultimately responsible for the preservation of law and order, for the observance of ritual functions, and for the general welfare of the community. By the time of the reign of Kosoko, just before the British intrusion, Lagos royalty was in its golden age of wealth, power, and status. The oba was simultaneously an astute political head, a prosperous trader, an aggressive warrior, a prestigious re-ligious leader, and a refined and sophisticated aristocrat, reputed to be "bold, dashing, and impressive."[8]

IMPACT OF COLONIAL RULE

Although Lagos had reached its peak of power and prosperity by the mid-nineteenth century, the town was highly vulnerable to outside intervention because of the bitter succession dispute between Kosoko, the incumbent, and his uncle, Akitoye, whom Kosoko overthrew in 1845. Aware that this internal struggle weakened Lagos and could be exploited by enterprising emigrants or British merchants who posed a serious economic threat to the traditional elite, Kosoko dealt ruthlessly with his enemies in defense of his throne. In capturing the stool, he killed as many of Akitoye's family and followers as he could find; he demanded an extortionate tax from the Amaros and butchered those who refused to pay.[9] Kosoko likewise did his best to keep out unfriendly foreign traders, including Saro emigrants, and stubbornly refused to cooperate when the British requested him to sign a treaty abolishing the slave trade.

By driving his opponents into a common corner, however, Kosoko unwittingly united his foes behind the British plan to conquer Lagos, a scheme that would simultaneously reinstate Akitoye, stamp out the slave trade, and open the town to missionaries, traders, and emigrants who would enjoy the protection of the British navy. At Akitoye's request for intervention, the British launched an attack on Lagos on December 1, 1851. Forced to withdraw in the face of stiff resistance, they staged a second offensive the day after Christmas with a combined force of 400 British soldiers, 3 warships, and 650 of Akitoye's warriors. After a two-day battle Kosoko fled to Epe, and Lagos was occupied by the British. Akitoye, formally reinstated on New Years Day, signed a treaty promising to abolish the slave trade, to permit the British to use force to crush any attempt at its revival, to destroy all barracoons, to liberate all known slaves, to abolish human sacrifice, to protect missionaries, and to assist in the construction of British chapels, schools, and homes.

All was not peaceful after the conquest; difficulties were encountered, during the next ten years, under British consular rule. First, Kosoko was a constant threat to the progress and security of the town. He was able to continue his slaving activities owing to his good connections in the areas around Lagos, and he clearly intended to recapture his throne through force of arms, Second, Akitoye proved unable to cope with the influx of foreigners, with the new traffic in agricultural produce over which he had no control, and with continuing unrest among Kosoko's partisans. The British, moreover, used the threat of Kosoko's return as a device to keep Akitoye a willing collaborator while consolidating their position on the coast. In so doing, they reinforced the popular belief that Akitoye was a usurper who had captured the throne only through foreign intervention. When Kosoko launched an attack on

Lagos in September 1853, he had the support of a substantial segment of the population. And although he failed to reclaim the throne, he did precipitate Akitoye's death. It is not clear whether Akitoye died from shock at the prospect of Kosoko's reinstatement or from ritual suicide. In any event, as soon as Akitoye's death was announced, a select group of kingmakers hastily convened by the British authorities chose Docemo, Akitoye's son, as successor.[10]

It was during Docemo's reign that the formal rights and privileges of traditional chiefs were relinquished in toto. Over Docemo's objections, the British began to make concessions to Kosoko, substantially reversing their former policy in an effort to get him to accept the new regime. They used him as an intermediary in the palm-oil trade; they allowed him to collect duties from the port of Palma where he had securely established himself; and in 1854 they recognized him as head of the territories in and around Lekki and Palma—all in the hope that he would finally renounce his claim to the Lagos stool and permit trade to flow freely into Lagos without interference. Meanwhile, heavier migration to Lagos was changing the economic structure of the town, shifting the distribution of wealth. Revenues now flowed into the hands of Africans who sold agricultural produce from the interior and to astute urban traders, particularly emigrants who had strong European and African connections. Prosperous settlers who occupied valuable waterfront sites were able, under the system of crown grants, to obtain proprietary rights to these areas, depriving the traditional landowners of their customary tenure. During the period of consular rule the oba's main income was narrowed down to the revenue derived through an agreement reached between Akitoye and foreign merchants in 1852. The oba was entitled to collect a 3 percent duty on imports and a 2 percent duty on exports, promising in return that merchants could set up warehouses in Lagos and have debtors prosecuted through traditional procedures.[11] Docemo continued the arrangement, but in 1854 the import duty was dropped. Docemo's net annual income at that time was £1,300 to £1,500, in addition to market dues, special duty on imported oil, fines, and confiscations to which he was entitled.[12]

The most serious problems encountered during the consular

period, however, derived not from the economic changes but from the ambiguity surrounding the seat of political authority. Since Britain did not declare Lagos a colony or protectorate in the ten years following the invasion, the British authorities were still nominally under the jurisdiction of the local sovereign. Unless a British cruiser happened to be in port, they had to depend upon the oba to protect their interests, clearly an unsatisfactory situation. The threat of civil disorder was not abated by the earlier concessions made to Kosoko; he was still pursuing his slaving activities and adamantly claimed he was the rightful heir to the throne. Moreover, the emigrants pouring into Lagos "made use of the protection but evaded the responsibilities of British law."[13] Many of them bought slaves for domestic purposes, and some Brazilian repatriates indulged surreptitiously in the slave trade. Portuguese slavers and African middlemen began to filter back into Lagos to resume the slave trade with friendly inland chiefs. Akitoye and Docemo both attempted to follow the wishes of the British consul, but they paid heavily for it in popularity. Akitoye, for example, arrested two slave dealers to demonstrate his good faith and as a consequence drove other slavers into Kosoko's camp, giving his enemy ample access to arms and ammunition from abroad with which to reconquer Lagos. At the request of the British consul, Docemo executed four men for stealing palm oil, an act viewed by his people as an excessive demonstration of loyalty to the British.[14]

Cognizant of the difficulties in relying upon traditional rulers whose status was compromised by their association with an external power, the British finally came around to the view that only direct annexation of Lagos would achieve their primary objectives of putting an end to the slave trade, bringing peace to the town, and opening inland routes for legitimate commercial transactions. Since Docemo's tenure was already wholly dependent on British support, it was argued that no injustice would be inflicted on him by this act. Indeed, if Lagos was ceded to the British Crown, it was asserted, Docemo would actually have much to gain: the British presence would guarantee him protection from raiders, assure him an annual income, and commit the British to uphold his claim to the throne and check advances by Kosoko.[15]

In addition, the cession would clarify the power relationships inherent in the 1851 invasion, giving the British the capability as well as the responsibility to protect and patrol the coast.

Accordingly, after being "persuaded" by the guns of a British warship and the landing of marines near the oba's palace, Docemo agreed on August 6, 1861, to sign the Treaty of Cession along with four of his subsidiary chiefs. Although Docemo thus lost his sovereignty, his trade, and his claims to territory in the town, he was allowed "the use of the title of King in its usual African signification" and was permitted "to decide disputes between natives of Lagos with their consent, subject to appeal to British laws."[16] Docemo's pension was fixed at an annual rate of 1,200 bags of cowries, then equivalent to £1,030 sterling, if he continued to abide by the terms of the treaty. But shortly afterward the Idejo chiefs expressed anxiety over the treaty provision that canceled their land rights. Docemo, having second thoughts, petitioned Queen Victoria three times for annulment of the treaty. Receiving no response, he led an uprising in 1863 supported by elements in the emigrant community.[17] The revolt was quickly crushed and, in retaliation, Docemo's pension was suspended.

Meanwhile, the British had again reopened negotiations with Kosoko. Instead of responding to Docemo's appeals to use military force to end harassment of the town, the British deceitfully invited his archrival back to Lagos. Kosoko, returning triumphantly with his chief advisers and an entourage of "several hundred people,"[18] was granted an annual pension of £400 and allowed to conduct legitimate trade.[19] All he had to do in return was formally recognize de facto British sovereignty over the town and its surroundings, including Lekki and Palma. Humiliated, Docemo watched helplessly as the British justified their stand by describing Kosoko as the "rightful heir to the throne" whose return to his native land was based on "sheer justice," and would, they hoped, restore "that confidence in British rule which . . . the occupation of this Island has shaken so much."[20]

Kosoko still had a large following in Lagos and his return revived old cleavages in the town, further weakening Docemo's efforts to resist the British intrusion. Thus, only ten years after the British invasion of Lagos, the confidence of interior Yoruba states in the traditional rulers had collapsed, the primary sources of wealth of Lagos chiefs had been abolished, and their formal political authority had been reduced to the barest rudiments of power. Unable to match the superior capabilities, skills, and wealth of the foreign forces that had seized control of the town, Lagos chiefs submitted peacefully, if unwillingly, to their own displacement. Not until the 1920s was their cause again resurrected, this time by a new generation of Nigerian nationalists.

By 1920, even the meager concessions reluctantly granted to Docemo had almost completely withered away. Oyekan I, Docemo's successor, was placed on a yearly pension of £300, and the oba was known simply as head of the House of Docemo or, in the case of Eshugbayi Eleko, simply as the Eleko. Under the policy of direct rule applied to the Colony of Lagos, there were no native authorities, no native courts, no native treasuries, institutions that existed in every other part of British Africa as integral units of colonial administration. The entire colony was placed under the jurisdiction of the Nigerian Supreme Court, and executive functions were carried out by district officers acting in lieu of native authorities. The policy "meant that there has been practically no assistance from the community chiefs as such and the staff has had to rely on the good citizenship of a few chiefs and others of strong personality and proved loyalty."[21] By the time the nationalist movement began, the position of chieftaincy had reached an all-time low. J. E. Egerton-Shyngle, who protested the deportation of the oba of Lagos in 1925, vividly described the Eleko's helplessness:

> There has never been any time at which Eleko's status has been defined. Meetings are called at his palace over which he presides, and there they go on chatting about one thing or another without their coming to any definite conclusions. He has ... no power to enforce anything that he may decide. Every member of the community is left to do just as he likes. Suppose a palaver is taken to him for settlement and, after going into it, he gives a decision. Well, none of the parties concerned thinks himself bound by it. He cannot, obviously, therefore, have that respect which is due to him in the position he occupies. If he should be held responsible

by Government for any breach of the peace and good order of the town, such as in the case of the Mohammedans, then he should be backed up with some substantial power so that, if he says one thing, it can be carried out. As matters are at present, if, for example, in the case of the Mohammedan trouble, he gives a certain decision, he has no power to compel the Mohammedans to act in accordance with that decision if they refuse to do so.[22]

Throughout most of the remaining years of the colonial period, the government regarded Lagos chiefs as political nonentities, having the official status of "private persons in the same way as any other citizens of the town."[23] Recognition was extended to Lagos chiefs only as lineage or family heads, an "act of courtesy" which, it was repeatedly pointed out, had "no political significance."[24] Economically, traditional authorities had been reduced to the status of "beggar chiefs" with no independent income; they relied upon voluntary gifts and fees from followers in Old Town to supplement their meager allowance, which predictably was suspended whenever they became involved in local disputes to the displeasure of the government. In stark contrast, the rest of the town prospered rapidly, particularly in the areas of administrative and commercial concentration and of European settlement immediately surrounding Isale Eko. Untouched by modernity, the indigenous quarter stood virtually frozen in time, waiting for the thaw that would release the deep frustrations and grievances that had accumulated in years of neglect and domination.

The opportunity for expressing collective discontent was provided when the issue of chieftaincy was raised by emerging nationalists who realized that the oba of Lagos was still regarded as the "father of his people." Moreover, the oba retained a degree of legitimacy that many other traditional rulers in southern Nigeria had lost under indirect rule. Since he was not an agent or a functionary in the colonial regime, the oba could easily be identified by the nationalists as a victim of imperialism. Some incumbents, such as the much maligned Eshugbayi Eleko, a close associate of Herbert Macaulay, endured suspension or banishment as the price of opposition and became popular folk heroes for the urban masses. The six-year struggle for Eshugbayi's reinstatement, directed mainly by the leaders of the NNDP, brought widespread publicity to the plight of the traditional authorities in Lagos and resulted in the vindication of the Eleko and the termination of his exile in 1931. From that time on, the oba of Lagos has remained close to the hearts of his people, not only as a high-ranking member of the Yoruba hierarchy of chiefs, but as an important leader of the traditional elements of the community.

POLITICS OF SUCCESSION

Popular sentiments toward chieftaincy were easily exploitable by politicians, as the question of royal succession aptly shows. Filling a vacancy for the stool never failed to attract widespread interest in Lagos or resurrect ancient cleavages that have affected royal competition since the mid-eighteenth century. Fundamentally, dynastic disputes arose because there were no clear traditions for choosing successors, a situation arising from the peculiar origin of Lagos. It is generally believed that the principle of primogeniture applied at the outset, as in Benin, but the principle came into disuse as the power of Benin waned and more candidates began to assert their claims in closer conformity to Yoruba tradition. Similarly, as the domination of Benin weakened, the committee of kingmakers, which selects the candidate from the progeny of ruling obas, became more inclusive; eventually representatives of all classes of chiefs were brought in to participate in the installation procedures.

Owing to the confusion surrounding these developments, there has never been a fixed number of royal houses or any criterion other than royal blood for determining candidacy. Succession has been influenced by such factors as divination, palace intrigue, factional rivalry, personal popularity of the nominees, their attitudes toward important local issues, and their political skills. So complex and so hotly disputed had competition for the throne become that by the late eighteenth and early nineteenth centuries the contest was settled through violent rebellion and open civil war within the community, and twentieth-century rivalry for the throne has escalated into marathon litigation that reached up to the Judicial Committee of the Privy Council. Figure 2 shows the genealogy of the obas of Lagos and the order of their succession from the time of Ado, the first supreme ruler, to Oyekan II, the reigning oba of Lagos.

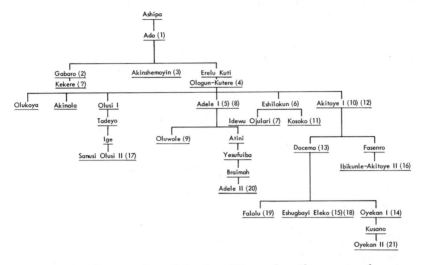

Fig. 2. Complete genealogy of the obas of Lagos, from the seventeenth century to the present. Numbers in parentheses show the sequence in which chiefs held office.

Three major chieftaincy disputes have arisen in the twentieth century, one as an outgrowth of British intervention during colonial rule and two as extensions of traditional dynastic rivalries complicated by modern party politics. The first may be traced to the activities of an aggressive chief, Eshugbayi Eleko, who broke the pattern of submissive obedience to colonial rule established by his predecessors. Upon ascending the throne in 1920, Eshugbayi became a popular champion of royal rights and eventually a budding nationalist actively encouraged by Herbert Macaulay. In 1916 he had publicly opposed the water rate; in 1919 he intervened in the Muhammadan Unrest; and in 1920 he openly came to Macaulay's defense. Finally, in 1925, Eshugbayi was removed from office and replaced by Ibikunle Akitoye II; after the latter's death Sanusi Olusi became oba, but neither he nor Ibikunle was descended from Docemo, as all previous obas had been after the British seizure of Lagos. It was an ironic twist of fate that, in attempting to reduce the power of the oba, colonial officials in-

213

sisted that he be restyled head of the House of Docemo in deference to the preferred royal family; yet in forcing their will upon the chiefs they found themselves turning instead to candidates who were not, in fact, of the favored Docemo line. A new governor, Sir Donald Cameron, corrected this anomaly under pressure of popular protest and restored Eshugbayi to the throne in 1931, just a year before his death. But by that time the damage had been done. Martyred by his exile, the oba returned more beloved by his followers than ever before. Rival lineages, however, which had resented the dominance of the Docemo faction were encouraged to press harder for the stool in subsequent contests. Aided by Macaulay's influence, Prince Falolu, Eshugbayi's brother and a decidely more docile ruler, was selected to keep the throne in the hands of the Docemo line. He remained in office until 1949, when Lagos was on the threshold of local self-government.

At this point the rival candidates began attracting strong political backers from the educated classes, who realized that the oba could have a significant bearing on the results of the first election based on universal suffrage. It was against this background that the most sensational chieftaincy dispute in modern times arose between the House of Docemo, backed by members of the NNDP and the NCNC, and the House of Adele, supported by the Nigerian Youth Movement. Modern politics stiffened competition for the traditional office, with repercussions that went beyond the confines of the indigenous quarter.

Upon the death of Falolu in 1949, the House of Docemo nominated Adedoyin Dosunmu, who died in 1950 after failing to claim the stool. The kingmakers, following the precedent set by the British, chose as candidate a chief who was not of the Docemo lineage, Adeniji Adele II, an educated Muslim who clearly had the endorsement of the city's most popular nationalist leaders. Responsibility for redeeming the throne for the Docemo family passed to Prince Adeyinka Oyekan II, who for the next fifteen years made pursuit of the crown his life ambition.

On behalf of Oyekan and the House of Docemo, Adeleke Adedoyin, a leading NNDP barrister, filed suit against Adele. Technically, Adele's candidacy for the stool could not be challenged, since he had been duly appointed according to custom. Alternatively, his opponents charged him with unlawful tenancy of the royal palace on the ground that it was the private property of the Docemo family, which had been paying rates and maintaining the house without state support for nearly a century. While this tactic would not have deposed Adele, it constituted a symbolic challenge to his authority and, if successful, would have been a severe blow to his prestige.[25] Defended by Sir Adeyemo Alakija and Chief H. O. Davies, leading members of the Nigerian Youth Movement, Adele argued that the Iga was public property which the oba was entitled to occupy by virtue of his office. Obviously, Adele's position was the stronger one, but Oyekan appealed through the Nigerian courts up to the Judicial Committee of the Privy Council, where the case was finally settled in 1957 in favor of Adele. In 1959, as an aftermath, the federal government passed legislation prohibiting future succession disputes from going to court and specifying that they be settled by the Ministry of Lagos Affairs. Government also assumed the maintenance of the Iga as a public building and, with the cooperation of the LTC, exempted the palace from payment of rates.

The competition between Adele II and Oyekan II was a throwback to earlier succession disputes, but there was a new dimension of modern partisan support. Adele II branded the Docemo family as one that had sold out to the British and unfairly dominated the throne ever since. Certainly the Docemo line had monopolized the throne for nearly a hundred years, except for the period 1925–1931, when the government installed two substitute candidates in place of the deposed Eshugbayi. Oyekan argued, however, that the dominance of the Docemo line showed that the other royal houses were not so popular as his own. Furthermore, he asserted that Adele's claim was weaker than his, since Adele's royal linaeage was traced through four generations to Adele I, a ruler whose own appointment had been highly controversial.[26]

The dispute was kept alive for several years not only by the protracted legal battle, but by the burgeoning political alignments in the town. As noted earlier, in 1949 Adele formed his own party, the Area Councils, and in 1950 he ran for the LTC, hoping to be elected mayor. Failing to achieve a majority, he then threw his support to the Action Group, staying with that party until 1958, when it refused to grant his request to increase the number of traditional chiefs entitled to hold office on the council. Oyekan had also, but to a lesser extent, become politically active. He ran as an NCNC candidate for the council in 1950, but his name was withdrawn when it appeared that the succession dispute would be carried to the ballot box. In 1959 Oyekan narrowly lost an election for a parliamentary seat on the NCNC ticket.

Both Adele and Oyekan, in becoming active in partisan politics, were trying to enhance the role of chieftaincy as well as advance their own careers. In some respects this objective was partly achieved. Through his political activities, Adele eased the transition from colonial rule to local self-government for his followers. By the end of his reign he had raised the prestige of his office, demonstrated the solidarity of the traditional community, and succeeded in recapturing certain ceremonial powers. The oba of Lagos was made statutory president of the Lagos Town Council in 1953 and an ex officio member of the Nigerian Senate in 1960. In 1959 the oba's annual stipend was fixed at £1,800, instead of the £300 token allowance of the colonial era. Finally, the title "oba of Lagos" replaced the misleading colonial designation, "head of the House of Docemo," and the Iga was modernized and expanded with the help of the federal government.

Thus the institution of chieftaincy experienced a brief revival during the 1950s, mostly through the sheer force of Adele's dynamic personality. A former civil servant and World War I veteran, Adele had served in the army in Nigeria and the Cameroons. He was vice-president of the Ahmadiya Movement in Nigeria and a member of the conference on revising the Richards Constitution in 1949. In the course of his political career, he served as a Lagos member of the Western House of Chiefs in 1951 and became vice-president of the Nigerian Senate in 1960. In 1959 he was awarded the CBE by the Queen of England. He was unquestionably one of the most colorful and active personalities ever to occupy the throne, a sophisticated, educated Muslim who had modernized the institution in the new age of nationalism and independence.

Yet by participating in partisan politics, Adele also deprived the institution of chieftaincy of the dignity associated with political neutrality. It was no longer possible to uphold the fiction that the oba was an uncommitted spectator, viewing the political activities of his community as a dispassionate onlooker. He was, in fact, a key member of a local caucus of political notables whose influence was almost wholly a function of their links with the dominant party. Although the privileges restored to the oba greatly enhanced his prestige, they did not substantially enhance the powers of his office. For this reason, to many observers, Adele stripped the office of the respect it had once enjoyed. People felt that the oba, as father of his people, should be above politics, not in the thick of the battle. Adele exposed himself as well as his office to recriminations that would inevitably affect the status of chieftaincy as well as the career of the incumbent.

The events following Adele's defection from the Action Group in 1958 showed how easily chieftaincy could be used for the purposes of political victimization. Among the incentives designed to lure Adele to the opposition was a bill passed by the federal legislature which empowered the oba of Lagos to recommend successors for subsidiary chieftaincies as they became vacant, including hereditary chieftaincies whose occupants were normally selected by their families. This measure was described in the local press as "a blow to the liberty of Lagos chiefs ... that might also enslave the chiefs and bring them under the thumb of the Oba of Lagos ... [to] make them no more than ... [his] sycophants."[27] Adele, on the other hand, cheerfully welcomed the measure, stating that this and other amenities offered by the federal government gave him "freedom from the control of the ruling political party in the LTC."[28] In 1962 Adele invoked his newly acquired privilege and requested that five of his subordinate chiefs be deposed on the grounds of disloyalty.[29] The federal government granted Adele's request; after his death on July 12, 1964, however, these chiefs were restored because some of them were among the kingmakers needed to choose Adele's successor.

The third competition for the stool in the twentieth century occurred after Adele's death. Two of the twenty-one contestants were Professor Oladele Ajose, then vice-chancellor of the University of Ife, and Prince Adeyinka Oyekan II. Once again divided in their sympathies, the kingmakers delayed their decision for more than six months while eligible families lobbied hard for their respective nominees. Prince Oyekan's candidacy was buttressed by the six years of publicity in his previous pursuit of office, by his being the nominee of the prestigious Docemo family, and by his attractive personal qualities. Like his predecessor, Oyekan also had a dynamic and colorful personality. A Christian, who qualified as a pharmacist, Oyekan undoubtedly impressed the kingmakers, many of whom had become enemies of Adele. Oyekan's commitment and sincerity in upholding tradition were beyond question. He had repeatedly urged expansion of the powers of traditional rulers, and he held himself somewhat aloof from the indignities of party politics, his previous electoral efforts notwithstanding.

It is difficult to know to what extent the kingmakers' decision was affected by Oyekan's past opposition to the Action Group, a stance he adopted in order to oppose Adele. But they undoubtedly were well aware that Oyekan's appointment would be welcomed by the federal government, then controlled by the Northern Peoples' Congress, a party that was dominated by traditional rulers and had, along with the NCNC, supported his earlier bid for the stool. The upcoming federal and local elections could also have influenced their decision. In the spirit of cooperation fostered by the new coalition between the NCNC and the AG, Oyekan's installation may have been seen as an opportunity to heal old wounds in the community. Thus, on March 11, 1965, Adeyinka Oyekan II, the great-grandson of Docemo I, became the twenty-first candidate and the first after Nigeria's independence to be coronated oba of Lagos.

## CHIEFTAINCY IN A MODERN URBAN COMMUNITY

Assuredly, for the majority of urban residents—immigrants who either maintain loyalty to chiefs in their own towns or who reject traditional authority altogether—the oba of Lagos is little more than a distant celebrity who makes a negligible impact on their daily lives. But for the cohesive and indigenous residents of Isale Eko, the oba continues to be a father figure who evokes warm sentimental feelings. For this segment of the population, chieftaincy has survived as a meaningful, albeit profoundly altered, part of the urban political structure, an institution that still fulfills political as well as social functions.

The current political functions of the oba of Lagos may be classified in two categories: residual functions that have been maintained or extended as part of the traditional prerogatives attached to his office, and acquired functions that have been gradually delegated to the oba as the institution modernized. Residual functions apply to the internal affairs of the town and carry informal powers of limited local influence. In this category, the oba's most extensive authority derives from the judicial powers he exercises in settling local disputes brought before him by lineage heads, market women, or religious leaders. Unlike the rest of the country, Lagos has no customary courts or other judicial machinery with jurisdiction in matters relating to local customs and practices of the community. The oba fills this gap admirably, but his decisions, of course, are only as binding as the people recognize them to be. In all probability this function will dwindle in importance as time goes on. As the supreme traditional head, the oba also conducts rites and rituals and presides at major ceremonies and public meetings, including such celebrations as the "capping" or coronation of chiefs. He has the power to appoint hereditary chiefs in consultation with the appropriate community leaders whenever vacancies arise. The appointment of a new class of titled or honorary chiefs is an extension of this prerogative. Unknown before the reign of Eshugbayi Eleko, honorary chieftaincies have become a means of bestowing status on prominent persons, a practice widely popularized since the reign of Adele II.

Certain acquired functions have been specifically delegated by the government to the oba in order to give him due recognition without actual executive control. In local government the oba acts in a capacity analogous to that of the lord mayor of London, whose prestige far exceeds his decision-making authority. The oba of Lagos has been statutory president of the municipal council since 1953, but he appears at council meetings only to deliver an annual address, leaving the responsibilty of representing his interests to the four ex officio traditional members who were given voting rights in the council in 1959. Before military rule, the oba was also an ex officio member of the Nigerian Senate, a position giving him a public voice on national issues. As a venerated figure in the nation's capital, he is also occasionally called upon as a "domestic statesman," mediating and advising on issues of local or national concern. In June 1966 he was appointed adviser to the federal military government, drawing a stipend of £4,000 ($11,200) a year.

Undoubtedly many members of the more sophisticated urban elite consider even these concessions to traditional rulers unnecessary. For them, chieftaincy is little more than a relic of the past. A prominent Lagos journalist expressed this point of view in describing Oyekan's installation in 1965:

> As a social event, the coronation was a superb anachronism. Ministers of state and diplomatic corps, civic and professional leaders, members of secret cults, market women, voluntary helpers and professional traditionalists were gathered to lend magnificence and be at his disposal on the occasion. . . . Nobody who was anybody was excluded and like a drove of benevolent locusts they swarmed the heart of Lagos to demonstrate their respect for the culture, superstitions and talismans of yesteryears. . . . But I am concerned at the price Oyekan has had to pay to achieve this meaningless success. It is reported that the cost to his famliy in solid cash is about £10,000. And there is his personal ordeal. What does Oyekan gain in return? His salary from the Lagos City Council was £1,800. As an ordinary senator he will receive £840 from the Federal Government. In addition, Oba Oyekan will administer the traditional Estates of the king of Lagos. His total financial reward will hardly compensate for the commitments which [will] confront him henceforth. . . . In his glorified office, Oba Oyekan will neither be taken into confidence on State matters nor will he face any official challenges. Instead, this one-time successful chemist and druggist is now to spend the rest of his life practically living off the begging bowl. When you think that this man has spent more than a third of his lifetime fighting for this moribund imperial, it seems to me that victory has come to him as an enemy. . . . As Oba in an era of faded royalty, he is no more than a tourist attraction, side by side with our museum pieces.[30]

Such sentiments are not without some basis of truth. Nevertheless, they belie the facts that the institution of chieftaincy, though stripped of most of its formal powers, is not without political significance and that it is not, in all respects, a static or reactionary structure. The oba of Lagos is an impressive individual in his own right, a man in whom the community can easily feel pride and place its trust. He and his immediate predecessor exemplify the community's current preference for an educated and distinguished oba. Adele's political activities have also demonstrated how a traditional chief with modern ambitions can be a useful agent of political mobilization, for it was he who first channeled the particularistic interests of the indigenes into concrete goals to be pursued through modern institutions. This is no trivial accomplishment in a community like Lagos, where the indigenes have been separtated from, and sometimes hostile to, their environment. A progressive oba is a bridge of communication between the old and new worlds that meet in the city; he is one of the few individuals who can cushion the impact of modernization which will inevitably fall hardest on his most ardent admirers in the traditional quarter.

In the final analysis, however, the oba's role is a transitional one that begs the question of the political future of his office. Like most constitutional monarchs today, the oba must find his influence more in the strength of his personality than in the strength of his office. Oyekan seems fully equipped and deeply committed to make the most of his position, although his immediate opportunities have been curtailed by the advent of military rule shortly after his appointment. Certainly his educational background is surperior to that of most traditional rulers in Nigeria. Born in 1910, Oyekan attended the best schools in Lagos, finishing his secondary education at King's College in 1929 and then going on to the School of Pharmacy, Yaba, where he qualified in 1933. He has old connections with Herbert Macaulay's NNDP and with its successor, the NCNC. From the days of his nomination for local office in 1950 and of his candidacy for the federal legislature in 1959, he has tasted both the excitement of political battle and the bitterness of electoral defeat. His suggestions for increased powers for traditional rulers are pragmatic proposals for participation, rather than empty political slogans designed to win votes.[31] Oyekan has likewise earned the admiration and friendship of intellectuals, is regarded as a member of the city's top social elite, and has indicated his intentions to go into business in order to reduce his dependency on his subjects. Disdaining further perpetuation of the dynastic dispute in which he was a primary protagonist, he has recognized the ethical as well as the legal complexities of his historic fifteen-year battle for the throne. "My own belief," he once remarked, "is that legally our case was right but perhaps morally and factually, no. When you have been enjoying something for more than a hundred years [as the Docemo family has], it is difficult to give it up."[32]

This sense of social justice has made Oyekan a popular and respected leader, a man who has sown unity rather than discord among a people who have been badly divided by dynastic loyalties. It is also possible that he may profit from the rising influence of the indigenes, especially now that Lagos State has been created. As he recently commented, "it is impossible to insulate the institution of Obaship from the politics of [its] ... locality." While this statement might suggest his expectation of expanded political influence, he is also conscious of the fact that, with rapid modernization, "the institution of Obaship is being killed slowly from all angles,"[33] an admission that the erosion of traditional authority may well be an unfinished process.

CHAPTER 8

*Market Women: Unassertive Influence*

Nearly all trade in Lagos is conducted through a network of thousands of small-scale vendors who, like generations of traders before them, follow traditional Yoruba marketing patterns.[1] From two-thirds to three-fourths of these traders are market women, the most highly organized, socially cohesive, and probably the most class-conscious occupational group in the city whose numbers, economic resources, and significance in the commercial affairs of the town have vastly increased.

Politically, however, market women are an unconventional interest group. Although exhibiting an exceptionally high degree of internal solidarity, they rarely lobby for specific measures or directly attempt to initiate public policies of particular concern to themselves. The nature of their influence lies, rather, in the widespread public awareness of their collective potential strength which could be marshaled for political protest, electoral victory, or material support. Government and political parties alike are sensitive to the reactions of market women to major political programs and adjust their policies and strategies accordingly. Through this type of unassertive influence, market women have indirectly shaped the character and outcome of electoral contests, the internal organization of political parties, and the administration of public policy.[2]

TRADITIONAL MARKETS IN LAGOS

The city's traditional market system has been remarkably resilient in the face of the pressures of modernization. Obviously, the number, location, and size of urban markets have changed to suit the needs of the shifting population, but the majority of African consumers still depend on petty traders who sell their goods in nearly every available open space where customers are to be found.

Opinion varies as to what actually constitutes a market, or *oja*, in Lagos. Some people regard as a market any collectivity of sellers who regularly congregate at fixed sites, including small groups of perhaps one or two dozen street traders who sell their wares from counters or tables set up along the pavements of major thoroughfares. Others think of markets as only those large congregations of traders who sell from permanent stalls, squarish wooden enclosures about the size of a telephone booth or a closet. There is also some dispute over the boundaries of neighboring markets that have overflowed into one continuous stream of traders, some people maintaining that these now constitute a single market entity, others holding that customary distinctions between markets are still valid, even if two or more have physically merged. Confusion also arises from differing legal and structural criteria. The Lagos City Council, for example, recognizes only legally "established," or gazetted, markets, while the market women's association accepts a broader definition based on its own leadership structure. Many markets in Lagos are also known by more than one name, and official designations do not always correspond to popular names or labels that have come into common usage. For these reasons, any attempt to set a precise figure for the total number of markets in Lagos depends upon the authority one consults or the criteria one chooses to accept. According to the LCC, eighteen established markets have been legally recognized, plus ten "wares" markets, clusters of street traders who have received licenses to sell along designated roads.[3] According to the Lagos City Markets and Women's Organization, with a claimed membership of 63,000, a total of thirty-three markets operate in Lagos.[4] Since this figure, based on a consensus of market leaders, is probably the most reliable one, it is here used as a working total.

The most popular market in Lagos is Jankara, a commercial complex actually consisting of three or four contiguous markets located in the heart of Isale Eko. Technically, Jankara is the provisions section of Idumagbo Market, but the two names are

used interchangeably and are now commonly regarded as referring to one and the same unit. Idumagbo has expanded so that it
now embraces Idera and Oko Awo markets. This sprawling
shopping center is one of several multipurpose markets which
sell the widest possible range of goods, including everything from
textiles, foodstuffs, jewelry, toiletries, and sundry provisions to
pottery, hardware, machine parts, furniture, fish nets, and so on.

Before products come for final sale to the consumer, they usually
pass through a long chain of intermediaries—importers, wholesalers, warehouse owners, and a number of supplementary
merchants who sell both in bulk and in small quantities—a practice
that blurs the distinction between wholesale and retail operations.
Imported goods are obtained from large European firms or from
Lebanese or Indian traders, many of whom have participated in
the retail trade along with the African traders.

Women function at all levels of trade but tend to specialize in
foodstuffs, textiles, provisions, and related commodities. Some
market activities requiring heavy labor or special skills, such as
the sale of lumber or fresh meat, are reserved for men. Commodity
specialization is reflected in the physical layout of markets, which
are divided into sections based on related product ranges. Although the Yorubas dominate the city's trade, some ethnic specialization appears in certain product lines which are favored by
particular consumers or are supplied from distant regions. Ibo
traders, for example, have been deeply involved in the distribution
of rice yams produced in the eastern provinces. Ijebu women tend
to specialize in gari from the west and the north and in palm oil;
Egba women, in rice; and Oyo women, in foodstuffs.[5] Locally
produced supplies pour into the city from all parts of the country:
yams from Abakaliki, groundnut oil and beans from Kano, and
fish from Maiduguri. Gari and other staples, which probably account for the largest volume of trade, originate from some 140
village groups in nearby Ijebu Province, principally in the Abigi,
Ilusen, Oni Ado, and Ibiade areas.[6] Lacking refrigeration and having to break down their stock into small, quickly disposable
quantities, traders must resell to other vendors to get produce to
the consumer as efficiently, rapidly, and profitably as possible. The
prosperous market woman who sells in bulk and extends substan-

tial credit to her customers is therefore linked through perhaps three or four other traders with the "penny-penny" hawker or itinerant vendor who sells a few kola nuts, cigarettes, matchsticks, peeled oranges, or other items from a head tray she carries from door to door.

Because the market system relies so heavily on middlemen, it has been criticized for driving up prices, diverting productive labor, and encouraging duplication in the distributive process.[7] Actually, even in an urban economy, the system should be viewed as an effective adaptation to special conditions imposed by the environment: a hot tropical climate, high population density, and low per capita purchasing power. Large quantities of perishable items must be distributed in small units for quick consumption by traders who have little capital to invest in display or preservation facilities. The existence of large numbers of middlemen is thus a functional means of solving the problem. In addition, the market system encourages keen competition which helps push down price levels, stimulates the use of available resources, and keeps cash in constant circulation. It also provides an outlet for the commercial talents of women, for whom trading is a means of obtaining economic independence without sacrificing family responsibilities. Women take their children with them to market, babies tied to their backs, older children helping in the business. A trader's profits are her own, and she spends them as she wishes, perhaps on her children's education, in investment in property, in purchasing clothing or jewelry, or in paying for a pilgrimage to Mecca. Besides being a lucrative practice, trading is also socially functional; it brings women together to gossip, share problems, and reinforce the esprit de corps that makes the traditional marketplace the nerve center of the community—crowded, noisy, colorful, and bustling with activity.

As in all Yorubaland, Lagos markets are either daily or periodic and either general or specialized. Ita Faji and Obun Eko, for example, are the two oldest markets in the city: Ita Faji is held daily and specializes in fresh meat, whereas Obun Eko is held periodically and deals in general goods. Jankara is a daily general market; Ebute Ero, a periodic textile market; and Oyingbo, a periodic general market. Periodic markets function partly as wholesale and redistribution centers which supply the daily markets. In Lagos, following Yoruba patterns, they are held in a double "ring" system according to a sequence based on a four- or eight-day market "week" in which only one market in the ring meets each day. In the first ring, the four periodic markets, Oyingbo, Obun Eko, Mushin, and Ebute Ero, meet in rotation; in the second ring, Oyingbo, Apapa, Mushin, and Agege markets are held successively.[8] In the next round, Oyingbo leads off again, activating the first ring, and so on. Thus, if the cycle begins on the first day of a calendar month, Oyingbo and Mushin meet every fourth day, Oyingbo on the 1st, 5th, 9th, 13th, 17th, 21st, 25th, and 29th, and Mushin on the 3rd, 7th, 11th, 15th, 19th, 23d, and 27th. Obun Eko, Ebute Ero, Apapa, and Agege markets are held every eighth day in staggered rotation.[9]

The ring system is designed so that one periodic market at a time serves each vicinity, but in practice there is some overlap. It is also not uncommon for some sections of a periodic market to remain open every day to supply the city with essential items, such as foodstuffs. Except for these minor deviations, the periodic market operates in Lagos with as much regularity and disciplined organization as it does in rural areas. Except for a few small traders who sell in the evening from their doorsteps or within their neighborhoods, night markets which are traditional in Yorubaland have disappeared in Lagos. All markets in the city are open during the daytime, usually from 8:00 or 9:00 in the morning to 4:00 or 5:00 in the afternoon.

It is difficult to assess the value of trade in the traditional sector as a proportion of the total commercial activity in Lagos. There is little doubt, however, that a substantial percentage of the community's wealth can be found in the traditional markets, usually strapped safely around the waists of the market women in money belts, which are heavy, knotted stockings tied under skirts or wrappers. In Jankara Market, which has about 2,000 occupied stalls, the value of one day's trading may vary from an estimated £5,000 to £25,000 or more, a range that suggests the large volume of business transacted. The profit margin of a trader may vary from a low of about £1 to £3 a month earned by the penny-penny hawkers to a high of about £100 or more earned by large-scale traders during peak market months. A sample survey of working women in Isale Eko reveals that a trader's average income ranges from £6 to £40 a month.[10] Earnings soar much higher, however, for larger businesswomen, particularly textile traders who sell a wide variety of materials, including traditional handwoven Bida, Okene, or Iseyin cloth, tie-dye Adire cloth, imported Indian silks, English woolens, Dutch wax prints, and expensive laces, satins, velvets, and brocades. As a whole, textile traders tend to be the city's most aggressive and hard-driving saleswomen, and they have a reputation for being the most prosperous of all traders. Some export to other West African ports and travel regularly up and down the coast to collect orders. Being in a highly competitive and lucrative line which requires comparatively large capital outlays and a broad range of customers, successful textile traders are accorded the highest degree of respect and prestige by their colleagues and, not surprisingly, have risen to become the most influential group of market leaders.

Market women have always maintained a distinct and exclusive sense of group solidarity, partly because their internal organization is strong and partly because trading is the only profit-making activity regarded by both sexes and by several ethnic groups as a culturally acceptable female occupation. The women's separate social consciousness, however, has been further reinforced by urbanization. The influx of large numbers of immigrants with mixed social backgrounds has brought into sharper relief the homogeneous socioeconomic character of the market women, a quality of sameness that accounts to a large extent for the internal cohesion they display. The great majority of market women are nonliterate; a large proportion are polygamously married;[11] and nearly all are Muslim or animist. The overwhelming majority are and always have been Yorubas, and immigration has not altered this pattern of ethnic dominance. Male immigrants to Lagos tend to leave their wives behind until they get established in the city. Even after wives are brought to Lagos, they often return home to have their babies, to attend social functions, and to maintain contacts with their families. Of the 287,687 females in Lagos in 1963, 75 percent were Yoruba, 13 percent were Ibo, and

3 percent were Edo.[12] Each of the other ethnic groups represented less than 2 percent of the total female population.

Since the turn of the century, the total number of male and female traders in Lagos has increased nearly fivefold, and since 1921 the number has nearly tripled. At the latest count in 1963, nearly 50,000 female "sales workers" were recorded, a figure that probably does not include young girls serving as apprentices to their mothers, maids or assistants working for a small allowance, and casual or itinerant traders who evade enumerators for fear that the census may be related to taxation. As far as possible, trade is handed down to younger girls from generation to generation, daughters sometimes inheriting from their mothers not only an established clientele, but also their stalls and tools of the trade as well, such as a valued pepper-grinding stone.

Obviously, there is little necessity in this business for modern education or skills. Of all the urban population, therefore, market women have been the least touched by the skyscraper culture that surrounds them, and "the grip of tradition on . . . [their] way of life is still very strong."[13] Yet it would be wrong to assume that market women have no ambition or lack a sense of achievement motivation. The profit incentive is very strong, and market women compete as keenly as any other occupatonal group for individual success. Their aspirations for their children are likewise very high; it is by no means unusual to find a prosperous trader boasting proudly of one or two sons whom she has put through a university abroad with her accumulated savings. More often than not, however, a trader expects her daughters to follow in her own footsteps, pursuing a trade for which they have been groomed since childhood.

### POLITICAL AUTHORITY IN THE MARKETS

Market women are organized around a powerful hierarchy of traditional market leaders who maintain strict supervision over all the main markets in the city. This traditional feminine elite still remains the single most effective mechanism for resolving conflict and enforcing discipline among the thousands of urban traders who are in daily competition.

At the top of the leadership pyramid is the supreme head of the market women, the Iyalode ("Mother of the Markets"), an official chieftaincy title last conferred by Oba Falolu on a venerable Muslim trader, Alhaja Rabiatu Eyiowuawi. After inheriting her mother's textile business, Alhaja Rabiatu became one of the largest exporters in the city. Now over eighty years old, she has held the post for more than twenty-five years, combining with it the respected title of Iyaeko ("Mother of Lagos"). According to traditional protocol, the Iyalode is second in status only to the oba of Lagos in whose appointment and installation she participates as the leading female chief in the city.

Under the Iyalode are the Alagas or market chairmen, with whom she regularly consults. Alagas and subsidiary market leaders are selected by the traders themselves on the basis of such criteria as wealth, character, birth, trading skill, and personal popularity. Two or three leaders may coexist for some time in a single market, but usually one of them eventually emerges as a predominant Alaga. The responsibilities of the Alaga are manifold, but she receives no remuneration other than the prestige that derives from her status.

The Alaga regulates and coordinates market affairs and arbitrates disputes, including personal conflicts that disturb the peaceful conduct of trade. In one instance, for example, an Alaga decided a case in which the husband of one of her traders made advances to the market woman occupying the stall next to his wife's. After a fight broke out, the Alaga banned both women from the market for six months and forbade the husband to enter the market for an indefinite period of time. Both her judgment and her sentence were unchallenged by the parties affected. Appeals from such rulings may be made in extraordinary circumstances to the Iyalode, but she rarely intervenes in petty disputes. The Alaga is empowered to penalize a market woman by levying fines or driving her out of the market altogether for chronic offenses such as price slashing. In addition, the Alaga is responsible for the overall supervision and maintenance of the market, looking after its sanitation and providing for the care and maintenance of the women and their children. Alagas may sometimes dip into their personal funds to aid a market woman in distress, and progressive leaders have been known to inaugurate literacy courses, establish nursery schools, and demonstrate the proper techniques of cooking and child care at their own expense.

At the next level, market leadership passes to the section head, the Iya Egbe Oja ("Mother of the Market Association"), who leads a section of traders in a particular product range, such as china, textiles, or grains. Like the Alagas, section heads may also arbitrate disputes brought before them by women in their group, but they are generally more concerned with the supply, sale, preparation, and processing of their merchandise. For example, they may set minimum prices to avoid unfair competition. A trader may lower her prices through bargaining, but persistent underselling will not be tolerated for very long.

Finally, below the section head in the leadership hierarchy are the commodity heads, the O-lo'ri Egbe, each of whom is in charge of the sellers of a particular item, such as peppers, yams, or cassavas. A market, depending upon its size, may also have a number of subsellers who work with established leaders. If a product passes through the hands of several intermediaries, for example, brokers may be designated to represent each step in the distributive process—wholesaling, warehousing, redistributing, and so on. Reporting to the Iyalode directly are also regional and ethnic group leaders who speak for cultural minorities. This chain of command, reaching from the Iyalode down to market chairmen, section leaders, commodity heads, and subsellers, applies throughout the markets of Lagos. Most of the leaders meet whenever necessary and are in almost daily contact. The Alagas hold formal monthly meetings at the home of the Iyalode, and an inner core of top Alagas and market representatives who are active in the Lagos City Markets and Women's Organization meet late every Friday afternoon, after Muslim prayers, at the association's headquarters near Jankara Market. There they discuss the thrift or credit (*esusu*) associations, the supply and the quality of their produce, the means of handling inflation, discipline problems, social functions, or political party activities. Collectively, the leaders exercise a remarkable degree of control over the markets, levying dues as deemed necessary, keeping rivalry within tolerable limits, maintaining order and peace, and directing affairs of group interest.

This efficient authority structure, combined with the economic independence and corporate solidarity of the traders, makes the market women one of the most autonomous and self-sufficient interest groups in Lagos.

### MARKET ADMINISTRATION

Despite the efficiency and the power of the traditional hierarchy of leadership, the market structure is only loosely connected with market administration as supervised by the council. The authority of market leaders, an extralegal dimension of the market system, has yet to be effectively related to the formal government of Lagos.

The council, though given the authority to establish and maintain markets by a special ordinance passed in 1922, did not exercise its prerogative until the early 1930s. At that time several of the main markets already in existence—Oyingbo, Faji Meat, Moloney Bridge Street, and Apapa—were recognized by the council and fees were levied on stall holders. By 1942 the ten established markets yielded £3,400 in annual revenue. By the sixties, the eighteen established and ten wares markets recognized by the council were yielding a yearly income of approximately £100,000.

Since the jurisdiction of the council extends only to established markets, thousands of street traders receive no market services from the government. Street traders are, in fact, officially regarded as illegal merchants. Periodically driven away from their places of trade by the authorities, they drift back after the campaign against them subsides. Nearly every elected council has wrestled with the problem of street trading, which officials tend to regard as an eyesore that creates unsanitary conditions in the capital city. Invariably, however, the council has been unable or, for political reasons, unwilling to enforce the ban on street trading, although punitive raids have occasionally been launched against traders suspected of siding with the opposition party.

The markets that do come under the jurisdiction of the council are grievously neglected. The council, viewing markets primarily as a source of revenue, provides a minimum of maintenance; the meager staff of cleaners and sweepers was supervised, until April 1, 1967, by the Town Clerk's Department. On the recommendation of the *Saville Tribunal Report*, markets were transferred to the

Public Health Department and two health superintendents and two assistant superintendents were added to the staff. In addition, the Markets Council was formed to link the local government system more directly with the traditional market structure.[14]

Most familiar to the market women are the municipal officials who enforce market bylaws and collect fees. Heading the staff is the market superintendent, who is responsible for the administration of all markets in the city. Assisting him are senior market masters, who issue stallage receipt books and supervise their respective market sections. Under them are the Grade I market masters, who keep the records, and a number of assistants who collect fees and tolls. In March 1967 a total of twenty-three market masters (seven of them in training), thirty-five assistants, and thirty-six sweepers, cleaners, and laborers were employed in Lagos markets by the council. But wares markets and some established markets had no cleaners or laborers at all, and some of the least sanitary and most crowded markets, such as Moloney Bridge Street, Iddo, and Oyingbo, had only one cleaner each. Hence much of the necessary maintenance has been the responsibility of the market women, who hire their own night watchmen, sweepers, and laborers.

The council's most important market function is the construction and allocation of stalls, until 1967 the sole responsibility of the Town Clerk's Department. When stalls are to be assigned in a new market, applications are invited by the council through advertisements in gazettes and newspapers and in notices posted throughout the town. Vacancies created by the death of stall holders, however, are generally filled from standing applications. Allocations are supposedly based on experience, type of commodity, and ability to pay stallage fees, but preference is sometimes given to descendants of deceased stall holders.[15] Although councilors are expected not to meddle in stall assignments, they have been known to exert influence on behalf of supporters of the dominant party.

The council levies fees on stalls it has constructed and on those that come under municipal control. No distinction is made between different kinds of markets in grading stalls for the fixing of rates. Rental fees vary on the basis of market quality and in accordance with type of stall: lockup, permanent open, temporary open,

233

or casual. Permanent lockup stalls—enclosed sheds with cement floors, steel pillars, and asbestos roofing—exist only in Ebute Ero and Iddo markets and rent for £3 each a month. (Smaller lockup stalls in Ebute Ero, Iddo, and Alayabiagba markets range from £1 to £2 each.) Permanent open stalls, with concrete floors and asbestos or tin roofing, rent for 15s. a month. Temporary open stalls are allocated to traders when the council is unprepared to erect permanent facilities; a plot of land is usually rented for 10s. a month, and the occupant erects her own stall. Traders renting permanent and temporary open stalls, the most common types, carry their entire inventory home at night and restock the next market day. Thousands of casual traders rent available open spaces in or near the main markets at 3d. a day, selling from a tray, mat, or narrow counter. In June 1967 the 12,958 occupied stalls in the established and wares markets yielded the council £7,564.5.6 in fees.[16] (There were also 2,053 stall holders in arrears and 2,954 vacant stalls, mostly in Alayabiagba, Oko Awo, and Ebute Ero markets.) This amount is only a fraction of the revenue that could have been raised if all the traders in the city had been subject to the council's jurisdiction.

The overall attitude of the market women toward the council is understandably negative, ranging from cynicism to indifference. To the traders, the council is not a dispenser of amenities but a regulatory institution that limits, restricts, and taxes their activities; its only meaningful function is the provision of stalls. Not surprisingly, the traders feel that their markets are controlled by the political party dominant in the council, rather than by the council itself.

### MARKET POLITICS

No political party can afford to ignore the interests of the market women. This fundamental axiom was appreciated by Herbert Macaulay, who was the first to mobilize feminine influence in behalf of his own partisan activities. Macaulay inspired the organization of the Lagos Market Women's Guild in the early 1920s when he was agitating against the imposition of a water rate. Madam Alimotu Pelewura, the Alaga of Ereko Market, was instrumental in forging a strong link between Macaulay and the traders; she was first associated with the Nigerian Union of Young Democrats, which eventually allied itself with the NNDP.[17] In due course the market women became the financial backbone of the NNDP and ardent admirers of its leader, who alone of the native foreigners spoke to them in Yoruba, championed the cause of the traditional chiefs to whom they were deeply devoted, and supported the Jam'at Congregation, the fastest-growing Muslim sect in Lagos, which raised the status of women.

The market women, like most of the indigenous population at the time, were politically loyal to Macaulay because of his personal magnetism. After his death the nationalist leaders of the NCNC failed to capture the imagination of the traders, who were estranged from the new breed of young, radical, Christian professionals espousing unfamiliar political slogans. Two years before Macaulay's death, in 1944, a small group of progressive women attempted to bridge the gap by launching the Nigerian Women's Party, headed by Lady Olayinka Abayomi. When party membership rose to only 500, however, it was clear that the female masses were as far removed from this association as from others run by modern educated elites. They found a new political hero in the oba of Lagos, Adeniji Adele II, who as a Muslim, a traditional chief, and an educated civil servant was the natural successor to Macaulay. Adele quickly seized the opportunity to mobilize the women, and in the 1950 election, the first with female suffrage, the Nigerian Women's Party threw its support to his Area Councils. Weeks before the election the Lagos Market Women's Association, claiming to represent 8,000 market women, denounced the leadership of the NNDP as "irresponsible and unworthy."[18] Only a few faithful members of the old Lagos Market Women's Guild continued to honor Macaulay's memory by remaining loyal to the NNDP and its new allies, the NCNC and the Nigerian Labour Congress.

The defeat of the Area Councils, the chieftaincy dispute between Adele and Oyekan, and the competition for the mayoralty in the early 1950s deepened the political divisions that began to appear among the market women after Macaulay's death. In an effort to generate stronger support, the NNDP-NCNC alliance which captured control of the council refused to follow a subcommittee recommendation to increase the rent for stalls; instead, it launched a program of construction and improvement of urban markets.[19] Traders in Ebute Ero Market, however, alleged that the council was demanding an additional tax of 2d. on every commodity displayed for sale in order to penalize those who did not support the alliance.[20] Meanwhile, Adele had joined forces with the opposition Nigerian Youth Movement, laying the groundwork for the rise of the Action Group, the party that eventually had the most success in winning the market women's support.

Recognizing the strength of the newly enfranchised female electorate, the major parties made systematic attempts to curry the favor of the Lagos traders. Some of the techniques used were uncovered by the 1958 investigation into alleged council irregularities in collecting fees and allocating market stalls, described in detail in the *Rapson Report*. Even though the government ultimately rejected the report,[21] the findings of the investigative commission smeared the Action Group, contributing to its defeat in 1959 and leading to dismissal of the town clerk. These events demonstrated how much influence market women could wield when their vital interests were at stake.

The investigation had been prompted by petitions submitted by the NCNC Market Women's Wing and the United Muslim Party Women's Wing. The substance of the complaint was that the council had allowed market dues to be collected in advance from traders who were promised stalls at proposed temporary sites in Ereko and Oko Awo in central Lagos; that applicants for stalls had first to join the Action Group, then in control of the council; and that they paid their dues to party workers who issued no receipts and kept no records. These charges were verified by the *Rapson Report*, which also described how lists of applicants were submitted. Market leaders and councilors submitted separate lists, containing 3,347 names in all. Adisa Oshodi, a paid clerk in the Action Group secretariat and a secretary of the Lagos Market Women's Association, an AG affiliate, prepared the lists for the market leaders. Councilors' lists, provided by members of both parties, were not checked against those presented by the market leaders, and no remittances accompanied them. Thus the money collected was not matched with the names, nor were the lists checked to see if any names appeared more than once.

When the Alaga of Ereko Market raised money from the traders in her market, after being instructed by the town clerk to collect dues, she was told that "the money [would] . . . be used to prepare the ground and build stalls . . . so that the site could be turned into a temporary market. . . . She asked various group leaders . . . to collect £6 from each individual member. The group leaders commenced the collection and called on Mr. Oshodi to assist them generally and keep records."[22] One trader, asked who had been invited to pay, replied: "Those of us who are old members of the group and who have suffered at the hands of the police. Those people who do not pay money occupy spaces along the drain."[23] According to the *Rapson Report,* £9,492 was collected from 1,582 traders, but only eight bulk receipts were issued by the town clerk. One receipt for £4,392, clumsily made out to Dr. J. Akanni Doherty, chairman of the Lagos Action Group, was later altered by substituting the words "town clerk" for Dr. Doherty in order to dissociate the party from the collection.

These irregularities impelled the federal government to order the money refunded to the women, but the lack of accurate records made that impossible. To this day the money remains on deposit with the council, which is powerless to reappropriate it since it was illegally collected in the first place. To add to the irony, hundreds of stalls eventually allocated to traders in Oko Awo Market, a former swamp, and the larger of the two proposed sites, have been abandoned because of seasonal flooding. The cost of reclaiming the market is conservatively estimated at £40,000, a prohibitively expensive undertaking.

An aspect of the case more relevant to Lagos politics is the attempt of the Action Group to get the women to commit themselves to the party while the money was being raised. Several market women testified that their traditional leaders had summoned them to the home of "Dr. Daddy" (Dr. J. Akanni Doherty), where they were asked to contribute a shilling for an Action Group membership card. Believing that compliance would enhance their chances of getting stalls in the new market sites, the market women obediently enrolled as AG members. Thus the AG used the prospect of expanded markets as bait to increase its rank-and-file membership. As the *Rapson Report* points out, Oshodi and "his party merely took full advantage of a situation presented to them, and no evidence was advanced to show that they acted illegally. . . . It must be remembered that identical action could have been taken by other political parties if they had so wished."[24] The town clerk, bearing the onus for the impropriety of his party's actions, suffered the severest consequences. Nevertheless, the Action Group, though sustaining a temporary electoral setback after publication of the *Rapson Report*, did gain a foothold among the market women. In the long run this achievement proved to be a pivotal factor in its later success.

After this episode the Action Group vigorously stepped up its efforts to incorporate the women as a meaningful wing of the party. Working through market supervisors and the Lagos Market Women's Association (later known as the Lagos City Markets and Women's Organization),[25] the party won the support of leading traders, particularly market chairmen and section heads. By 1964 the AG had a branch in every urban market, each equal in status to a ward or precinct organization. The party concentrated on soliciting grass-roots membership rather than on giving market women representation on the council or in the party executive. As a result, only one female AG councilor has attained prominence in the party; Mrs. Elsie Femi-Pearse, an Egba Yoruba and former teacher, served on the council for five years before she resigned from the party allegedly in protest against the award of an abattoir contract. More important for the party, however, about 75 percent of the market women, a strategically useful bloc vote, had become firmly pro-AG. In 1962 the AG acknowledged "especially the market women for voting the party into power in the LTC"[26] when all hope seemed lost. NCNC leaders openly agreed that the women's vote was a decisive factor in the electoral outcome. The women voted as they did primarily because they believed, rightly or wrongly, that the 1962 AG crisis, climaxed by the treason trial of Chief Awolowo, had been instigated by the federal government.[27]

Having been out of power for all but six years after female suffrage had been introduced, the NCNC was in a less advantageous position to offer inducements to the market women for their political support. In recapturing control of the council in 1959, just after publication of the *Rapson Report*, the NCNC promised to "rescue helpless market women from the avaricious exploitation of the AG" and to "provide more modern markets for the women of Lagos without having to demand any advance payment from them."[28] About this time the NCNC also made an effort to incorporate the women into the party structure. Unlike the AG, which had aimed at mass membership, the NCNC strove for group representation of women in both the party hierarchy and the council. Except for Mrs. Elsie Femi-Pearse, all successful female councilors in Lagos have been members of the NCNC. Consistent with the party's diversity, NCNC women councilors included three Lagosian traders, one Ibo seamstress, and one Ibo trader, all of them Christian. Rather than work through traditional leaders or natural market divisions, as the AG had done, the NCNC created a cumbersome set of leadership positions for women in different geographical zones, some of which overlapped or conflicted in jurisdiction.[29] Moreover, the formation of two separate women's wings—the NCNC Women's Association and the NCNC Market Women's Association—suggests that class divisions between educated and uneducated women were transferred into the party. As a result, the NCNC could not match the efficiency and intensity with which its opposition mobilized the bulk of city traders.

The strength among market women of the breakaway NNDP, controlled in Lagos by former leaders of both the AG and the NCNC, had too little time for testing before the imposition of military rule. Under the direction of Chief O. A. Fagbenro-Beyioku, former secretary of the NCNC Market Women's Wing, the party made a strenuous, if belated, effort to bring the women into the embryonic organization. Four NNDP women's committees functioned at the parliamentary constituency level, and Madam Sinotu Alaga was designated as the key organizer to win members by working through market branches of the party. Each constituency committee had a chairman and a secretary, kept its own accounts, raised its own funds, and developed its own strategy. That the party succeeded in gaining some influence among market women is evidenced by the events that followed the establishment of a military regime, particularly the struggle over naming a women's representative to the newly appointed caretaker committee.

After the military coup d'etat of January 15, 1966, all elected local councils in the country were dissolved and interim administrative committees were appointed to take over their functions. In Lagos the caretaker committee was to include representatives of all relevant administrative departments, federal ministries, and community interest groups. One out of twenty-five seats was to be reserved for the market women. Despite the ban on political activities, all the market women's factions previously allied with political parties immediately began to lobby for their respective nominees. The Lagos City Market and Women's Organization, which rightly claimed to have the largest membership, nominated its administrative secretary, Chief E. O. Dare, a male herbalist who had worked with the association for some thirty-four years.[30] The rival United Market Women's Association, claiming to be the only organization competent to represent the traders, nominated Madam Abibatu Mogaji. It further argued that its members had suffered at the hands of other women's organizations which "have the corrupt backing of a Godfather in the LCC."[31] A third association, the Ebutero-Alakoro-Elefun Market Women's League, denounced Madam Mogaji on the grounds that she was not a trader, had no stall of her own, was an illiterate who would not be able to follow council proceedings, and was an AG politician, "a campaigner of a first class order who is well known from Lagos to every corner of the Western Provinces. Her composition and political songs and utterances during the last Western and Federal Elections of 1964/65 are still fresh in everybody's memory." Chief Dare, the league claimed, was also a well-known AG organizing secretary who, along with Adisa Oshodi, had been placed in the markets "to coordinate and propagate the ideologies of their party. By allowing any of these people to represent the market women's interest is just another way the politicians will inject themselves into the Council again, therefore defeating the aims for which the Council was dissolved."[32] Accordingly, the Market Women's League put forward as its candidate Madam Ige Ogunbiyi, a trader in Oko Awo Market. Significantly, if Madam Ogunbiyi failed to be elected, the league wanted the government to cancel representation of the market women on the caretaker committee altogether.

The military regime had been advised by the senior market master and the council's information officer to accept the recommendation of the Lagos City Markets and Women's Organization, despite the strong objections of rival associations, which demanded equal representation. Calling for more information on the membership and structure of the competing unions, the government delayed its decision until July 26, 1966, just three days before the second military coup d'etat. At that time, Major General J. T. U. Aguiyi-Ironsi, head of the military regime, confirmed Mrs. Modupe Caxton-Martins, the Alaga of Tejuoso Market, the wife of a High Court judge, and a former NNDP ward leader, as a member of the caretaker committee.

In retrospect, one can appreciate the extent to which the role of the market women has changed since the time of Macaulay. Before 1950 the women lacked the vote, had no representation, and were not officially incorporated into any party structure, even though they contributed financially and gave mass popular support to Macaulay. After 1950 the politicization of the market women had progressed to the point where they formed an auxiliary wing in every major party in Lagos, establishing factions that continued to be meaningful even after the imposition of military rule. Although it might be an exaggeration to claim, as did E. A. Oluyele Bright, the deputy mayor of Lagos, that "any person supported by the women must be successful at the polls,"[33] it is true that the dominant party in the city has had the majority support of the market women. In 1962, when victory appeared to be certain for the NCNC, the market women were considered to have been the decisive factor in giving victory to the AG. Earlier, they had successfully protested council abuses, provoking a probe that affected local elections and resulted in the dismissal of the town clerk. It is not surprising that politicians fear the potential impact of the market women, for on the few occasions when they have been aroused, their political influence has been significant.

In light of their collective resources—an aggressive spirit of competition, economic independence, and a strong sense of group solidarity—it is curious that the market women have not been more assertive on a broader range of issues. Market women tend to react to, rather than innovate, public policies. They act as a pressure group only when their vital interests are directly at stake. They have not agitated, for example, for lower taxes, better education, or increased public medical facilities, issues one might expect to be of special concern to them.

The unassertiveness of the market women's political activities may be attributed to three primary factors: a traditional view of politics, a high degree of self-sufficincy, and a lack of modern leadership. Basically, market women still retain a traditional conception of politics as a face-to-face relationship in which individual political favors are distributed by recognized authorities with whom they can identify personally. For this reason, the women are still attached to traditional market heads and to the oba and chiefs of Lagos—protective leaders to whom they can relate on familiar and friendly terms—in contrast with the impersonal bureaucratic leadership of municipal institutions. At bottom, the women do not believe in the efficacy (perhaps not even in the legitimacy) of local government machinery as a means of furthering their own interests. Individual councilors or dominant parties that can present the "face"of the council in the markets may bridge the gap, using personal relationships to solicit endorsement through the ballot box. But until the market women are more assimilated into the modern urban culture, they will lack the motivation for sustained and autonomous activity in issue areas not related to their immediate interests.

Second, the market women have achieved a high degree of self-sufficiency as an occupational group. Except for the construction of market stalls and minimum sanitation control, the women carry on their commerce almost without reference to local government control. Problems arising in connection with the everyday concerns of traders are resolved through the market women's own leadership hierarchy, which has served them well for years. In effect, this leadership structure, functioning as a political subsystem within the larger political community, is governed by rigid rules and regulations for conflict resolution and for the provision of public welfare. With this degree of independence, the women see no need to pursue abstract goals of group representation or to agitate for reforms that would only peripherally affect their lives.

Finally, the market women are not so assertive as they might be because they lack aggressive modern leadership. To utilize their resources to the fullest they would need a female counterpart of Oba Adele, a market woman with acknowledged status, with the respect of the mass of traders, and with the ability to function as meaningfully in the corridors of city hall as in the crowded alleys of urban markets. Thus far, outstanding females active in the modern sector have been drawn chiefly from the ranks of the urban upper class, not from among the traders. These educated and wealthy women have little or no identity with the traditionalistic Muslim women. It is reasonable to assume, however, that when the market women do develop modern leadership, they will begin to utilize their collective resources more fully and become a formidable political force. They would then certainly emerge as one of the most influential and independent economic interest groups in Lagos.

# CHAPTER 9

*The Constitutional Status of Lagos*:
*Internal and External Influences*

For years the constitutional status of Lagos has been of crucial importance to local, regional, and central government authorities as well as to leaders of major political parties. No other local issue has loomed so large on the stage of Nigerian politics or elicited such widespread and occasionally contradictory responses, contributing toward unity, secessionist agitation, intergovernmental conflict, and the growth of community consciousness.

The historic position of Lagos as the nation's administrative and economic capital has accounted in large part for the intensity of political activity over this issue. But the rapid pace of urbanization has stimulated even greater interest in the city's constitutional status. The seacoast town exercises economic dominance over the hinterland as a leading port, commercial center, and industrial complex, wherein reside most of the country's foreign population, diplomatic corps, and African elite. The group or interest that controls Lagos, the wealthiest and most modern community in the country, obviously has a strong claim to prestige, revenue, and power.

These political and economic advantages have shaped the question of urban political control more directly than have administrative or functional considerations. Indeed, the status of the capital is essentially a question of how to divide a national asset among sectional interests. Not until the 1950s, with the full emergence of a Lagos state movement, were the needs of the urban inhabitants considered an important criterion, and never have the requirements of city planning or urban development guided the decision-making process as to what direction the community's growth should take.

Three basic policy options are available to decision makers in determining how a federal capital is to be governed.[1] First, if the city is placed under the jurisdiction of a state or regional government, it could function as either a state or a federal capital or as both. This experiment has been tried twice in Nigeria: between 1951 and 1954 Lagos and its outlying districts were incorporated into the Western Region; since 1967 the city has been the capital of Lagos State. Lagos is now both a federal and a state capital, a status held by only five other cities in the world.[2] Second, the federal capital may itself be made a state equal in status to all other component parts of the federation. Lagos has never experienced this form of government, although during the agitation for a Lagos state this alternative was considered. The city-state type of urban government exists only in Austria, where Vienna is one of the country's nine provinces and is the federal capital as well. Finally, the most widely used option is to give the capital a unique status as a federal territory, a special district owing no allegiance to any state or component part of the union.[3] Most federal systems have adopted this alternative, though with varying degrees of local autonomy. For example, Washington, D.C. is largely deprived of local self-government, whereas Lagos, through most of its history as a self-governing municipality, has enjoyed a substantial measure of autonomy in local matters.

Despite the apparent simplicity of these options, certain complications limit freedom of choice. Is the capital to be carved out of an area that a state would resist giving up, or is it for geographical convenience to be merged with a state with which it has had no previous association? What ethnic or cultural ties between the capital and the surrounding area, and what historical connections, affect the situation? Suppose, as a port or an industrial area, the town is a vital economic complex on which remote areas of the country depend for export of agricultural produce and for international trade. Are such factors as access to the sea, a profitable consumer market, and the productive capacity of a city legitimate bases for determining the future of urban government? Finally, how can the desire for political neutralization and the equitable division of resources be balanced against the demands for local representation and communal home rule? All these dilemmas were pertinent to Lagos. Each time the Lagos issue arose, the particular solution adopted was interpreted by one or more parties as an alternative designed to favor one sectional interest over another. Perhaps inevitably, the question of the status of Lagos came to turn on determining, not what form of government the city should have, but to whom the prize of political control would ultimately be awarded.

GROWTH OF REGIONAL INTERESTS

Had Lagos not been made the capital under the colonial regime, much of the subsequent controversy over its status might have been avoided, since only the Western Region, geographically contiguous to Lagos, could have claimed control. But because Lagos was the natural gateway to the interior and a logical center of administrative operations, both during and after colonial rule, all regions felt they had a vested interest in the city's status. After the 1914 amalgamation, Lord Lugard intended to move the country's capital to Kaduna, capital of the Northern Provinces, but the Colonial Office denied his request because of inadequate communications with and transportation to a town nearly 600 miles upcountry. After Lagos began to develop as a commercial and trading center, the argument was that it was too late to change, since heavy public and private investments made a shift to the north uneconomical. By the 1950s, when transferral of the capital was seriously reconsidered, the cost of moving would have been exorbitant. For the first ninety years of British rule, therefore, Lagos was governed as a special administrative unit separate from the rest of the country.

From 1886 until 1951 the municipal district, or the urban area subsequently known as the Federal Territory, was joined to three colony districts (Badagry, Ikeja, and Epe) to form the Lagos Crown Colony. Lagos town always dominated the affairs of this colony and remained a distinct community, having a character that sharply distinguished it from the rural areas. Unlike the rest of the country, the colony was placed under direct rule, a form of administration that continued in the city even after the native authority system was introduced in the colony districts in 1938. The Crown Colony status of Lagos also contrasted with the protectorate status applied to the Northern and Southern Provinces. The distinction was a legal one, suggesting a stronger and presumably perpetual imperial domain over the coastal enclave. Thus, until the nationalist period, the status of Lagos was carefully defined so that the town owed allegiance only to the central government, not to any constituent part of the federation, and shared a political identity with no other region. Protectively guarded as a strategic outpost of the British Empire, Lagos was deliberately and effectively insulated from the hinterland and, at the same time, was portrayed as a city whose benefits all Nigerians were entitled to share.

The postwar birth of the nationalist movement and the new policy of granting gradual self-government to Britain's colonies forced reexamination of the privileged status of Lagos in light of anticipated constitutional reforms. From all parts of Nigeria, covetous eyes turned toward this important town, now the comparatively rich and sophisticated home of the nation's first-generation nationalists. Each of the three regions formed in 1945 had its own particular reasons for wanting control of or, at the very least, a voice in the affairs of the most advanced community in the nation.

The first to assert its claim to the city was the Western Region, the least populous of the three at the time of the 1950 Ibadan General Conference on the Review of the Nigerian Constitution. At that conference the Western Region argued its case for the incorporation of Lagos within its own borders, defending its proposal on the grounds of cultural affinity and administrative expediency. Lagos Yorubas were ethnically related to the majority of the west's Yoruba population, and the town had historical connections with the ancient kingdom of Benin, then situated in the eastern part of the Western Region. Moreover, since the colony shared its inland boundaries with the west, it was through that region that the bulk of the nation's export produce had to pass en route to the harbor. It was natural, argued the western delegation, that Lagos be absorbed into the region with which it had the closest cultural and economic ties.

The opponents of this proposal—the Lagos and Eastern Region delegations—argued vehemently for preserving the city's independence in fairness to all sections of the country. At the most, they allowed, the colony districts might be merged with the west, but the concentration of national facilities and investments in the city required that the capital stay under federal control. In reply, the western delegation claimed that Lagos was too small and too weak financially to be self-sufficient, an argument supported by the northern delegation. The conference finally recommended as a compromise solution the merger of the colony districts with the Western Region, leaving the city of Lagos as a federal territory.[4] On the findings of a select committee of the Legislative Council, however, the recommendation was overruled and in 1951 the entire colony was merged with the west, as the latter had originally proposed. For the first time in its history, Lagos lost its identity as a separate political entity. Its administrative and legislative institutions were placed under regional control, except that central services, such as the port and railways, remained under federal supervision.

The political differences that emerged over the status of Lagos at this first constitutional conference were relatively mild compared with the conflict that arose shortly afterward, when the basic interests of the three regions and of the dominant parties governing them finally crystallized into concrete goals and objectives. Having won control of the government machinery of Lagos, the Action Group regime in the Western Region quickly embarked upon a program designed to solidify its popularity in the community and to undermine the influence of its rival, the NCNC, which had recently won a landslide victory in the 1950 urban elections. Political institutions in Lagos were made to conform in broad outline with the regional pattern of local government. This change entailed raising the status of the popular oba of Lagos, Adeniji Adele II; reserving seats on the council for traditional chiefs; expanding the council's membership from twenty-four to forty-two; redrawing electoral districts; and redesigning voting procedures. Under the shrewd planning of Chief Obafemi Awolowo, then Action Group minister of local government for the Western Region, in the short span of only three years these moves gave the AG electoral as well as administrative control of the city. But just as the party's penetration of Lagos appeared to be making significant headway, a second constitutional conference was called to review the provisions of the Macpherson Constitution, under which Lagos had been merged with the west. It was at the 1953 London Conference that entrenched regional interests clashed most bitterly over the status of the capital city.

It is important to understand how the positions adopted at the London Conference were related to the events that precipitated constitutional review in the first place and made the question of Lagos a sensitive national issue. On March 31, 1953, Anthony Enahoro, an Action Group member of the legislature from Benin, proposed that the House of Representatives endorse "as a primary political objective the attainment of self-government for Nigeria in 1956,"[5] a goal endorsed by his party three months earlier at its annual convention. In response, Alhaji Ahmadu Bello, the Sardauna of Sokoto and leader of the Northern Peoples' Congress, offered an amendment that the specific date of 1956 be replaced by the phrase "as soon as practicable." After a heated debate the NCNC and the AG walked out of the session to protest the north's refusal to push ahead with the nationalists' demands. Alluding to the amalgamation that had created the Nigerian nation, the Sardauna also left the session embittered, with his famous closing remark that "the mistake of 1914 has come to light and I should like to go no further."[6] Accusing the NPC of collusion with the colonial regime, the NCNC and the AG formed an alliance in order to continue the fight for self-government, thus isolating the insular and traditionalistic Northern Region in its conservative stance.

The treatment received by northern representatives from the crowds of Lagos during this episode did as much to shape their attitudes on the Lagos question and to deepen the split between the north and the south as did the ideological differences separating the major political parties. Sedate, reserved, and aristocratic northern leaders had been subjected to degrading ridicule from the indignant urban masses, who contemptuously jeered at the

Sardauna and his entourage as "imperialist stooges" with "no minds of their own." During their stay in the city the northern members—many of them in Lagos for the first time in their lives— were sharply criticized in the Lagos press and openly insulted in the streets as they emerged from the halls of parliament. These humiliating experiences convinced them of the fundamental incompatibility between their feudalistic northern culture and the radical and undisciplined south.[7] Accordingly, as recounted by the Sardauna,

> There were agitations in favour of secession; we should set up on our own; we should cease to have anything more to do with the Southern people; we should take our own way. I must say it looked very tempting. ... We had no sentimental illusions about leaving the others; they had acted in such a way that it was abundantly clear to us that they would sooner see the back of us.[8]

Any lingering doubts about the depth of hostility in the country at this time were put to rest by the violent reception given to an untimely southern delegation sent by the NCNC and the AG, shortly after the parliamentary debate, to campaign for self-government in northern cities. Six weeks after the Sardauna had left "the screams and insults of the large crowd of Lagos thugs,"[9] rioting broke out in Kano, the north's largest city, where an Action Group political rally was being planned. In the wake of a four-day purge of southern residents in the *sabon gari*, the secretary of state for the colonies summoned Nigerian leaders to the London Conference to review the constitution. It was during the tense months following these acrimonious events that regional leaders reevaluated their positions as to the form of political association they favored and as to the status of Lagos in the future constitutional structure.

The sharpest turnabout at this conference was made by members of the Northern Region delegation. The largest and least developed unit in the federation, the north was especially concerned about the threat of domination by the southerners after the achievement of self-government, because skilled manpower was in far greater supply in the commercial and administrative sectors of the Western and Eastern regions. Hundreds of thousands of southerners had already migrated northward, contributing to the insecurity that led to the Kano riots. Now the prospect of independence raised further fears that unfriendly southerners would hold influential positions in crucial regional institutions, flouting their achievements in the face of the less qualified northerners whom they had supplanted. With the scars of maltreatment in Lagos fresh in their memories, northerners introduced an eight-point program at the London Conference which, "if implemented, would have meant virtual secession of the Northern Region from Nigeria."[10]

The north was inclined toward a path of separatism, but, in the words of the Sardauna,

> there were . . . two things of the most vital importance [standing] in our way. The first was that the greatest part of the revenue of Nigeria comes from customs duties collected on the coast on all goods brought over the wharves. Obviously we would have to collect our own duties at our own borders [if the federation broke up]. This would be more difficult than collecting at the waterside, but it was not impossible.
>
> The second difficulty was similar to it. . . . Would it be possible to send our goods down to the coast for shipment by rail or road, and what guarantee would there be that they would get there at all? . . . We would have to use the southern roads and they are built and maintained from southern funds. . . . What about this transport difficulty?[11]

Since access to the sea was absolutely essential for the landlocked north, its interest in remaining in the federation was inextricably tied to the position of Lagos. The region's political ambitions for the capital were based entirely on economic grounds, for "who-[ever] . . . holds Lagos . . . could withhold our trade."[12] Accordingly, after extended discussions, the northern representatives, along with the other regional delegations, agreed to continued federal association with political power residing primarily in the regions. With regard to Lagos, however, the north reversed its original support of a merger of the capital with the west, demanding neutralization of its vital economic lifeline. If the west should secede from the federation, the northern leaders realized, they could be completely cut off from the port through which most of the region's groundnut and cotton produce were exported.[13] The north's new position was that Lagos should be separated from the west to assume a neutral status as an autonomous federal territory, toward which all regions could jointly contribute and from which all could jointly benefit.

The north's proposal was in line with that of the Eastern Region, which all along, but for different reasons, had advocated a separate status for Lagos. The NCNC had regarded Lagos as its political stronghold, a place where Azikiwe had built up immense popularity and the NCNC had enjoyed landslide electoral successes. As a stepping-stone from which nationalists had risen to higher office, Lagos had been NCNC headquarters since the time of the party's formation. Not until the city was placed under the control of the west did the party's fortunes begin to decline in the capital. First, Azikiwe's attempt to enter the House of Representatives had been thwarted by the Action Group's refusal to nominate him as a Lagos representative from the Western House of Assembly in 1951, a tactic that Azikiwe had warned of before the merger (see chap. 5). The ensuing party crisis resulted in open defiance of the NCNC hierarchy by local leaders and a split in the party's representation on the council. With the introduction of new local government reforms in the 1950s, with the growing popularity of an oba who was campaigning for the AG, and with the NCNC defeat in the 1953 local elections, the NCNC clearly saw that its best interests lay in supporting the north's proposal to remove Lagos from control of the west. Thus, while the north urged federalization of Lagos for reasons of economic self-interest, the east supported the move for reasons of political self-interest. On the Lagos issue, the conservative northern and radical eastern leaders were in substantial harmony.

The Action Group predictably fought the movement to withdraw Lagos from its jurisdiction, and the strength of the party's resistance was underestimated by its opponents. Naturally, the tenuous alliance between the Action Group and the NCNC formed after the self-government debate dissolved over this issue after only a few months of existence. The Western Region, determined to keep its grip on the city at all costs, adamantly refused to agree to the separation of Lagos at the 1953 London Conference. When all attempts at a compromise failed, the delegations agreed to allow the colonial secretary, Oliver Lyttleton (Lord Chandos), to decide the matter. Lyttleton supported the north's demand for federalization, emphasizing his desire to protect the interests of all Nigerians. While urging the west to yield for the sake of national unity, he noted that an example of compromise had already been set by the northern delegation by its agreement to stay in the federation after it had been assured of access to the sea. The federalization of Lagos therefore appeared to be not a neutral act, but a necessary compromise to keep the north in the union.

This outcome further enraged the western delegation, whose leaders, despite their prior agreement to accept the verdict of the colonial secretary, launched a vigorous campaign to reverse his decision. To them, Lagos had been ripped out of their control through the combined offensive of two rival parties. In addition, since the north was the largest region, the net effect of federalization was northernization. Recalling events at the conference, Awolowo bitterly described the controversy as a conspiracy between his political enemies and the colonial government: "One morning, the Sardauna, who had not until then uttered a word, broke his silence and declared that he agreed that Nigeria should continue as a federal union. He was cheered; and for his generous 'concession' in this regard Lord Chandos awarded Lagos to him as a Federal Territory!"[14]

Ironically, in quelling the drive toward secession in one part of the country, the Lagos issue had spawned a similar drive in another. As part of its campaign the Action Group published a thirty-page tract reviewing the history of Lagos, its social composition, its economic role in the country, and the arguments submitted by different interests. Entitled *Lagos Belongs to the West*, the document claimed that Lagos was "not a cosmopolitan territory, but a Yoruba town pure and simple."[15] Citing the previous passivity of the north, the pamphlet argued that until the west became active the north had shown "complete indifference as to where Lagos was."[16] Nor did the economic argument that the north needed an outlet to the sea convince the AG of the value of federalization, since Nigeria had other ports through which produce

253

could be shipped. Lagos was more important to the people of the Western Region than those of the Northern Region: it was to the west "precisely what the head is to the body of an individual."[17] Finally, the AG blamed the decision to federalize Lagos not on the northerners, but on "a class of Ibo politicians [who] . . . had occasionally described Lagos as a 'no-man's land.'"[18] The document concluded with an ominous threat:

> Unless Her Majesty's Government is going to use force to deny the people of the Western Region the right of self-determination— to remain within or outside Nigeria as they desire—we believe we have said enough to show that this solution can have no other effect than the disintegration of Nigeria.[19]

In reply, the NCNC published a ten-page pamphlet entitled *Gedegbe L'eko Wa* ("Lagos Is Free"), which repeated the colonial secretary's arguments and refuted the AG's position.[20] Hoping to get the decision changed before resumption of the Constitutional Conference in 1954,the AG relentlessly persisted in its campaign, drawing upon all its resources to demonstrate the seriousness of its position. The AG Youth Association passed a resolution endorsing the secession of the Western Region should the colonial secretary fail to reverse his decision on Lagos.[21] Similar mandates were confirmed by the obas and chiefs of the Western Region, the Western House of Chiefs, and the Egbe Omo Oduduwa.[22] Backed by these expressions of mass support, Awolowo defiantly cabled the colonial secretary a sharply worded threat of regional withdrawl based on the right of self-determination. The colonial secretary, in a reply published in the local press, warned Awolowo that "any attempt to secure alteration of [the Lagos] . . . decision by force will be resisted, and . . . any attempt to secure the secession of the Western Region from the federation would be regarded as the use of force."[23] The Action Group, though refraining from raising the question at the resumed 1954 Constitutional Conference, did try to have the right of regional secession written into the new constitution. The proposal was roundly defeated, but it served as a warning that Nigerian unity was still being threatened. The decision to sever Lagos from the west went into effect with the introduction of the Lyttleton Constitution in 1954, ending a brief three-year period of Western Region control over Lagos.

It is difficult to say whether the Action Group's refusal to accept the loss of Lagos was motivated by injured pride or by the quest for material gain. Certainly Awolowo's assertion of cultural affinity between the Yorubas of Lagos and those of the west was incontestable, and his endorsement of a merger on this ground was consistent with his advocacy of a federation of linguistic states. But this is the weakest explanation of the AG's policy, for even Awolowo recognized the legitimacy of internal demands for autonomy, as his evolving views on this point make clear.[24] It is likely that the party's inflexibility on the Lagos issue can be traced to the loss of revenues and the political setback incurred as a result of federalization. As late as 1957, long after the question had been settled by the colonial secretary, Awolowo told a party conference that he "did not regard the demand for merger as an end in itself, but as a means only to remove certain political disabilities of the Lagos people and to eliminate adverse financial effects on the Western Region which result from separation."[25] To this end, the Action Group had even suggested during the 1953 controversy that the federal capital be moved to a site near Kafanchan in the heart of the Northern Region, offering generous compensation for federal establishments, such as the harbor, railway, customs, and other agencies, which it would then take over.[26] This plan would have satisfied neither the north nor the east, for moving the capital would not have ended the struggle for control of the economic assets of Lagos. Regional competition for Lagos continued, particularly on the part of the west, long after 1954. Meanwhile, internal agitation for creation of a Lagos state—for autonomy as an alternative to regionalization or federalization—began to make itself felt.

URBAN COMMUNAL NATIONALISM

Agitation for an autonomous status for Lagos originated in the early 1950s not as an isolated phenomenon stemming from the particular circumstances of the city alone, but as part of a wider trend in Nigeria for minority groups to press for their rights as the country progressed toward independence. The pattern was always the same: one or more related minority groups wanted governmental protection against the threat of domination from a larger ethnic group in their immediate vicinity. Such protection was sought through the creaton of more states by dividing each of Nigeria's three regions into smaller units. The process would undercut the power of the three largest ethnic groups—Hausa-Fulani, Yoruba, and Ibo—an unstable but powerful triumvirate that precluded meaningful political participation by more than 200 minority groups which together constituted approximately 40 percent of Nigeria's total population. The "big three," although differing widely in other respects, shared the common goal of maintaining their strongholds of power in their respective regions. Nevertheless, a tactic used by all of them in interparty competition was to support the movement for more states in other regions while resisting dismemberment of their own. Once Lagos was separated from the west, however, regional interests had little cause to support separatist demands in the capital, for autonomy would benefit only the local inhabitants.

To indigenous Lagosians, the demand for a region or a state was clearly as justifiable as were the demands for autonomy arising from Nigeria's other cultural minorities. But since Lagos was not even part of a region, its residents felt they were more deprived than most minorities: they lacked proportional representation in government institutions at both regional and national levels; they had few opportunities for employment in the civil service and in statutory agencies; they gained less benefit from regional development programs; and they were vulnerable to exploitation from external groups through federal interference. Moreover, they were being governed by non-Lagosians, principally northerners who occupied the top positions in the federal ministries overseeing Lagos.[27] From the Lagosian point of view, the demand for a Lagos state was self-evidently just. Gradually, as communal consciousness intensified among indigenous Lagosians, these sentiments hardened into open political activity by organized pressure groups. Eventually the agitation for a Lagos state took on a special form of its own, related to but distinguished from other minority movements. It became an urban populist movement designed to uplift the misunderstood, underprivileged, and widely neglected urban poor, the Lagos indigenes who regarded the national capital as their home.

The sentiments of these "true Lagosians" were shared by few other Nigerians, not even by other minorities. The reasons for rejecting the demands for autonomy, besides the obvious economic ones, stemmed from the conflict between two different conceptions of an urban dweller. Most Nigerians have regarded Lagos as a land of opportunity to which people migrate to pursue material or utilitarian objectives; it is a place to get a job, to seek adventure, to improve one's station in life. Thus a "Lagos man" is a "modern man" who may or may not be a long-term resident, but one who in any event has probably not been born in the city and who maintains his rights, privileges, obligations, and loyalties to his homeland elsewhere in the country. The indigenes, by contrast, are viewed by the average Nigerian primarily as lowly slum-dwellers of little or no importance. Lagos has been described by most immigrants as a "no man's land," meaning, in African terms, a land belonging to no communal group.

The true Lagosians were therefore a faceless minority whose communal identity had a political impact only when challenged by other outgroups. Political consciousness was primarily a defensive response to the immigrant invasion, after the indigenes realized that strangers were grabbing the land, jobs, trade, and political control of their community. But to claim equal rights as a minority is not necessarily to have them recognized as legitimate by others. Lagosians found it far more difficult to claim authentic minority distinction, for they spoke the same language, were of the same ethnic stock, owed allegiance to the same political rulers, and shared the same traditional religious beliefs as the Yorubas of the Western Region, a people noted for the cultural variations and political divisions of their subgroups. No other segment of the Yoruba people had previously claimed the status of a cultural minority or demanded political autonomy as the Lagosians were beginning to do in the 1950s.

In many respects, then, the demand for a Lagos state was unique. It expressed the sentiments of a people closely related to a larger ethnic group rather than the complaints of an oppressed minority with distinct cultural differences from their neighbors. Economically, the indigenes were agitating for a state that would be the smallest unit in the federation, possessing virtually no natural resources; yet as an outlet to the sea, it would be one of the nation's most important states, with a comparatively wealthy and highly educated population. Politically, the state movement had no exact parallel elsewhere, for it concerned government at every level; each region had an interest in the status of the capital, in control of the nation's primary seaport, and in the location of federal administrative headquarters. It is remarkable that, despite the inherent complications and the stiff resistance of external groups, a lower-class urban minority of approximately 175,000 people succeeded in establishing their own state about twenty years after they began to agitate for local autonomy.

The first stirrings of communal nationalism in Lagos were evidenced in the development of communal associations exclusively concerned with the interests of indigenous citizens. Associations such as the Lagos Aborigines Society, the Egbe Omo Oba, the Lagos Royalists, and the Egbe Omo Ibile Eko intensified the particularistic loyalties of the indigenes, clarified their corporate identity, and helped generate political activity. The Egbe Omo Ibile Eko, for example, encouraged native sons to press for stronger representation on government boards, to lobby for increased responsibilities and higher status for the oba and chiefs of Lagos, and to work for the creation of a Lagos state.[28] The association also provided an operational definition of Lagosians as (1) descendants of past and present obas, (2) persons whose families possess a compound (*agbo-ile*) in Lagos and who lay no claim to any other part of Nigeria, and (3) persons whose ancestors settled in Lagos before 1900 and had abandoned their domicile of origin (i.e., descendants of native foreigners).

The most politically effective communal organization was the Lagos Citizens' Rights Protection Council (LCRPC), also known as the Egbe Eko Parapo. Formed in 1962 by the merger of the Egbe Omo Ibile Eko and the Lagos Aborigines Society, and led by Chief T. A. Doherty, the LCRPC was an organization working for "the welfare of Lagosians in all its aspects."[29] Claiming a membership of 7,000 and boasting an eighty-one-member executive council of prominent citizens, this association stimulated mass support for statehood for Lagos by advertising in the press, by publishing lists of the grievances of Lagosians, and by presenting formal proposals for the structure of a Lagos state government.[30] Many of the LCRPC's rank-and-file members came from the new generation of Muslims educated in the progressive Islamic schools run by the Ahmadiya and Ansar-ud-Deen societies. Since the association's goals included a higher status for the oba and chiefs of Lagos, these traditional leaders joined enthusiastically in the campaign for autonomy. Market women, landowners, and small businessmen, having been exploited by externally controlled political parties were attracted by the prospect of local leadership. As the movement for autonomy gradually gained momentum, nearly every major sector of the indigenous community supported it. It cut across party lines, religious groups, dynastic factions, and class boundaries.

A formal demand for autonomy was made by indigenous elements at the 1957 Constitutional Conference. The state advocates were supported by the NCNC, an alliance of easterners and indigenes reminiscent of the old coalition between Herbert Macaulay's followers and the nationalist NCNC union in early Lagos. Also speaking for the indigenes was the United Muslim Party, dominated by Lagos Muslims who specifically attacked the AG, then controlling the Town Council, for denying equal rights to Lagos citizens. The UMP asserted that "any proposals from the Lagos Town Council should be regarded as representing a nonpolitical organization or as expressing the wishes of an individual body under the influence of the AG and therefore seeking the duplication of the submission of the AG." The UMP added that "Lagos should never be merged with the West."[31] Affirming this position were other local associations representing traditional interests, as well as the Lagos and Colony State Movement, an NCNC affiliate created in 1953 "to give articulation to the views and feelings of the Lagos and Colony populace at the forthcoming Pan-Nigerian Conference."[32] The movement for a Lagos state had at this point become irredentist: it pressed not only for a new constitutional status but for reunion with the colony districts of Badagry, Ikeja, and Epe, which had been left under the jurisdiction of the Western Region when Lagos was separated from that region in 1954. The Lagos state movement urged the creation not only of a city-state, but also of a unit that would mean a further loss of territory for the west.

In the opposite corner at the 1957 conference was the Action Group, still lobbying for a return to the 1951 arrangement under which Lagos was part of the Western Region. To appease the demands of the indigenes, however, the AG agreed that additional responsibilities could be transferred from the federal government to the council, that Lagosians should be represented more fully on government agencies, and that the status of the oba and chiefs of Lagos should be raised. These measures were designed to redress the grievances of Lagosians while at the same time undercutting their demand for autonomy.[33] Only groups closely affiliated with the Action Group, such as the Central Area Council, the executive arm of the Area Councils which was then a wing of the Action Group, supported this position.[34] The oba of Lagos, torn between deference to his party's position and his personal sympathy for political autonomy, was significantly silent.

The 1957 conference decided that Lagos should retain its status as a federal territory, a compromise that pleased the north and conveniently avoided favoring either the west or the east, though neither region was altogether satisfied with the outcome. In accordance with the Action Group's proposals, the conference also decided to grant Lagos proportional representation in the House of Representatives and to include one Lagos member of the house in the federal cabinet. These decisions did not satisfy the indigenes, however, and more demands were made the following year to the Minorities Commission appointed to investigate the fears of minority groups and the means of allaying them. A combined submission, forwarded by the Lagos and Colony State Movement, the United Muslim Party, and the Aborigines of Lagos and Colony Provinces, aired local grievances. Under existing arrangements, the petitioners argued, lack of land cramped the fast-growing urban population into an enclave that could barely provide sufficient space for development; metropolitan services were apportioned among separate governments, creating jurisdictional conflict; and citizens living in Lagos were more conscious than ever before of their lack of political and economic opportunities. The Minorities Commission, concurring with the view of most of Nigeria's decision-making elite, rejected these complaints:

> It was ... suggested that there should be a Lagos and Colony State including the municipal area of Lagos, which is now Federal, and the three Divisions of the old Colony. The formation of a new state of this nature, *representing no discernible minority interest* [italics mine], seemed to us quite outside our terms of reference, nor, as is elsewhere explained, did we think that the proceedings of the Conference would justify us in reopening without specific instructions a question so recently settled as that of the boundary between the Federal Territory of Lagos and the immediately surrounding area.[35]

Disappointed but resolute, the supporters of the Lagos state movement continued to pursue their objective. The NCNC promised in the 1959 election campaign to expand the boundaries of Lagos for 20 miles if it was returned to office, a promise the NPC nominally supported in order to undermine AG dominance in the capital.[36] Disillusioned with the AG, Oba Adele withdrew his support from his traditional ally months before the electoral contest; though failing to affiliate with the NCNC, he did lend support to the swelling ranks of Lagosians asserting communal independence. Following his example, several other Lagosian supporters of the AG began to waver in their loyalties. As noted earlier, Lagosians had by then begun to filter into the ranks of the AG, constituting a pivotal inner circle of local leaders shaping the party's policy and wielding control on the Town Council. For the most part, harmony had prevailed between Action Group Lagosians and westerners. But when the interests of the west collided with the interests of Lagosians, party solidarity quickly evaporated. Indigenous Lagosians were determined not to be second-class citizens, even if it meant breaking with their fraternal brothers.

Intra-Yoruba conflict on this issue appeared openly in what came to be the final round of maneuverings in the two years immediately preceding the creation of a twelve-state structure. A national political crisis provided the opportunity to review the federal structure once again, a process that exposed the depths of dissatisfaction and disillusionment among Lagosians. In September 1965 the prime minister, Alhaji Abubakar Tafawa Balewa, appointed a constitutional review committee under the chairmanship of the attorney general (now chief justice), Dr. T. O. Elias. Again the stage was set for the proponents of a Lagos state to put forth their case. In an unusual display of unity, the broadly based Lagos delegation submitted a memorandum signed by representatives of key interest groups and political parties, all lending support to the idea of raising the status of Lagos.[37] The newly appointed oba of Lagos, Adeyinka Oyekan II, similarly called for a Lagos state, a cause to which he was now firmly committed.[38] The deliberations of the Constitutional Review Committee, however, were rapidly overtaken by events: the coup d'etat of January 15, 1966, took the lives of top civilian leaders and plunged Nigeria into a whirlpool of violent recriminations leading to a brutal civil war seventeen months later. During the uncertain months between September 1965 and the creation of the twelve-state structure in May 1967, the conflict between Lagos and the west could no longer be concealed.

On May 24, 1966, the first military regime, headed by Major General J. T. U. Aguiyi-Ironsi, abolished Nigeria's federal structure and created a unitary state by decree, a move that altered the nominal status of Lagos from a federal territory to a capital territory. After a second military coup d'etat on July 29, 1966, Major (now Brigadier) Mobolaji Johnson, administrator for Lagos, summoned an emergency meeting of the Lagos City Council to review the unitary decree issued by the Ironsi regime and to discuss the position of Lagos. The council's opinion was that

> a great proportion and a good number of Nigerians were not keen on the unitary form of government. [The council wanted a federal form of government] . . . which should be more liberal than the type before January 15, 1966, . . . [under which Lagos] should have her own state or region or province on . . . the same basis and with all rights and privileges as other states. [Lagos State] . . . should embrace a substantial part of the old Colony Province. In the event of an unpleasant situation whereby the other states decide to split away and become autonomous, a referendum should

be held in Lagos to determine the wishes of the people as to which state they would join.[39]

On September 1, 1966, the second military regime, under Lieutenant Colonel (now Major General) Yakubu Gowon, revoked the unitary form of government and returned Nigeria to the old federal structure based on four regions, with Lagos reverting to its former status as a federal territory. On September 7 an ad hoc committee on constitutional review convened; it comprised delegates from all four regions and from Lagos who were to work out constitutional arrangements agreeable to all sections of Nigeria. Heading the Lagos delegation was Lateef Jakande, a Lagosian journalist and top Action Group aide who had been released from prison immediately after the second coup d'etat, along with Chief Awolowo and others convicted of treason after the 1962 Western Region crisis. The statement issued by the Lagos City Council (quoted above), and the subsequent controversy over the proposals of the Lagos delegation, suggest that Jakande's thinking at the time was more in line with the old policy objectives of the Action Group than with the preferences of the Lagosians, who soon became aware of the distance between themselves and those acting in their behalf on the ad hoc committee.

Under Jakande's direction, the Lagos delegation decided to submit proposals jointly with the western delegation. This move, creating the impression that the views of the two delegations on most matters were identical, irritated Lagosians who were by now understandably wary of the west's stand in favor of merger. Their fears proved to be justified when substantive proposals were submitted. The western delegates held that the ideal solution was to create a federation of eighteen linguistically based states, each to control its own armed forces. Since this arrangement was admittedly impractical and unlikely, the next best would be a commonwealth of Nigeria in which each of the four regions would be a sovereign state, having the right to secede at any time.[40] Although the western delegates also advocated the creation of a Lagos state, they stipulated that its formation would be desirable or feasible only under a federal system of government. Since the western and Lagos delegations were advocating creation of a confederation, however, a Lagos state would be inconsistent with their overall scheme. Essentially, then, the west was suggesting that Lagos should merge with it to form one of four regions in a new confederal association that would give the west more control over Lagos than ever before.[41] It was this position that alienated a substantial section of the Lagos community, provoking an unprecedented degree of conflict among Yorubas in Lagos.

Indigenous Lagosians claimed that the obas, chiefs, and people of the community had never consented to the merger with the west, under either a federal or a confederal system, and that Jakande had therefore misrepresented their views at the conference. Oba Oyekan publicly denounced the constitutional delegation, declaring that "the people do not like to be pushed to the West by some ambitious leaders." In explanation, he said that "what we agreed with Chief Awolowo was that in the event of the country being disintegrated, we would merge with the West. But now, all the Military Governors including the Supreme Commander had come out in support of Nigeria remaining a political entity. Therefore, we in Lagos want a separate state."[42]

Oyekan's statement was a typical minorities position, one that looked to the central government for protection of minority interests. Not surprisingly, Lagosians were in substantial accord with the position adopted by the small Mid-Western Region, pinched between the east and the west. Like Lagos, this region was vulnerable to domination by a majority ethnic group or by a larger neighboring region in the event of national disintegration. To minorities, the only meaningful alternatives facing the country were federation and fragmentation. If Nigeria was to remain united, protection of and opportunities for minorities could be assured only by a strong central government, particularly if more states were created. If the country should break up, minorities would revert to their historic position of being subject to domination by neighboring groups. To suggest a confederation based on regional sovereignty was to invite the worst situation of all, for a minority would then have neither the security of a superior body as a counterweight to local domination nor the freedom to fight for autonomy if it wished to create a separate state.[43] In short, to Lagosians, the type of confederation suggested by the west guaranteed regional domination and the subjugation of their rights.

Oyekan's second memorandum, pledging support for a federation and calling for a Lagos state, was sent "on behalf of the chiefs and people of Lagos" to the supreme commander.[44] Jakande described Oyekan's criticism as "reckless and false," claiming that he had carried out his mandate faithfully.[45] Stubbornly defending his position, Jakande continued to adhere to the position adopted by the west as the crisis worsened.

By October 3, 1966, when the constitutional talks were adjourned for three weeks to give the delegates time for discussion, three of the four delegations (the east reserved its position) had agreed in principle on the need to create more states if the country stayed together. During the adjournment riots broke out in the north, claiming thousands of lives of eastern Nigerians and driving the respective regions further apart. On October 22 the Eastern Region delegation announced that owing to fears for their safety, they could no longer attend the conference unless northern troops in Lagos went home or the conference was held outside Nigeria. Despite attempts to move the meetings to Benin or to a Nigerian ship, a mutually agreeable solution was not forthcoming and the conference was adjourned indefinitely on November 1, 1966.

Events over the next six months paved the way for the de facto secession of the east. On July 4 and 5, 1967, the military governors of all the regions met at Aburi, Ghana, in a session that ended in a false sense of harmony. Confusion over what had transpired made the Aburi talks similarly unfruitful. Step by step, the Eastern Region proceeded to inch its way out of the federation, withholding federal revenues collected in the region, refusing to market produce through the Nigerian Produce Marketing Board, and taking other measures that effectively cut it off from the rest of the country. Meanwhile, in a demonstration of support for the east, the heads of the Western Region and Lagos delegations to the ad hoc committee resigned in April 1967, shortly before the conference was to be reconvened at Benin in hopes of an eleventh-hour reconciliation. As a protest over the government's refusal to remove troops from Lagos, this move by Awolowo and Jakande fueled the fires of opposition within Lagos. Jakande was now under attack by indigenes on three counts: for loyally following the west in disregard of Lagosians; for advocating a confederation that would deny them statehood; and for supporting the east's insistence on the removal of troops from Lagos. On the latter point in particular, there was widespread fear in Lagos that the west might follow the east out of the federation, as Awolowo threatened on May 5, 1967. To Lagosians, the retention of troops in the capital was concrete proof of the commitment of the federal government to keep Nigeria united and was a safeguard against the possibility that the west would pull Lagos into an unwanted secession.

On May 4, 1967, a meeting of "Lagos leaders of thought" was called at the oba's palace to discuss the situation in the country. Minutes before the meeting was to convene, it was announced that the oba had decided to postpone the discussion in view of the cancellation of the ad hoc committee, scheduled to meet in Benin. At this point Jakande emerged from the audience, mounted the rostrum, and attempted to address the crowd. For the first time, he was shouted down by his own people as a puppet of the west. In spite of this evidence of his unpopularity, Jakande afterward reiterated the threat recently made by Awolowo that "in the event of any region seceding, Lagos and Western Nigeria would also secede."[46]

Probably more than any other stand adopted by former Action Group leaders in this crisis, this threat drove home to the Lagosians the reality of their helplessness if abandoned to the west. Pressure was exerted more than ever before for the creation of a Lagos state. The frantic pace of events in May 1967 indicated the degree of tension in Nigeria as the secession of the east approached. In Lagos, Chief T. A. Doherty, a "Lagos Elder," asserted that under no conditions should Lagos "be an appendage of the West." He demanded that, in the event of a breakup, "Lagos should stand alone as a state."[47] The Lagos Elders' Committee, an offshoot of the Lagos Citizens' Rights Protection Council, which had been banned along with political parties and other civic associations after the first military coup, passed a resolution opposing both "the idea of secession by Lagos from the federation under any circumstance" and the evacuation of troops from Lagos.[48]

A week later, thirty former Action Group councilors adopted a seven-point resolution calling for a referendum on the Lagos question. Torn between party and communal loyalties, the ex-councilors asserted that "the people of Lagos will not accept any constitutional decision imposed on them by any authority with or without the connivance of traditional chiefs," but they "do not wish to perpetuate their present status as 'Second Class' citizens as desired by certain persons for their own personal aggrandisement."[49] Supported by a committee of thirty Lagos elders, including Dr. Oladele Ajose, former vice-chancellor of Ife University, Alhaji Elias, a Lagos transporter, and Chief H. O. Davies, a former federal minister, Doherty once again called for a Lagos state, this time urging the federal government to do so by decree "without any further delay."[50] The "Lagos Youths," headed by Dr. F. O. Onipede, a lecturer in political science at the University of Lagos, reaffirmed the proposal, adding that leaders from the west should "desist from further speaking on behalf of the people of Lagos because they have not been mandated to do so."[51]

Vindicating those Lagosians who claimed he was not a true representative of the community, Jakande reacted to these events with spiteful threats of recrimination. "Isolationists" who passed "frivolous resolutions" in "the bedrooms of certain individuals" could only invite the hostility of the west, he declared.[52] Under these conditions, a separate state "will not survive if the West closes its border with Lagos." Moreover, "without the active support of Western Nigeria, a Lagos State cannot be created either by decree or otherwise."[53] The day after Jakande's statement was published, the head of the federal military government promulgated a decree creating twelve states, including Lagos State, comprising the colony districts of the former Western Region and the federal capital. Four days later the Eastern Region seceded from the federation.

Clearly the issue of the status of Lagos, from the time it was first raised, had been influenced by external factors. The city's unique role as an economic and political capital, and the way Lagos was administered during the colonial period, contributed toward the feeling that it belonged to all Nigerians. Once active regional competition for control of the city emerged, it became evident that the status of Lagos was tied to the central question of the continued existence of Nigeria as a single political entity. Regionalization had been urged by the west because Lagos was a wealthy, geographically contiguous Yoruba city. Federalization had been advocated by the north because that region depended upon the city for an outlet to the sea. As the birthplace of the nationalist movement, Lagos had been seen by the east as a town that would best be left under federal supervision, rather than placed in the hands of its southern rival. Against these external forces, only the Lagos indigenes consistently pressed for autonomy, a political status that would directly benefit only the urban inhabitants.

Thus, although the timing of the creation of Lagos State was largely determined by external events, the driving force behind the movement for statehood emanated solely from internal pressure. The indigenes, frustrated by lack of equal opportunity within the federation and fearful of domination by the west in the event of fragmentation, exploited the national situation. The creation of the twelve-state structure was a gesture aimed at relieving some of the deep-seated grievances that had existed among a number of peoples since colonial rule, in the hope that it would demonstrate to the minorities that their own best interests lay in continuance of the federation. With statehood, however, Lagos also ceased being a pawn in the chess game of federal politics, and the indigenes gained a new respectability as citizens with equal rights and opportunities. And for the first time since the mid-nineteenth century, they were given control over their own political affairs.

# PART IV

## Conclusion

# CHAPTER 10

# Urbanization and Political Change

## PATTERNS OF POLITICAL CHANGE

Four historical stages of political change may be discerned in the fifty-year period examined in this work, during which time Lagos grew from a colonial town of less than 100,000 people to a metropolis of 1,250,000, the largest city in tropical Africa. Each stage is distinguished by transformations in some or all of the political variables treated in this study: the types of ruling strata; the distribution and use of political resources; the patterns of political behavior; and the formal structure of government. Political change took two general directions: first, toward democratization of the political system, with wider and more meaningful participation from a broader range of social groups; and second, toward localization of urban politics, with community control shifting steadily away from national or external interests in favor of resident groups, a process that ultimately resulted in political domination by indigenous Lagosians.

In the first period (1917–1938), urban political control was monopolized by an Anglo-African oligarchy consisting of European colonial administrators and a small group of educated Africans. The latter were descendants of nineteenth-century liberated slaves and were mostly professional men of Yoruba ancestry who shared the Victorian values of British officialdom. The majority of local inhabitants were unable to match the cumulative resources of this privileged minority, which alone of the urban African population had wealth, education, competence, social rank, access to public office, and the right to vote. Under the policy of direct rule applied to Lagos, traditional chiefs representing the urban majority received no formal recognition, were assigned no administrative functions, and were legally barred from political activities. These constraints meant that indigenous Lagosians were politically impotent; they constituted a subject people wholly dependent on the benign paternalism of the colonial regime and of members of the emigrant elite, most of whom, despite their ethnic connections, stood aloof from the Yoruba masses. Partisanship and political competition took the form of personal rivalries among the outstanding leaders of the African upper class; and the few voluntary associations in existence had exclusive memberships, reinforcing the sharp class distinctions and social cleavages that divided the town. Local government was in the hands of a small municipal council, created in 1917 as an upgraded sanitation board, with limited responsibilities and weak financial resources. The few Nigerians recruited to serve on the local council and on the central Legislative Council were drawn from those members of the colonial establishment who came to be designated as "native foreigners," a closed aristocracy of westernized Africans loyal to the British Crown.

In the second period (1938–1950) a more youthful class of educated Nigerians, professional men of mixed social origin, including non-Yoruba nationals and some third- and fourth-generation native foreigners, refused to support the colonial establishment. Imbued with racial consciousness and a radical ideology, this new generation constituted an aspirant elite with superior organizational talents. By forming mass political parties based on urban voluntary associations and appealing to emergent class and ethnic identities, they mobilized the settler groups then migrating by the thousands to Lagos in search of jobs. Through them, education and competence were separated from wealth and social rank, and the means for overturning the old-guard aristocracy were provided. Buttressed by the gradual introduction of constitutional reforms and increasing social differentiation, these resources enabled the nationalists to achieve ascendancy in the capital. Partisanship and political competition were elevated from petty personal antagonisms to a higher level of ideological and social rivalry. To be sure, urban democracy had not yet arrived: a limited franchise still prevented direct participation by the indigenous masses; access to public office was still restricted to the politically articulate upper classes; and local government institutions were still largely non-representative bodies closely linked to the colonial administration. But this period represented a significant turning point in that political influence passed from the dominant aristocracy to leaders of the nationalist movement, and the foundations were laid for more permanent forms of party-oriented political competition.

The sharpest break with the past occurred in the third period (1950–1959). After the introduction of a fully elective town council and universal suffrage, elements of the urban population which had been standing in the wings for decades suddenly appeared as active participants in urban politics. The group to benefit most immediately from constitutional reforms was the one with the combined resources of numerical strength, residential stability, and organizational capabilities—the "new men" of urban Africa, consisting of middle-class and middle-aged Yoruba settlers who had migrated to the city during the interwar years, mostly salaried white-collar workers, and only a few professionals. Additional groups that made their political debut in the 1950s were Muslims, indigenes, Ibos, women, members of the urban lower class, and traditional chiefs; for the first time in its history, the Town Council boasted a heterogeneous and representative character. Elite domination of local politics had been overcome through the subordination of the resources of the few to the resources of the multitudes: numbers, use of the ballot box, residence, ethnic solidarity, and occupational achievement, the latter with the important qualification that it referred to the accomplishments of men who earned rather than inherited their status, individuals who had the economic security with which to contest, but not to monopolize, public office.

In this age of nonelite politics, partisanship and political competition also assumed new dimensions. Particularistic interests attempted to exert influence as independent forces in local politics: political associations, representing separate residential, ethnic, or nationalist groups, contested the first election held on the basis of a universal franchise. But these disparate associations soon amalgamated or dissolved, giving rise to a two-party system in the community. The most popular nationalist association in Lagos, the

National Convention of Nigerian Citizens, which had fused the three major social groups in the city (settler Yorubas, indigenous Lagosians, and immigrant Ibos) into one anticolonial front, began to drop in strength, retaining solid support only in the Ibo and other minority areas. Displacing it was a rising Yoruba party, the Action Group, which cut across class, religious, and communal lines to forge a union based on Yoruba solidarity. In this new age, community politics had come to focus on ethnic politics, and the principal instrument of group influence came to be the urban political party.

Mass public participation also increased during this period as heavy immigration accompanied constitutional reforms. Voluntary associations became more directly involved in political activities, either as wings of major political parties or as independent agents of political agitation. Voting turnout rose sharply, increasing nearly twice as fast between 1953 and 1957 as the rate of growth in the voting population. By 1959, just one year before independence and nine years after the introduction of universal suffrage, voter turnout in the city reached an all-time high of 58 percent. Grassroots activity was made all the more meaningful when wider responsibilities were granted to the Lagos Town Council in 1953, which thereafter functioned as a representative, multipurpose public service agency instead of as a weak colonial institution.

In the fourth period (1959–1967), another distinctive pattern of political change emerged as a product of intra-Yoruba factionalism and the rising communal consciousness of Lagos indigenes. The political awakening of the urban masses now touched the indigenous population, a delayed response to postwar immigrant invasions. The Lagosian trader realized that he had to meet stiffer competition in trade; the Lagosian clerk discovered that it was becoming more difficult to find employment; the Lagosian landowner found that he was losing property that had been in his family for centuries; and the Lagosian resident of Isale Eko—the traditional indigenous quarter—became aware of the vast inequality between his standard of living and that of residents of the more developed areas surrounding him.

The indigenes lacked the conventional political resources, such as education, wealth, prestige, and numbers, usually deemed necessary to a group fighting for its rights. But they had one strength that no other group could employ with equal force—an unusually strong sense of corporate solidarity based on a plurality of social ties, deriving from a common history, origin, kinship, locality, ethnicity, ownership of land, and, for the most part, religion. Even Lagosians of different religious affiliations shared the same group loyalties and the same sense of deprivation felt by most indigenes. By 1963 indigenous Lagosians had proportionally declined to about 27 percent of the municipal population, or about 175,000 people, approximately 125,000 of whom lived on Lagos Island. Among them, the core of Lagos Muslims, numbering about 75,000, were the most cohesive of all. They sustained a traditional "urban village" existence, experienced the deepest poverty, and evidenced the strongest sense of communal patriotism. The drive for community control spearheaded by Lagos Muslims brought Lagosians as a whole to a position of unprecedented importance in local affairs.

The leadership of the town during the sixties was thus dominated by those who were born and bred in Lagos, mostly self-employed workers such as entrepreneurs, contractors, artisans, and traders with a modest level of education and a modest income. Unlike the disadvantaged in many Western cities, the Lagos Muslims worked through, rather than against, the system, capturing the machinery of the dominant Yoruba party, filling key positions on the municipal council, and exerting presure on higher government authorities regarding matters of local concern, a strategy that allowed them to exert influence in the community to a far greater extent than their numbers or their socioeconomic importance would suggest. Lagosians had achieved a double legitimacy to rule: as native-born inhabitants with the strongest attachments to the town, and as the duly elected pivotal group controlling governmental institutions.

During this period partisanship and political competition came to focus on intraethnic and, to some extent, on intracommunal rivalry. Primary political conflict centered on the competition between settlers and indigenes, but intracommunal cleavages followed the lines of lineage or dynastic factionalism. Some traces of religious division also were evident, as in the rise of the Lagos

Muslims at the expense of the Lagos Christians on the council. These intracommunal differences, however, were submerged in the face of the threat of settler domination, as Lagosians closed ranks for mutual group advantage.

Curiously, when the enthusiasm of the nationalist period died in the postindependence years, mass participation in local politics dropped sharply, particularly among immigrants. The rate of voter turnout fell far behind the rate of increase in voting population, in a pattern precisely opposite to that of the preceding period. The increase in number of voters between 1959 and 1965 was negligible, although in that period the voting population increased by nearly 100,000. Settlers tended to be apathetic toward urban politics, and many who were previously active failed to sustain their interest. Only in the traditional wards did the public continue to participate at a rate higher than the urban average. Diminished political activity by immigrants, coupled with the devolution of additional powers for the council, further enhanced the opportunities for indigenous Lagosians to exert influence in their own town. As the city grew larger in scale, therefore, political influence passed to lower socioeconomic elements of the population and urban politics concentrated increasingly on communal tensions.

### INDIGENIZATION OF URBAN POLITICS

These patterns of political change indicate that the structure of power in Lagos shifted not from oligarchy to pluralism, as in New Haven,[1] but from oligarchy to communalism. Pluralism posits a type of power structure in which several leadership hierarchies are identified in different issue areas. As used here, the term "communalism" refers to a form of political domination which is not vested in competing sets of interest-group leaders or, as the stratification school asserts, in a dominant socioeconomic class, but rather in a particular communal group, a cultural aggregate whose members share a common identity and a common sense of corporate solidarity.[2]

Communalism is an original model of community power which contrasts markedly with conventional formulations. The following propositions summarize its major features and the conditions under which it operates:

276

1. Communalism may be said to exist in a culturally hetero-geneous community where the primary political actors are corporate or communal groups rather than "influentials" or occupational classes.
2. Political conflict occurs chiefly between these communal groups, as each aspires exclusively for the benefits of wealth, status, and power for its own members.
3. Each communal group may compete in all sectors of the community for these rewards, but, owing to uneven de-velopment, communal primacy eventually appears, or is believed to appear, in different spheres.
4. Subjective interpretations of communal primacy in com-munity life are based on symbols of group achievement, such as the capture of public office, appointment to high-status jobs, acquisition of wealth or education, concentra-tion of public attention on particular group issues, and so on.
5. These subjective interpretations of group achievement (whether based on real or imagined success) give a new meaning to communal identities, transforming them from ascriptive categories of horizontal social differentiation to achievement categories of vertical social rank—a process, in short, through which communal groups come to be per-ceived in class terms.
6. In this new social context, traditional communal identities may also be revised in terms of sub- or supragroup affilia-tions, depending upon the nature of intergroup conflict and the perceptions of group achievement among the respective communal competitors.
7. Communal revision (i.e., redefinition of communal identity through fusion, expansion, division, or compartmentaliza-tion) will likely occur according to a pattern of communal balancing, with larger groups fragmenting and smaller groups combining into more or less structurally equivalent segments.
8. New inputs into the community—additional waves of im-migration, redistribution of resources, changing perceptions of group deprivation—will stimulate communal revision

and a search for a new equilibrium, as communal competitors reassess fresh sources of opposition.

9. Among communal competitors, the group whose members share a plurality of social ties and exhibit the strongest and most sustained sense of communal solidarity will probably exert a disproportionately large influence in the political sector.

10. Uneven development will encourage communalism: a group that has either advanced rapidly in socioeconomic development and displays pride in its accomplishments or, conversely, has remained far behind other groups and harbors deep frustrations because of its retardation will in all likelihood evidence a heightened sense of communal patriotism, leading eventually to more aggressive efforts to achieve political influence.

This model of communalism explains the configuration of power that emerges from the interaction of traditional communal loyalties and modern socioeconomic aspirations. It suggests that because the quest for modernization occurs along communal lines, traditional loyalties are not destroyed in the urban environment. They may undergo variation and acquire a new meaning as categories of group achievement, but they remain crucial determinants of community influence in two important respects. First, communal solidarity may outweigh socioeconomic resources and numerical superiority as an instrument of achieving political influence; second, uneven modernization may reinforce traditional social ties by encouraging communal nationalism, a movement stemming either from a bloated sense of communal pride or, at the other extreme, from the painful crush of communal frustration at the relative rates of group advancement.[3]

In Lagos, communalism replaced less egalitarian forms of political domination through a process that resulted in the indigenization of local politics. Lagosians exhibited a unique degree of communal cohesion which compensated for their numerical inferiority and lack of socioeconomic resources. Their underprivileged status gave rise to a heightened sense of communal nationalism which led to a successful drive for community control.

Evidence of the indigenization of Lagos appeared increasingly over the last two historical periods discussed above. At a time when the indigenes were proportionally declining in number, they were gaining stronger and more meaningful representation on the council, capturing more than a third of the seats when they constituted only about a quarter of the population. Similarly, while the Action Group was fighting for national survival, it rose to be the most popular party in the Yoruba-dominated capital, controlled by an inner circle of Lagos Muslims who had achieved top posts in the local branch organization. Electoral patterns also became increasingly favorable for the Lagosians, partly because of their role in the Action Group, partly because of malapportionment, and partly because they constituted a solid bloc vote in the two central constituencies in the city. Lagosians sustained a higher rate of consistent political participation than settlers, who displayed a surge of popular enthusiasm in the nationalist period followed by general apathy after independence. Evidence of the indigenization of local politics was also apparent in the proliferation of politically oriented voluntary associations representing the interests of Lagosians. Closer attention was paid to local issues, such as the Central Lagos Slum Clearance Scheme, the exploitation of the market women, the role of traditional chiefs, and the Lagos state movement. The achievement of statehood in the face of powerful opposition from external groups was the ultimate expression of the political influence captured by this indigenous cultural minority.

Several social characteristics unique to Lagosians gave them an advantage over the communal competitors in the quest for political primacy. First, as permanent residents who traced their ancestry to seventeenth-century founders or nineteenth-century immigrants, Lagosians had deeper sentimental attachments to the community. Transients tended to view the city in instrumental terms, channeling their aspirations for communal achievement toward socioeconomic goals that were not dependent upon political control. Lagosians considered political primacy an immediate objective preparatory, and perhaps even preferable, to communal achievements in other directions.

Second, as a host population, Lagosians could claim greater

legitimacy to rule, particularly since they constituted a significant landowning class, lived in the central districts, and had historical connections which gave them the right to call themselves "true Lagosians." Moreover, the corporate solidarity of Lagosians had been concretized in the continuing existence of Old Town. Isale Eko had changed very little throughout the rapid urbanization of the surrounding districts. Traditional face-to-face relations between members of extended lineages have been maintained in the inner city, reinforcing the intimacy and cohesion characteristic of this communal enclave.

Finally, since the imposition of colonial rule, Lagosians have constituted the least privileged communal group in the city. Instead of trying to catch up in all respects with more socially advanced groups, however, Lagosians singled out the political sector as the most promising avenue to communal achievement. They pursued a selective and concerted drive in a particular sphere of community life which was of intense psychological importance to them. The drive for community control thus took the form of an urban populist movement, with indigenes seeking to control their hometown after having been deprived of influence for nearly a century.

In light of these advantages, why were the indigenes quiescent for so long? Why did they not assert themselves at an earlier point in the development of the city? One reason is that, although they maintained a latent group indentity, the indigenes did not conceive of themselves as a collective political force until the presence of other communal groups stirred them to reevaluate their status in the community. Perceptions of group identity and communal competition were revised relative to the group in opposition. In the early years of colonial rule, indigenes had conceived of themselves as Africans dominated by European aliens and native foreigners. With the influx of new ethnic groups, Lagosians conceived of themselves principally as Yorubas. Subsequently, when settler domination appeared, Lagosians conceived of themselves as indigenes. Only in the face of direct threats to their position—when they realized that they were a dwindling minority—did they feel it imperative to assert themselves politically as a distinct social group. In doing so, they plunged into a sector of modern urban life in which they had had little or no previous experience. To this extent, communalism contributed toward political integration, for it stimulated active participation by a traditional population in modern urban politics.

Another factor accounting for the earlier political dormancy of the indigenes was the harsh form of colonial rule imposed on their community. Lagosians had the longest history of colonial domination of any group in Nigeria. But contrary to usual expectations of early advancement on the part of a group that had had early exposure to westernization, Lagosians were a forgotten minority. After colonial conquest, their economic resources and political independence were destroyed. Prosperity passed to other segments of the community, leaving the indigenes in a state of poverty which has remained a permanent feature of their urban condition. In addition, colonialism eroded traditional institutions, as the case study of chieftaincy has shown. Under direct rule, traditional chiefs were excluded from even perfunctory participation; and a restricted franchise and limited representation further isolated what was then the urban majority, effectively preventing the indigenes from playing a significant role in administrative procedures.

The third factor that contributed to the political unassertiveness of the indigenes was the role of an intervening elite. Emigrant Africans stood between colonial officials and the indigenous masses as an educated and wealthy upper class that acted as a privileged group of political intermediaries. Since the status of the intervening elite could be sustained only by the continued weakness of the masses, the British found the emigrants a willing group of African collaborators who shared the goal of political repression of the masses. Even Herbert Macaulay's successful campaigns in favor of popular local issues were carefully designed to emphasize the importance of his own role. Cumulatively, then, these three factors—failure to conceive of themselves as a collective political force, political exclusion and neglect under direct rule, and the presence of an intervening African elite—account for the unaggressive political behavior of the indigenes during the first half of the twentieth century. These factors also explain the indigenes' determination to retrieve political influence once conditions began to

*Conclusion*

change and the era of communal politics began.

POLITICAL CORRELATES OF URBANIZATION

Insofar as communalism is an outgrowth of population growth, social differentiation, and economic development, it may be said to be a direct correlate of urbanization. As such, it is a model of community power which may be applicable to many rapidly developing cities with culturally heterogeneous populations. The particular form of political domination which may emerge from communal conflict will vary according to several factors: the existence or absence of an indigenous host population, the nature and pace of immigration, the structural opportunities for group achievement in different institutional sectors, and so on. But whatever political structure emerges, the urban political process may be expected to conform to the model of communalism in terms of the nature of the particular actors involved, the forms of competition which come into play, and the perceptions of group achievement which affect the pursuit of influence.

In a broader context, communalism may be seen as part of a larger trend toward "urban neotraditionalism," a process of social change in which traditional social norms, values, and loyalties are reinterpreted in the context of modern situations. Conventional formulations of modernization postulate an inherent incompatibility between modern and traditional values which empirical studies have increasingly found to be misleading, if not wholly inaccurate, explanations of sociopolitical change in developing areas.[4] The findings of this study lend support to this criticism. In Lagos, modern socioeconomic identities have not been substituted for traditional communal identities. Rather, primordial loyalties have been reinterpreted in light of modern necessities and continue to have relevance in the urban milieu. Urban neotraditionalism was evidenced not only in the political sphere, but in other sectors of urban life as well, particularly among indigenes. Extended family ties and the retention of lineage relationships, communal ownership of land, the rise of Islam, the control by market women of the urban retail trade, the prestige of chieftaincy, and other cultural practices point up the resilience of traditional norms and structures in an urban environment. Theories of modernization which predict an inevitable and comprehensive tide of sweeping social change in areas of rapid urban growth neither explain the successful resistance of indigenes to modernization in these diverse areas nor their rise to political power at the peak years of urban growth and development.

The survival of traditional loyalties in the urban milieu further suggests that the African city is not an anomic society of rootless and alienated individuals who present potential pockets of political unrest, but a community of cohesive corporate groups through which newly arrived immigrants can derive a sense of belonging, secure employment and shelter, and find companionship, friendship, and links with fellow townsmen. This communal social structure tends to reduce the potential for political instability insofar as it may arise from local conditions.

It is true that the African urban community is typically a plural community, consisting of "a medley of peoples living side by side, but separately, within the same political unit."[5] This does not mean, however, that it is an atomized society without any basis for internal social cohesion. Communalism suggests that the community is a heterogeneous aggregate of corporate groups whose individual members maintain interlocking group affiliations through which they aspire for wealth, status, and power. These multiple group affiliations prevent excessive fragmentation and provide a foundation for interaction and interdependence among the various segments of the community. It is possible, and under certain conditions likely, that a cultural minority will achieve political primacy; but it will do so through collective social mobilization, not through the use of force or political repression. Indeed, one of the salient features of the change that occurred in Lagos is the relatively peaceful nature of the transformations over the fifty-year period. The indigenization of Lagos politics was a quiet revolution achieved through legitimate channels at the local level; it was a process, it may be noted in addition, which contrasted sharply with more dramatic and disruptive events at higher levels of Nigerian society.

But if communalism may be said to be functional in overthrowing less egalitarian forms of political domination, in aiding the integration of rural immigrants into the urban milieu, in reducing the potential for political unrest, and perhaps even in cushioning the impact of urban poverty, it must also be recognized as having equally dysfunctional consequences in other respects. Because of the narrow view of political competition and the rapid rise of less qualified ruling strata, communalism lowers the standards of leadership, competence, and efficiency in urban administration. Local government and the municipal bureaucracy are regarded as private domains of particular communal groups, each in pursuit of its own special objectives. Governmental performance tends to be measured in terms of the degree to which public policies confer benefits on the dominant communal group. Inevitably, this system militates against the professionalization of urban government and introduces partiality and favoritism into the decision-making process.

Related to the lowered standards of urban administration is the type of political ethos that emerges from communalism. Generally, it may be described as a view of politics which emphasizes partisanship over efficiency, group interests over public interests, immediate gratification of the needs of the controlling few rather than long-range welfare of the community as a whole. In a word, there fails to arise a conception of "public-regardingness,"[6] a civic spirit or norm of public responsibility so desperately needed to satisfy the pressing social demands caused by rapid urbanization.

Finally, communalism tends to feed on itself, to contribute in a vicious spiral to continued social inequalities. Communalism is simultaneously a cause and a product of uneven development, arising out of the disparities that provoke a heightened sense of deprivation and resulting in a further sharpening of urban social cleavages by fostering a narrow, parochial view of achievement. In this regard, communalism widens the gap between the haves and the have-nots within the community, between the elites and the masses, and between different communal components of the city. Once communalism takes hold, therefore, it tends to be a self-sustaining political process, a political correlate of urbanization with mixed implications for African development.

*Appendixes*

# APPENDIX I

| | Origin | Ethnic identification | Religion | Occupation | Years in office | Party affiliation |
|---|---|---|---|---|---|---|
| **1920** | | | | | | |
| A. Folarin | Saro | Yoruba | Christian | Barrister | 3 | Ind. |
| R. A. Savage | Saro | Yoruba | Christian | Doctor | 3 | Ind. |
| G. D. Agbebi | Saro | Yoruba | Christian | Civil eng. | 6 | Ind. |
| **1923** | | | | | | |
| J. Egerton-Shyngle | Gambian | Yoruba | Christian | Barrister | 3 | NNDP |
| G. D. Agbebi | Saro | Yoruba | Christian | Civil eng. | 6 | NNDP |
| O. Alakija | Amaro | Yoruba | Christian | Barrister | 3 | NNDP |
| **1926** | | | | | | |
| T. A. Doherty | Saro | Yoruba | Christian | Barrister | 9 | NNDP |
| J. B. Benjamin | Saro | Yoruba | Christian | Civil eng. | 3 | NNDP |
| J. C. Zizer | Saro | Yoruba | Christian | Barrister | 3 | NNDP |
| **1929** | | | | | | |
| A. Williams | Saro | Yoruba | Christian | Barrister | 10 | NNDP |
| T. A. Doherty | Saro | Yoruba | Christian | Barrister | 9 | NNDP |
| A. S. W. Shackleford | Jamaican | Yoruba | Christian | Business mgr. | 9 | NNDP |
| **1932** | | | | | | |
| A. Williams | Saro | Yoruba | Christian | Barrister | 10 | NNDP |
| T. A. Doherty | Saro | Yoruba | Christian | Barrister | 9 | NNDP |
| A. S. W. Shackleford | Jamaican | Yoruba | Christian | Business mgr. | 9 | NNDP |
| **1935** | | | | | | |
| A. Williams | Saro | Yoruba | Christian | Barrister | 10 | NNDP |
| A. L. Johnson | Saro | Yoruba | Christian | Barrister | 3 | NNDP |
| C. C. Adeniji-Jones | Saro | Yoruba | Christian | Doctor | 6 | NNDP |
| A. S. W. Shackleford | Jamaican | Yoruba | Christian | Business mgr. | 9 | NNDP |

APPENDIX I—*Continued*

| | Origin | Ethnic identification | Religion | Occupation | Years in office | Party affiliation |
|---|---|---|---|---|---|---|
| **1938** | | | | | | |
| A. Maja | Saro | Yoruba | Christian | Doctor | 6 | NYM |
| J. A. Ladega | Lagos | Yoruba | Christian | Govt. dispenser | 3 | NYM |
| C. C. Adeniji-Jones | Saro | Yoruba | Christian | Doctor | 6 | NNDP |
| I. Caxton-Martins | Saro | Yoruba | Christian | Barrister | 3 | NYM |
| **1941** | | | | | | |
| A. Maja | Saro | Yoruba | Christian | Doctor | 6 | NYM |
| H. A. Subair | Saro | Yoruba | Christian | Accountant | 6 | NYM |
| A. Williams | Saro | Yoruba | Christian | Barrister | 10 | NNDP |
| S. H. A. Baptist | Saro | Yoruba | Christian | Barrister | 1 | NNDP |
| **1942 by-election** | | | | | | |
| H. S. A. Thomas | Saro | Yoruba | Christian | Barrister | 2 | NYM |
| J. T. A. White | Saro | Yoruba | Christian | Commercial agent | 2 | NNDP |
| **1944** | | | | | | |
| A. Bola Cole | Saro | Yoruba | Christian | Surveyor | 6 | NYM |
| H. A. Subair | Saro | Yoruba | Christian | Accountant | 6 | NYM |
| I. Olorun-Nimbe | Lagos | Yoruba | Muslim | Doctor | 9 | NNDP |
| R. A. Dawodu | Lagos | Yoruba | —— | Pensioner | 1 | NNDP |
| **1945 by-election** | | | | | | |
| H. A. G. Thompson | Saro | Yoruba | Christian | Surveyor | 5 | NNDP |
| **1947** | | | | | | |
| A. Bola Cole | Saro | Yoruba | Christian | Surveyor | 6 | NYM |
| I. Olorun-Nimbe | Lagos | Yoruba | Muslim | Doctor | 9 | NNDP |
| A. Ibikunle Akitoye | Lagos | Yoruba | Christian | Company dir. | 3 | NNDP |
| A. Adedoyin | Ijebu | Yoruba | Christian | Barrister | 6 | NNDP |
| H. A. G. Thompson | Saro | Yoruba | Christian | Barrister | 5 | NNDP |

# APPENDIX II

## SOCIOECONOMIC AND POLITICAL PROFILES OF LAGOS COUNCILORS, 1950–1966

| | Age last birthday (1967)[a] | Hometown[b] | Father's hometown | Highest education achieved | Years resident in Lagos | Ethnic identification | Religion | Occupation | Years in office (rounded) | Party affiliation |
|---|---|---|---|---|---|---|---|---|---|---|
| **1950** | | | | | | | | | | |
| *Ward A* | | | | | | | | | | |
| J. A. Ogunbiyi | 75 | Lagos | Lagos | Attended secondary | 62 | Yoruba | Christian | Pensioner | 7 | AC |
| Y. A. Williams | 67 | Lagos | Ijebu | Grad. primary | Since birth | Yoruba | Muslim | Trader | 3 | AC |
| A. Y. Ojikutu | 68 | Lagos | Lagos | Grad. secondary | Since birth | Yoruba | Muslim | Contractor and butcher | 9 | AC |
| *Ward B* | | | | | | | | | | |
| Adeniji-Adele II | 70 | Lagos | Lagos | Grad. secondary | Since birth | Yoruba | Muslim | Civil servant | 1 | AC |
| F. R. A. Williams | (est.) 53 | Abeokuta | Abeokuta | University | — | Yoruba | Christian | Barrister | 7 | AC |
| A. O. Lawson | 43 | Lagos | Abeokuta | University | Since birth | Yoruba | Christian | Solicitor and company dir. | 12 | AC |
| *Ward C* | | | | | | | | | | |
| I. Olorun-Nimbe | (est.) 60 | Lagos | Lagos | University | Since birth | Yoruba | Muslim | Doctor | 9 | NNDP/NCNC |
| A. Ajala | (est.) 60 | Abeokuta | Abeokuta | Grad. primary | 46 | Yoruba | Christian | Clerk and printer | 1 | NNDP/NCNC |
| N. Eze | — | Asaba | Asaba | —— | — | Ibo | Christian | Secretary | 7 | NNDP/NCNC |
| *Ward D* | | | | | | | | | | |
| M. Ojike | — | Aro | Aro | —— | — | Ibo | Christian | Corp. dir. | 3 | NNDP/NCNC |

| | | | | | | | | | | |
|---|---|---|---|---|---|---|---|---|---|---|
| M. Martins | — | — | — | — | — | Yoruba | Christian | Trader | 3 | NNDP/NCNC |
| J. I. Talabi | 57 | Epe | Epe | Attended secondary | 35 | Yoruba | Christian | Tailor | 12 | NNDP/NCNC |
| *Ward E* | | | | | | | | | | |
| E. A. O. Bright | 65 | Ile-Ife | Ile-Ife | Attended secondary | 55 | Yoruba | Christian | Office asst. | 3 | NNDP/NCNC |
| A. J. Marinho | — | — | — | — | — | Ibo | Christian | Pensioner | 3 | NNDP/NCNC |
| L. U. Agonsi | 48 | Orlu | Orlu | — | — | Ibo | Christian | Labor leader | 3 | NNDP/NCNC |
| *Ward F* | | | | | | | | | | |
| T. O. S. Benson | (est.) 55 | Ikorodu | Ikorodu | University | Since birth | Yoruba | Christian | Lawyer | 3 | NNDP/NCNC |
| F. Anyiam | — | — | Orlu | — | — | Ibo | Christian | Trader | 4 | NNDP/NCNC |
| C. N. Gogo | — | — | — | — | — | Ibo | Christian | Trade union secretary | 1 | NNDP/NCNC |
| *Ward G* | | | | | | | | | | |
| S. O. Maduike | (est.) 60 | Orlu | Orlu | — | (est.) 35 | Ibo | Christian | Contractor and pensioner | 12 | NNDP/NCNC |
| G. Awobiyi | — | Ondo | Ondo | Grad. primary | 28 | Yoruba | Christian | Clerk | 3 | NNDP/NCNC |
| D. Awode | 66 | Ijebu | Ijebu | Grad. secondary | 48 | Yoruba | Christian | Asst. supt. of police | 3 | NNDP/NCNC |
| *Ward H* | | | | | | | | | | |
| A. Adedoyin | 61 + | Ijebu | Ijebu | University | — | Yoruba | Christian | Barrister | 6 | NNDP/NCNC |
| Mrs. H. Lawson | 54 | Lagos | Lagos | Attended secondary | Since birth | Yoruba | Christian | Contractor | 3 | NNDP/NCNC |
| L. Moore | (est.) 55 | Lagos | Abeokuta | University | Since birth | Yoruba | Christian | Barrister | 3 | NNDP/NCNC |

APPENDIX II—Continued

| | Age last birthday (1967)[a] | Hometown[b] | Father's hometown | Highest education achieved | Years resident in Lagos | Ethnic identification | Religion | Occupation | Years in office (rounded) | Party affiliation |
|---|---|---|---|---|---|---|---|---|---|---|
| **1951** | | | | | | | | | | |
| *Ward A* | | | | | | | | | | |
| Y. A. Williams | 67 | Lagos | Ijebu | Grad. primary | Since birth | Yoruba | Christian | Trader | 3 | AG |
| *Ward B* | | | | | | | | | | |
| A. O. Lawson | 43 | Lagos | Abeokuta | University | Since birth | Yoruba | Christian | Solicitor and company dir. | 12 | AG |
| J. A. Doherty (by-election) | — | Lagos | Lagos | University | Since birth | Yoruba | Christian | Doctor | 2 | AG |
| *Ward C* | | | | | | | | | | |
| H. Kaine | 58 | Onitsha | Onitsha | — | — | Ibo | Christian | — | 2 | NCNC |
| *Ward D* | | | | | | | | | | |
| J. I. Talabi | 57 | Epe | Epe | Attended secondary | 35 | Yoruba | Christian | Tailor | 12 | NCNC |
| *Ward E* | | | | | | | | | | |
| A. K. Blankson | — | In Ghana | In Ghana | — | — | — | Christian | Company dir. | 6 | NCNC |
| *Ward F* | | | | | | | | | | |
| O. Phillips | 53 | Lagos | Abeokuta | Grad. secondary | Since birth | Yoruba | Christian | — | 2 | NCNC |
| *Ward G* | | | | | | | | | | |
| T. Afinneh | 58 | Badagry | Badagry | Attended secondary | 48 | Yoruba | Muslim | Contractor | 2 | NCNC |
| *Ward H* | | | | | | | | | | |
| F. S. McEwen | 49 | Lagos | In Sierra Leone | University | Since birth | Yoruba | Christian | Company dir. | 14 | NCNC |

| | Age | Birthplace | | Education | Years in Lagos | Ethnicity | Religion | Occupation | | Party |
|---|---|---|---|---|---|---|---|---|---|---|
| *1952* | | | | | | | | | | |
| *Ward A* | | | | | | | | | | |
| M. A. Ogun | 59 | Ijebu | Ijebu | Grad. secondary | 42 | Yoruba | Christian | Business mgr. | 10 | AG |
| *1953* | | | | | | | | | | |
| *Ward A* | | | | | | | | | | |
| J. A. Ogunbiyi | 75 | Lagos | Lagos | Attended secondary | 62 | Yoruba | Christian | Pensioner | 7 | AG |
| J. A. Ajao | (est.) 60 | Oyo | Oyo | Grad. primary | (est.) 50 | Yoruba | Christian | Trader | 6 | AG |
| M. A. Ogun | 59 | Ijebu | Ijebu | Grad. secondary | 42 | Yoruba | Christian | Business mgr. | 10 | AG |
| T. Thompson | 52 | Lagos | Lagos | Attended secondary | Since birth | Yoruba | Muslim | Company dir. | 6 | AG |
| S. A. Durojaiye | — | —— | —— | —— | — | Yoruba | — | Company dir. | 6 | AG |
| A. Y. Ojikutu | 68 | Lagos | Lagos | Grad. secondary | Since birth | Yoruba | Muslim | Contractor and butcher | 9 | AG |
| *Ward B* | | | | | | | | | | |
| L. O. Bello | 53 | Abeokuta | Abeokuta | Grad. primary | 40 | Yoruba | Muslim | Trader | 6 | AG |
| H. O. Idewu | 58 | Lagos | Lagos | Grad. secondary | Since birth | Yoruba | Muslim | Journalist | 9 | AG |
| F. R. A. Williams | (est.) 53 | Abeokuta | Abeokuta | University | — | Yoruba | Christian | Barrister | 7 | AG |
| E. F. A. Dada | 63 | Ijebu | Ijebu | University | 50 | Yoruba | Christian | Pensioner | 4 | AG |
| L. J. Dosunmu | 48 | Lagos | Lagos | University | Since birth | Yoruba | Muslim | Barrister/judge | 6 | AG |
| A. O. Lawson | 43 | Lagos | Abeokuta | University | Since birth | Yoruba | Christian | Solicitor and company dir. | 12 | AG |
| *Ward C* | | | | | | | | | | |
| O. Ajayi | 60+ | Lagos | Lagos | Grad. secondary | Since birth | Yoruba | Muslim | Clerk | 4 | AG |

| | Age last birthday (1967)[a] | Hometown[b] | Father's hometown | Highest education achieved | Years resident in Lagos | Ethnic identification | Religion | Occupation | Years in office (rounded) | Party affiliation |
|---|---|---|---|---|---|---|---|---|---|---|
| **1953** | | | | | | | | | | |
| *Ward C* | | | | | | | | | | |
| Mrs. K. A. Fashina | 56 | Lagos | Lagos | Grad. secondary | Since birth | Yoruba | Christian | Trader | 10 | NCNC |
| T. S. Calfos | 58 | Lagos | Lagos | Attended secondary | Since birth | Yoruba | Muslim | Transporter | 4 | AG |
| C. Okun | — | — | — | ---- | — | Efik | Christian | Clerk | 4 | NCNC |
| N. Eze | — | Asaba | Asaba | ---- | — | Ibo | Christian | Secretary | 7 | NCNC |
| *Ward D* | | | | | | | | | | |
| J. I. Talabi | 57 | Epe | Epe | Attended secondary | 35 | Yoruba | Christian | Tailor | 12 | NCNC |
| E. A. Ladega | 59 | Ijebu | Ijebu | Grad. secondary | 43 | Yoruba | Christian | Hotel owner | 9 | NCNC |
| C. B. Ndukwe | — | — | — | ---- | — | Ibo | Christian | Trader | 4 | NCNC |
| *Ward E* | | | | | | | | | | |
| F. S. McEwen | 49 | Lagos | In Sierra Leone | University | Since birth | Yoruba | Christian | Company dir. | 14 | NCNC |
| K. Balogun | — | Oshun | Oshun | University | — | Yoruba | Christian | Barrister | 4 | NCNC |
| A. K. Blankson | — | In Ghana | In Ghana | ---- | — | — | Christian | Company dir. | 6 | NCNC |
| S. A. Onitiri | 50 | Lagos | Lagos | Grad. secondary | 49 | Yoruba | Christian | Landlord | 4 | AG |
| L. Aborisade | 70 | Lagos | Lagos | Grad. secondary | Since birth | Yoruba | Christian | Trader | 4 | AG |
| F. M. Moronu | — | — | — | ---- | — | Ibo | Christian | Tech. clerk | 9 | NCNC |
| *Ward F* | | | | | | | | | | |
| A. Akinyemi | 54 | Lagos | Lagos | Attended secondary | Since birth | Yoruba | Muslim | Trader | 4 | AG |

| | | | | | | | | | | |
|---|---|---|---|---|---|---|---|---|---|---|
| J. U. Isuman | — | — | — | — | — | Beni | Muslim | Company dir. | 4 | NCNC |
| J. Takuro | — | Benin | Benin | — | — | Ibo | Christian | Teacher | 4 | NCNC |
| C. B. Williams | 77 | Abeokuta | Abeokuta | Grad. primary | Since birth | Yoruba | Christian | Civil servant | 4 | AG |
| M. Abina | 60 | Lagos | Lagos | Grad. secondary | Since birth | Yoruba | Muslim | Printer | 9 | AG |
| F. A. Tejuoso | 71 | Abeokuta | Abeokuta | University | 51 | Yoruba | Christian | Solicitor | 6 | AG |
| *Ward G* | | | | | | | | | | |
| S. O. Maduike | (est.) 60 | Orlu | Orlu | Grad. T.T.C.[e] | (est.) 35 | Ibo | Christian | Contractor and pensioner | 12 | NCNC |
| L. Benedict | 53 | Ijebu | Ijebu | Grad. secondary | 46 | Yoruba | Christian | Teacher | 9 | NCNC |
| M. S. Joaquim | 60 | Lagos | Lagos | — | Since birth | Yoruba | Christian | Clerk | 4 | AG |
| *Ward H* | | | | | | | | | | |
| N. A. Cole | — | Warri | Warri | — | — | Urhobo | Christian | Tr. union sec. | 4 | NCNC |
| O. A. Fagbenro-Beyioku | (est.) 55 | Ikorodu | Ikorodu | — | Since birth | Yoruba | Muslim | Trade unionist | 4 | NCNC |
| J. A. George | 73 | Abeokuta | Abeokuta | Grad. secondary | 60 | Yoruba | Christian | Cable operator | 4 | AG |
| F. Rufai | — | — | — | — | — | Yoruba | — | Trader | 4 | AG |
| J. K. Randle | — | Lagos | Lagos | — | — | Yoruba | Christian | Business dir. | 4 | AG |
| R. Ajayi | — | — | — | — | — | Yoruba | — | Company dir. | 4 | AG |
| *1954 by-election* | | | | | | | | | | |
| *Ward B* | | | | | | | | | | |
| N. A. Taiwo | 64 | Lagos | Lagos | Grad. secondary | Since birth | Yoruba | Christian | Sawmiller and pensioner | 8 | AG |
| *Ward H* | | | | | | | | | | |
| N. A. Cole | — | Warri | Warri | — | — | Urhobo | Christian | Tr. union sec. | 4 | NCNC |

## APPENDIX II—Continued

| | Age last birthday (1967)[a] | Hometown[b] | Father's hometown | Highest education achieved | Years resident in Lagos | Ethnic identification | Religion | Occupation | Years in office (rounded) | Party affiliation |
|---|---|---|---|---|---|---|---|---|---|---|
| **1955 by-election** | | | | | | | | | | |
| *Ward A* | | | | | | | | | | |
| M. Animashaun | 70 | Lagos | Lagos | Grad. primary | Since birth | Yoruba | Muslim | Civil servant | 4 | AG |
| *Ward B* | | | | | | | | | | |
| H. A. B. Fasinro | (est.) 50 | Lagos | Lagos | University | Since birth | Yoruba | Muslim | Solicitor | 2 | AG |
| K. B. Shomade | 56 | Lagos | Lagos | Grad. secondary | Since birth | Yoruba | Muslim | Pensioner | 2 | AG |
| *Ward C* | | | | | | | | | | |
| N. A. Taiwo | 64 | Lagos | Lagos | Grad. secondary | Since birth | Yoruba | Christian | Pensioner | 8 | AG |
| *Ward E* | | | | | | | | | | |
| Mrs. E. Femi-Pearse | 59 | Lagos | Abeokuta | Grad. secondary | 54 | Yoruba | Christian | Teacher | 5 | AG |
| *Ward F* | | | | | | | | | | |
| S. I. Martins | 48 | Lagos | Lagos | Grad. primary | Since birth | Yoruba | Christian | Trader | 10 | AG |
| **1957** | | | | | | | | | | |
| *Ward A* | | | | | | | | | | |
| J. A. Ajao | (est.) 60 | Oyo | Oyo | Grad. primary | (est.) 50 | Yoruba | Christian | Trader | 6 | AG |
| M. A. Ogun | 59 | Ijebu | Ijebu | Grad. secondary | 42 | Yoruba | Christian | Business mgr. | 10 | AG |
| T. Thompson | 52 | Lagos | Lagos | Attended secondary | Since birth | Yoruba | Muslim | Company dir. | 6 | AG |

| Name | Age | | | | | | | | Party |
|---|---|---|---|---|---|---|---|---|---|
| M. Animashaun | 70 | Lagos | Lagos | Grad. primary | Since birth | Yoruba | Muslim | Civil servant | 4 | AG |
| S. A. Durojaiye | — | — | — | — | — | Yoruba | — | Company dir. | 6 | AG |
| A. Y. Ojikutu | 68 | Lagos | Lagos | Grad. secondary | Since birth | Yoruba | Muslim | Contractor and butcher | 9 | AG |
| *Ward B* | | | | | | | | | |
| H. O. Idewu | 58 | Lagos | Lagos | Grad. secondary | Since birth | Yoruba | Muslim | Journalist | 9 | AG |
| L. O. Bello | 53 | Abeokuta | Abeokuta | Grad. primary | 40 | Yoruba | Muslim | Trader | 6 | AG |
| N. A. Taiwo | 64 | Lagos | Lagos | Grad. secondary | Since birth | Yoruba | Christian | Sawmiller and pensioner | 8 | AG |
| A. O. Lawson | 43 | Lagos | Abeokuta | University | Since birth | Yoruba | Christian | Solicitor and company dir. | 12 | AG |
| N. A. Agiri | 54 | Lagos | Lagos | Grad. primary | Since birth | Yoruba | Muslim | Trader | 2 | AG |
| L. J. Dosunmu | 48 | Lagos | Lagos | University | Since birth | Yoruba | Muslim | Barrister/judge | 6 | AG |
| *Ward C* | | | | | | | | | |
| E. A. Manuel | 41 | Abonema | Abonema | Attended secondary | Since birth | Kalabari/Ijaw | Christian | Shipping agent | 5 | NCNC |
| M. S. Oshodi | 71 | Lagos | Lagos | Grad. primary | Since birth | Yoruba | Christian | Clerk | 2 | NCNC |
| A. B. Yesufu | 52 | Lagos | Lagos | Attended secondary | Since birth | Yoruba | Muslim | Trader | 8 | NCNC |
| R. A. Balogun | 47 | Lagos | Abeokuta | Grad. primary | Since birth | Yoruba | Muslim | Contractor | 8 | NCNC |
| H. O. Davies | 62 | Lagos | Lagos | University | Since birth | Yoruba | Christian | Barrister | 2 | NCNC |
| *Ward D* | | | | | | | | | |
| O. O. Soleye | 53 | Abeokuta | Abeokuta | Grad. T.T.C.[c] | 24 | Yoruba | Christian | Teacher | 5 | NCNC |

APPENDIX II–Continued

| | Age last birthday (1967)[a] | Hometown[b] | Father's hometown | Highest education achieved | Years resident in Lagos | Ethnic identification | Religion | Occupation | Years in office (rounded) | Party affiliation |
|---|---|---|---|---|---|---|---|---|---|---|
| **1957** | | | | | | | | | | |
| **Ward D** | | | | | | | | | | |
| E. A. Ladega | 59 | Ijebu | Ijebu | Grad. secondary | 43 | Yoruba | Christian | Hotel owner | 9 | NCNC |
| J. I. Talabi | 57 | Epe | Epe | Attended secondary | 35 | Yoruba | Christian | Tailor | 12 | NCNC |
| **Ward E** | | | | | | | | | | |
| F. S. McEwen | 49 | Lagos | In Sierra Leone | University | Since birth | Yoruba | Christian | Company dir. | 14 | NCNC |
| H. P. Adebola | 53 | Ijebu | Ijebu | — | — | Yoruba | Muslim | Trade unionist | 8 | NCNC |
| I. Obiajulu | — | — | — | — | — | Ibo | Christian | Clerk/steno. | 5 | NCNC |
| F. M. Moronu | — | — | — | — | — | Ibo | Christian | Tech. clerk | 9 | NCNC |
| A. Ogunsanya | 49 | Ikorodu | Ikorodu | University | 47 | Yoruba | Christian | Barrister | 8 | NCNC |
| G. Oparah | — | — | — | — | — | Ibo | Christian | Business mgr. | 9 | NCNC |
| M. Tijani | — | — | — | — | — | Yoruba | — | Trader | 2 | NCNC |
| **Ward F** | | | | | | | | | | |
| J. A. Idowu | 60 | Shagamu | Shagamu | Grad. primary | 55 | Yoruba | Christian | Pensioner | 5 | AG |
| S. I. Martins | 48 | Lagos | Lagos | Grad. primary | Since birth | Yoruba | Christian | Trader | 10 | AG |
| E. A. Molajo | 47 | Abeokuta | Abeokuta | University | 28 | Yoruba | Christian | Trader | 2 | AG |
| A. Akodu | — | — | — | — | — | Yoruba | — | Trader | 1 | AG |
| M. Abina | 60 | Lagos | Lagos | Grad. secondary | Since birth | Yoruba | Muslim | Printer | 9 | AG |
| A. Tejuoso | 71 | Abeokuta | Abeokuta | University | 51 | Yoruba | Christian | Barrister | 6 | AG |

| | | | | | | | | | | |
|---|---|---|---|---|---|---|---|---|---|---|
| **Ward G** | | | | | | | | | | |
| S. O. Maduike | (est.) 60 | Orlu | Orlu | — | (est.) 35 | Ibo | Christian | Contractor and pensioner | 12 | NCNC |
| L. Benedict | 53 | Ijebu | Ijebu | Grad. T.T.C.ᵉ | 46 | Yoruba | Christian | Teacher | 9 | NCNC |
| I. Salu | — | — | — | — | — | Yoruba | — | Jockey | 2 | NCNC |
| **Ward H** | | | | | | | | | | |
| S. O. Martins | — | — | — | — | Since birth | Yoruba | Christian | Debt collector | 2 | AG |
| G. O. Dawodu | 34 | Lagos | Lagos | Grad. secondary | Since birth | Yoruba | Muslim | Clerk | 9 | AG |
| M. Grillo | 59 | Lagos | Lagos | Attended secondary | Since birth | Yoruba | Muslim | Builder | 5 | AG |
| S. O. Ajose | 59 | Lagos | Lagos | Grad. primary | Since birth | Yoruba | Muslim | Trader | 5 | NCNC |
| Z. A. Balogun | 68 | Lagos | Ilesha | Attended secondary | 58 | Yoruba | Muslim | Debt collector | 2 | AG |
| E. A. Bankole-Olemoh | — | — | — | — | — | Yoruba | — | Contractor | 2 | AG |
| *1958 by-election* | | | | | | | | | | |
| **Ward F** | | | | | | | | | | |
| A. Layeni | 44 | Abeokuta | Abeokuta | Attended secondary | Since birth | Yoruba | Christian | Hotel owner | 4 | AG |
| *1959* | | | | | | | | | | |
| **Ward A** | | | | | | | | | | |
| A. D. Williams | 55 | Lagos | Lagos | Grad. secondary | Since birth | Yoruba | Muslim | Personnel officer | 3 | AG |
| A. F. Masha | 49 | Lagos | Lagos | Attended secondary | Since birth | Yoruba | Muslim | Trader | 7 | AG |
| J. A. Odeku | 41 | Oyo | Oyo | University | Since birth | Yoruba | Christian | Barrister | 6 | AG |
| I. A. S. Adewale | 51 | Lagos | Lagos | University | 15 | Yoruba | Muslim | Barrister | 3 | AG |
| **Ward B** | | | | | | | | | | |
| N. A. Taiwo | 64 | Lagos | Lagos | Grad. secondary | Since birth | Yoruba | Christian | Sawmiller and pensioner | 8 | AG |

APPENDIX II—Continued

| | Age last birthday (1967)[a] | Hometown[b] | Father's hometown | Highest education achieved | Years resident in Lagos | Ethnic identification | Religion | Occupation | Years in office (rounded) | Party affiliation |
|---|---|---|---|---|---|---|---|---|---|---|
| **1959** | | | | | | | | | | |
| *Ward B* | | | | | | | | | | |
| H. O. Idewu | 58 | Lagos | Lagos | Grad. secondary | Since birth | Yoruba | Muslim | Journalist | 9 | AG |
| S. A. R. Anifowoshe | 57 | Lagos | Lagos | Attended secondary | Since birth | Yoruba | Muslim | Contractor | 6 | AG |
| A. O. Lawson | 43 | Lagos | Abeokuta | University | Since birth | Yoruba | Christian | Solicitor and company dir. | 12 | AG |
| M. O. Oseni | 49 | Lagos | Lagos | University | Since birth | Yoruba | Muslim | Barrister | 3 | AG |
| T. B. Lawal | 43 | Lagos | Lagos | Attended secondary | Since birth | Yoruba | Muslim | Clerk | 6 | AG |
| *Ward C* | | | | | | | | | | |
| R. F. Jakande | 62 | Lagos | Lagos | Grad. secondary | Since birth | Yoruba | Muslim | Builder | 3 | AG |
| A. B. Yesufu | 52 | Lagos | Lagos | Attended secondary | Since birth | Yoruba | Muslim | Trader | 8 | NCNC |
| E. A. Manuel | 41 | Abonema | Abonema | Attended secondary | Since birth | Kalabari/Ijaw | Christian | Shipping agent | 5 | NCNC |
| R. A. Balogun | 47 | Lagos | Abeokuta | Grad. primary | Since birth | Yoruba | Muslim | Contractor | 8 | NCNC |
| Mrs. K. A. Fashina | 56 | Lagos | Lagos | Grad. secondary | Since birth | Yoruba | Christian | Trader | 10 | NCNC |
| *Ward D* | | | | | | | | | | |
| H. P. Adebola | 53 | Ijebu | Ijebu | —— | — | Yoruba | Muslim | Trade unionist | 8 | NCNC |
| J. I. Talabi | 57 | Epe | Epe | Attended secondary | 35 | Yoruba | Christian | Tailor | 12 | NCNC |

| Name | Age | | | Education | | Ethnicity | Religion | Occupation | | Party |
|---|---|---|---|---|---|---|---|---|---|---|
| O. O. Soleye | 53 | — | Abeokuta | Grad. T.T.C.[c] | 24 | Yoruba | Christian | Teacher | 5 | NCNC |
| Mrs. B. Ogamba | — | — | — | — | — | Ibo | Christian | Trader | 3 | NCNC |
| *Ward E* | | | | | | | | | | |
| B. Sadipe | 39 | Ilesha | Ilesha | University | 13 | Yoruba | Christian | Barrister | 6 | NCNC |
| G. Okigbo | — | — | — | — | — | Ibo | Christian | Banker | 3 | NCNC |
| I. Obiajulu | — | — | — | — | — | Ibo | Christian | Clerk/steno | 5 | NCNC |
| G. Oparah | — | — | — | — | — | Ibo | Christian | Business mgr. | 9 | NCNC |
| M. A. Giwa | — | — | — | — | — | Yoruba | Muslim | Trader | 3 | NCNC |
| F. M. Moronu | — | — | — | — | — | Ibo | Christian | Tech. clerk | 9 | NCNC |
| A. Ogunsanya | 49 | Ikorodu | Ikorodu | University | 47 | Yoruba | Christian | Barrister | 8 | NCNC |
| F. S. McEwen | 49 | Lagos | In Sierra Leone | University | Since birth | Yoruba | Christian | Company dir. | 14 | NCNC |
| *Ward F* | | | | | | | | | | |
| M. A. Ogun | 59 | Ijebu | Ijebu | Grad. secondary | 42 | Yoruba | Christian | Business mgr. | 10 | AG |
| M. Abina | 60 | Lagos | Lagos | Grad. secondary | Since birth | Yoruba | Muslim | Printer | 9 | AG |
| H. O. Coker | — | — | — | — | — | Yoruba | Christian | Clerk | 3 | AG |
| S. I. Martins | 48 | Lagos | Lagos | Grad. primary | Since birth | Yoruba | Christian | Trader | 10 | AG |
| M. D. Ilesanmi | 38 | Ilesha | Ilesha | Grad. primary | 20 | Yoruba | Christian | Storekeeper | 3 | NCNC |
| J. A. Idowu | 60 | Shagamu | Shagamu | Grad. primary | 55 | Yoruba | Christian | Pensioner | 5 | AG |
| *Ward G* | | | | | | | | | | |
| S. O. Maduike | (est.) 60 | Orlu | Orlu | — | (est.) 35 | Ibo | Christian | Contractor and pensioner | 12 | NCNC |
| C. Biaduo | — | — | — | — | — | Ibo | Christian | Clerk | 3 | NCNC |
| Mrs. L. M. Joseph | 49 | Lagos | Lagos | Grad. primary | Since birth | Yoruba | Christian | Trader | 3 | NCNC |

## APPENDIX II—Continued

| | Age last birthday (1967)[a] | Hometown[b] | Father's hometown | Highest education achieved | Years resident in Lagos | Ethnic identification | Religion | Occupation | Years in office (rounded) | Party affiliation |
|---|---|---|---|---|---|---|---|---|---|---|
| **1959** | | | | | | | | | | |
| *Ward H* | | | | | | | | | | |
| M. Grillo | 59 | Lagos | Lagos | Attended secondary | Since birth | Yoruba | Muslim | Builder | 5 | AG |
| G. O. Dawodu | 34 | Lagos | Lagos | Grad. secondary | Since birth | Yoruba | Muslim | Clerk | 9 | AG |
| M. G. Salvador | 62 | Lagos | Lagos | Attended secondary | Since birth | Yoruba | Muslim | Contractor | 3 | AG |
| K. O. Giwa | 44 | Ibadan | Ibadan | Grad. primary | 28 | Yoruba | Muslim | Trader | 6 | AG |
| S. O. Ajose | 59 | Lagos | Lagos | Grad. primary | Since birth | Yoruba | Muslim | Trader | 5 | NCNC |
| B. Agusto | 47 | Lagos | Lagos | University | Since birth | Yoruba | Muslim | Barrister | 3 | NCNC |
| **1961 by-election** | | | | | | | | | | |
| *Ward A* | | | | | | | | | | |
| J. A. Odeku | 41 | Oyo | Oyo | University | Since birth | Yoruba | Christian | Barrister | 6 | AG |
| **1962** | | | | | | | | | | |
| *Ward A* | | | | | | | | | | |
| T. A. O. Olusi | 30 | Lagos | Lagos | Grad. secondary | 28 | Yoruba | Muslim | Clerk | 4 | AG |
| A. F. Masha | 49 | Lagos | Lagos | Attended secondary | Since birth | Yoruba | Muslim | Trader | 7 | AG |
| R. A. Williams | 37 | Lagos | Lagos | Grad. secondary | Since birth | Yoruba | Muslim | Contractor | 4 | AG |
| M. L. Onigbanjo | 46 | Lagos | Lagos | Attended secondary | Since birth | Yoruba | Muslim | Lab. tech. | 4 | AG |

*Ward B*

| M. A. Bashua | 38 | Lagos | Lagos | University | Since birth | Yoruba | Muslim | Barrister | 3 | AG |
|---|---|---|---|---|---|---|---|---|---|---|
| W. A. Ojikutu | 38 | Lagos | Lagos | University | Since birth | Yoruba | Muslim | Barrister | 3 | AG |
| S. A. R. Anifowoshe | 57 | Lagos | Lagos | Attended secondary | Since birth | Yoruba | Muslim | Contractor | 6 | AG |
| I. Laniyan | 51 | Ibadan | Ibadan | Attended secondary | Since birth | Yoruba | Muslim | Contractor | 3 | AG |
| H. A. Hakeem-Habeeb | 40 | Lagos | Lagos | University | Since birth | Yoruba | Muslim | Barrister | 4 | AG |
| T. B. Lawal | 43 | Lagos | Lagos | Attended secondary | Since birth | Yoruba | Muslim | Clerk | 7 | AG |

*Ward C*

| A. S. Motajo | 44 | Lagos | Lagos | Grad. primary | Since birth | Yoruba | Muslim | Trader | 3 | AG |
|---|---|---|---|---|---|---|---|---|---|---|
| A. B. Yesufu | 52 | Lagos | Lagos | Attended secondary | Since birth | Yoruba | Muslim | Trader | 8 | NCNC |
| A. L. Jimoh | 38 | Lagos | Lagos | Attended secondary | Since birth | Yoruba | Muslim | Trader | 3 | AG |
| R. A. Balogun | 47 | Lagos | Abeokuta | Grad. primary | Since birth | Yoruba | Muslim | Contractor | 8 | NCNC |
| Mrs. K. A. Fashina | 56 | Lagos | Lagos | Grad. secondary | Since birth | Yoruba | Christian | Trader | 10 | NCNC |

*Ward D*

| H. P. Adebola | 53 | Ijebu | Ijebu | —— | — | Yoruba | Muslim | Trade unionist | 8 | NCNC |
|---|---|---|---|---|---|---|---|---|---|---|
| E. A. Ladega | 59 | Ijebu | Ijebu | Grad. secondary | 43 | Yoruba | Christian | Hotel owner | 9 | NCNC |
| G. O. Oladipo | 47 | Abeokuta | Abeokuta | Attended secondary | 36 | Yoruba | Christian | Debt collector | 3 | AG |
| Mrs. C. Iwunze | — | —— | —— | —— | — | Ibo | Christian | Seamstress | 3 | NCNC |

## APPENDIX II—Continued

| | Age last birthday (1967)[a] | Hometown[b] | Father's hometown | Highest education achieved | Years resident in Lagos | Ethnic identification | Religion | Occupation | Years in office (rounded) | Party affiliation |
|---|---|---|---|---|---|---|---|---|---|---|
| **1962** | | | | | | | | | | |
| *Ward E* | | | | | | | | | | |
| B. Sadipe | 39 | Ilesha | Ilesha | University | 13 | Yoruba | Christian | Barrister | 6 | NCNC |
| E. T. Macaulay | 61 | In Sierra Leone | In Sierra Leone | Attended secondary | Since birth | Yoruba | Christian | Pensioner | 3 | AG |
| Mrs. E. Femi-Pearse | 59 | Lagos | Abeokuta | Grad. secondary | 43 | Yoruba | Christian | Housewife | 5 | AG |
| G. Oparah | — | ——— | ——— | Grad. ——— | — | Ibo | Christian | Business mgr. | 9 | NCNC |
| J. A. Ogun | 50 | Okitipupa | Okitipupa | Grad. secondary | 30 | Yoruba | Christian | Shoemaker | 4 | AG |
| L. S. Solomon | 40 | Calabar | In Lebanon | Grad. technical | 17 | Efik | Christian | Contractor | 4 | NCNC |
| A. Ogunsanya | 49 | Ikorodu | Ikorodu | University | 47 | Yoruba | Christian | Barrister | 8 | NCNC |
| F. S. McEwen | 49 | Lagos | In Sierra Leone | University | Since birth | Yoruba | Christian | Company dir. | 14 | NCNC |
| *Ward F* | | | | | | | | | | |
| F. Oshin (Oshinkanlu) | 61 | Ijebu | Ijebu | Grad. technical | 45 | Yoruba | Christian | Engineer | 4 | AG |
| J. O. Showemimo | 44 | Abeokuta | Abeokuta | Grad. T.T.C.[e] | 33 | Yoruba | Christian | Teacher | 4 | AG |
| A. Layeni | 44 | Abeokuta | Abeokuta | Attended secondary | Since birth | Yoruba | Christian | Hotel owner | 4 | AG |
| S. I. Martins | 48 | Lagos | Lagos | Grad. primary | Since birth | Yoruba | Christian | Trader | 10 | AG |
| J. A. Odeku | 41 | Oyo | Oyo | University | Since birth | Yoruba | Christian | Barrister | 6 | AG |
| T. A. Tokan | 43 | Ijebu | Ijebu | Attended secondary | 25 | Yoruba | Muslim | Contractor | 3 | AG |

*Ward G*

| Name | | | | | | | | | | |
|---|---|---|---|---|---|---|---|---|---|---|
| L. Benedict | 53 | Ijebu | Ijebu | Grad. T.T.C.^e | 46 | Yoruba | Christian | Teacher | 9 | NCNC |
| W. Owukori | — | — | — | — | — | Ibo | Christian | Storekeeper | 4 | NCNC |
| G. Chilaka | — | — | — | — | — | Ibo | Christian | Cook | 3 | NCNC |

*Ward H*

| | | | | | | | | | | |
|---|---|---|---|---|---|---|---|---|---|---|
| O. Imoru | 55 | Ilorin | Ilorin | Attended secondary | 49 | Yoruba | Muslim | Trader | 4 | AG |
| G. O. Dawodu | 34 | Lagos | Lagos | Grad. secondary | Since birth | Yoruba | Muslim | Clerk | 9 | AG |
| J. K. Ekisola | 36 | Ijebu | Ijebu | Attended secondary | 11 | Yoruba | Christian | Trader | 4 | AG |
| K. O. Giwa | 44 | Ibadan | Ibadan | Grad. primary | 28 | Yoruba | Muslim | Trader | 6 | AG |
| R. S. Shittu (Bajulaiye) | 31 | Lagos | Lagos | Attended secondary | Since birth | Yoruba | Muslim | Electrician | 3 | AG |
| T. Cole | 38 | Lagos | Lagos | Attended secondary | Since birth | Yoruba | Muslim | Storekeeper | 4 | AG |

*1965*

*Ward A*

| | | | | | | | | | | |
|---|---|---|---|---|---|---|---|---|---|---|
| T. A. O. Olusi | 30 | Lagos | Lagos | Grad. secondary | 28 | Yoruba | Muslim | Clerk | 4 | AG |
| A. F. Masha | 49 | Lagos | Lagos | Attended secondary | Since birth | Yoruba | Muslim | Trader | 7 | AG |
| R. A. Williams | 37 | Lagos | Lagos | Grad. secondary | Since birth | Yoruba | Muslim | Contractor | 4 | AG |
| M. L. Onigbanjo | 46 | Lagos | Lagos | Attended secondary | Since birth | Yoruba | Muslim | Lab. Tech. | 4 | AG |

*Ward B*

| | | | | | | | | | | |
|---|---|---|---|---|---|---|---|---|---|---|
| T. A. Lawal | 47 | Lagos | Lagos | Grad. primary | Since birth | Yoruba | Muslim | Plumber | 1 | AG |
| B. Ishmail | 36 | Lagos | Lagos | Attended secondary | Since birth | Yoruba | Muslim | Clerk | 1 | AG |

APPENDIX II—Continued

| | Age last birthday (1967)[a] | Hometown[b] | Father's hometown | Highest education achieved | Years resident in Lagos | Ethnic identification | Religion | Occupation | Years in office (rounded) | Party affiliation |
|---|---|---|---|---|---|---|---|---|---|---|
| **1965** | | | | | | | | | | |
| **Ward B** | | | | | | | | | | |
| T. B. Kotun | 63 | Lagos | Lagos | Attended primary | Since birth | Yoruba | Muslim | Contractor | 1 | AG |
| B. A. Kuku | 30 | Ijebu | Ijebu | Attended secondary | Since birth | Yoruba | Muslim | Clerk | 1 | AG |
| H. A. Hakeem-Habeeb | 40 | Lagos | Lagos | University | Since birth | Yoruba | Muslim | Barrister | 4 | AG |
| T. B. Lawal | 43 | Lagos | Lagos | Attended secondary | Since birth | Yoruba | Muslim | Clerk | 7 | AG |
| **Ward C** | | | | | | | | | | |
| D. Pitan | 32 | Epe | Epe | Attended secondary | 21 | Yoruba | Christian | Tailor | 1 | AG |
| A. W. Jawando | 35 | Abeokuta | Abeokuta | Attended secondary | Since birth | Yoruba | Muslim | Trader | 1 | AG |
| E. O. Ferreira | 34 | Lagos | Lagos | Attended secondary | Since birth | Yoruba | Christian | Company mgr. | 1 | AG |
| M. Bamgbelu | 38 | Epe | Epe | Grad. primary | 25 | Yoruba | Muslim | Contractor | 1 | AG |
| A. Oguntuga | 39 | Ijebu | Ijebu | Attended secondary | 24 | Yoruba | Christian | Printer | 1 | AG |
| **Ward D** | | | | | | | | | | |
| B. A. Animashaun | 28 | Lagos | Lagos | University | Since birth | Yoruba | Muslim | Trade unionist | 1 | AG |
| A. Adesakin | 47 | Oyo | Oyo | Attended secondary | 39 | Yoruba | Christian | Transporter | 1 | AG |

| Name | Age | | | Education | Years | Ethnicity | Religion | Occupation | No. | Party |
|---|---|---|---|---|---|---|---|---|---|---|
| M. A. Lawal | 39 | Ekiti | Ekiti | Attended secondary | Since birth | Yoruba | Muslim | Storekeeper | 1 | AG |
| A. Adegoke | 36 | Ibadan | Ibadan | Attended secondary | 20 | Yoruba | Christian | Contractor | 1 | NCNC |
| *Ward E* | | | | | | | | | | |
| E. Ogunmayin | 38 | Okitipupa | Okitipupa | Attended secondary | 36 | Yoruba | Christian | Trader | 1 | NCNC |
| E. Ilebiyi | 50 | Oyo | Oyo | Attended secondary | Since birth | Yoruba | Christian | Contractor | 1 | AG |
| J. B. Alli | 35 | Abeokuta | Abeokuta | Attended secondary | 20 | Yoruba | Muslim | Area supervisor | 1 | AG |
| G. Oparah | — | —— | —— | — | — | Ibo | Christian | Business mgr. | 9 | NCNC |
| J. A. Ogun | 50 | Okitipupa | Okitipupa | Grad. secondary | 30 | Yoruba | Christian | Shoemaker | 4 | AG |
| L. S. Solomon | 40 | Calabar | In Lebanon | Grad. technical | 17 | Efik | Christian | Contractor | 4 | NCNC |
| F. Anyiam | (est.) 60 | Orlu | Orlu | —— | (est.) 35 | Ibo | Christian | Company dir. | 4 | NCNC |
| B. Onyekwere | — | —— | —— | —— | — | Ibo | Christian | Barrister | 1 | NCNC |
| *Ward F* | | | | | | | | | | |
| F. Oshin (Oshinkanlu) | 61 | Ijebu | Ijebu | Grad. technical | 45 | Yoruba | Christian | Engineer | 4 | AG |
| J. O. Showemimo | 44 | Abeokuta | Abeokuta | Grad. T.T.C.[c] | 33 | Yoruba | Christian | Teacher | 4 | AG |
| J. Kalejaiye | 43 | Ijebu | Ijebu | Grad. T.T.C.[c] | 19 | Yoruba | Christian | Teacher | 1 | AG |
| S. Olaleye | 32 | Abeokuta | Abeokuta | Attended secondary | 15 | Yoruba | Christian | Draftsman | 1 | AG |
| L. Ekundayo | 36 | Ikorodu | Ikorodu | Grad. primary | 15 | Yoruba | Muslim | Trader | 1 | AG |
| K. Gbenro | 38 | Abeokuta | Abeokuta | Grad. secondary | 20 | Yoruba | Muslim | Contractor | 1 | AG |

| | Age last birthday (1967)[a] | Hometown[b] | Father's hometown | Highest education achieved | Years resident in Lagos | Ethnic identification | Religion | Occupation | Years in office (rounded) | Party affiliation |
|---|---|---|---|---|---|---|---|---|---|---|
| **1965** | | | | | | | | | | |
| **Ward G** | | | | | | | | | | |
| A. A. Animashaun | 34 | Abeokuta | Abeokuta | Grad. primary | Since birth | Yoruba/Hausa | Muslim | Pools agent | 1 | AG |
| W. Owukori | — | | | — | — | Ibo | Christian | Storekeeper | 4 | NCNC |
| L. Odunsi | 37 | Lagos | Lagos | Attended secondary | Since birth | Yoruba | Muslim | Trader | 1 | AG |
| **Ward H** | | | | | | | | | | |
| O. Imoru | 55 | Ilorin | Ilorin | Attended secondary | 49 | Yoruba | Muslim | Trader | 4 | AG |
| G. O. Dawodu | 34 | Lagos | Lagos | Grad. secondary | Since birth | Yoruba | Muslim | Clerk | 9 | AG |
| J. K. Ekisola | 36 | Ijebu | Ijebu | Attended secondary | 11 | Yoruba | Christian | Trader | 4 | AG |
| A. K. Jinadu | 62 | Lagos | Lagos | Grad. primary | Since birth | Yoruba | Muslim | Pensioner | 1 | AG |
| S. K. Jenmi | 37 | Lagos | Lagos | Attended secondary | Since birth | Yoruba | Muslim | Contractor | 1 | AG |
| T. Cole | 38 | Lagos | Lagos | Attended secondary | Since birth | Yoruba | Muslim | Storekeeper | 4 | AG |

a If a councilor died before 1967, his age at death is given.

b In Africa, one's hometown does not usually mean one's place of birth or residence, but rather one's place of origin, that is, where one's ancestors originated. Communal loyalties are determined by descent rather than by actual residence. For example, a councilor may have been born and raised in Lagos and may plan to remain there for the rest of his life, but he still replied to the questionnaire by saying that he considers his hometown to be his father's place of origin. This explains the seeming inconsistency when a councilor reported a place other than Lagos as his hometown, but said that he had lived in Lagos "since birth." Indigenes of Lagos, of course, are those who reported that Lagos was both their hometown and their fathers' hometown, regardless of the number of years they lived in the city. Some councilors displayed a more "westernized" image by identifying their hometown and their fathers' hometown as two different places, adopting the definition of "hometown" as one's place of birth or residence. It is significant that only eight individuals replied in this way, not including the one naturalized Nigerian and Africans with native foreigner backgrounds.

c Teacher training college.

## Appendix III

## Major Political Events in the History of Lagos

1849    Appointment of John Beecroft as first British consul for the Bights of Benin and Biafra.

1851    British naval squadron bombards Lagos to depose Oba Kosoko and install Akitoye who had been ousted by his nephew in 1845. Akitoye's installation marks the beginning of direct British intervention in Nigeria.

1853    Beecroft's jurisdiction limited to the Bight of Biafra. Benjamin Campbell appointed first full-time consul in Lagos. Akitoye's son, Docemo (Dosunmu), accedes to the throne with British support.

1859    Campbell replaced by Consul George Brand who urges Foreign Office to seize Lagos as a protectorate.

1861    Brand replaced by Consul Henry G. Foote who supports his predecessor's suggestion, adding that military occupation is the only way to contain the Yoruba warfare interrupting legitimate trade. Foote succeeded by Acting Consul William McKoskry who receives final approval from Foreign Office to annex Lagos. On August 6, 1861, Oba Docemo signs Treaty of Cession and McKoskry becomes acting governor. Lagos now officially known as a Crown Colony.

1862    H. Stanhope Freeman appointed first governor of Lagos. He pursues a policy of expansion against orders of Foreign Office, annexing Palma and Lekki from Kosoko, repressing resistance in Epe where there is much sympathy for Kosoko, and seizing control of Badagry.

1866    Colony of Lagos placed under administration of governor of West African Settlements in Sierra Leone. Captain John H. Glover appointed administrator of Lagos. He continues to pursue a policy of unauthorized expansion and involvement in the interior in order to gain control of trade routes from the Niger. Glover recalled in 1872.

1886    Lagos merged with outlying provinces to form Colony and Protectorate of Lagos administered directly by the governor.

1906    Lagos Colony administratively joined to Protectorate of Southern Nigeria and placed under the jurisdiction of a provincial commissioner.

1914    Amalgamation of Northern and Southern Protectorates of Nigeria. An administrator appointed to replace provincial commissioner of Lagos.

1916    Lieutenant governor of Southern Provinces adds to his own title that of administrator of Lagos. Dr. Henry Carr appointed provincial commissioner (later changed to resident) of Lagos. Water rate introduced after repeated local agitation against it.

## Appendix

1917    Creation of Lagos Town Council.

1920    Nigeria's first election for three members of LTC is held; franchise restricted to adult male property owners.

1923    First election for Legislative Council. Nigeria's first political party, Nigerian National Democratic Party, inaugurated by Herbert Macaulay.

1925    Eshugbayi Eleko banished to Oyo by the government.

1927    Lieutenant governor of Southern Provinces relieved of his title as administrator of the colony and a new administrator appointed who is directly responsible to the governor of Nigeria. Income tax introduced in Lagos.

1928    Creation of Lagos Executive Development Board.

1931    Eshugbayi Eleko allowed to return to Lagos and restored to the throne one year before his death.

1934    Lagos Youth Movement (later changed to Nigerian Youth Movement) formed.

1938    Indirect rule introduced in colony provinces. Lagos Town Council becomes financially independent.

1941    Lagos Town Council empowered to levy rates.

1944    National Council of Nigeria and the Cameroons (later changed to National Convention of Nigerian Citizens) organized in Lagos.

1946    Herbert Macaulay dies.

1949    Prince Adeniji Adele becomes oba of Lagos and inaugurates Area Councils.

1950    Mayor-council system of local government introduced. For first time in British West Africa, all representatives on a local council are elected by universal adult suffrage. Dr. I. Olorun-Nimbe elected first mayor of Lagos.

1951    Lagos merged with Western Region. Title of commissioner of the colony (formerly administrator) changed back to administrator. Action Group organized in Lagos.

1952    Lagos Town Council dissolved by Western Region government and caretaker committee appointed under Sir Kofo Abayomi.

1953    Sweeping reforms in local government introduced by Western Region government. The mayoralty is abolished; traditional rulers are given ex-officio membership on council; and oba of Lagos is made president of Lagos Town Council. This is the first time official responsibilities and recognition are given to traditional rulers in the town.

1954    Lagos separated from Western Region and given a new status as a federal territory. Badagry, Ikeja, and Epe provinces remain part of the west. Administrator of colony becomes chief administrative officer, Lagos.

1957    Alhaji Mohammadu Ribadu appointed the first minister of Lagos Affairs, Mines and Power.

1960    Nigeria becomes independent. Alhaji Musa Yar'Adua appointed minister of of Lagos affairs.

1963    Lagos achieves city status when Nigeria becomes a republic. Thereafter Lagos Town Council is known as Lagos City Council.

1965    Prince Adeyinka Oyekan II becomes oba of Lagos.

1966    Lagos City Council dissolved in April after the crisis precipitated by military coup d'etat of January 15. Ministry of Lagos Affairs is abolished.

1967    Creation of Lagos State on May 27 when a new twelve-state structure is set up in Nigeria. Lagos State, a 5,747-square-mile area, comprises enlarged divisions of Badagry, Ikeja, and Epe which were part of old Lagos colony; its population at time of formation said to be 1,443,567. Colonel Mobolaji Johnson appointed military governor.

# Abbreviations:

Dosunmu-Stapleton Report
: The *Dosunmu-Stapleton Commission of Inquiry Report* (1958)

Hoskyns-Abrahall Report
: *Report of the Lagos Town Planning Commission with Recommendations on the Planning and Development of Greater Lagos* (1946)

Imrie Report
: *Report by Sir John Imrie, C. B. E., into the Relationship between the Federal Government and the Lagos Town Council* (1959)

Jones and Lucas Report
: G. C. Jones and Keith B. Lucas, *Report on the Administration of Lagos Town Council* (1963)

Price Report
: *Report of a Commission of Inquiry Regarding the House of Docemo* (1933)

Rapson Report
: *Report of an Inquiry by Mr. R. N. Rapson, M. V. O., into Alleged Irregularities by the Lagos Town Council in Connection with the Collection of Money and the Issue of Permits and the Allocation of Market Stalls in Respect of Proposed Temporary Markets at Ereko and Oko-Awo* (1959)

Sagoe Tribunal Report
: *Report of the Tribunal of Inquiry into the Affairs of the Lagos Executive Development Board for the Period 1st October 1960 to 31st December 1965* (1968)

Saville Tribunal Report
: *Report of the Tribunal of Inquiry into the Affairs of the Lagos City Council for the Period October, 15, 1962 to April 18, 1966* (1966)

Storey Report
: *Report of the Commission of Inquiry into the Administration of the Lagos Town Council* (1952)

UN Report
: UN Technical Assistance Program, *Metropolitan Lagos*, report prepared for Ministry of Lagos Affairs (1964)

*Notes*

# Notes

CHAPTER. 1: *Introduction*

[1] Lucy Mair, *New Nations* (Chicago: University of Chicago Press, 1963), pp. 130–131.

[2] Edward Shils, *Political Development in the New States* ('s-Gravenhage: Mouton, 1962), p. 45.

[3] P. C. W. Gutkind, "The African Urban Milieu: A Force in Rapid Social Change," in Peter J. M. McEwan and Robert B. Sutcliffe, eds., *Modern Africa* (New York: Thomas Y. Crowell, 1965), p. 345.

[4] The paucity of research on African urban politics may be illustrated by reference to the bibliography on "Urban Politics in Africa, 1965–1969," compiled by Ronald R. Stockton for *African Urban Notes*, IV, 4, Bibliographical Supplement, no. 9, (December 1969), 67–75. Of the total of 115 works listed, 53 are country or regional studies; 48 are concerned with subjects that are only indirectly relevant to local politics (such as labor, elite recruitment, ethnic unions, etc.); 9 deal with non-political urban subjects (such as religion or family life); and only 4 focus specifically on urban politics in Africa.

[5] P. C. W. Gutkind, "Orientation and Research Methods in African Urban Studies," in D. G. Jongmans and P. Gutkind, eds., *Anthropologists in the Field* (Assen, Netherlands: Van Gorcum, 1967), p. 139.

[6] *African Urban Notes* and *Manpower and Unemployment Research in Africa,* two newsletters that concentrate exclusively on urban Africa, indicate the shift in attention. Horace Miner, ed., *The City in Modern Africa* (New York: Praeger, 1967), is a pioneering effort in the field. It is noteworthy, however, that only one contribution to Miner's book is concerned with the political structure of African cities. Most of the research on urban Africa has been conducted by anthropologists.

[7] See Horace Miner, *The Primitive City of Timbuctoo* (New York: Anchor Books, 1965); Hortense Powdermaker, *Coppertown: Changing Africa* (New York: Harper Colophon Books, 1962). Recent notable exceptions, indicating a departure from this narrow view, are the works by Abner Cohen, *Custom and Politics in Urban Africa* (Berkeley and Los Angeles: University of California Press, 1969), and David Parkin, *Neighbours and Nationals in an African City Ward* (Berkeley and Los Angeles: University of California Press, 1969).

[8] James S. Coleman, "The Politics of Sub-Saharan Africa," in Gabriel A. Almond and James S. Coleman, eds., *The Politics of the Developing Areas* (Princeton: Princeton University Press, 1960), pp. 536–537.

[9] Richard L. Sklar, "A Note on the Study of Community Power in Nigeria" (paper read at annual conference of African Studies Association, Washington, D. C., October 13, 1962), p. 2.

[10] Seymour Martin Lipset, *Political Man* (New York: Doubleday Anchor Books, 1963), pp. 34–38.

[11] Coleman, *op. cit.*, pp. 536–544.

[12] Samuel P. Huntington, *Political Order in Changing Societies* (New Haven and London: Yale University Press, 1968), pp. 72–73.

[13] Hilda Kuper, ed., *Urbanization and Migration in West Africa* (Berkeley and Los Angeles: University of California Press, 1965), p. 4.

[14] See Gerald Breese, *Urbanization in Newly Developing Countries* (Englewood Cliffs, N.J.: Prentice-Hall, 1966); UNESCO, *Social Implications of Industrialization and Urbanization in Africa South of the Sahara* (Paris, 1956).

[15] See William Bascom, "Some Aspects of Yoruba Urbanism," in Pierre L. van den Berghe, ed., *Africa: Social Problems of Change and Conflict* (San Francisco: Chandler Publishing Co., 1965), pp. 369–384. Elsewhere Bascom has written that "urbanization can . . . be considered a traditional Yoruba pattern and not the outgrowth of European acculturation" ("Urbanization among the Yoruba," *American Journal of Sociology*, 60 [1955], 447).

[16] A primate city has been identified as an extremely large city in a developing country in which major national institutions and resources are concentrated (Breese, *op. cit.*, pp. 48–49).

[17] According to the 1963 census, Ibadan had 627,379 inhabitants and an estimated metropolitan population of 1 million, and Lagos had 665,246 inhabitants with an estimated metropolitan population of 1.25 million.

[18] For a series of essays reviewing theories of urbanization, see Philip M. Hauser and Leo F. Schnore, eds., *The Study of Urbanization* (New York: John Wiley and Sons, 1965).

[19] Leonard Reissman, "Urbanism and Urbanization," in Julius Gould, ed., *Penguin Survey of the Social Sciences* (London: Penguin Books, 1965), pp. 45–46.

[20] Horace Miner, "The City and Modernization: An Introduction," in Miner, *The City in Modern Africa*, p. 9.

[21] J. Clyde Mitchell, "Theoretical Orientations in African Urban Studies," in Michael Banton, ed., *The Social Anthropology of Complex Societies* (London: Tavistock Publications, 1966), p. 45.

[22] *Ibid.*, p. 48.

[23] The study of community power has given rise to other mixed approaches that combine or borrow from the reputational and decision-making methods. A third type, the "positional" approach, investigates the persons and interests represented in formal institutional positions in the community. Although methodological refinements and experimentation have contributed toward the clarification of issues, they have not substantially affected the theoretical underpinnings that divide the two camps. For a discussion of the range of methods, see Terry Clark, *Community Power and Decision-making: Comparative Analyses* (San Francisco: Chandler Publishing Co., 1968). For discussions of the reputational and decision-making approaches, see Nelson W. Polsby, *Community Power and Political Theory* (New Haven: Yale University Press, 1963); Robert Presthus, *Men at the Top* (New York: Oxford University Press, 1964); Robert E. Agger, Daniel Goldrich, and Bert E. Swanson, *The Rulers and the Ruled* (New York: John Wiley and Sons, 1964); C. W. Gilbert, *Community Power Structure* (Gainesville: University of Florida Press, 1972).

[24] There have been relatively few attempts to test community power approaches in non-Western settings. For a review of such attempts in Latin America, see Francine Rabinowitz, "Sound and Fury Signifying Nothing," *Urban Affairs Quarterly*, 3 (March 1968), 111–122. Only William John Hanna and Judith Lyne Hanna have experimented with these methods in Africa ("The Political Structure of Urban-Centered African Communities," in Miner, *The City in Modern Africa*, pp. 151–184; "The Integrative Role of Urban Africa's Middle-Places and Middlemen," *Civilisations*, 15, no. 1 [1967], 12–29; "The Cross-Cultural Study of Local Politics," *Civilisations*, 16, no. 1, [1968], 81–96).

[25] See Thomas J. Anton, "Power, Pluralism and Local Politics," *Administrative Science Quarterly*, 7 (March 1963), 425-457, for an analysis of the theoretical assumptions of each school. Anton mars an otherwise balanced and perceptive dis-

cussion by somewhat overstating the images of society held by each school. Pluralists are portrayed as Hobbesian theorists who view society as an uncohesive collection of self-interested individuals free of any relationship with classes or institutions, while stratification theorists are described as analysts who view society as a fixed system of interacting roles through which individuals act invariably in terms of their class or institutional affiliations. Both presentations are caricatures. While not denying the relevance of contrasting models, scholars from both schools are critical of the methodological assumptions implied by such models. As Anton points out, the question to be asked of both schools is whether these assumptions influence investigational techniques so as to make the models self-fulfilling prophecies.

26 Floyd Hunter, *Community Power Structure* (Garden City: Anchor Books, 1963), pp. 11-12.

27 *Ibid.,* p. 13.

28 William John Hanna encountered this problem in Africa while attempting to use the Form-Miller technique of identifying community leaders by setting up a panel of two representatives each from the fields of mass communications, business, labor, welfare, education, government, and religion, these being the major institutional sectors in Western communities. Hanna remarks: "It would have been difficult to use identical techniques in Africa, but what is more important, it would not have been desirable. The underlying objective of the Form-Miller technique is to select representatives of the community's primary institutional sectors. Vary the culture and it is clear that the primary institutional sectors are also likely to vary" (Hanna and Hanna, "Cross-Cultural Study of Local Politics," pp. 87-88). Even though different institutional sectors were selected, Hanna observed that he was still left with the problems of (1) unbalanced representation of groups that, in the opinion of the researcher, are "knowledgeable," (2) an inability to weigh the equivalence of responses from groups of varying size and importance, (3) limitations imposed by the likelihood that only elite groups were sampled, (4) the lack of means of cross-checking, and (5) weakness in measurements that do not allow for time-free generalizations. For an explanation of the Form-Miller technique, see William H. Form and Warren L. Sauer, *Community Influentials in a Middle-Sized City* (East Lansing: Michigan State University, 1960).

29 Hunter, *op. cit.,* and Presthus, *op. cit.,* used this question.

30 Hanna and Hanna, "Political Structure of Urban-Centered African Communities," pp. 170-171.

31 Robert S. Lynd and Helen Merrell Lynd, *Middletown* (New York: Harcourt, Brace and World, 1929), and *Middletown in Transition* (New York: Harcourt, Brace and World, 1937).

32 Robert Dahl, *Modern Political Analysis* (Englewood Cliffs, N. J.: Prentice-Hall, 1963), p. 53. See Dahl, *Who Governs?* (New Haven: Yale University Press, 1961), for the original application of this methodology.

33 For further elaboration of this criticism, see Peter Backrach and Morton S. Baratz, "Decisions and Non-Decisions," *American Political Science Review,* 57 (September 1963), 632-642.

34 Hanna and Hanna, "Cross-Cultural Study of Local Politics," p. 81.

35 The degree of importance of each subject selected for detailed study was determined by the recurrence of controversy or by the significance of the subject to community or party leaders. The judgment had to be made by the researcher, but it can be fairly well substantiated by newspaper accounts, party records, government files, or evaluations by leading citizens.

# CHAPTER 2: *Growth of a City*

1 Jean Herskovits Kopytoff places the earliest settlement in the sixteenth century (*A Preface to Modern Nigeria: The "Sierra Leonians" in Yoruba, 1830–1890* [Madi-

son: University of Wisconsin Press, 1965], p. 11).

[2] For major events in early Lagos history, see John Losi, *History of Lagos*, first published in 1914, (Lagos: African Education Press, 1967).

[3] Quoted in Michael Crowder, *The Story of Nigeria* (London: Faber and Faber, 1962), pp. 151-152.

[4] Lord Hailey, *Native Administration in the British African Territories* (London: H.M.S.O. 1951), I, 24.

[5] Aku is probably a version of the root "Eku" used in Yoruba greetings: Ekãro ("Good morning"), Ekuòsáno ("Good afternoon"), and Ekualéo ("Good evening").

[6] Spencer H. Brown, "A History of the People of Lagos, 1852-1886" (Ph. D. dissertation, Northwestern University, 1964), p. 36.

[7] See S. O. Biobaku, *The Egba and Their Neighbours, 1842-1872* (Oxford: Clarendon Press, 1965), for a full treatment of relations between the Egbas and Lagos at this time.

[8] See John A. Payne, *Payne's Lagos and West African Almanack and Diary for 1884* (London, 1884), p. 42.

[9] P. A. Talbot, *The Peoples of Southern Nigeria*, IV (London: Oxford University Press, 1926), 178.

[10] The death rate in Lagos was 59 per thousand as against 19 per thousand in London (*Annual Colonial Reports: Lagos*, 1897).

[11] Cowrie shells were used as currency on the West African coast before the conversion to cash. European traders, by the mid-nineteenth century, maintained control of the supply. Jean Kopytoff notes (*op. cit.*, p. 104) that a German, Hermann Grote, was the Lagos agent for the distribution of the currency shipped from Zanzibar to several points along the Bight of Benin by William O'Swald and Company, a firm that held a monopoly on the shells which were available only in the Indian Ocean.

[12] Agreement of 10 Feb. 1859, in Kopytoff, *op. cit.*, p. 107.

[13] Akin L. Mabogunje, "Lagos: A Study in Urban Geography" (Ph.D. dissertation, University of London, 1961), p. 67.

[14] Quoted in Brown, *op. cit.*, p. 179 n. 133.

[15] *Ibid.*, p. 54.

[16] Kopytoff, *op. cit.*, p. 280.

[17] Brown, *op. cit.*, p. 37.

[18] *Ibid.*, p. 164.

[19] W. N. M. Geary, *Nigeria under British Rule* (New York: Barnes and Noble, 1965), pp. 24-67.

[20] *Ibid.*, p. 41.

[21] *Annual Colonial Reports: Lagos*, 1890, p. 20.

[22] See Payne's *Almanack* for lists of early organizations.

[23] Statistics on industrial location were calculated from *Industrial Directory*, 3d ed. (Lagos: Ministry of Industries, 1963), which gives figures for establishments with ten employees or more.

[24] R. A. Akinola, "Factors in the Geographical Concentration of Manufacturing in Greater Lagos," *Lagos Notes and Records*, 1 (June 1967), 34.

[25] UN Workshop on Urbanization in Africa, *Symposium on the Social Aspects of Urbanization*, April 25–May 5, 1962, Addis Ababa, Part I Report, "Introduction to the Problems of Urbanization in Tropical Africa," prepared by ECA Secretariat, March 7, 1962, p. 18.

[26] Akin Mabogunje, *Urbanization in Nigeria* (London: University of London Press, 1968), p. 252.

[27] *Ibid.*, p. 256.

[28] *Ibid.*, p. 261.

[29] All figures in this and subsequent quoted tables are reproduced as they appear in the original sources.

30 The 1963 census put the Ibo population in Lagos at 99,638, excluding the large Ibo settlements beyond the municipal boundaries in Ajegunle and Mushin. The 1968 figures are based on the number of Ibos who responded to the call to register and receive identity cards for their own protection during the civil war. At first, 17,000 Ibos in Lagos were said to have registered; several months later the Lagos State government speculated that about 38,000 Ibos, including those who failed to register, chose to remain in Lagos throughout the civil war.

31 The military governor of Lagos State, Colonel Mobolaji Johnson, announced on June 27, 1968, that the entire state of Lagos had an expatriate population of 28,000. Approximately 27,000 are located in the metropolitan area and, within the municipal area itself, about 23,000.

32 B. A. Williams and A. H. Walsh report that less than 5 percent of the metropolitan area is devoted to agricultural production; within the municipal boundaries only approximately 3 square miles of land is classified as undeveloped (*Urban Government for Metropolitan Lagos* [New York: Praeger, 1968], p. 4).

33 T. M. Yesufu, "Labour in the Nigerian Economy," lecture delivered on Nigerian Broadcasting Corporation program, October 1967 (mimeographed), p. 21. See also *Report of the Working Party on Statutory Corporations and State-owned Companies* (Lagos: Ministry of Information, 1966), App. II, "Analysis of Government and Corporations Salary Structures," p. 48.

34 *Report on Lagos Housing Enquiry* (Lagos: Federal Office of Statistics, 1961), p. 1.

35 *Ibid.*

36 *Urban Consumer Surveys in Nigeria: Lagos 1959–1960* (Lagos: Chief Statistician, 1963), pp. 18-19.

37 Yesufu, *op. cit.*, p. 7.

38 *Urban Consumer Surveys*, p. 31.

39 Akinola, *op. cit.*, p. 35.

40 See Mabogunje, "Lagos: A Study in Urban Geography," p. 44, for details of ethnic concentrations in different districts of the city. For details on central Lagos, see Peter Marris, *Family and Social Change in an African City* (London: Routledge & Kegan Paul, 1961).

41 Ethnic distribution data are derived from Mabogunje, "Lagos: A Study in Urban Geography," esp. pp. 148-150.

42 From the data on these five major groups it appears that the length of residence of immigrants is inversely proportional to the distance from region of origin. Frequent occasional visits to home villages or towns ease the strains of urban life for the Yoruba and permit longer residence, whereas groups like the Hausa and the Ibibio which cannot visit their homelands often, must bear long absences from family and friends.

CHAPTER 3: *The Ruling Strata*

1 The term "emigrants" denotes nineteenth-century liberated slaves and their descendants—the old Lagos elite—to be distinguished from twentieth-century settlers, who are called "immigrants."

2 *Population Census of Lagos, 1931* (Lagos: Federal Office of Statistics, 1932), p. 10.

3 *Nigerian Trade Report, 1921* (Lagos: Government Printer, 1922).

4 Margery Perham has succinctly described the attitudes of the Lagos elite: "The gradual and tentative advance of British power had left Lagos and other Yoruba people with a sense of self-confidence so that they did not regard themselves as a conquered people, but rather as torchbearers of progress who had kindled their flame at Britain's hearth and were eager to go into partnership with the government in its task of civilizing their more backward brethren" (*Lugard: The Years of*

*Austerity* [London: Collins, 1960], p. 585).

[5] "LTC Election, 1919/1920," files of the Lagos City Council, Town Clerk's Office. Some observers contend that most native foreigners were more liberal than these three. G. O. Olusanya, for example, has written that by 1917 "the government was ready to accede to the constant demand by the educated elements in Lagos for a Municipal Council" ("The Origin of the Lagos Town Council," *Lagos Notes and Records*, 2 [June 1968], 53). It is true, of course, that some Africans urged reform, but their requests were far from being "constant" or in the nature of a "demand." The evidence suggests, to the contrary, that the majority of educated Africans in Lagos were either apathetic or openly opposed to the principle of elective representation.

[6] *Nigerian Pioneer*, October 17, 1919, p. 7.

[7] *Ibid.*, September 21, 1917, p. 8.

[8] F. D. Lugard, *The Dual Mandate in British Tropical Africa*, 4th ed. (London: William Blackwood, 1929), p. 225.

[9] Lord Frederick Lugard was high commissioner of Northern Nigeria from 1900 to 1906, governor of Northern and Southern Nigeria from 1912 to 1914, and governor-general of Nigeria from 1914 to 1918.

[10] *Report on the Amalgamation of Southern and Northern Nigeria and Administration, 1912 to 1919*, Cmd. 468 (London: H.M.S.O., 1920), p. 19.

[11] For example, the government seized upon the Lagos riot over the water rate in 1916 to launch a general attack on the Lagos elite, even though the *Lagos Weekly Record*, a popular antigovernment newspaper, condemned the riot. In the Legislative Council debates, Governor Moorhouse cited this riot as the reason for not introducing elective representation in the colony (Minutes of the Legislative Council, April 23, 1917).

[12] Sir Hugh Clifford before the Nigerian Council, December 25, 1920, as quoted in Michael Crowder, *The Story of Nigeria* (London: Faber and Faber, 1962), p. 227.

[13] Spencer H. Brown, "A History of the People of Lagos, 1852–1886" (Ph.D. dissertation, Northwestern University, 1964), p. 37.

[14] *Legislative Council Debates*, June 12, 1934; August 23, 1927.

[15] Nnamdi Azikiwe, *Renascent Africa* (Accra: privately printed, 1937).

[16] The NEC was formed after the Iva Valley coal miners struck against the management in Enugu, Eastern Nigeria. Armed police, attempting to recover stockpiles of explosives in the mines, fired upon protesters who feared a lockout, killing twenty-one and wounding fifty-one. The nationalists were sufficiently unified to form a common front, the NEC, led by Dr. Akinola Maja and Mbonu Ojike, but the committee survived for only ten months before internal factionalism caused its dissolution. For further information see James S. Coleman, *Nigeria: Background to Nationalism* (Berkeley and Los Angeles: University of California Press, 1958), pp. 299–301, and Richard L. Sklar, *Nigerian Political Parties* (Princeton: Princeton University Press, 1963), pp. 76–79, 83–86.

[17] Three other Europeans ran as independents, but none of the expatriates won.

[18] *Daily Times*, September 12, 1950, p. 7.

[19] *Ibid.*, September 1, 1950, p. 5.

[20] Christianity and education were more widespread in the Eastern Region than in any other part of Nigeria. Comparatively speaking, the Ibos were the most modernized ethnic group in the country, and they adapted to urbanization with considerable ease. The position of the Ibos in Lagos is discussed further in chapter 4.

[21] The survey was conducted in three stages. First, one-page questionnaires were mailed to all councilors who served between 1959 and 1966. Seventy-three councilors, or 78 percent of the total, replied. The same procedure was followed for councilors who served between 1950 and 1959, but only about half of the group could be located. A number of councilors who were traced through inquiries were interviewed by a trained research assistant. Altogether, from mailed questionnaires and

interviews, information was obtained on 46 persons, or 51 percent of the councilors who served in the 1950s. For the final stage of the survey, two students from the University of Lagos were recruited to track down remaining councilors in both periods through family, friends, and colleagues, and to make personal contact with those who had failed to respond through the mail. Several councilors were found in this way. From close colleagues or relatives whose testimony could be deemed reliable, information was also gathered on councilors who were deceased or who had moved out of Lagos. Thirty-two questionnaires were completed in this manner, 28 through direct interviews and 6 through knowledgeable respondents.

Thus, of the 187 councilors who served between 1950 and 1966, full information was obtained on 151, or 81 percent of the total. Data were collected on each councilor's age, hometown, father's hometown, education, length of residence in Lagos, ethnicity, religion, occupation, number of years in office, and party affiliation. Partial information on the 36 councilors who could not be contacted was obtained through LCC records, nomination papers, and reliable respondents, particularly with respect to widely known characteristics such as occupation, ethnicity, and religion.

The use of these techniques during a two-year period yielded information on all the councilors who served between 1950 and 1966. Only a few were uncooperative and refused to provide information. Most were surprisingly responsive and many offered extensive follow-up assistance, some volunteering to comment on changes in the council's composition, on the state of local politics, and on their roles in local government. My research assistants and I were encouraged by the friendliness of these leaders, especially during a time of national crisis.

22 The rise of the Lagos Muslims occurred roughly in the period after the 1959 federal elections, when northern Nigerians captured control of the central government. This development, however, had little or no effect on the internal politics of Lagos, because northern Nigerians represented only about 2 percent of the urban population and their party, the Northern Peoples' Congress, had negligible local support, never won a seat on the council, and finally closed down its branch office in 1965, when indigenous Lagosians were nearing the peak of influence. Except for the constitutional status of Lagos (see chap. 9), northern Nigerians exercised political influence in the city almost entirely through the federal Ministry of Lagos Affairs, which existed from 1957 to 1966. During these years influence was limited to ministerial interference in land matters (see chap. 4) and to the withholding of mandatory financial contributions to the council (see chap. 6), a tactic designed to undercut the power of the opposition party, which controlled the council. Otherwise there is no evidence that northerners ever deliberately encouraged the Lagos Muslims to be more aggressive politically, nor is it likely that northerners were even aware of local changes within the ruling strata.

23 The change in the ratio of indigenes to immigrants at the time when the indigenes' political power was growing represents one of the most significant developments in Lagos politics in recent years. As table 28 shows, indigenes dropped from 80 percent of the total urban population in 1911 to 27 percent in 1963. By contrast, immigrants (Yoruba and non-Yoruba) rose from 20 percent in 1911 to 73 percent in 1963. One of the periods of heaviest immigration occurred after independence (see chap. 2). Indigenes, of course, could expand only through natural increase, but even in this respect immigrants tended to outpace indigenes, since migration was selective of young adults of reproductive age. While indigenes were declining as a proportion of the population (from 37 percent in 1950 to 27 percent in 1963), they were exerting stronger and more meaningful control on the council (from 33 percent of the councilors in 1950–1959 to 38 percent in 1959–1966, not counting near Lagosians). Immigrants, on the other hand, while increasing demographically (from 63 percent in 1950 to 73 percent in 1963) were declining politically (from 62 percent of the councilors in 1950–1959 to 57 percent in 1959–1966).

The impact of massive immigration on the composition of the ruling strata was thus diluted by the failure of the immigrants, particularly Yorubas, to translate their numbers into political control. They remained relatively stagnant while a cohesive minority ( Lagos Muslims, a particular faction of the indigenous population ) steadily advanced. Although immigrants collectively held the majority of seats on the council, they were internally divided by ethnicity, religion, and origin. Indigenes were divided by only one of these features—religion—and even this cleavage diminished as the Lagos Muslims displaced the Lagos Christians. The political consciousness of the indigenes grew in proportion to the influx of strangers who regarded the city in utilitarian or materialistic terms, retaining their links to their towns of origin. This was as true of Yoruba as of non-Yoruba immigrants and explains the inverse relationship between population and power in the urbanizing community.

24 Prince Tajudeen Oluyole Olusi, a Lagos Muslim elected as an Action Group councilor in 1962 and 1965, made this observation during the course of the 1967 social survey.

## CHAPTER 4: *Political Resources*

1 Herbert Macaulay, *Henry Carr Must Go*, open letter dated January 24, 1924, Kirsten Hall, p. 13.

2 Ellen Thorp, *Ladder of Bones* (London: Fontana Books, 1966), p. 212.

3 The tax rate was 1 percent on incomes of £30 or more and only male adults were taxed (*Annual Colonial Reports: Nigeria*, 1928, p. 11).

4 *Ibid.*

5 See P. A. Talbot, *The Peoples of Southern Nigeria*, IV (London: Oxford University Press, 1926), 185 (table 16).

6 See *Colonial Reports*, 1934 and 1935. For details on the structure of traditional political authority in the colony districts, see *Report of the Native Courts (Colony) Commission of Inquiry, 1949* (Lagos: Government Printer, 1952).

7 Obafemi Awolowo, *Awo: The Autobiography of Chief Obafemi Awolowo* (London: Cambridge University Press, 1960), p. 82. For a detailed account of the Nigerian press, see Increase Coker, *Landmarks of the Nigerian Press* (Lagos: Nigerian National Press, 1967).

8 Among the exceptions were two professional journalists: Thomas Horatio Jackson, who succeeded his father, John Payne Jackson, in managing and editing the *Lagos Weekly Record*; and Mohammed Ali, an Egyptian who edited the *Comet*, a weekly news review (see Coker, *op. cit.*, pp. 12–22).

9 *Ibid.*, p. 19.

10 *Ibid.*, p. 20.

11 See, for example, the discussion (*ibid.*, pp. 21–22) of the controversy over the *Pilot*'s attempt to establish a wireless station for receiving news items from independent services.

12 See Coker, *op. cit.*, for a list of newspapers and magazines published in Nigeria since 1859. The only paper concerned exclusively with Lagos affairs today is the *Lagos Weekend*, a weekly tabloid that directs its appeal to young, fun-loving, party-going city dwellers. It features sensational stories of sex scandals or of crime, covers major social functions in the city, and runs a column on "old Lagos" which focuses on personalities of the past. A comic strip, "Omo-Eko," depicts the life of a shiftless loafer seeking an easy urban existence.

13 *Population Census of Lagos, 1950* (Lagos: Federal Office of Statistics, 1950); *Statistics of Education in Nigeria*, 1964, no. 1, vol. 5 (Lagos: Ministry of Education, 1964).

14 *Population Census of the Western Region of Nigeria, 1952* (Lagos: Government Statistician, 1953–54).

15 Literacy was defined in the 1950 census as "the ability to write a short letter and to read a letter, or newspaper, or other written or printed document." No actual

test of literacy was given, but enumerators were instructed to conduct a "careful inquiry" before making any entry. Literates included persons who were able to read and write in any language. Three-quarters of the literate population of Lagos were found to read and write English, and 90 percent of the 15–24 age group were literate in English. The majority of literate Nigerians from the Western and Eastern regions were bilingual, able to read and write both an African language and English.

[16] Except for northerners, migration tended to be selective of persons with relatively high educational achievements. The percentage of educated northerners is low because the educational system in their region is poor and because many of them are traders, a calling that does not require formal education.

[17] Gutkind's research in 1966 led him to conclude that "almost any Ibo who comes to town can almost certainly expect food and shelter from another Ibo whether they are related in some manner or not. . . . This is perhaps to be contrasted with the Yoruba among whom a very large number of unemployed men expressed the view that it was quite unpredictable even whether a relative would act as a willing or friendly host. . . . The Ibo . . . have developed a complex network of non-kin-based associations which are particularly suitable to aid the new urbanite both during times of plenty and times of stress" (P. C. W. Gutkind, "The Energy of Despair: Social Organization of the Unemployed in Two African Cities, Lagos and Nairobi," *Civilisations*, 17, nos. 3 and 4 [1967], reprinted by Centre for Developing-Area Studies, McGill University, pp. 17–18).

[18] The Ibos evidenced a low rate of unemployment in Lagos because, more than other groups, they tended to return home when they could not find work (*Population Census of Lagos, 1950*, p. 20). The residency patterns of ethnic groups shown in table 6 confirm this generalization.

[19] For the role of Ibos in Nigeria, see Paul Anber, "Modernization and Political Disintegration: Nigeria and the Ibos," *Journal of Modern African Studies*, 5, no. 2 (1967), 163–179.

[20] This figure does not include Ibos who lived in districts beyond the municipal area, principally Ajegunle and Mushin. Although there are no precise figures, it is likely that the number of Ibos who held jobs in Lagos but lived outside the city did not exceed the number of Yorubas in the same situation. The majority of Ibos living in Ajegunle and Mushin were not in higher occupational categories nor, of course, were they part of the Lagos electorate. The 15 percent figure for Ibos as a proportion of the total Lagos population is therefore fairly accurate despite the overspill population beyond the city limits.

[21] The dominance of Yoruba women traders is also partly due to the sex ratio of Ibos in Lagos (18 males to 10 females) as compared with Yorubas, who have had an almost equal number of males and females since 1950.

[22] The Ibo exodus from Lagos began after the September 1966 riots in the Northern Region and continued until the roads were closed after the Eastern Region seceded in May 1967. The total stallage collection for September 1966 was £7,697.1.6, as compared with £7,587.7.6 for September 1967. The decrease was only £109.14.0. The markets most affected were Apapa Elemu, Alayabiagba, Iddo, Ijero, and Obalende, in or near Ibo residential areas. ("Market Monthly Statements for the Month of September, 1967," in report of the Market, Parks, and Cemetery Committee of the Lagos City Council Caretaker Committee, February 20, 1968, in papers prepared for the March 5, 1968, meeting of the LCC.) Since some stalls may have been reassigned after they were abandoned, however, the decrease is not a precise indication of the proportion of Ibos in Lagos markets.

[23] The survey, covering private homes, was conducted by Akin Mabogunje. Ownership of land is usually linked to ownership of houses, particularly in the older sections of the city.

[24] Allegations of Ibo domination also derive from supposed favoritism toward kinsmen in recruitment policies for institutions controlled by Ibos, many of them

federal establishments. There is ample evidence that Ibo clannishness or tribalism existed. For example, the Nigerian Railway Corporation, headed by an Ibo, was run as a "clannish institution" in which personnel "drawn from the same tribe and from the same division within the tribe" were given senior positions (*Report of the Nigerian Railway Corporation Tribunal of Inquiry Appointed under the Tribunal of Inquiry Decree, 1966, to Inquire into the Affairs of the Nigerian Railway Corporation* [Lagos: Ministry of Information, 1967]). But similar evidence of tribalism could be found in institutions run by Yorubas and other ethnic groups (*Report of the Electricity Corporation of Nigeria Tribunal of Inquiry* [Lagos: Ministry of Information, 1967]; *Sagoe Tribunal Report* [1968]; *Saville Tribunal Report* [1966]).

25 A notable exception to the standard models of community power is the interpretation presented by Robert O. Schulze, "The Role of Economic Dominants in Community Power Structure," *American Sociological Review*, 23 (February 1958), 3–9.

26 Charisma is used here in the Weberian sense, as "a certain quality of an individual personality by virtue of which he is set apart from ordinary men and treated as endowed with supernatural, superhuman, or at least specifically exceptional powers or qualities. These as such are not accessible to the ordinary person, but are regarded as . . . exemplary, and on the basis of them the individual concerned is treated as a leader" (Max Weber, *The Theory of Social and Economic Organization* [New York: Free Press, 1947], pp. 358–359).

27 Macaulay was ineligible for office because of two criminal convictions, one for embezzlement early in his career and one for libel at the height of his popularity. The latter resulted from his publication of the "gun-powder plot," alleging a plan to assassinate the exiled oba of Lagos, Eshugbayi Eleko.

28 See Richard L. Sklar's discussion of Adelabu in *Nigerian Political Parties* (Princeton: Princeton University Press, 1963), pp. 289–320.

29 The Jam'at Congregation, which separated from orthodox Muslims in 1916, became the most popular Muslim sect in Lagos (see pp. 105–110).

30 Coleman notes that Macaulay called for the "success of British arms" in 1940 and in his attacks on government policies invariably closed his remarks with the incantation, "God Save the King" (James S. Coleman, *Nigeria: Background to Nationalism* [Berkeley and Los Angeles: University of California Press, 1958], pp. 197, 456–457).

31 Weber warns (*op. cit.*, p. 360) that "if . . . [the charismatic leader] fails to benefit his followers, it is likely that his charismatic authority will disappear."

32 The role of land in Lagos politics is discussed later in this chapter. For his efforts in the Oluwa case, Macaulay received a fee of £2,083 (W. N. M. Geary, *Nigeria under British Rule* [New York: Barnes and Noble, 1965], p. 302).

33 Divisions within the Muslim community in Lagos are discussed later in this chapter.

34 Of all the incidents that brought fame to Macaulay, the Eleko's reinstatement is perhaps the most illustrative of his political style. The issue originated in 1921 when Macaulay was in London defending Chief Oluwa's petition before the Privy Council. During an interview with a journalist, Macaulay reportedly claimed that the oba of Lagos, Eshugbayi Eleko, was recognized by the 17 million people of Nigeria as king, to whom all revenues from the colony were due as personal property. Buell later argued that Macaulay actually meant that Nigerians regarded the oba as king of Lagos, not king of Nigeria. This was not clear at the time, however, and the local authorities were furious with Macaulay, interpreting his action as a deliberate attempt to embarrass the colonial government. The situation was complicated by the fact that Macaulay was then in possession of the silver-mounted staff of the Eleko, a gift from the British Crown to Oba Docemo at the time of the cession of Lagos. The staff had come to be recognized as a symbol of authority of the Lagos monarchy. As self-styled "Minister Plenipotentiary of the House of Docemo," Macaulay used the staff to lend authority to his statements. The government demanded

that the Eleko call for the immediate return of his staff and publicly denounce Macaulay. The Eleko refused, both because of his close personal ties with Macaulay and because of the embarrassment he would inevitably suffer by humiliating Macaulay. His continued defiance provoked the government to suspend him from office, terminate his pension, and deport him to Oyo. Macaulay then published a disquisition on the government's treatment of the royal house, *Justitia Fiat: The Moral Obligation of the British Government to the House of King Docemo of Lagos* (London: St. Clement's Press, 1921). Shortly thereafter he organized the NNDP and began agitating for the reinstatement of the Eleko. In 1925 the government placed a rival pretender, Prince Ibikunle Akitoye, on the Lagos throne. This action split the traditional community down the middle, reviving old enmities and giving Macaulay a strong platform for his antigovernment activities. In 1928 he was jailed for his story of a conspiracy to assassinate the Eleko. Undaunted, Macaulay began court proceedings against the government, petitioning for a writ of habeas corpus for Eshugbayi. The Nigerian court denied his petition. He appealed to the Privy Council which ruled that the petition be returned to Nigeria for a hearing. Just as the issue was reaching a new pitch, Governor Donald Cameron rescinded the deportation order and removed the incumbent, Sanusi Olusi, who had succeeded Akitoye.

On July 4, 1931, Eshugbayi returned to Lagos after a six-year exile. Celebrations lasted an entire week and Macaulay was heralded as a popular hero. A year later, Eshugbayi died. Macaulay exerted his influence among the chiefs to have Eshugbayi's brother, Prince Falolu, selected as successor, keeping the throne in the hands of the Docemo line. Falolu was recognized by the governor in "an act of grace" after much bickering over procedures of succession. (For further details see Margery Perham, *Native Administration in Nigeria* [London: Oxford University Press, 1937], pp. 264–271; T. O. Elias, "Makers of Nigerian Law," *West Africa*, June 9, 1956, p. 367: E. A. Akintan, *The Closing Scene of the Eleko Case and the Return of Chief Eshugbayi Eleko* [Lagos: Tika-Tore Press, 1931]; "Proceedings of the Prince Eshugbayi Eleko Case," *Nigerian Daily Telegraph*, January 16–19, 1929; Raymond Leslie Buell, *The Native Problem in Nigeria* [New York: Macmillan, 1928], I, 662–667.)

35 Macaulay's son, Oged (Ogedengbe), recalled one occasion when his father became involved in events that were usually beyond his scope of activity. In 1901, when the choice of a successor to the stool was delayed, members of one of the rival dynasties buried the royal staff of office and a document entitled *Laws for the Government of Lagos*, drawn up by the colonial government, in a grave of a recently deceased relative, thus depriving Eshugbayi Eleko of the symbols of office establishing his rightful claim to the throne. One of the persons privy to the plot informed Macaulay who, under cover of night, traveled to the grave site, exhumed the body, and retrieved the staff and the document. Thanks to this daring act, the Eleko was able to produce the symbols of office when challenged by his rivals, and he thereby acceded to the throne. Eshugbayi, eternally indebted to Macaulay, refused to repudiate him when the government insisted he do so some years later (*Sunday Post*, April 6, 1969, p. 13).

36 *Annual Colonial Report: Nigeria*, 1927, p. 4.

37 Lord Hailey, *Native Administration in the British African Territories* (London: H.M.S.O., 1951), I, 35.

38 Herbert Macaulay, *Henry Carr Must Go* (Kirsten Hall, January 24, 1924).

39 It was reported that, by 1938, 80 percent of the members of the Democratic Party had fallen out with Macaulay. An example of the disaffection was the reaction of some of his associates to the supposed deal between Macaulay and the government for reinstatement of the Eleko. The government, addressing a delegation consisting of T. A. Doherty, Eric Moore, and Adeniji-Jones, all Legislative Council members, had offered to allow the Eleko to return to Lagos on the conditions that the existing head of the House of Docemo would receive a house and a pension and that

the Eleko would not take part in political affairs. The governor gave the leaders of the Democratic Party three days to answer. Macaulay immediately accepted the offer, regarding it as a personal victory in a long six-year battle. After the Eleko's return, however, when the estimates were drawn up to provide compensation for the deposed ruler, Macaulay instructed the elected members of the Legislative Council to refuse to endorse the appropriation. Adeniji-Jones did not sign the bill, but Doherty and Moore both honored their agreement in defiance of Macaulay's instructions, signaling for the first time an open break between Macaulay and his lieutenants.

[40] Coleman's comparison of the two men (*op. cit.*, p. 266) is an excellent summary: "On the one hand, Macaulay was more in the tradition of Victorian radicalism and thus was more conservative and 'constitutional' than Azikiwe would probably have been. Where Macaulay would demand his rights as a British subject, Azikiwe would talk of natural rights. In a sense, therefore, Macaulay in the early period served as a brake upon Azikiwe's leadership of the NCNC. On the other hand, although a Yoruba, Macaulay was a poor instrument for gaining widespread Yoruba support. Azikiwe, leveler and iconoclast that he was, had already done much to alienate the old conservative Yoruba families through his journalism. By joining with Macaulay, however, Azikiwe and the NCNC inherited all the enmities and personal rivalries accumulated by Macaulay during his forty-year domination of Lagos politics. The alliance gave them both power over the masses in Lagos, but it also exacerbated the tension between them and the educated Yoruba middle class."

[41] In his autobiography, Awolowo clearly expressed disdain for Macaulay's leadership (*op. cit.*, pp. 114–115): "'H.M.' was, in his time, a political colossus: and all those who assembled under the shade of his giant structure obeyed his words without question. Anything short of this was unthinkable and unacceptable to the 'Monghul'. ... To the masses of the people in Lagos and in the southern parts of Nigeria the 'Wizzard of Kirsten Hall' ... was something of a superman. But to most of the elite and intellectuals in Lagos who knew him intimately, he was not quite ɪᴛ. ... As time went on, ... more and more of the intelligentsia in Lagos drifted away from him. The admiration for the doughty fighter was there all right, but they denied him their political association and collaboration. Consequently, ... the Lagos Youth Movement was inaugurated, in preference to and as distinct from the Democratic Party, as the rallying platform for mass protest."

[42] Awolowo reported (*ibid.*, p. 127) that in 1937 "We approached Herbert Macaulay, Dr. the Hon. C. C. Adeniji-Jones, and Sir Adeyemo Alakija. ... When [Macaulay] ... learnt that we had also enlisted the assistance of Sir Adeyemo Alakija, he was enraged, drove us away from his house, and threatened to break up the strike. He then wrote an article ... calling upon the government to enact a law making strikes illegal."

[43] Ogedengbe Macaulay is Herbert Macaulay's second eldest son. The first son died at a young age in a car accident. When the NCNC tour resumed after Macaulay's funeral, Oged took his father's place. He played a minor official role in the NCNC as an assistant secretary and has memorialized his father in a series of articles on old Lagos published in the local press.

After Macaulay's death a dispute lasting twenty-one years arose among his children over division of his estate. One faction claimed that the offspring of Macaulay's alliances with women he did not marry should not inherit his property. The court upheld this view in 1952, depriving Oged and other children of their inheritance. The Lagos High Court nullified the judgment in 1967, declaring that all offspring "acknowledged by [a man] ... as his children are entitled to share equally when he dies intestate" (*Lagos Weekend*, April 21, 1967, p. 3).

[44] *West African Pilot*, May 8, 1946. See also Isaac B. Thomas, *Life History of Herbert Macaulay*, 3d ed. (Lagos: privately printed, 1948), pp. 67–77.

[45] Obadia Adegboyega Sobande, *Notes and Comments on the Life of Mr. H.*

*Macaulay* (Lagos, n.d.), as quoted in *Coleman, op. cit.*, p. 291.

[46] See William L. Riordon, ed., *Plunkett of Tammany Hall* (New York: E. P. Dutton, 1963).

[47] See Oged Macaulay in *Lagos Weekend*, May 26, 1967, p. 8; T. O. Elias, *Nigerian Land Law and Custom* (London: Routledge & Kegan Paul, 1951); G. B. A. Coker, *Family Property among the Yoruba* (London: Sweet and Maxwell, 1962); C. K. Meek, *Land Tenure and Land Administration in Nigeria and the Cameroons* (London: H.M.S.O., 1957).

[48] Oged Macaulay has provided the only available summary of the holdings of each chief, although even his account (in *Lagos Weekend*, May 26, 1967, p. 8) is not precise.

[49] Daryll Forde, *The Yoruba-speaking Peoples of South-Western Nigeria* (London: International African Institute, 1951), pp. 25–26.

[50] Elias (*Nigerian Land Law*, p. 102) defined the following customary rules of succession among Lagos Yorubas:

"(1) When the founder of a family dies, the eldest surviving son called the 'Dawodu' succeeds to the headship of the family with all that implies, including residence and the giving of orders in his father's house or compound;

"(2) On the death of the eldest surviving son, the next eldest surviving child of the founder, whether male or female, is the proper person to succeed as head of the family;

"(3) If there is going to be any important dealing with family property all branches of the family must be consulted, and representation on the family council is . . . according as there are wives with children;

"(4) The division is into equal shares between the respective branches, regard being had to any property already received by any of the founder's children during his life-time;

"(5) The founder's grandchildren only succeed to such rights as their immediate parents had in the family property;

"(6) The founder's compound or house is usually regarded as the 'family house' which must be preserved for posterity."

[51] Article III reads: "In the transfer of Lands, the stamp of Docemo affixed to the document will be proofs [*sic*] that there are no other native claims upon it, and for this purpose he will be permitted to use it hitherto."

[52] Meek, *op. cit.*, p. 63.

[53] *Ibid.*

[54] None of the earlier sporadic attempts to resist government expropriation of property were nearly so successful or gained such widespread publicity as the Apapa case (see, e.g., Oged Macaulay, "Lands Acquisition Act Inflames Agitation," *Sunday Post*, March 30, 1969, p. 13). The Democratic Party noted sometime after this episode that "Land and all that appertaineth to land are matters of life and death with the Natives of West Africa. . . . The shortest and easiest way to start a conflagration in West Africa is to make an attempt at depriving the Native of his land or inherent rights thereto." (*West Africa*, April 10, 1927, p. 415).

[55] "Where the Cession passes any proprietary rights, they were rights which the ceding king possessed beneficially and free from the usufructuary qualification of title in favor of his subjects' (*Amodu Tijani [Chief Oluwa]. v. Secretary, Southern Provinces*, 1921, 2 A.A., The Privy Council, pp. 295–302).

[56] Increase Coker, *op. cit.*, pp. 182–204.

[57] S. R. Simpson, *A Report on the Registration of Title to Land in the Federal Territory of Lagos* (Lagos, 1957), p. 7.

[58] For details on the background of these ordinances, see Increase Coker, *op. cit.*, chaps. 9, 10. Perhaps the best illustration of the complexities of land tenure is the Glover Settlement Ordinance. In 1866 the Glover Settlement was established in order to absorb the Abeokuta refugees fleeing from a religious dispute provoked, in

part, by the government. Sir John Glover, the administrator of the colony, obtained a concession of land from Chief Olotu with the aid of Oba Docemo. The area, covering approximately 1 square mile in Ebute Metta, was bordered on the north by Glover Street, on the west by Denton Street, and on the east and south by the Lagos lagoon. No compensation was paid to the Olotu family. Settlers were given individual tickets for each plot, copies of which were later lost or destroyed by the surveyor general. Hence, as time went on it became impossible to verify the specific holding of each settler or of his descendants. Eventually two interests claimed ownership: the Ebute Metta Aborigines' Society, representing the Egba refugees, and the Olotu family represented by Chief Olotu. The Glover Settlement Ordinance provided that an officer determine the validity of competing claims and issue certificates of title to the rightful owners. Those who were given title, however, were not permitted to alienate their property without the consent of the Olotu family. If the family of the titleholder became extinct, ownership of the land reverted to the Olotu family. In essence, the titleholders became occupants having only usufruct rights in conformity with customary law, but they were not owners in the sense of having the right of alienation. The solution, acceptable to both sides, was a reversion to the original pattern of Yoruba land tenure. (See Mervin Tew, *Report on Title to Land in Lagos* [Lagos: Government Printer, 1939], and W. Fowler, *A Report on the Lands of the Colony District* [Lagos, 1949].)

[59] Peter Marris, *Family and Social Change in an African City* (London: Routledge & Kegan Paul, 1961), p. 23.

[60] *Ibid.*, p. 29.

[61] *Daily Service*, May 19, 1962, p. 14.

[62] Data on the Central Lagos Slum Clearance Scheme were collected from a variety of sources. The principal references used were the *UN Report* (1964); the *Sagoe Tribunal Report* (1968); and Marris, *op. cit.*

[63] "Stones, bottles and sticks were thrown at the police, who in retaliation, used their batons to beat up a number of people. . . . Many were arrested" (*Daily Service*, June 29, 1956). The same day the *Daily Times* reported one man as saying, "This is my father's house, and only my dead body can be removed from this place." The chairman of the LEDB, Sir Kofo Abayomi, related his experience at the inception of the scheme: "I told the Prime Minister that all what [*sic*] I was doing was not for the monetary profit, but to have the happiness that I contributed to the development of this country from slum to what it is now. In the early days . . . I was stoned; they broke my car when we were arranging to move these slum dwellers. They said we wanted to move them for commercial interest (*Lagos Executive Development Board Tribunal of Inquiry Proceedings* [1967], p. 29).

[64] Letter from J. E. King to the chief executive officer, LEDB, May 22, 1961 (*LEDB Tribunal Proceedings*, p. 87).

[65] *UN Report*, pp. 174–196.

[66] From May 1963 all meetings of the Ex-gratia Compensation Committee became shop allocation exercises administered by the Ministry of Lagos Affairs, heightening conflict between the ministry and the board. Each authority advertised separately for applications from the general public for allocation of temporary shops. This situation placed the board in a very embarrassing position (*LEDB Tribunal Proceedings*, p. 91).

[67] *Morning Post*, February 9, 1967, p. 1; *New Nigerian*, February 9, 1967, p. 2. The list of names of those who received allocations were tendered at the LEDB probe by the acting principal lands officer in the federal Ministry of Lands and Housing. In some instances as many as six plots were merged, renamed, and allocated to one person.

[68] *West African Pilot*, December 7, 1966, p. 1.

[69] The Association of House Owners and Tenants of the Olowogbowo Area, representing some 10,000 persons displaced when the second mainland bridge was

built, joined the Association of Central Lagos Residents in condemning the treatment of displaced persons. Remaining communal land designated by the LEDB for future development is likely to be the source of persistent conflict between traditional landowners and local authorities. For example, Chief Yesufu Abiodun, the Oniru of Lagos, publicly warned that he would "resist to the bitter end" attempts of the LEDB or the government to acquire Maroko Village, which is part of the family's property (*Morning Post*, March 16, May 27, 1967). The determination of traditional landowners to keep their land is also indicated by the suit that 42 members of Lagos royal families brought against the oba of Lagos, Adeyinka Oyekan II, for land located in the traditional quarter, bounded by Great Bridge Street and Reclamation Road. The plaintiffs argued that the oba, in leasing this land to an oil company, had acted in violation of native law and custom (*West African Pilot*, October 27, 1967).

70 On the conservative assumption that from three-fifths to three-fourths of the 250,000 people living on Lagos Island are indigenes, the total number of Lagos Muslims can be estimated at about 75,000. Before 1921 many indigenes were animists and, strictly speaking, could not be identified as Lagos Muslims. For the purpose of analyzing the role of this social group over time, however, the ancestors of today's Lagos Muslims may be properly regarded as indigenes. In instances where no distinction between indigenes and Lagos Muslims is made, the two terms are used interchangeably.

71 *Hoskyns-Abrahall Report*, p. 17.

72 Community leaders interviewed in Old Town were very close, both physically and emotionally, to other family members. I was often referred to other family members who lived just around the corner or down the block. A brother or a cousin who might be of help could be found in a matter of minutes. This practical ease of instant communication, which is not typical of Lagos generally, undoubtedly adds to a large extent to the intimacy of the community. For details of life in central Lagos, see Marris, *op. cit.*, pp. 1–81; see also Peter Marris, "African City Life," in *Nkanga*, no. 1 (Kampala, Transition Books, 1968).

73 Marris, *Family and Social Change*, pp. 32–33.

74 The incidence of polygamy was highest among Muslims. Many women felt that the practice provided social, domestic, and economic advantages in the running of the household. In central Lagos most marriages were solemnized under customary or Muslim law, and a bride-price was usually paid. Marriage customs in the urban environment have therefore not greatly deteriorated, but have assumed a new social function. Heavy investments in marriage or engagement parties, in bride-price, or in gifts are taken as indications of a man's status or wealth. (See P. O. Ohadike, "A Demographic Note on Marriage, Family, and Family Growth in Lagos, Nigeria," paper read at First African Population Conference, University of Ibadan, January, 1966.)

75 Data on the history of Islam in Lagos were derived from Jean Comhaire, "La Vie Religieuse à Lagos," *Zaïre*, 3 (May 1949), 549–556; J. S. Trimingham, "Islam and Christianity among the Yoruba," *East and West Review*, 19 (October 1953), 109–111; Humphrey J. Fisher, "The Ahmadiyya Movement in Nigeria," in *African Affairs*, no. 1, ed. Kenneth Kirkwood (London: Chatto and Windus, 1961), pp. 60–88; Adam I. Animashaun, *The History of the Muslims* [sic] *Community of Lagos* (Lagos: Hope Rising Press, n.d.); and from personal interviews with local religious leaders.

76 Another sensational incident occurred when Lemomu Braimah turned down the Jam'at's request to use the Central Mosque for a meeting in 1919. When the Jam'at arrived to hold the meeting anyway, they found the doors of the mosque locked. In retaliation, they double-locked the doors, compelling members of the Lemomu faction to have to force their way in when they returned.

77 Fisher, *op. cit.*, p. 67.

78 J. S. Trimingham (*The Influence of Islam upon Africa* [London: Longmans,

1968], p. 44) hypothesized three major stages of Islamic conversion in Africa: "In religious change the family rather than the individual is the natural and significant unit. The process takes more than one generation and is a reciprocal interaction between three generations. We may express it in this way. A pagan family (generation 1) is subject to Islamic radiation. This affects their children (generation 2) who become Muslims in name, without discarding much of the old, but their children (generation 3), under the influence of clerics, learn to despise the old inheritance, and generation 1, in order to preserve its authority and maintain the unity of the family, now become Muslims. So the cycle is complete." Islam in Lagos might be interpreted in the context of this model, with generation 3 comparable to the Jam'at which did, in fact, "despise the old inheritance." The model, however, stops short of explaining the evolution of Islam once it becomes integrated into the community. For Lagos, such a model would have to take into account the special features of urban Islam, with its status and class associations. Trimingham touches upon this point in his last chapter (*ibid.*, pp. 103–125).

[79] The Jam'at claims ownership of the Central Mosque, the old Muhammadan cemetery at Oke Suna, and the praying grounds at Obalende, all said to be covered by crown grants issued by the colonial government (see Animashaun, *op. cit.*, p. 2).

[80] The Ansar-ud-Deen Society, formed in 1923, first established a primary school for Muslim children in Lagos after the Anglican Synod decided in 1922 to exclude them from Christian schools because they were "debased, untrained and come only to corrupt the morals" of Christian children (Fisher, *op. cit.*, p. 72).

[81] "Islamic culture was based on urban civilization and Africa had relatively few towns and cities; and where no towns existed, as among Bantu and Nilotic tribes, it could not penetrate at all. All the same, Islam in Africa flourished where there was some basis of urban culture, together with trading relations which ultimately stemmed from the city" (Trimingham, *Influence of Islam upon Africa*, p. 3). Elsewhere Trimingham notes that the advances made among the Yoruba represent "the first conquest of Islam over peoples in the forest region" of Africa ("Islam and Christianity," p. 110).

[82] Lacking precise knowledge, religious leaders estimate that there are approximately 70 to 80 mosques in Lagos. Most are simple accommodations, such as a room reserved in a house, a separate courtyard, or a raised platform in the street. These small mosques function as subsidiary branches of the parent societies and are led by district prayer leaders, who serve on the governing councils of the main mosques in their respective sects. Each congregation is headed by a chief imam or priest, the senior regional cleric who leads Friday prayers, teaches Islam to the young, performs the main sacrifices at the great feasts, christens the newborn, and conducts marriage and funeral ceremonies. In most Muslim societies, the imam is designated for life and can be displaced only at the risk of splitting the congregation. He is usually nominated by the district prayer leaders and selected by the congregation at mass meetings. Disputes among Lagos Muslims cannot be resolved by any central authority as in the north, where emirs act as judges. For that reason, many religious conflicts have ended up in secular courts. Each of the major ethnic groups from the north also have their own religious hierarchies in Lagos.

[83] In a parallel way, religion sometimes becomes a measure of social location. Will Herberg (*Protestant, Catholic, Jew* [New York: Anchor Books, 1960]) shows how religion became a means of social affiliation among European immigrants in America; the melting-pot model of assimilation was, in actuality, a "triple melting pot" based on religious categorization. In Dar es Salaam, Islam played a similar role: "The attraction of Islam in Dar es Salaam is that it is the religion of the majority and the donning of a *kanzu* is a simple but effective membership card enabling the country bumpkin to be accepted as a civilized man; it is also in sympathy with Bantu conservatism and reliance on elders, tradition and continuity, its accent on the community rather than on the individual; it has enabled its adherents to laugh off the material success of the 'new man' and to retain their own self-respect though lacking

in wealth, education and hustle" (J. A. K. Leslie, *A Social Survey of Dar es Salaam* [London: Oxford University Press, 1963], pp. 11–12).

84 *Saville Tribunal Report*, p. 160.

85 An Ibo in Lagos is quoted as saying: "You see, we all belong to this [union] once we come to a city. If you don't people will say you are not sociable and will not respect you. And, if you didn't join, when you get in trouble, you won't have anyone to help you. So you can see why all of us belong to it" (Hugh H. Smythe and Mabel M. Smythe, *The New Nigerian Elite* [Stanford: Stanford University Press, 1960], p. 30; also see Kenneth L. Little, *West Africa Urbanization* [Cambridge: The University Press, 1965]).

86 The role of ethnicity in urban society is discussed more fully by Immanuel Wallerstein, "Ethnicity and National Integration in West Africa," *Cahiers d'Etudes Africaines* (October 1960), 129–138.

87 "Everyone recognized that the notion of 'being a Nigerian' is a new kind of conception. But it would seem that the notion of 'being a Yoruba' is not very much older" (Thomas Hodgkin, "Letter to Dr. S. O. Biobaku," *Odu*, no. 4 [1957], 59).

88 T. M. Yesufu has summed up the conflict between ethnicity and labor unity: "In the tribal 'unions' . . . the worker can speak and be spoken to in a language he understands well, against a background of customs and traditions which he comprehends. Those with whom he has to deal can give him that due personal respect to which the African attaches so much importance. In one word, the worker feels that in the gathering of his tribal organization, he truly 'belongs.' In the trade union meeting on the other hand, matters are often discussed against an industrial and economic background which the worker hardly understands; the secretary of the trade union may be of a different tribe; and if, in addition, he belongs to a rival political party, all the seeds of failure have been sown" (*Daily Times*, April 14, 1958). Roger Scott, examining the relationship between tribal and labor unions in East Africa, makes a similar comment: ". . . unions tend to be weak where tribal associations hamper their operation by dividing the loyalty of the union membership" ("Trade Unions and Ethnicity in Uganda," *Mawazo*, 1, no. 3, p. 45).

89 P. C. W. Gutkind, "The Poor in Urban Africa: A Prologue to Modernization, Conflict, and the Unfinished Revolution," in *Power, Poverty and Urban Policy*, II (Hollywood: Sage Publications, 1968), 381–382.

90 The five central labor bodies were the United Labour Congress, headed by Alhaji H. P. Adebola; the Nigerian Trade Union Congress, headed by Wahab Goodluck; the Labour Unity Front, headed by Michael Imoudu; the Nigerian Workers' Council, headed by N. Chukwura; and the Nigerian Federation of Labour, formed by A. Bassey Etienam. Of the 642 registered unions, only 19 had a membership of 500 or more. For fuller details on the Nigerian labor movement, see T. M. Yesufu, "Labour in the Nigerian Economy," lecture delivered on Nigerian Broadcasting Corporation program, October 1967, mimeographed (Lagos: Ministry of Information), and his "Manpower and Educational Objectives for Nigeria's Reconstruction and Development," paper read at Conference on National Reconstruction and Development, University of Ibadan, March 1969.

91 There have been two notable exceptions to the low political effectiveness of labor. In 1945 a 37-day general strike, protesting low wages and racial discrimination in the civil service, ended when the government agreed to appoint a commission of inquiry to look into the grievances, the first such concession made by the colonial regime. Another general strike was called in 1964, after independence, to protest the government's failure to implement the recommendations of the Morgan Report, which set minimum wage standards throughout the country. The strike forced the government into a compromise solution which resulted in a wage increase, but not to the full extent called for by the Morgan Report.

92 Ferdinand Tönnies, *Gemeinschaft and Gesellschaft*, trans. with introd. by Charles P. Loomis (East Lansing: Michigan State University Press, 1957).

CHAPTER 5: *Political Behavior*

¹ For early political associations in Lagos see James S. Coleman, *Nigeria: Background to Nationalism* (Berkeley and Los Angeles: University of California Press, 1958), chaps. 7, 8; Richard L. Sklar, *Nigerian Political Parties* (Princeton: Princeton University Press, 1963), chap. 1; Takena N. Tamuno, *Nigeria and Elective Representation, 1923-1947* (London: Heinemann, 1966), chap. 4.

² From 1923 to 1947 Lagos had three elective seats, and Calabar had one, on the Nigerian Legislative Council; elections were held every five years.

³ Minor parties in Lagos allied with the NNDP were the Union of Young Nigerians, formed in 1923 by Dr. Moses da Rocha, and the Nigerian Union of Young Democrats, launched in 1938 by Ayodele Williams, former secretary of the UYN.

⁴ NNDP Legislative Council nominees were required to take an oath pledging loyalty to the king of England and to the NNDP (from Macaulay's private papers).

⁵ "Constitution of the Nigerian National Democratic Party" (n.d.), sec. 1-5.

⁶ The officers and members of the NYM in 1938 were Kofo Abayomi, president; Ernest Ikoli, vice-president; H. O. Davies, secretary; H. A. Subair, treasurer; O. Caxton-Martins, legal adviser; Paul Cardozo, editor of the *Daily Service* (the NYM newspaper); Akinola Maja; Nnamdi Azikiwe; Jibril Martins; Mobolaji Bank-Anthony; Adjudant Jones; H. S. A. Thomas; Obafemi Awolowo; S. L. Akintola, J. A. Tuyo; F. Ogugua-Arah; S. O. Shonibare; and L. Duro Emmanuel. Azikiwe was an Ibo, Ikoli was an Ijaw, and Martins was a Lagos Muslim. The other members were all Yorubas, either of Saro origin or from the provinces. "Without exception, they were men of substance, engaged in business, law, medicine, or journalism" (Sklar, *op. cit.*, p. 52; see also Coleman, *op. cit.*, p. 22).

⁷ Chief H. O. Davies's checkered career reveals a restlessness characteristic of many Lagosians. Born in 1905, he attended the Olowogbowo Methodist School, the Methodist Boys' High School, and King's College, where he taught for a year before entering the civil service. He earned a Bachelor of Commerce degree at the London School of Economics and returned to Nigeria in 1937 to become secretary of the NYM and a leading nationalist figure. Davies received his law degree in 1947 and later distinguished himself in defending Jomo Kenyatta, a personal friend, at the trial of Mau Mau conspirators in Kenya. When Davies broke with the NYM in 1951 over the proposed Lagos-west merger, he formed his own party, the Nigerian People's Congress, which failed to win much support. Davies had been a member of the Egbe Omo Oduduwa, closely linked with the NYM, and later joined the Action Group. He subsequently switched to the NCNC, becoming its legal adviser and chairman of its Western Working Committee. In 1958 Davies participated in the abortive effort of a rebel faction of the NCNC to remove Azikiwe from the party's leadership. After the 1962 Action Group crisis, he joined forces with the Nigerian National Democratic Party, a splinter faction of the AG. While serving as chairman and managing director of Nigerian National Press Ltd. in 1961 and 1962, he commenced publication of the *Morning Post* and the *Sunday Post*. Chief Davies is a director of Total Oil Products (Nigeria) Ltd., Safrap (Nigeria) Ltd., Arbico Ltd., and W. H. Biney and Company Ltd. He is the author of *Nigeria: The Prospects for Democracy* (1961). He was appointed a minister of state in the Ministry of Industries in 1965, shortly before the military coup d'etat in January 1966.

⁸ In 1951 the NCNC shifted from organization to individual membership. In 1961 it changed its name to the National Convention of Nigerian Citizens.

⁹ Azikiwe was formerly a member of the NYM but left it in 1941 after a crisis erupted over the nomination of a candidate to replace Kofo Abayomi on the Legislative Council. The then president of the NYM, Ernest Ikoli, and the vice-president, Samuel Akinsanya, were competing for the nomination. When Ikoli was chosen,

Azikiwe and Akinsanya charged the NYM with tribalism. Akinsanya, an Ijebu Yoruba, was unacceptable to the Yoruba elite based in Lagos, who were contemptuous of hinterland Yorubas. Despite the fact that Ikoli (an Ijaw) was supported by Awolowo (an Ijebu), Azikiwe (an Ibo) maintained that anti-Ijebu bigotry was responsible for the outcome of the nomination and therefore resigned in protest. When Azikiwe left the NYM he sealed the division of the nationalist movement into permanent ethnic factions. (See Sklar, *op. cit.*, pp. 52–55.)

[10] Nnamdi Azikiwe, an Onitsha Ibo, was born in Zungeru, Northern Nigeria, where he learned to speak Hausa. At the age of eight he was sent to Lagos for his primary education. He attended Wesleyan Boys' High School, where he acquired fluency in Yoruba, and the Hope Waddell Training Institute in Calabar. At the age of twenty-one he traveled to the United States for further studies. There he earned his nickname, "Zik," which became the rallying cry of militant nationalist youths who formed the Zikist Movement in the late 1940s. Racial discrimination in the United States and his own poverty drove him into a deep depression. Once he attempted to commit suicide by lying across some railway tracks; he was saved by a passerby who, with the aid of a clergyman, helped him find lodging and employment. During his years abroad Azikiwe worked as a dishwasher, a coal miner, and a laborer. He attended Howard University, was graduated from Lincoln University, and earned a certificate in journalism from Columbia University. He also received an M.A. in political science from Lincoln. His first job when he returned to Africa was with the *African Morning Post*, published in Accra, Ghana. In 1930 Azikiwe started his own newspaper, the popular *West African Pilot*, which became a publicity organ for his nationalist activities, and in 1944 he founded the first Pan-Nigeria political party, the National Council for Nigeria and the Cameroons. He is the author of *Liberia in World Politics* (1934), *Renascent Africa* (1937), *My Odyssey* (1970), and of forthcoming works on the Nigerian Civil War. In 1953 Azikiwe became premier of the Eastern Region, and after independence he became president of the Federal Republic of Nigeria.

Azikiwe recorded some of his sentimental attachments to Lagos in a series of autobiographical remembrances written for his column, "Inside Stuff," in the *West African Pilot* in 1938 and 1939. From 1916 to 1920 he had lived in the Brazilian Quarter of Lagos, where holidays were celebrated by masquerades, with each section of the community putting on its own. He and a friend refused to join the Aguda (Brazilian) masquerade because they were alleged to be too rough. Instead they joined the Olowogbowo masquerade, thus becoming marked boys in the neighborhood (August 2, 1938, no. 6). In a later issue he wrote: "Living at Lagos where about ¾ of the population were Muslims, and having been educated with them throughout the major stages of my education, and having worked with them during my brief experience in the Nigerian Civil Service, I had learnt to admire their humanity" (August 16, 1938, no. 17).

[11] In April 1950 Adele sent invitations to chiefs and prominent citizens to attend a meeting at the Iga (palace), where he proposed formation of the Area Councils. The proposal was overwhelmingly supported and the party was organized at once (*Daily Service*, August 30, 1950, pp. 6–7).

[12] *Daily Times*, October 7, 1950, p. 3.

[13] *Ibid.*, September 28, 1950, p. 7.

[14] *Ibid.*, September 6, 1950, p. 3.

[15] Zik's name did not appear on the voters' list because at the time of registration he was in Enugu for the budget session of the Legislative Council. Since he had been told that his name was on the list, he protested his disqualification, arguing that he had been resident in Lagos for thirty years and had been a landlord for ten years (*ibid.*, September 29, 1950, p. 1).

[16] The A Ward Voters' Association, formerly the A Ward Ratepayers' Association, was a faction in the indigenous community which rebelled against the Area

Councils. Most likely it comprised supporters of Prince Oyekan, Adele's rival, and Macaulay loyalists. M. A. O. Makanja, once a branch secretary of the Area Councils, left the party "when he refused to sabotage the efforts of the Association as requested by members of the Area Councils" (*ibid.*, October 7, 1950, p. 15). The association particularly appealed to the landlords in the traditional wards, claiming that "one of the most spectacular things the Voters Association candidates had taken up, and which they still were fighting against, was the acquisition of slum houses" (*ibid.*, October 14, 1950, p. 11). Azikiwe indirectly endorsed the association, exempting it from the category he called "opponents of the Triple Alliance," but he urged it to align with a more prominent political party.

Five women were contestants in the 1950 election. One was an NCNC candidate, Mrs. H. Lawson. The other four were candidates of the Nigerian Women's Party, led by Lady Olayinka Abayomi. They were Lady Alakija, wife of Sir Adeyemo Alakija; Mrs. Ore Jones; Mrs. Ayo Manuwa, principal of the Girls' Muslim Academy; and Mrs. Toro John.

The F Ward Ratepayers' Association expressed the communal patriotism of the second oldest section of the city, Ebute Metta, which had just been demarcated as a separate electoral constituency (it had been part of Ward D). The campaign style of this election was well demonstrated by the exhortations of E. A. O. Bright, an NCNC candidate, who urged constituents to "beware of the activities of some over-zealous residents of 'D' Ward who have been and are still seeking that the 'F' and 'D' Wards be formed into one union and that matters and affairs of the two separate Wards be managed and conducted jointly" (*ibid.*, September 10, 1950, p. 1).

[17] *Ibid.*, October 11, 1950, p. 5.

[18] The Macpherson Constitution gave the regional governments partial autonomy but made no commitment to a federal or a unitary system. Difficulties in the operation of the constitution soon became apparent, and a new constitution was introduced in 1954. The period when Lagos was part of the Western Region is coterminous with the life of the Macpherson Constitution (1951–1954). For further information on Nigeria's constitutional history see Kalu Ezera, *Constitutional Developments in Nigeria* (Cambridge: The University Press, 1964), and Eme O. Awa, *Federal Government in Nigeria* (Berkeley and Los Angeles: University of California Press, 1964).

[19] The results of the Lagos election held in November 1951 were: I. Olorun-Nimbe (NCNC), 12,875; N. Azikiwe (NCNC), 12,711; A. Adedoyin (NCNC), 12,539; H. P. Adebola (NCNC), 12,340; T. O. S. Benson (NCNC), 12,249; F. R. A. Williams (AG), 7,070; A. Maja (AG), 7,005; H. O. Davies (Nigerian People's Congress), 884; Magnus Williams (Independent), 406; and O. A. Fagbenro-Beyioku (NPC), 269 (*Daily Times*, November 22, 1951).

[20] Minutes of Lagos Town Council, February 5, 1951.

[21] *Daily Times*, February 23, 1952.

[22] After Olorun-Nimbe's term ended, the council fixed the mayor's salary at £800. On September 5, 1958, long after the mayoralty had been abolished, the AG-controlled council decided that as "an act of grace" it should pay Olorun-Nimbe £1,600 for the two years he had served as mayor.

[23] Supporters of the NNDP were then split into three factions: those who remained with the NCNC and retained the official name of the party, those who followed Olorun-Nimbe and kept an active wing of the party going until 1959, and those who transferred their loyalties to Adele and the Action Group. The 1957 local election was the last one in which the NNDP-NCNC banner was used.

[24] Minutes of Lagos Town Council, February 22, 1952, p. 2.

[25] Awolowo was born in 1909 at Ijebu Remo in the Western Region. After completing his secondary education in parochial schools, he worked as a schoolteacher, a shorthand typist, and a correspondent with the Nigerian *Daily Times*. In order to obtain enough money to study abroad, Awolowo also ventured into business

enterprises, including moneylending, letter writing, taxi ownership, produce marketing, and transport. Earning a Bachelor of Commerce degree from the University of London through correspondence courses, he rose to influential positions in a number of labor organizations: the Nigerian Motor Transport Union, the Nigerian Produce Traders' Association, and the Nigerian Trade Union Congress. In the early 1940s Awolowo revived the Ibadan branch of the Nigerian Youth Movement, which had been moribund for some time. It was during these years, before he left Nigeria to study law in Britain, that his fundamental political ideas hardened into concrete strategic goals, such as constitutional reforms and a revised federal system based on the principle of linguistic states. He argued strongly for these objectives in *Path to Nigerian Freedom* (1947) and continued to advocate them in *The People's Republic* (1968).

While in London pursuing his legal education, Awolowo and some of his fellow students founded the Egbe Omo Oduduwa, a Yoruba cultural organization that became the foundation stone of the Action Group. When he returned to Nigeria in 1946 he set up a flourishing legal practice and entered into national politics with a vengeance, playing on the theme of Yoruba nationalism, partly to counteract Ibo chauvinism and partly to acquire a regional power base. In 1950 Awolowo initiated the Action Group, an organ of Yoruba strength which propelled him into the premiership of the Western Region and subsequently into the role of leader of the Opposition in the federal Parliament. With Nnamdi Azikiwe in the east and Alhaji Ahmadu Bello, the Sardauna of Sokoto, in the north, Awolowo became one of the three top men in the tripolar regional balance of power.

In 1962 Awolowo's fortunes suffered a severe reversal. A schism in the ranks of the Action Group exploded into a sensational treason trial in which Awolowo and twenty others were charged with plotting to overthrow the government by a coup d'etat. Awolowo was convicted and sentenced to ten years in prison. A splinter faction of the Action Group led by Awolowo's former lieutenant, S. L. Akintola, formed the United People's Party, later restyled the Nigerian National Democratic Party, which assumed the mantle of Yoruba leadership in the Western Region. In January 1966, in Nigeria's first military coup d'etat, the Sardauna of Sokoto and Akintola were assassinated. Six months later a second military coup d'etat resulted in the assassination of the Ibo supreme commander, Major General J. T. U. Aguiyi-Ironsi, and his replacement by Lieutenant Colonel (now Major General) Yakubu Gowon, a young and relatively unknown army officer from the northern Angus tribe. In a decree reputedly initiated by Ironsi and ratified by Gowon, Awolowo was released from prison in August 1966. He was subsequently made commissioner of finance and vice-chairman of the Federal Executive Council of the Federal Military Government, a position he resigned in 1971.

In a personal statement of his political ambitions, Awolowo declared himself "irrevocably committed to federal politics. [Yet] I am, by nature, too proud to descend from the pedestal of being the first premier of the Western Region, which embraced practically the whole of the present Western, Mid-Western and Lagos States, to the lower level of being the premier or governor of the present Western State. . . . I aspire, and will continue, until I am 75, to aspire to participate effectively in government activities. . . . So, if, on the return of civilian rule, I am in government, well and good. If not, I will mount a most vigorous campaign to the end that those who are in power should give very serious, sincere, and favorable consideration to what I believe should be done to cater to, and advance, the welfare and the best interest of the masses of our people. Fortunately . . . the country has reached a stage of enlightenment . . . under which it is not going to be easy . . . to silence the voice of reason and progress which, under God, many right-thinking people and I claim to typify" (*Sunday Times*, March 30, 1969, p. 2).

[26] These reforms included redistricting, inclusion of traditional chiefs on the council, and expansion of council membership, all of which would have reduced the

proportional strength of the NCNC on the council.

[27] Minutes of Lagos Town Council, August 8, 1952.

[28] In his autobiography, Awolowo wrote: "By the end of August 1949, I was certain in my own mind that Dr. Azikiwe was not a conscientious member of the Nigerian Youth Movement, and that for some reasons best known to himself, he was bent on destroying this nationalist organization. At the same time, it seemed clear to me that his policy was to corrode the self-respect of the Yoruba people as a group; to build up the Ibos as a master race; to magnify his own vaunted contributions to the nationalist struggles; to dwarf and misrepresent the achievements of his contemporaries; and to discount and nullify the humble but sterling quota which older politicians had made to the country's progress" (*Awo: The Autobiography of Chief Obafemi Awolowo* [London: Cambridge University Press, 1960], p. 135). Time and again Awolowo recounts the petty squabbles that flourished among Lagos leaders during the nationalist period, many of which he directly attributes to Azikiwe's inspiration. Of Zik's personal character, Awolowo wrote: "You only had to disagree with him on any issue, however minor, and you at once qualified to go on the black-list. . . . He observed neither modesty nor reck in inflating his own ego or in deflating that of his opponent. In this connection he is in the first line of succession to Herbert Macaulay, whom Dr. Azikiwe had claimed to be his journalistic and political father" (*ibid.*, p. 137).

[29] Coleman, *op. cit.*, p. 350. Ken Post argues that "the fact that so many of the original members [of the AG] had business and other interests in Lagos makes it difficult to agree that the new party 'shunned Lagos' as Professor Coleman puts it. The AG . . . from the beginning used its NYM connections to play a full part in Lagos local politics" (*The Nigerian Federal Election of 1959* [London: Oxford University Press, 1963], pp. 35–36). Sklar, on the other hand, concludes that "oddly, the leaders of the Action Group were reluctant initially to include Lagos within the scope of their operations, a reflection of the fact that opposition to the new party within the Egbe [Omo Oduduwa] and the Nigerian Youth Movement was centered in the seacoast capital. However, the major objectives of the Action Group were identical to those of the Lagos Yoruba elite, and leaders of the Youth Movement concluded that the political aims of Azikiwe might be thwarted by placing his metropolitan base under the jurisdiction of an anti-NCNC government in the Western Region" (*op. cit.*, pp. 111–112).

The AG did use its NYM connections to influence Lagos politics, but Post exaggerates the degree of its involvement. The principle actors in Lagos politics at the time of the Action Group's formation were the Area Councils and the NNDP-NCNC, with the NYM playing a secondary role in support of the Area Councils. Moreover, Post overlooks the fact that the NYM leaders in Lagos, centering on Chief H. O. Davies, were opposed to the regionalization and Yorubanization of the NYM when it melted into the Action Group's organization. Post likewise ignores Awolowo's personal distaste for Lagos politics. As Sklar implies (*ibid.*) these factors were evaluated against the strengths of more rational arguments: the need for Yoruba unity, the opportunity to gain a foothold in the capital when the NCNC had suffered a setback, and the compliance of Oba Adele who was willing to join forces with a larger party, realizing the weakness of his own organization. Many of the original reservations among the Action Group's leaders were revived some years later when the movement for a Lagos state was launched.

[30] It is ironic that the Action Group's national headquarters were located in a city that became an NCNC stronghold in the Western Region, owing to the efforts of Adegoke Adelabu, a flamboyant but effective charismatic Ibadan leader who became the leader of the Opposition in the Western House of Assembly (see Sklar, *op. cit.*, pp. 284–320; George Jenkins, "An Informal Political Economy," in *Boston University Papers on Africa*, ed. Jeffrey Butler and A. A. Castagno [New York: Praeger, 1967], pp. 166–194).

[31] Nearly all the top leaders of the Lagos Action Group were drawn from the ranks of the Lagos NYM. The first fifteen names in the membership book were Dr. Akinola Maja, Chief J. A. Doherty, Chief Bode Thomas, Chief J. A. O. Obadeyi, S. L. Akintola, Arthur Prest, Sir Kofo Abayomi, F. R. A. Williams, Alhaji Jibril Martins, Alhaji S. O. Gbadamosi, M. A. Ogun, Alfred Rewane, Lady Olayinka Abayomi, S. O. Shonibare, and Ladipo Amos (Sklar, *op. cit.*, p. 112 n. 52).

[32] NCNC files reveal a protest to the Council of Ministers in 1957 that political parties had to direct voters to the polling stations and assist election officials in finding their names on the voters' list. This opened the way for corruption: "With the financial resources of the AG and the vast number of field secretaries drafted into Lagos from the Western Region, it was easy for them not only to compile a list of non-existent voters at different addresses, but also to retain the cards prepared for such persons whose names appeared on the Voters' List and give the cards to paid impersonators for use."

[33] The Lagos NCNC was to raise £2,000; the Eastern Region Parliamentary Party, £1,000; the Federal Parliamentary Party, £1,200; and the Western Parliamentary Party, £500.

[34] The general secretary of the Ibo National Progress and Welfare Association, Patrick Nwokobia, distributed a circular dated January 8, 1957, urging a boycott of the LTC election of that year because of (1) the inquiry into the African Continental Bank which was closely linked with NCNC interests, (2) the death shortly after the inquiry of Mazi Ojike, an Ibo confidant of Azikiwe's and former deputy mayor of Lagos, and (3) the NCNC's support for a Lagos state movement, which he claimed was a Yoruba-inspired plan.

[35] Letter from A. Ogunsanya to the secretary of the Ibo NCNC Elements' Shomolu Union, October 11, 1964, in reply to complaints that Ibos were not being fairly treated by the party.

[36] Meeting of the NNDP-NCNC alliance on October 19, 1956. This decision was never implemented.

[37] *Rapson Report.*

[38] *West African Pilot*, July 7, 1965, p. 1. The lack of a meaningful constituency may also have been a reason for closing the local NPC office. Sometime later, Chief A. D. S. Yaro, head of the Hausa community in Lagos, requested the oba of Lagos to propose that one special Hausa member be appointed to the LCC, just as, in some northern cities, special seats on local councils were reserved for stranger communities living in the *sabon garis*. The modesty of the request revealed the weakness of the Hausa community in Lagos. Chief Yaro observed that since the "numerical strength of the Hausa is scattered [in Lagos] . . . it [would be] difficult for them to win even if they decide to contest elections in the City Council. Tradition is sometimes considered in apportioning of amenities to a community, and unless the Hausa community in Lagos area has a spokesman in the council, it may not be possible for them to have their fair share of things" (*Morning Post*, October 6, 1965, p. 9).

[39] *Daily Express*, November 13, 1965, p. 1.

[40] Some of the goals set forth were the adoption of compulsory education, the repeal of the provincial courts ordinance, the creation of an independent court of appeals in civil and criminal cases to serve all British West African colonies, the creation of a "full-blown municipality wherein municipal revenue and expenditure are under the definite and entire control of the rate-payers," the establishment of party branches and auxiliaries in all parts of Nigeria subject to the parent body in Lagos, and the raising of funds by regular contributions ("Constitution of the Nigerian National Democratic Party," in Macaulay's private papers).

[41] Max Weber, *The Theory of Social and Economic Organization* (New York: Free Press, 1947), pp. 363–372, discusses the routinization of charismatic authority.

[42] Thomas Hodgkin, *African Political Parties* (London: Penguin Books, 1961), p. 69.

[43] *Ibid.*, pp. 50–51.

[44] Among the 128 organizations in the NCNC in 1944 were 101 tribal unions, 11 social clubs, 2 affiliated political parties (NNDP and Young Democrats), and 2 trade unions (Coleman, *op. cit.*, pp. 264–265). In 1958 the NCNC included 143 organizations, among them 120 ethnic group associations, 95 of which had Lagos addresses (Sklar, *op. cit.* p. 408 n. 69).

[45] In 1965 the top officers of the Lagos NCNC were Chief Adeniran Ogunsanya (federal minister of housing and surveys), chairman; Councilor R. A. Balogun (chairman of Lagos South constituency), vice-chairman; Abiola Oshodi (federal minister of state) secretary; F. M. Moronu, treasurer; Chief F. U. Anyiam, publicity secretary; C. B. Onikoyi, financial secretary; Councilor Bola Sadipe (secretary of Western Working Committee), legal adviser; Councilor E. A. A. Ladega, auditor; and B. K. Johnson, senior executive secretary. Elected triennially they duplicated exactly the number and hierarchical ranking of party officials in each of the regional executives.

[46] The ward unit was the lowest in the NCNC organization. In 1965 the ward leaders were: A and B: W. A. Giwa and G. O. Soneye, chairmen, and S. M. Ogunlabi, secretary; C and G: A. A. Oshodi, chairman, and R. A. Fakunle, secretary; D: J. I. Talabi, chairman, and P. O. Offem, secretary; E: B. K. Blankson and F. M. Moronu, chairmen, and C. E. Nwoko, secretary; H and F: R. A. Balogun, chairman, and Kunle Ogunbiyi, secretary. Some strategic wards were divided between two chairmen. J. I. Talabi was chief whip of the NCNC councilors.

[47] The NEPU's secretary-general in Lagos was M. Adamu Ibrahim Kano. The party had five branches in Lagos: (1) NEPU Lagos, (2) NEPU Obalende, (3) NEPU Mushin idi Araba, (4) NEPU Apapa, and (5) NEPU Ebute Metta. In 1965 the party requested one LEDB shop as an office and two seats on the LCC (in G1 and E8) from the NCNC.

[48] After Olorun-Nimbe's expulsion from the NCNC in 1952, the NNDP affiliate of the NCNC was headed by Pa Joachim, president, and B. B. Salami, secretary. Pa Joachim, a "Lagos Elder," also represented the Market Women's Guild.

[49] The 1962 defeat also caused national headquarters to forbid meetings of branch committees without written approval from the national secretary, F. S. McEwen.

[50] Letter from Mbadiwe to McEwen, March 12, 1963.

[51] In 1957 an executive committee of the NNDP-NCNC alliance decided that henceforth all candidates seeking party nomination must apply in writing with a contribution of £10, and that each nominee must be a well-known party member and a maximum vote getter and must have an impeccable character. It also suggested that a committee of elders—Chief Afolabi, Pa Joachim, Pa Kakawa, Pa Abijo, and N. B. Soule—be appointed as a nominating body.

[52] One of Mbadiwe's earlier proposals was to widen the role of the constituency executive committees to make them nominating committees. With 15 members from 8 wards, 120 individuals would be involved. The size was justified on the ground that "it would be almost impossible for any prospective candidate to bribe all the members of the Constituency Executive Committee" (App. B, par. 2b, of Mbadiwe's Commission of Inquiry Report on LTC elections of October 1962).

[53] Letter from Mbadiwe to Okpara, April 2, 1963.

[54] Letter from Fagbenro-Beyioku to Mbadiwe, April 4, 1963.

[55] "Income and Expenditure Account During 13 November, 1965, LCC Elections for the NCNC, Lagos Region."

[56] "There is no doubt that the conservancy contracts of 1960–61 and 1962–63 were awarded to Commercial and Industrial Transport Services because that firm was, in a sense, an extension of the NCNC and its members on the council, and that both the party and some of its individual members benefited from the award of the contracts" (*Saville Tribunal Report*, p. 34).

[57] Of the 63 NCNC councilors who served after 1950, 51 were Christian, 10 were Muslim, and 2 were of unknown religion. Of a total of 96 AG councilors, 54 were Muslim, 31 were Christian, and 5 were of unknown religion.

[58] *Action Group of Nigeria Programme of Organization (Lagos Branch)*, April 4, 1964.

[59] In 1964 all the major ward leaders in Lagos were Yoruba. The officers of branch subcommittees to oversee party elections in each ward were: A: Chief G. B. A. Akinyede, chairman; E. O. Ferreira, secretary; B: Hon. L. J. Dosunmo, chairman; R. A. Williams, secretary; C: Councilor J. A. Odeku, chairman; J. O. Showemimo, secretary; D: P. Ade Okesojo, chairman A. A. Layeni, secretary; E: Alhaji A. F. Masha, chairman; Abayomi Eshilokun, secretary; F: L. K. Jakande, chairman; Mrs. Elsie Femi-Pearse, secretary; G: A. O. Okuribide, chairman (subsequently removed); J. Ola Oki, secretary; H: S. A. Onitiri, chairman; S. O. Akinwunmi, secretary.

[60] I am grateful to Richard L. Sklar for permitting me to use his field notes to get information on the Lagos AG in 1957 and 1958.

[61] Before the 1965 election, 13 members of the Lagos AG who had been improperly selected as candidates were expelled from the party. A 15-man selection committee had been established in some wards at the direction of some members of the Divisional Executive who wanted their preferred nominees to bypass the party election. Protests from rank-and-file members who were being deprived of their rights to participate in nominations prompted the party hierarchy to investigate. The nominees selected by the committee all ran as independents after their expulsion and all were badly defeated.

[62] *Constitution of the Action Group of Nigeria* (Lagos: Amalgamated Press, 1962), pp. 9-10.

[63] During the inquiry by the Saville Tribunal, Dawodu submitted a statement of his assets and income to the authorities. He noted that he had been paid only from March 1962 to June 1962 and that he had received no regular income from June 1962 to January 1963, during which period he "was living mainly on the generosity of friends and relatives" (letter to chairman and members of the Lagos City Council Tribunal of Inquiry, December 31, 1966).

[64] Ayo Fasanmi in *Daily Express*, November 13, 1965, p. 1.

[65] *Saville Tribunal Report*, p. 11.

[66] The AG and the NCNC nominated separate candidates because they could not agree on a division of seats between the parties. The AG, with 27 seats on the outgoing council, wanted each party to maintain the number of seats won at the preceding election. The NCNC leaders insisted, however, on an equal division of seats. Apparently the Western Region NCNC argued for the AG plan, urging its Lagos branch to be satisfied with its quota of 15 seats. Michael Okpara flew to Lagos and, with top AG leaders, convened a special UPGA meeting to resolve the dispute. As it happened, the NCNC ended up with only 7 seats. The selection of the chairman of the council also reflected the autonomy of the local AG. Masha urged cooperation with the NCNC, including giving it a fair share of committee chairmanships. Dawodu, after having worked hard to win a sweeping victory, refused; he subsequently became chairman of the council despite Masha's seniority in the party.

[67] Township Ordinance of May 29, 1919 (*Nigerian Handbook*, 1919, p. 96). Technically, the franchise was limited to those "whose names appear in the rates ledgers as being responsible for payment of rates on tenements" so assessed.

[68] The Lagos assessment area, defined in 1924 in terms of areas with taxable populations, was revised in 1927.

[69] Lagos Township Ordinance, 1941.

[70] The comment was made by H. A. Subair (minutes of the Lagos Town Council, September 28, 1943).

[71] For example, the commissioner for the colony explained that the "number of

voters under the existing franchise should run into the thousands, and it is hoped that before further elections are due, there will be a greater indication of interest in the value of the franchise on the part of the rate-payers and tenants of property in the township. The lack of interest is likely to retard any proposals for the extension of the franchise" (*Annual Report of the Lagos Town Council*, 1941–42, p. 2). For a more extensive discussion of voter apathy, see Tamuno (*op. cit.*) who considers other factors such as the absence of a proxy vote, inadequate transport facilities on polling day, registration regulations requiring annual claims, the use of printed forms confusing to an illiterate population, the impact of the great depression of 1929–1932, and so forth. In effect, Tamuno considers every possible explanation including the fact that "light showers and 'uncertain weather' at Lagos on polling day were reported in 1923 and 1940" (*ibid.*, pp. 110–111). While all these elements can, in their own small way, play a role in keeping voters at home, they can hardly be taken as serious explanations of a pattern that lasted for thirty years.

72 The distribution of population by ward in 1950 was: A, 17,700; B, 18,400; C, 14,700; D, 9,000; E, 14,300; F, 16,200; G, 7,400; and H, 17,000.

73 Letter from civil secretary's office, Ibadan, Western Region, to administrator of the colony, March 26, 1953.

74 The allocation of seats for the 1953 election by ward was: A, 6; B, 6; C, 5; D, 3; E, 6; F, 6; G, 3; and H, 6.

75 The allocation of seats in 1957 was: A West, 3; A East, 3; B East, 3; B West, 3; C West, 3; C East, 2; D, 3; E East, 3; E West, 4; F North, 3; F South, 4; G, 3; H North, 3; and H South, 3.

76 Files of Town Clerk's Office, LCC.

77 Letter from Mayaki, town clerk, to permanent secretary, Ministry of Lagos Affairs, June 9, 1965 (files of Town Clerk's Office, LCC).

78 Robert Lane, *Political Life* (New York: Free Press, 1959), pp. 267–270.

79 The size of an increase in voter population was determined by comparing the rate of change in a particular constituency with the municipal average. If the rate of increase for the constituency was less than the municipal average, it was considered small. If it was above the average, it was considered relatively large. The same measure was used to compare degrees of voter turnout. Since turnout declined generally in 1965, a high turnout was indicated by the smallest percentage decline.

80 Voter turnout in pre-1962 elections is not available by ward breakdowns except for the 1957 election which was conducted with plural voting and multimember districts. All wards then had a turnout of between 33 and 34 percent, except for E West, where it was only 24.99 percent. Generalizations about voter participation in this discussion have been made primarily on the basis of data gathered for the elections of 1962 and 1965.

C H A P T E R 6: *Formal Structure of Government*

1 See Gabriel A. Almond and James S. Coleman, eds., *The Politics of the Developing Areas* (Princeton: Princeton University Press, 1960), pp. 33–38; Lucian W. Pye, *Aspects of Political Development* (Boston and Toronto: Little, Brown, 1966), pp. 81–85.

2 *Annual Report of the Lagos Town Council*, 1917. The ordinance providing for the establishment of the council was the Lagos Township Ordinance, 1917.

3 *Annual Report of the Lagos Town Council*, 1917.

4 "No matter shall be discussed or determined at ... [each] meeting other than the matters specified in the written request [submitted in advance to the chairman], and no resolution passed at the meeting shall be acted upon or have any effect unless and until it has been submitted to and received the Governor's approval" (*Township Ordinance*, 1917, sec. 7, subsec. 2). "No question shall be debated

or resolution moved which is not concerned with control, sanitation, public services or good order of the Township except with permission of the President" (*ibid.*, sec. 8, subsec. 1).

[5] Memo from administrator of the colony, January 14, 1932, files of Town Clerk's Office, LCC.

[6] Meeting of the Committee on the Financial Position of the LTC and Connected Matters, January 20, 1932, files of Town Clerk's Office, LCC.

[7] Throughout this period, there was considerable reshuffling and reorganization at top administrative levels. Lagos was partly ruled by the Legislative Council for the Colony frrom 1914 until 1922, when it was absorbed by the Legislative Council for the Southern Provinces. In 1946 the whole of Nigeria was placed under one legislative council. Administratively, the municipality was part of the colony of Lagos which included three rural provinces, Epe, Ikeja, and Badagry, all of them now in Lagos State. For the most part, the township (or municipality) was treated as a separate entity by the colonial authorities. Indirect rule, for example, was introduced in the provinces in 1938 to allow the establishment of native treasuries and native courts. Indirect rule was never introduced in the township.

The post of administrator of the colony was created in 1914, the year the Legislative Council for the Colony was established and the Northern and Southern Provinces were amalgamated into one administrative unit by Lord Lugard. In 1916 the lieutenant governor of the Southern Provinces assumed the responsibilities and the title of the administrator of the colony. He was assisted by a resident and a subordinate district officer. In 1914 and 1915 the staff of the administrator consisted of two secretaries, a traveling district officer, and two assistant district officers. In 1916 the secretaries were absorbed by the Southern Provinces and the duties of the traveling district officer were turned over to the resident. In 1927 the office of administrator of the colony was separated from the office of the lieutenant governor of the Southern Provinces. The administrator was made chairman of the LTC and given the responsibility of handling all land matters and income tax collection (just introduced in 1927); he was assisted by two district officers (one of whom was substituted for the resident of the colony) and an assistant district officer. The colony provinces were formed into a separate unit for administrative purposes and put in charge of another assistant district officer station in Ikeja. In 1933 the title of administrator of the colony was changed to commissioner of the colony.

[8] *Annual Report for the Colony*, 1932, p. 2.

[9] *Annual Colonial Reports*, 1939, p. 4.

[10] *Hoskyns-Abrahall Report*, p. 35.

[11] "Despatch by the Secretary of State for the Colonies to the Governors of the African Territories," February 25, 1947, in *The Principles of Native Administration in Nigeria: Selected Documents*, ed. with introd. by A. H. M. Kirk-Greene (London: Oxford University Press, 1965), pp. 238–239.

[12] By comparison, before the 1950 reforms, the performance record of the LTC was described as follows: "Lagos Council functions with considerable efficiency, chiefly owing to the efforts of its highly qualified executive officers. Experience has shown that the African members very seldom make use of their majority, partly owing to a general reluctance to accept responsibility for major issues likely to be unpopular with the African citizens and partly owing to a conflict of opinion between elected and nominated members. The nominated members for the most part show a considerable spirit of public service while the elected members tend to display a marked degree of irresponsibility which is possibly due in part to the knowledge that they are a minority. Although every effort is made by the European element to educate the African members by arrogating to them the greatest possible measure of responsibility, there is still among the latter far too great an insistence on personal issues and a tendency to abstain from voting on matters of importance. Thus, at present the greater part of the initiative in local government matters in-

# Notes to Chapter 6

evitably comes from the European Council members or from the executive officers" ("The Development of Local Government for Africans in Urban Areas," in *African Administration* [n.p., 1949], p. 85–97).

[13] *Local Government in Africa*, summer conference at King's College, Cambridge, August 28–September 9, 1961, published by Cambridge University Overseas Studies Commission, p. 5. Arthur Creech Jones, in his 1947 dispatch, affirmed that the "essential and permanent objective of the British policy is to bring forward the African territories to self-governing responsibility within the Commonwealth. . . . In this, local government plays a conspicuous part. . . . It is through these organs of government that the African may acquire experience in civil responsibility and handling his own affairs, factors essential to his effective work in the central political institutions of his territory" ("Despatch by the Secretary of State," p. 245).

[14] The English county borough is created by an act of Parliament, whereas other English local government units are established by the Ministry of Local Government. It operates under a mayor-council plan, with councilors elected for three-year terms from single-member districts. The councilors, in turn, co-opt a third as many aldermen who serve for six-year terms. One-third of the councilors retire annually, and one-half of the aldermen retire triennially in rotation. The mayoralty is a non-executive but prestigious office filled by the councilors' election of one of their own number. The chairman of the council is usually the leader of the majority party. Business is conducted in committees, which make most of the decisions. Only important items of general policy come before the full council. The most distinguishing feature of the county borough is the degree of autonomy it enjoys; its powers are shared with no subordinate or superior authorities, other than the central government.

[15] Lagos Local Government Law, 1953, Supplement to the Western Regional Gazette, vol. 2, no. 25 (July 16, 1953), sec. 140, 141, pp. 55–59.

[16] The Lagos Local Government Law of 1959 was based on recommendations made in the *Imrie Report*.

[17] Lagos City Council (Dissolution) Decree, 1966, Supplement to Official Gazette Extraordinary, vol. 53, no. 38 (April 20, 1966), Part A.

[18] *Report of the Tribunal of Inquiry into the Reorganization of Local Government Councils in the Lagos State* (Lagos: Lagos State of Nigeria, 1970).

[19] Testimony given by G. Opara (*Saville Tribunal Report*, p. 11).

[20] *Standing Orders*, Lagos City Council, made under the Lagos Local Government Act, 1959.

[21] Low attendance at council meetings is one indication of boredom. Between October 22, 1952, and February 3, 1953, attendance varied from a high of 32 meetings (by the mayor) to none at all. The majority of councilors were present at only 1 to 10 meetings. One councilor explained that many "found their vocation or business was being affected [if they attended too many meetings]. . . . They received no remuneration and their enthusiasm for free civic duties has been considerably dampened by the realization that members of the House of Assembly in the . . . Regions are being paid appreciable salaries and allowances monthly, and these Members do not attend meetings as frequently as Councilors have to do" (*Storey Report*, p. 12).

Poor remuneration has also had other negative effects in addition to contributing toward apathy. Like elected representatives at other levels, councilors feel they should be compensated for time invested in community service. If their compensation is not fixed in the form of salaries, councilors feel free to accept kickbacks. The primary reason for withholding remuneration from representatives derives from the English aristocratic tradition that local councilors should not become politically active for reasons of material gain; by withholding remuneration, precisely the opposite effect has been produced in Lagos.

[22] Minutes of LTC, June 3, 1958, p. 3.

[23] *Ibid.*

[24] Minutes of LTC, October 3, 1963, pp. 1–2.

[25] In 1957 the AG chairman of the LTC, A. O. Lawson, openly advocated that this distinction be minimized: "In the past we . . . had adversely drawn a very distinct line between our duties and those of the officers of the council, a distinction between what was frequently referred to as 'Policy Making' and 'Matters of Administration.' We modify our views on this distinction. . . . Although we shall observe all lawful distinctions and refrain from any unlawful interference with the duties of the officers of the Council, we shall, however, go further than we have done in the past by taking all steps that may be necessary not only to formulate policies but also to see that all our decisions are executed . . . promptly and efficiently. . . . Perhaps our line of distinction was rather thickly drawn; we may make it a wee bit finer this time" (Minutes of LTC, January 22, 1957, pp. 5–6). When the NCNC gained control of the council in 1959, the new chairman, F. S. McEwen, similarly warned that "an NCNC controlled Lagos Town Council will not tolerate officers of the council using their positions to thwart or sabotage our policies and decisions" (Minutes of LTC, November 5, 1959, p. 5).

[26] An excellent summary is provided in G. O. Orewa, "The Development of Local Government Service in Nigeria and the Problem of the Local Civil Servant" (paper read at Nigerian Institute of Public Administration Conference, Lagos, July 7, 1967).

[27] The letter (dated December 11, 1950) from Mayor Olorun-Nimbe to Sho-Silva informing him of the council's decision gives a vivid impression of how newly elected councilors viewed their position immediately after the local government reforms were initiated (*Storey Report*, p. 7):

"Realising as I do that you must have been extremely tired after the last Municipal Elections, and having regard to the fact that you have rendered faithful and meritorious services to the Lagos Town Council for almost forty years, and having regard also to the incontrovertible fact that the Lagos Town Council today is unquestionably a democratic assembly, having replaced the old inglorious bureacratic institution of which Mr. Edward Arthur Carr was the head, I have the honour to request you to proceed on local leave for 10 days on the 23rd December, 1950, as requested by you, and further to proceed on vacation leave pro rata—preparatory to retirement, having reached and exceeded the age limit of 55 years, para. 70 of the Lagos Local Government Ordinance of 1950 refers.

"You will no doubt appreciate the necessity for this long over-due request because,

"(1) This is a new regime, and the old order must inevitably change yielding place to the New.

"(2) Mr. Carr has relinquished his seat as the erstwhile President of the old Council, and as the faithful convert and loyal adherent of the late President, it is desirable that you follow Mr. Carr to 'voluntary exile.'

"(3) I honestly cannot, for the life of me, see how you can work cooperatively with me, nor do I see what useful purpose you will serve in the New Constitutional setup in the New Lagos Town Council.

"(4) I would be grateful therefore, if you will arrange as early as possible, say within 48 hours (forty-eight hours) to get your leave papers ready for my signature in order to expedite matters.

"(5) Please take notice that a new Town Clerk will be appointed at the Establishment Committee on the 20th December, 1950, in keeping with the provisions of the Lagos Local Government Ordinance of 1950.

"Finally, I wish to say on behalf of the Council that the public are grateful for your services, and I shall not fail to bring this to the Notice of the Council and the Public in due course.

"I sincerely hope you will enjoy your well-earned pension through the years that lie ahead."

[28] In the interim between Martin's departure and Akinbiyi's confirmation, A. I. McNab, a South African who had been treasurer of the LTC, acted as town clerk.

[29] *Dosunmu-Stapleton*, p. 8. According to the report, Akinbiyi insisted that standards always be as high as they were at Oxford, where he was educated: "The qualifications he suggested for the posts of Deputy Town Clerk and Senior Assistant Town Clerk were such that in fact no Nigerian, save he, possesses them, yet at this moment it would be politically difficult, if not impossible, to appoint expatriates to the posts. . . . At this moment in time we must all be prepared (for sound political reasons) to sacrifice some degree of efficiency for the sake of Nigerianization."

[30] *Saville Tribunal Report*, esp. pp. 232–250.

[31] *Morning Post*, May 10, 1967, p. 2.

[32] Letter from acting town clerk, M. A. Sho-Silva, to commissioner of the colony, July 18, 1947 (files of Town Clerk's Office, LCC).

[33] "Report on the Personnel Department," submitted to the administrator for Lagos by J. A. Adeyemo, personnel officer of LCC, September 8, 1966.

[34] Staff recruitment is based on the following regulations: appointments with salaries of less than £198 a year may be made by the heads of departments; those with salaries ranging between £198 and £476 a year may be made by the heads of departments with the approval of the town clerk; those with salaries ranging between £476 and £900 may be made by the council with the prior approval of the Lagos State government (formerly by the minister of Lagos affairs).

[35] Meeting of Establishment Sub-Committee, June 15, 1964, LCC; letter from town clerk dated August 11, 1964, to permanent secretary of Ministry of Lagos Affairs.

[36] The Saville Tribunal urged the establishment of a Lagos city services commission "composed of citizens of Lagos appointed on a part-time and strictly non-political basis." This suggestion does not vary much from Imrie's proposals in 1959, but while Imrie was silent about the relationship of the Establishment Committee to the Service Commission, the Saville Tribunal proposed that the former deal only with "matters of principle and not with individuals" (*Imrie Report*, pp. 247–248).

[37] See budget speech delivered by Colonel Mobolaji Johnson, June 27, 1968 (Lagos: Lagos State Government, 1968), pp. 8–9.

[38] *Morning Post*, March 31, 1967, p. 1.

[39] In varying degrees, the *Storey Report*, the *Dosunmu-Stapleton Report*, the *Imrie Report*, the *Jones and Lucas Report*, and the *Saville Tribunal Report* gave a high rating to the general quality of administrative performance, particularly by the senior staff. Administrative faults were attributed to federal interference, inadequate financial resources, or political mismanagement.

[40] The administrator of the colony request clarification of the jurisdiction of the LEDB in a letter to the Land Department, January 6, 1932 (files of Town Clerk's Office, LCC).

[41] Letter to administrator of the colony from Nigerian Land Department, Lagos, January 13, 1932 (files of Town Clerk's Office, LCC).

[42] *Hoskyns-Abrahall Report*, p. 26.

[43] *Ibid.*, pp. 27–28.

[44] *Ibid.*, p. 32. This report is as interesting for its inconsistencies as for its insights. While arguing for conformity with Yoruba tradition and control of the council by the city's elected representatives, the commission was also extremely disdainful of slum dwellers. The colonial attitude toward the urban poor is revealed by a passage dealing with government-subsidized housing: "Government . . . is still faced with the problem of those who cannot afford to pay an economic rent for accommodation in a modern house, those who have lived rent free, or practically rent free, in a hovel. Quite a large proportion are not natives of Lagos, giving no benefit to Lagos, and they should be got rid of. Others with whom we are concerned here can claim to be Lagosians, though the mere fact of their being unable to pay a reasonable rent

proves them to be of no great value as citizens. There can, I believe, be no place in a replanned and largely rebuilt capital for people of this kind. The face of Lagos is to be changed, we hope, from slum to modern town, and it must follow that the type of people living in it must change too. . . . Twenty years or so should clear the slums and rebuild Lagos and twenty years should also be sufficient to rid the island of the unwanted" (*ibid.*, p. 33).

An addendum to the report stressed the government position by referring to the experience with council houses in England, where also it was allegedly shown that "the adult slum mind cannot be changed" (*ibid.*, p. 50).

45 Minutes of LTC, May 3, 1949, p. 17 (files of Town Clerk's Office, LCC).

46 Governor's communication to LTC, July 3, 1951 (files of Town Clerk's Office, LCC).

47 Minutes of LTC, April 3, May 10, 1951 (files of Town Clerk's Office, LCC).

48 Cf. Lagos Town Planning Ordinance, cap. 103 of 1928, and Lagos Town Planning Act, cap. 95 of the Law of the Federation of Nigeria and Lagos, 1958.

49 The levying of rates was the only power delegated to the LEDB which was not exercised. The board was financed primarily through grants from the federal government and income derived from its own housing settlements. To the public, LEDB rates would have appeared as double taxation and the LCC, as the collection agent, would inevitably have been the target of protest against the levy.

50 The major LEDB projects have been the Yaba Town Planning Scheme (1929), the Central Lagos Slum Clearance Scheme (1951), the Apapa Town Planning Scheme (1953), the Lagos Re-Housing Scheme (1955), the Surulere Town Planning Scheme (1955), the Southwest Ikoyi Town Planning Scheme (1958), the Freehold Plots Scheme (1958), the Leasehold Plots Scheme at Iganmu Industrial Estate, the Surulere Light Industries Scheme, and the Freehold Housing Scheme (1956). In 1966 the LEDB reported that its projects included the Iganmu Industrial Estate, the Olowogbowo Resettlement Area, the Olowogbowo Land-Lord's Site, the Metropolitan Housing Scheme, the Lagos Workers' Estate, and the Rehousing Estates-Hogan Bassey Service Industry. In addition, the board carried out projects for the federal government, among the largest having been the enormous Victoria Island Reclamation and Development Project. Future schemes include Maroko Village Development, Okesuna Development, Iponrin Village Development, Falomo Village Development, and a central Lagos shopping district, to be executed by the successor Lagos State Property and Development Corporation.

51 *Sagoe Tribunal Report*, p. 30.

52 *Ibid.*, p. 31, Sir Kofo Abayomi is also an associate of the Ibadan University Teaching Hospital, a director of many private firms, and an optometrist with a thriving practice in Lagos. His remuneration as LEDB chairman was £1,200. The chief executive officers of the LEDB were on a scale of £3,800–£4,500.

53 The relationship between the LEDB chairman and the federal government was explained to the Sagoe Tribunal by Sir Kofo. The dialogue that was particularly instructive on this point revealed that the minister of Lagos affairs assigned land to the LEDB chairman, who in turn allocated plots to the LEDB chief executive officer, who likewise was empowered to give others land, all in order to keep people from saying that officials did not act correctly by appropriating property directly to themselves. The minister could also interfere at any time in land allocations. *LEDB Tribunal of Inquiry Proceedings*, no. 64, May 22, 1967, pp. 18–23.

54 *Sagoe Tribunal Report*, p. 34.

55 *Ibid.*, p. 5.

56 *Annual Report of the Lagos City Council*, 1965–66, p. 23.

57 *UN Report*.

58 In 1965 nearly 85 percent of all deaths from pneumonia in Lagos occurred among children five years of age or less (*Annual Report of LCC, 1965–66*, p. 48). The high incidence of intestinal parasites is also linked to unhygienic environmental

conditions: in 1960, among schoolchildren, the rate of infestation by roundworms and hookworms was a shocking 85 percent, and examination of a sample of government workers revealed a 96 percent rate of infestation among adults (*UN Report*, pp. 198–199).

[59] The inadequacies of health facilities were outlined in a letter dated August 20, 1962, submitted to the council by Dr. O. Adeniji-Jones, the medical officer of health. Dr. Adeniji-Jones also presented a detailed memorandum on the council's services to the Saville Tribunal (see *Saville Tribunal Report*, pp. 94–102, for summary).

[60] "Memorandum Submitted by the Medical Officer of Health" (1966), files of the Town Clerk's Office, LCC.

[61] In a letter dated December 9, 1969, Lord Lugard wrote: "The people here are seditious and rotten to the core. They are masters of secret intrigue and they have been plotting against the government ceaselessly. . . . I could show you that Lagos has for 20 years past opposed every Governor and has fomented strife and bloodshed in the Hinterland. . . . I have spent the best part of my life in Africa; my aim has been the betterment of the Natives for whom I have been ready to give my life. But after some 29 years, and after nearly 12 years as Governor here, I am free to say that the people of Lagos are the lowest, the most seditious and disloyal, the most prompted by purely self-seeking money motives of any people I have met" (quoted in Margery Perham, *Lugard: The Years of Austerity* [London: Collins, 1960], pp. 593–594).

[62] For comments on Lugard's plans, see *ibid.*, p. 588.

[63] Quoted from C. L. Temple, *Native Races and Their Rulers* (Capetown, 1918), by A. H. M. Kirk-Greene, ed., *The Principles of Native Administration in Nigeria: Selected Documents* (London: Oxford University Press, 1965), p. 48.

[64] For a comparison of British and French colonial policies, see L. Gray Cowan, *Local Government in West Africa* (New York: Columbia University Press, 1958).

[65] *Annual Colonial Report*, 1936, p. 2.

[66] "Nigeria: A Preliminary Report on the Administrative Reorganization of the Colony Districts of Nigeria" (1939), in Colonial Office Library, London, p. 1.

[67] Minutes of LTC, October 15, 1957.

[68] The Nigerian Building Society is a federally controlled savings and loan agency owned jointly by the federal government, the former Eastern Region government, and the Commonwealth Development Corporation. It was formed to provide capital for housing developments in Lagos, supplementing the activities of the LEDB, but thus far private deposits have remained low and the NBS has had to rely on heavy subsidies for its operations. It is estimated that approximately 60 percent of its gross profits flow back to the federal government through dividends and taxes.

[69] From 1960 to 1966 the Registry Division dealt with almost double the number of titles dealt with in the twenty-four years before independence.

[70] *Saville Tribunal Report*, p. 232.

[71] Other federal departments besides the Ministry of Lagos Affairs have exercised control over Lagos. In 1965 the Ministry of Works operated the Lagos water supply, the Ministry of Internal Affairs had jurisdiction over places of public entertainment including hotels and horse racing, the Ministry of Health was responsible for curative health and medical services, the Ministry of Natural Resources and Research took care of animal health and fisheries, the Ministry of Housing and Surveys supervised rent control and government quarters, the Ministry of Education was in charge of secondary education and the University of Lagos, and the Ministry of Labour controlled labor and social welfare. Except for rent control, these functions did not constitute a significant source of influence. Cumulatively, however, they represented a wide range of subjects over which the city government had little control, although many of them would normally be regarded as local government matters.

72 Information on the early financial resources of the LTC was obtained from files in the Town Clerk's Office, particularly a 1942 memorandum, "Information asked for by the Financial Secretary and based on rough notes handed by him to the Secretary of the LTC"; a report of June 3, 1942, ostensibly based on the memorandum, "Lagos Town Council Finances"; and a brief dated January 20, 1932, "Report by the Committee on the Financial Position of the LTC and Connected Matters."

73 Ordinance no. 9 of 1941 was passed "to make provisions for the Constitution of and the appointment and election of members of the LTC and to empower the Council to levy rates for township purposes."

74 "Memorandum Submitted by the City Treasurer" (1966), files of the Town Clerk's Office, LCC.

75 The council's main source of income is property rates or taxes levied on the capital, annual, or unimproved value of tenements in the city. In practice, the "assessed annual value," ranging between a fifth and a third of the actual rent paid on a tenement, is used. Property assessment, initially handled by the town clerk and later by the town engineer, was transferred in 1958 to a government appraiser, the principal valuation officer, attached to the Ministry of Lagos Affairs. All council files on property assessment were removed at that time to the ministry, which continued, however, to work with the city's valuation officers.

The general rate in 1957–58 was 7s. 4d. on the pound (i.e., about a third of the assessed annual value of the tenement). In 1963 the rate was raised to 10s. (or half the assessed annual value). So desperate was the council's financial situation by 1966 that Mr. Coker warned: ". . . unless the Council is willing to increase the rates to be levied, we cannot proceed to discharge our duties as a Local Authority efficiently under the present circumstances" (Minutes of the LCC Financial Committee, December 30, 1965). It was estimated that the council, in order to finance its proposed expenditures for 1966–67, would have to increase the rate to 19s. on the pound. The council set the rate at 12s., asking the ministry to approve it. Permission was denied on the grounds that £700,000 in rate arrears had not been collected and that a raise in rates would inflate wages and prices. Some of the government's arrears in grants were paid up, although not the total due the council. As a result, various municipal projects, such as covering of drains, road maintenance, new drainage, and street lighting, had to be suspended. Schemes postponed indefinitely were the Surulere swimming pool, the acquisition of a new abattoir site, the Surulere Library, the Maroko Bridge, the LCC Health Center, and the Macgregor Canal Bridge.

## CHAPTER 7: *Chieftaincy*

1 For details on the origin of Lagos royalty, see John Losi, *History of Lagos*, first published in 1914 (Lagos: African Educational Press, 1967). Other sources for this chapter include J. F. Ade Ajayi, "Political Organizations in West African Towns in the Nineteenth Century: The Lagos Example," in *Urbanization and African Social Change*, proceedings of inaugural seminar held at Center of African Studies, University of Edinburgh, January 1963; J. F. Ade Ajayi, "The Beginnings of Modern Lagos," *Nigeria*, 69 (August 1961), 122–127; and *Price Report*. I am grateful to Adeyinka Oyekan II, oba of Lagos, for granting me interviews from which I obtained additional information.

2 Losi, *op. cit.*, p. 12.

3 The exact origin of the Ogalede and Abagbon chiefs is unclear: "The Akarigbere and Ogalede chiefs are said to have been originally strangers from Benin and elsewhere, who later on were also given white caps to be tokens of their authority. There is no evidence of any appointment of the leading Akarigbere chief as the

exofficio senior chief of Lagos; or even of the establishment of the Akarigbere as a higher rank than either the Idejos or the Ogaledes. It is claimed that the Akarigbere is the superior class because they came from Benin, whose patronage Lagos acknowledged; it is also claimed that the Idejo is the superior class because they own the land, and their rights were never disturbed by Benin. But there is nothing to support either view. The order of precedence of these classes was never decided upon, most probably because any decision would have caused jealousy and might result in setting one class against another and so disrupt the town" (*Price Report,* p. 6).

4 Oba Akinshemoyin was given "a costly piece of deep-satin-velvet. This piece of velvet being placed in his room made the room dark in the day and bright at night. He was so much astonished at this that he sent the cloth to the King of Benin as [a] present, adding that it was worthy of being only in the possession of His Majesty. The King of Benin, on receiving this present was exceedingly glad, and encouraged him to continue his friendship with the Portuguese slave dealers. . . . It was in this way that Lagos became prominent among the Yoruba countries as the great centre of trade" (Losi, *op. cit.,* p. 13).

5 *Ibid.,* p. 14. The wealth amassed by Lagos chiefs from the slave trade is suggested by the value of the slaves aboard each ship. A slave in the early nineteenth century was said to be worth about $1,200, and each ship carried more than 1,000 prisoners. By 1852 "the island [of Lagos] was full of slave traders, Brazilian, Spanish, Portuguese, French, and possibly even an occasional Briton. . . . 'Those were merry days,' remarked Richard Burton, 'the slaver had nothing to do but sleep and smoke, with an occasional champagne tiffin on the beach. The trade man made all the bargains; the doctors examined the "contraband"; they were shipped off by the captain and crew, and in due time came a golden return' " (Ellen Thorp, *Ladder of Bones* [London: Fontana Books, 1966], pp. 36–37).

6 For further discussion of the links between Lagos politics and the slave trade, see Ajayi, "Political Organization in West African Towns in the Nineteenth Century," pp. 166–173.

7 Jean Herskovits Kopytoff, *A Preface to Modern Nigeria: The "Sierra Leonians" in Yoruba, 1830–1890* (Madison: University of Wisconsin Press, 1965), p. 101.

8 S. O. Biobaku, "Prince Kosoko of Lagos," in *Eminent Nigerians of the Nineteenth Century* (Cambridge: The University Press, 1960), p. 32.

9 W. N. M. Geary, *Nigeria under British Rule* (New York: Barnes and Noble, 1965), p. 29. For additional details on Kosoko's exploits, see Kopytoff, *op. cit.,* pp. 44–62; J. F. Ade Ajayi, "The British Occupation of Lagos, 1851–1861: A Critical Review," *Nigeria,* 69 (August 1961), 102.

10 Kopytoff, *op. cit.,* p. 320 n. 72.

11 *Ibid.,* pp. 106–107; Geary, *op. cit.,* p. 27.

12 Geary, *op. cit.,* p. 35.

13 *Ibid.,* p. 33.

14 *Ibid.,* pp. 34, 36.

15 *Ibid.,* p. 38.

16 Treaty of Lagos, 1861, Art. II.

17 Kopytoff, *op. cit.,* p. 177.

18 *Ibid.,* p. 146.

19 Geary, *op. cit.,* p. 40.

20 Kopytoff, *op. cit.,* p. 146.

21 *Annual Colonial Report: Nigeria,* 1928–29, p. 11.

22 J. E. Egerton-Shyngle, "Mr. Egerton-Shyngle Interviews Sir Hugh Clifford," in Herbert Macaulay, *Justitia Fiat: The Moral Obligation of the British Government to the House of King Docemo of Lagos* (London: St. Clement's Press, 1921), p. 61.

23 *Price Report,* p. 2. The designation of obas as "private persons" was made official in a Gazette Extraordinary, August 10, 1925.

[24] In 1901, in a feeble attempt to accord a measure of recognition to chiefs, the government created the Central Native Council, a body of traditional authorities with weak advisory powers. It met infrequently and died in 1912, having had no affect on administrative policy.

[25] As Oyekan later described the meaning attached to the palace, "the ceremony of moving into the Iga Idunganran . . . is thought to be the most important stage [in acceding to the throne]. . . . People don't always believe what they read in the newspapers or hear on the radio. They have to see the Oba move in with their own eyes" ("The King of Lagos," *West Africa*, January 8, 1966, p. 35).

[26] Some of Oyekan's supporters also alleged that the son of Adele I, Atini, through whom Adele II traced his descent, was really a Hausa slave, not a legitimate off-spring of the royal family. If true, Adele's heritage would have been based on a fictional genealogical connection, disqualifying him from office.

[27] *Daily Service*, August 1, 1959, p. 1.

[28] *Daily Times*, August 3, 1959, p. 1.

[29] The rift between Adele and his chiefs involved the Obanikoro of Lagos (senior religious chief), the Olumegbon of Lagos (senior landowning chief), and three other hereditary chiefs, two of whom were members of the Akarigbere class of kingmakers. The dispute was also extended to four titled or honorary chiefs, including the prominent Action Group members, Dr. J. Akanni Doherty (Otun Eko) and Dr. Akinola Maja (Baba Eko).

[30] Peter Enahoro, "After the Ordeal . . . ," *Daily Times*, March 15, 1965, p. 10.

[31] For example, Oyekan has urged the employment of chiefs in suitable positions, the appointment of chiefs to local boards and agencies such as rent tribunals, and the creation of welfare courts to include traditional members.

[32] "The King of Lagos," p. 35.

[33] *Lagos Weekend*, August 1, 1969, p. 12.


CHAPTER 8: *Market Women*

[1] On traditional markets in West Africa, see B. W. Hodder, "The Markets of Yorubaland" (Ph.D. dissertation, University of London, 1963); B. W. Hodder, "The Markets of Ibadan," in P. C. Lloyd, A. L. Mabogunje, and B. Awe, eds., *The City of Ibadan* (London: Cambridge University Press, 1967), pp. 173–190; Daryll Forde, *The Yoruba-speaking Peoples of South-Western Nigeria* (London: International African Institute, 1951); Raymond W. Baker, "Marketing in Nigeria," *Journal of Marketing*, 29 (July 1966), 40–48; Paul Bohannan and George Dalton, *Markets in Africa* (Evanston, Ill.: Northwestern University Press, 1962); and P. T. Bauer, *West African Trade* (Cambridge: The University Press, 1954).

[2] This type of influence is described as "unassertive" in preference to "potential" or "latent," two related terms that have received wider acceptance in the literature. Both of them, however, imply that such influence might in the future have a meaningful impact on community politics, whereas "unassertive" influence has already affected the political process.

[3] The eighteen established markets are Apapa Elemu, Apapa General, Anikantamo, Abule Ijesha, Alayabiagba (Ebute Elefun), Ebute Ero, Oyingbo, Egerton, Gbaja (Lawanson), Iddo, Idumagbo (Jankara), Ijero, Lewis Street (Araromi or Sandgrouse), Moloney Bridge Street (Idumagbo Marina), Oko Awo, Obalende, Obada, and Oju Elegba (Tejuoso or Ojuelegba). The ten wares markets are Agarawu Street, Docemo Street, Daddy Alaja Street, Egerton Street, Ijaiye Street, Iddo, Idumagbo (Idera), Palm Church Street, Porter Street, and Mosalasi Street.

[4] Chief E. O. Dare, secretary to the Lagos City Markets and Women's Organization, listed thirty-three markets in the city: Ajengunle, Ajelogo, Alakoro, Araromi (Sandgrouse or Lewis Street), Araromi Odo, Apapa Elemu 1, Apapa Elemu 2, Apapa Elemu 3, Apapa Elemu 4, Apapa Elemu 5, Ebute Elefun, Ebute Ero, Ebute

Saka Olowo, Elegbata (Daddy Alaja Street), Ereko (Egerton), Gbaja (Lawanson), Idera, Ijero (Ademuyiwa), Iddo, Idumagbo (Jankara), Idumagbo Marina, Ita-Faji, Ita Omo, Makoko, Obalende, Obun Edo, Oke Arin Olowo, Oke Arin Oni, Oko Awo, Olorun Sogo, Oyingbo, Sabo, and Tejuoso (Ojuelegba). He made no distinction between established markets and wares markets.

[5] A. L. Mabogunje, "Lagos: A Study in Urban Geography" (Ph.D. dissertation, University of London, 1961), pp. 202–220. For another discussion of markets, see Suzanne Comhaire-Sylvain, "Le Travail des Femmes à Lagos, Nigérie," *Zaïre*, 5 (February and May 1951), 169–187, 475–502.

[6] This information was obtained from officers of the Lagos City Markets and Women's Association. Many details on the operations of Lagos markets were generously supplied by these officials and other prominent market traders.

[7] See Bauer, *op. cit.*, for a thorough examination of this argument. Peter Marris, *Family and Social Change in an African City* (London: Routledge & Kegan Paul, 1961), pp. 72–76, also discusses it briefly. Both authors reject the criticism and seem to agree that the traditional market system is, in fact, appropriate for the present needs of the African economy.

[8] Mushin and Agege markets, though not within the official city limits, nevertheless function as part of the urban ring system serving Lagos. Obun Eko and Ebute Ero are the only two periodic markets on Lagos Island.

[9] That is, Obun Eko would meet on the 2d, 10th, 18th, and 26th; Ebute Ero, on the 4th, 12th, 20th, and 28th; Apapa, on the 6th, 14th, 22d, and 30th; and Agege, on the 8th, 16th, and 24th.

[10] Marris, *op. cit.*, p. 70. Because of the concentration of traders in Isale Eko, "the slum clearance area is probably one of the most prosperous communities in the town" (*ibid.*, p. 71).

[11] P. O. Ohadike, "A Demographic Note on Marriage, Family, and Family Growth in Lagos, Nigeria," paper read at First African Population Conference, University of Ibadan, January 1966. Ohadike conducted a survey of married women of all classes in 1964, finding that 62.8 percent of them were self-employed traders, "almost half of whom were polygamously married" (*ibid.*, p. 1). About a third of those interviewed defended polygamy because it provided social, domestic, and economic assistance in the household.

[12] *Population Census of Lagos, 1963* (Lagos: Federal Office of Statistics, 1963), p. 9.

[13] Ohadike, *op. cit.*, p. 9.

[14] The original members of the Markets Council were two traditional chiefs (Chief Ogundimu, the Oloto of Otto, and Chief Aminu Kosoko, the Oloja of Lagos), the alaga of each established market, the Iyalode of Lagos, two representatives of each market women's association, two representatives of the National Council of Women's Societies, the city engineer, the medical officer of health, and the senior health superintendent who is secretary to the Markets Council.

[15] For details of the controversy over allocating meat stalls on a hereditary basis, see *Saville Tribunal Report*, pp. 57–63.

[16] Report of the Markets, Parks and Cemeteries Sub-Committee of the Lagos City Council, July 18, 1967.

[17] Takena N. Tamuno, *Nigeria and Elective Representation, 1923–1947* (London: Heinemann, 1966), p. 55.

[18] *Daily Times*, October 14, 1950, p. 11.

[19] *Storey Report*, pp. 45–46.

[20] *Daily Times*, September 5, 1952, p. 1.

[21] The federal government rejected the *Rapson Report* because it approved of collecting money in advance for the construction of markets. The government deemed this procedure illegal and financially unsound. It also claimed that the Rapson recommendations were based on misstatements of fact. The basic objection

to collecting in advance, however, was tied to the question of the culpability of the town clerk, D. M. O. Akinbiyi, widely regarded as an AG sympathizer who permitted the party, however reluctantly, to use his office for partisan purposes. Had the basic plan of collecting dues in advance been endorsed, Akinbiyi would have been relieved of complicity in the matter, an outcome that was unacceptable to the new 1959 coalition government formed by the opposition NCNC and NPC.

[22] *Rapson Report*, p. 14.

[23] *Ibid.*, p. 16.

[24] *Ibid.*, p. 20.

[25] The origins and development of most of the market women's organizations are obscure. Many arose in response to a particular event in support of a protest; women would form an ad hoc association, borrowing a name from the markets to which most of them were attached. It is difficult to trace the history of such associations and of their transformation into more formal organizations. The only associations that seem to achieve permanence and to sustain a continuous organizational structure are those affiliated with political parties. The Lagos City Markets and Women's Organization, which was linked with the AG, includes the majority of traditional market leaders; associations linked with the NCNC or the UMP represent dissenting factions. Others, like the Ebutero-Alakoro-Elefun Market Women's League, are smaller and weaker spontaneous bodies that originated for a particular purpose.

[26] *Daily Telegraph*, October 12, 1962, p. 1.

[27] *West African Pilot*, October 30, 1962, p. 3.

[28] Chairman's address, annual inaugural meeting of LTC, November 5, 1959, pp. 4, 6.

[29] The positions included the president-general of the NCNC Market Women's Association (Madam Rabiatu Erelu); the leader of the NCNC Market Women's Association, Lagos Island Markets (Madam Bintu Kotun); the leader of the NCNC Market Women's Association, Mainland Markets (Madam M. Ifedirah); the chairman of the NCNC Women's Association, Lagos Branch (Mrs. K. A. Fashina); the chairman of the NCNC Women's Association, Lagos South Zone (Mrs. A. Reis); the chairman of the NCNC Women's Association, Lagos North Zone (Alhaja Daniju); the chairman of the NCNC Women's Association, Lagos Middle Zone (Mrs. E. A. Bamijoko); the deputy leader of the NCNC Market Women's Association, Island Markets (Mama Ife); and the deputy leader of the NCNC Market Women's Association, Mainland Markets (Alhaja Anibaba).

[30] In a letter to Major General Aguiyi-Ironsi, dated May 6, 1966, the association described itself as a nonpolitical organization cutting across all the markets "without any of the boggy distinctions of tribalism that have plagued this blessed country of ours." The letter was signed, with thumbprints, by three of the city's leading traders, including Madam Sabalemotu Aduke Ologundudu, the alaga of Jankara Market.

[31] *Daily Telegraph*, June 6, 1966, p. 1.

[32] Letter to Major General Aguiyi-Ironsi from the Ebutero-Alakoro-Elefun Market Women's League, May 30, 1966.

[33] *Daily Times*, September 20, 1950, p. 1.

CHAPTER 9: *Constitutional Status of Lagos*

[1] For a fuller examination of this subject, see Donald C. Rowat, "The Problems of Governing Federal Capitals," *Canadian Journal of Political Science*, 1 (September 1968), 345–356.

[2] Belgrade, Bern, Bonn, Moscow, and Yaoundé are both federal and state capitals.

[3] Examples are Mexico City, Caracas, Brasília, Buenos Aires, Canberra, New Delhi, Islamabad (Pakistan), Kuala Lumpur, and Washington.

[4] For details on the constitutional conferences leading to independence, see Kalu

Ezera, *Constitutional Developments in Nigeria* (Cambridge: The University Press, 1964); Eme O. Awa, *Federal Government in Nigeria* (Berkeley and Los Angeles: University of California Press, 1964).

[5] *House of Representatives Debates*, 2d sess. March 19–April 1, 1953, p. 989.

[6] *Ibid.*, p. 1053.

[7] The Sardauna, with obvious restraint, commented: "The Northerners, being people of the same outlook for the most part, clung together.... We all found it very strange and did not care for our stay in Lagos. The whole place was alien to our ideas of life and we found that the Members for the other Regions might well belong to another world so far as we were concerned" (Ahmadu Bello, *My Life* [Cambridge: The University Press, 1962], p. 85).

[8] *Ibid.*, pp. 135–136.

[9] *Ibid.*, p. 134.

[10] James S. Coleman, *Nigeria: Background to Nationalism* (Berkeley and Los Angeles: University of California Press, 1958), p. 399. The program stipulated regional legislative and executive autonomy; no central legislative or executive body for Nigeria as a whole except for national defense, external affairs, customs, and West African research institutions; common services, such as communications and transport, to be managed by interregional, independent corporations; separate public services and separate revenues except that customs duties were to be collected by a central agency. See Richard L. Sklar, *Nigerian Political Parties* (Princeton: Princeton University Press, 1963), pp. 125–133, for a review of the self-government crisis.

[11] Bello, *op. cit.*, pp. 135–136.

[12] *Ibid.*, p. 156.

[13] The north's fear that the west might cut off its passage to the sea was more than imaginary. Awolowo, in a public statement, threatened that access to Lagos through the west would be denied the north if it seceded. Later, Awolowo claimed he had merely pointed out the disabilities the north might face if it was not part of Nigeria, including the possibility that the north would need the permission of the southern regions to send exports to Lagos.

[14] Obafemi Awolowo, *Awo: The Autobiography of Chief Obafemi Awolowo* (London: Cambridge University Press, 1960), p. 244.

[15] Action Group, *Lagos Belongs to the West* (London: Purnell and Sons, n.d.), p. 12.

[16] *Ibid.*, p. 9.

[17] *Ibid.*, p. 14.

[18] *Ibid.*, p. 9. Although the Action Group felt that federalization was essentially a concession to the north, it was eastern leaders who were blamed for instigating the plan.

[19] *Ibid.*, p. 27.

[20] NCNC, *Gedegbe L'eko Wa* (Yaba: Zik Enterprises, 1953).

[21] *Daily Times*, September 8, 1953, p. 4.

[22] See *ibid.*, September 12, 1953, p. 3; *Debates of the Western House of Chiefs*, October 19, 1953; and *Nigerian Tribune*, October 23, 1953.

[23] *Daily Times*, November 12, 1953.

[24] Awolowo advocated a linguistic basis for the division into states early in his career, but he has altered his views on Lagos several times. In *Path to Nigerian Freedom* (London: Faber and Faber, 1947) he did not specify the number of states he felt was suitable for Nigeria. In 1957, at a party conference, he argued that "every ethnic group in this country, and there may be as many as a hundred of them, should in the long run be constituted into a separate state. That is the ideal, and it is in our view a long term project" (address by Chief Obafemi Awolowo at Emergency Conference of Western Region Action Group, Ibadan, October 12, 1957, p. 7, quoted in Sklar, *op. cit.*, p. 266). A few years later Awolowo wrote that he had "felt very strongly on the [Lagos] issue, but my feelings were not based on

the mere sentiment of blood relationship between the indigenous inhabitants of Lagos and those of the Western Region. . . . I fought for the continued merger of Lagos with the Western Region for two reasons. First, it is difficult . . . to separate revenue attributable to the Western Region from that imputable to Lagos. Second, the scope for independent revenue through purchase or sales tax on imported goods is severely limited for the Government of the Western Region by the mere juxtaposition of the most populous and most prosperous parts of the Western Region to Lagos" (Awolowo, *Awo*, p. 247). Curiously, despite Awolowo's concern for raising revenues in Lagos, he argued somewhat contradictorily that "anyone who knows something of the expenditure now being incurred on Lagos by the Federal Government, will readily agree that it was in the best interest of the Western Region that Lagos was severed from it in 1954 [because] . . . Lagos was a financial liability to the Western Region" (*ibid.*). Later, Awolowo also conceded that in the interest of progress and peace the territory of Lagos should be made independent, should possibly be enlarged, and should be elevated to the status of a state; the linguistic principle, he felt, should give rise to eleven states, including Lagos (*Thoughts on the Nigerian Constitution* [London: Oxford University Press, 1966], p. 99). Developing this theme further, Awolowo advocated a federation of seventeen states, excluding Lagos, and asserted that the tendency of Lagos and the west to cohere "has grown stronger and stronger with the passage of time" (*The People's Republic* [London: Oxford University Press, 1968], p. 250). Nevertheless, in order to protect the interests of the "Eko tribe," Lagos should be regarded as a special case, worthy of becoming a state even though such a development would not be in keeping with the strict application of the linguistic principle. In sum, Awolowo's views on the status of Lagos evolved from denial of autonomy because of the need for ethnic or linguistic unity, to firm advocacy of a merger of Lagos with the west on the basis of cultural affinity, and finally to an admission that the demands for autonomy might have merit.

[25] Sklar, *op. cit.*, p. 135 n. 106.

[26] *Lagos Belongs to the West*, p. 28.

[27] From 1957 to 1960 the minister of Lagos affairs was Alhaji Mohammadu Ribadu. From 1960 to 1966 the ministry was headed by Alhaji Musa Yar'Adua. Both men were northerners. Before the creation of the Ministry of Lagos Affairs, federal responsibility for Lagos was vested in the Council of Ministers, also dominated by northerners.

[28] "Constitution and Rules for Egbe Omo Ibile Eko," mimeographed (London, n.d.), Clause III, secs. 1–5.

[29] *Daily Times*, November 7, 1964, p. 11.

[30] See, for example, the *General Manifesto on the Disabilities of the Citizens of Lagos* (Lagos: Lagos Press, n.d.).

[31] United Muslim Party Resolution, unanimously passed at a meeting at Glover Hall, July 4, 1956.

[32] A resolution passed at a meeting of the descendants of King Akitoye, King Dosunmu, and King Oyekan on March 3, 1957, cited the 1852 treaty obligations of the British as justification for the call for a Lagos state or a Lagos region. This type of resolution was duplicated by many local groups. A more formal proposal, "The Case for the Creation of a Lagos and Colony State within the Federation of Nigeria," was presented to the secretary of state for the colonies by the Lagos and Colony State Movement on November 19, 1956.

[33] "Memorandum Submitted by the Chairman of the Council," Adeyemi Lawson, 1957 (mimeographed). Basically, Lawson proposed increased powers of legislation for the LTC, adding that the council should be competent to establish scholarships for Lagosians, that Lagos should be deemed a region or a state for the purpose of representation on statutory boards or government committees, that the oba of Lagos and other council members should be represented in the Nigerian Senate, and that

the oba's status should be raised by making him ex officio president of the LTC. Many of these proposals were adopted in the 1959 Lagos Local Government Act. See chapter 6 for details.

[34] Resolution passed by the Central Area Council, Glover Hall, June 25, 1956.

[35] *Nigeria: Report of the Commission Appointed to Enquire into the Fears of Minorities and the Means of Allaying Them* (London: H.M.S.O., 1958), p. 29. The commission did not recommend the creation of new states in Nigeria, feeling that this solution would not allay the fears of minorities, but would only create further difficulties owing to the heterogeneity of the population. Instead, it recommended that the constitution include safeguards to protect minorities, that the federal police force be strengthened, and that political as opposed to constitutional means be used to protect minority rights. By endorsing the status quo, the Minorities Commission, to the satisfaction of the three dominant political parties, assured continuation of regional domination over smaller cultural groups.

[36] *Daily Times*, October 17, 1952.

[37] Significantly, the proposal urged autonomy for the Federal Territory only, leaving the issue of the colony districts an open question. This proposal was probably made in order to present a united front and thereby not provoke a split within the ranks of the Action Group. The proposal defined indigenous persons of Lagos as "all descendants of families of Yoruba origin known and recognized as Lagosians as at 1st January, 1900," and "all descendants of other Nigerians who since that date have continuously resided in Lagos for at least thirty years and do not claim any political rights or privileges in any other part of the federation." The document was signed by four traditional chiefs of Lagos, two titled chiefs of Lagos, and two representatives each from the Action Group, the NCNC, the NPC, the NNDP, the Lagos Citizens' Rights Protection Council, the Lagos State United Front, the Lagos Aborigines Society (in alliance with the Association of the Descendants of Lagos Chiefs), the Egbe Omo Oba, the Egbe Omo Eko, the Lagos Royalists, the Lagos League (London Branch), the United Market Women's Association, and all federal members of Parliament and federal senators from Lagos. The committee's secretary was Chief I. O. Bajulaiye. (See "Memorandum on Lagos by the Lagos Committee on the Review of the Constitution of the Federal Republic of Nigeria" [mimeographed, n.d.]).

[38] *Daily Times*, September 2, 1965, p. 16.

[39] Minutes of an Emergency Meeting of the Lagos City Council, August 8, 1966, p. 2.

[40] *Memoranda Submitted by the Delegations to the Ad Hoc Conference on Constitutional Proposals for Nigeria* (Lagos: Nigerian National Press, 1967), pp. 28–59, 136–152. Actually, two separate proposals were submitted by the west, one at the first session advocating a federation and another advocating confederation submitted after a three-week recess during which time there were disturbances in the north. It is not clear whether the delegation considered the change a reversal of policy or simply a shift in emphasis. In any event, the changes did mark substantive reformulations of the preferred form of political association by the west. The northern delegation similarly shifted its stand during the ad hoc committee talks, but explicitly stated that the change constituted "a modification of our stand as indicated in the original memo." In contrast with the west, the north changed from a confederal position to a federal position, and conceded in its second memorandum that the creation of states was necessary to allay the fears of domination by sections of the country (*ibid.*, p. 17). The mid-west delegation was the only one that consistently advocated a strong federation. At the final discussions, the western and Lagos delegations agreed substantially with the eastern delegation that the existing regions should be constituted as separate states having the right of secession.

[41] The part of the memorandum dealing with Lagos, "The Future Status of Lagos within the Federation, by Western Nigeria and Lagos Delegations," was a

verbatim reproduction of a booklet written by Lateef Jakande, somewhat misleadingly entitled *The Case for a Lagos State* (Lagos: John West Publications, 1966). The booklet was written in 1964 while Jakande was serving a seven-year prison sentence for treasonable felony and conspiracy. He argued against the control of Lagos by the federal government, rather than for the unconditional creation of a Lagos state. The position of Jakande, like that of Western Region leaders, was that Lagos should be a state under a federal system of government; but if this arrangement was not feasible, as the west claimed, Lagos should be merged with the west under a confederation. This position was clarified when Jakande was challenged by Lagosians after he resigned from the ad hoc committee in support of Chief Awolowo's resignation on April 25, 1967.

42 *West African Pilot*, November 28, 1966, p. 1.

43 A related point was raised by the Lagos Youths in a press statement of May 21, 1967 (mimeographed), denouncing the position of the Lagos and western delegations: "Those who want Lagos to be 'merged' with the West in the case of the disintegration of the Federation or in the so-called case of Confederation, have themselves conceded that the case for a Lagos State within the Federation is unassailable. The question we ask them is simple: supposing the Federation continues as we wish it to do, and the Lagos State is created. What happens if in the future the Federation breaks up? Would the Lagos State be automatically 'merged' with the Western Region? Those who think like this might as well ask that in the case of the disintegration of the Federation or of its breaking up into a Confederation, the Mid-West State should be merged back with the West. The idea is preposterous."

44 *Daily Times*, November 29, 1966, p. 1.

45 *West African Pilot*, November 11, 1966, p. 1.

46 *Daily Times*, May 4, 1967, p. 16.

47 *Ibid.*

48 "Resolution Adopted Unanimously at a Meeting of the Lagos Elders Committee, held at the Residence of Chief T. A. Doherty, Leader of the Committee, on Tuesday, 9th May, 1967" (mimeographed).

49 *West African Pilot*, May 12, 1967, p. 1.

50 *Daily Times*, May 15, 1967, p. 1.

51 *Ibid.*, May 22, 1967, p. 7.

52 *West African Pilot*, May 25, 1967, p. 1.

53 *Daily Times*, May 25, 1967, p. 4.

CHAPTER 10: *Urbanization and Political Change*

1 Robert Dahl, *Who Governs?* (New Haven: Yale University Press, 1961).

2 Robert Melson and Howard Wolpe ("Modernization and the Politics of Communalism: A Theoretical Perspective," *American Political Science Review*, 64 [December 1970], 1112) define communalism as "the political assertiveness of groups which have three distinguishing characteristics: first, their membership is comprised of persons who share in a common culture and identity . . . , second, they encompass the full range of demographic (age and sex) divisions within the wider society . . . , and, third, like the wider society in which they exist, they tend to be differentiated by wealth, status, and power." They argue further that "modernization, far from destroying communalism, in time both reinforces communal conflict and creates the conditions for the formation of entirely new communal groups" (*ibid.*, p. 1113). My findings substantially support their conclusions.

3 In this study the rise of communal nationalism in a disadvantaged group is examined. For the same phenomenon in an advantaged group, see Paul Anber, "Modernization and Political Disintegration: Nigeria and the Ibos," *Journal of Modern African Studies*, 5, no. 2 (1967), 163–179.

⁴ See S. N. Eisenstadt, "Review Article: Some New Looks at the Problems of Relations between Traditional Societies and Modernization," *Economic Development and Cultural Change,* 16 (April 1968), 436–450; C. S. Whitaker, Jr., *The Politics of Tradition: Continuity and Change in Northern Nigeria, 1946–1966* (Princeton: Princeton University Press, 1969); Joseph R. Gusfield, "Tradition and Modernity: Misplaced Polarities in the Study of Social Change," *American Journal of Sociology,* 72 (January 1967), 351–362; L. I. Rudolph and S. H. Rudolph, "The Political Role of India's Caste Associations," *Pacific Affairs,* 28, no. 3 (1955), 235–253; L. I. Rudolph and S. H. Rudolph, *The Modernity of Tradition* (Chicago and London: University of Chicago Press, 1967).

⁵ Leo Kuper, "Plural Societies: Perspectives and Problems," in Leo Kuper and M. G. Smith, eds., *Pluralism in Africa* (Berkeley and Los Angeles: University of California Press, 1969), p. 10.

⁶ Edward C. Banfield and James Q. Wilson (*City Politics* [Cambridge: Harvard University Press, 1963]) pose "private-regardingness" as the opposite of "public-regardingness." This polarity would be somewhat misleading here, for it suggests the primacy of individual interests over the group interests that prevail in Lagos.

*Bibliography*

# Bibliography

BOOKS

Agger, Robert E.; Daniel Goldrich; and Bert E. Swanson. *The Rulers and the Ruled.* New York: John Wiley and Sons, 1964.
Ajayi, J. F. Ade. *Christian Missions in Nigeria, 1841–1891.* London: Longmans, 1965.
Awa, Eme O. *Federal Government in Nigeria.* Berkeley and Los Angeles: University of California Press, 1964.
Awolowo, Obafemi. *Awo: The Autobiography of Chief Obafemi Awolowo.* London: Cambridge University Press, 1960.
———. *The People's Republic.* London: Oxford University Press, 1968.
———. *Thoughts on the Nigerian Constitution.* London: Oxford University Press, 1966.
Azikiwe, Nnamdi. *Renascent Africa.* Accra: privately printed, 1937.
Banfield, Edward C. *Big City Politics.* New York: Random House, 1966.
———*Political Influence.* New York: Free Press, 1961.
Banfield, Edward C. and James Q. Wilson. *City Politics.* Cambridge: Harvard University Press, 1963.
Bauer, P. T. *West African Trade.* Cambridge: The University Press, 1954.
Bello, Ahmadu. *My Life.* Cambridge: The University Press, 1962.
Biobaku, S. O. *The Egba and Their Neighbours, 1842–1872.* Oxford: Clarendon Press, 1957.
Bohannan, Paul, and George Dalton. *Markets in Africa.* Evanston, Ill. Northwestern University Press, 1962.
Breese, Gerald. *Urbanization in Newly Developing Countries.* Englewood Cliffs, N. J.: Prentice-Hall, 1966.
Buell, R. L. *The Native Problem in Africa.* 2 vols. New York: Macmillan, 1928.
Burns, Alan. *History of Nigeria.* 5th ed. London: George Allen and Unwin, 1955.
Carter, Gwendolyn M. *Independence for Africa.* New York: Praeger, 1962.
Clark, Terry. *Community Power and Decision-Making: Comparative Analyses.* San Francisco: Chandler Publishing Co., 1968.
Cohen, Abner. *Custom & Politics in Urban Africa: A Study of Hausa Migrants in Yoruba Towns.* Berkeley and Los Angeles: University of California Press, 1969.
Coker, G. B. A. *Family Property among the Yoruba.* London: Sweet and Maxwell, 1962.
Coker, Increase. *Landmarks of the Nigerian Press.* Lagos: Nigerian National Press, 1967.

357

# Bibliography

Coleman, James S. *Nigeria: Background to Nationalism.* Berkeley and Los Angeles: University of California Press, 1958.

Cowan, L. Gray. *Local Government in West Africa.* New York: Columbia University Press, 1958.

Crowder, Michael. *The Story of Nigeria.* London: Faber and Faber, 1962.

Dahl, Robert. *Modern Political Analysis.* Englewood Cliffs, N. J.: Prentice-Hall, 1963.

———. *Who Governs? Democracy and Power in an American City.* New Haven: Yale University Press, 1961.

Elias, T. O. *Nigerian Land Law and Custom.* London: Routledge & Kegan Paul, 1951.

Ezera, Kalu. *Constitutional Developments in Nigeria.* Cambridge: The University Press, 1964.

Forde, Daryll. *The Yoruba-speaking Peoples of South-Western Nigeria* London: International African Institute, 1951.

Furnivall, J. S. *Colonial Policy and Practice: A Comparative Study of Burma and Netherlands India.* London: Cambridge University Press, 1948.

———. *Netherlands India: A Study of Plural Economy.* Cambridge: The University Press, 1939.

Geary, W. N. M. *Nigeria under British Rule.* New York: Barnes and Noble, 1965. First published in 1927.

Hailey, Lord. *Native Administration in the British African Territories.* 5 vols. London: H. M. S. O., 1951.

Hauser, Philip M., and Leo F. Schnore, eds. *The Study of Urbanization.* New York: John Wiley and Sons, 1965.

Hodgkin, Thomas. *African Political Parties.* London: Penguin Books, 1961.

———. *Nigerian Perspectives.* London: Oxford University Press, 1960.

Hunter, Floyd. *Community Power Structure.* Garden City: Anchor Books, 1963.

Huntington, Samuel P. *Political Order in Changing Societies.* New Haven and London: Yale University Press, 1968.

Janowitz, Morris. *Community Political Systems.* New York: Free Press, 1961.

Kirk-Greene, A. H. M., ed. *The Principles of Native Administration in Nigeria: Selected Documents.* London: Oxford University Press, 1965.

Kopytoff, Jean Herskovits. *A Preface to Modern Nigeria: The "Sierra Leonians" in Yoruba, 1830-1890.* Madison: University of Wisconsin Press, 1965.

Kuper, Hilda, ed. *Urbanization and Migration in West Africa.* Berkeley and Los Angeles: University of California Press, 1965.

Kuper, Leo, and M. G. Smith, eds. *Pluralism in Africa.* Berkeley and Los Angeles: University of California Press, 1969.

Lane, Robert. *Political Life.* New York: Free Press, 1959.

Leslie, J. A. K. *A Social Survey of Dar es Salaam.* London: Oxford University Press, 1963.

Lipset, Seymour Martin. *Political Man: The Social Bases of Politics.* New York: Doubleday Anchor Books, 1963.

Little, Kenneth L. *West African Urbanization.* Cambridge: The University Press, 1965.

Lloyd, P. C.; A. L. Mabogunje; and B. Awe, eds. *The City of Ibadan.* Cambridge: The University Press, 1967.

Losi, John. *History of Lagos.* Lagos: African Education Press, 1967. First published in 1914.

Lynd, Robert S., and Helen Merrell Lynd. *Middletown.* New York: Harcourt, Brace, and World, 1929.

———. *Middletown in Transition.* New York: Harcourt Brace and World, 1937.

Mabogunje, Akin. *Urbanization in Nigeria.* London: University of London Press, 1968.

Mackintosh, John, ed. *Nigerian Government and Politics.* London: George Allen and

Unwin, 1966.

Mair, Lucy. *New Nations.* Chicago: University of Chicago Press, 1963.

Marris, Peter. *Family and Social Change in an African City.* London: Routledge & Kegan Paul, 1961.

Mayer, Philip. *Townsmen or Tribesmen: Conservatism and the Process of Urbanization in a South African City.* Cape Town: Oxford University Press, 1961.

Meek, C. K. *Land Tenure and Land Administration in Nigeria and the Cameroons.* London: H.M.S.O., 1957.

Miner, Horace. *The Primitive City of Timbuctoo.* New York: Anchor Books, 1965.

Mitchell, J. C. *The Kalela Dance.* Rhodes-Livingstone Papers, no. 27. Lusaka, 1956.

Parkin, David. *Neighbours and Nationals in an African City Ward.* Berkeley and Los Angeles: University of California, 1969.

Perham, Margery. *Lugard: The Years of Austerity.* London: Collins, 1960.

———. *Native Administration in Nigeria.* London: Oxford University Press, 1937.

Polsby, Nelson W. *Community Power and Political Theory.* New Haven: Yale University Press, 1963.

Powdermaker, Hortense. *Coppertown: Changing Africa.* New York: Harper Colophon Books, 1962.

Presthus, Robert. *Men at the Top.* New York: Oxford University Press, 1964.

Pye, Lucian W. *Aspects of Political Development.* Boston and Toronto: Little, Brown, 1966.

Riordin, William L. ed. *Plunkett of Tammany Hall.* New York: E. P. Dutton, 1963.

Shils, Edward. *Political Development in the New States.* 's-Gravenhage: Mouton, 1962.

Simms, Ruth P. *Urbanization in West Africa: A Review of the Literature.* Evanston, Ill.: Northwestern University Press, 1965.

Sklar, Richard L. *Nigerian Political Parties: Power in an Emergent African Nation.* Princeton: Princeton University Press, 1963.

Smythe, Hugh H., and Mable M. Smythe. *The New Nigerian Elite.* Stanford: Stanford University Press, 1960.

Southall, A. W., ed. *Social Change in Modern Africa.* London: Oxford University Press, 1961.

Talbot, P. A. *The Peoples of Southern Nigeria.* Vol. IV. London: Oxford University Press, 1926.

Tamuno, Takena N. *Nigeria and Elective Representation, 1923-1947.* London: Heinemann, 1966.

Temple, C. L. *Native Races and Their Rulers.* Cape Town, 1918.

Thomas, Isaac B. *Life History of Herbert Macaulay.* 3d ed. Lagos: privately printed, 1948.

Thorp, Ellen. *Ladder of Bones.* London: Fontana Books, 1966.

Tönnies, Ferdinand. *Gemeinschaft and Gesellschaft.* Trans. with introd. by Charles P. Loomis. East Lansing: Michigan State University Press, 1957.

Trimingham, J. S. *The Influence of Islam upon Africa.* London: Longmans, 1968.

Waith, Ronald. *Local Government in West Africa.* London: George Allen and Unwin, 1964.

Walsh, Annmarie Hauck. *The Urban Challenge to Government.* New York: Praeger, 1969.

Warner, Lloyd W.; J. O. Law; Paul S. Lurt; and Leo Srale. *Yankee City.* New Haven: Yale University Press, 1963.

Weber, Max. *The City.* Trans. and ed. Don Martindale and Gertrud Neuwirth. New York: Free Press, 1958.

———. *The Theory of Social and Economic Organization.* New York: Free Press, 1947.

Wheare, Joan. *The Nigerian Legislative Council.* London: Faber and Faber, 1950.

Whitaker, C. S., Jr. *The Politics of Tradition: Continuity and Change in Northern Nigeria, 1946-1966.* Princeton: Princeton University Press, 1969.

# Bibliography

Williams, B. A. and A. H. Walsh. *Urban Government for Metropolitan Lagos.* New York: Praeger, 1968.

Zolberg, Aristide. *Creating Political Order: The Party States of West Africa.* Chicago: Rand McNally, 1966.


ARTICLES, PAMPHLETS, AND NEWSLETTERS

Action Group. *Lagos Belongs to the West.* London: Purnell and Sons, n. d.

*African Urban Notes.* Newsletter published jointly by African Studies Center, University of California, Los Angeles, and Center for African Studies, Michigan State University, East Lansing.

Ajayi, J. F. Ade. "The Beginnings of Modern Lagos," *Nigeria,* 69 (August 1961), 106–121.

———. "The British Occupation of Lagos, 1851–1861: A Critical Review," *Nigeria,* 69 (August 1961), 96–105.

———. "Political Organization in West African Towns in the Nineteenth Century: The Lagos Example," in *Urbanization and African Social Change,* proceedings of inaugural seminar at Centre of African Studies, University of Edingburgh, January 1963.

Akinola, R. A. "Factors in the Geographical Concentration of Manufacturing in Greater Lagos," *Lagos Notes and Records,* 1 (June 1967), 30–47.

Akitan, E. A. *The Closing Scene of the Eleko Case and the Return of Chief Eshugbayi Eleko.* Lagos: Tika-Tore Press, 1931.

Amicus. *Who's Who in Nigeria.* Lagos, 1949.

Anber, Paul. "Modernization and Political Disintegration: Nigeria and the Ibos," *Journal of Modern African Studies,* 5, no. 2 (1967), 163–179.

Animashaun, Adam I. *The History of the Muslims Community of Lagos.* Lagos: Hope Rising Press, n. d.

Anton, Thomas J. "Power, Pluralism and Local Politics," *Administrative Science Quarterly,* 7, no. 4 (March 1963), 425–457.

Anyiam, Fred U. *Men and Matters in Nigeria Politics (1934–1958).* Lagos: privately printed, 1959.

Azikiwe, Nnamdi. *The Development of Political Parties in Nigeria.* London: Office of the Commissioner in the U. K. for the Eastern Region, 1957.

———. "My Odyssey," *West African Pilot,* 1938–1939.

Backrach, Peter, and Morton S. Baratz. "Decisions and Non-Decisions," *American Political Science Review,* 57 (September 1963), 632–642.

Baker, Raymond W. "Marketing in Nigeria," *Journal of Marketing,* 29 (July 1966), 40–48.

Bascom, William. "Some Aspects of Yoruba Urbanism." In Pierre L. van den Berghe, ed. *Africa: Social Problems of Change and Conflict,* pp. 369–384. San Francisco: Chandler Publishing Co., 1965.

———. "The Urban African and His World," *Cahiers d'Études Africaines,* 4 (1963), 163–185.

———. "Urbanization among the Yoruba," *American Journal of Sociology,* 60 (1955), 446–454.

Biobaku, Saburi. "Prince Kosoko of Lagos." In *Eminent Nigerians of the Nineteenth Century,* pp. 25–32. Cambridge: The University Press, 1960.

*The Case for the Creation of a Lagos and Colony State within the Federation of Nigeria.* Lagos, [ca. 1958].

Coleman, James S. "The Politics of Sub-Saharan Africa." In Gabriel A. Almond and James S. Coleman, eds. *The Politics of the Developing Areas.* Princeton: Princeton University Press, 1960.

Comhaire, Jean. "L'Organisation Municipale à Lagos," *Revue Coloniale Belge,* no.

92 (August 1949), 494–496.

———. "Leopoldville, Lagos and Port au Prince: Some Points of Comparison." In *Nigerian Institute of Social and Economic Research Conference Proceedings*, pp. 73–83. Ibadan: Caxton Press, 1960.

———. "La Vie Religieuse à Lagos," *Zaïre*, 3 (May 1949), 549–556.

Comhaire-Sylvain, Suzanne. "Associations on the Basis of Origins in Lagos, Nigeria," *American Catholic Sociological Review*, 11 (December 1950), 234–236.

———. "Le Travail des Femmes à Lagos, Nigérie," *Zaïre*, 5 (February and May 1951), 169–187, 475–502.

Daland, R. T. "Political Science and the Study of Urbanism," *American Political Science Review*, 51 (June 1957), 491–509.

Davidson, A. "The Origin and Early History of Lagos," *Nigerian Field*, 19 (April 1954).

Davis, Kingsley. "The Origin and Growth of Urbanization in the World," *American Journal of Sociology*, 60 (March 1955), 429–437.

Deniga, Adeoye. *The Nigerian Who's Who for 1919*. Lagos: "Herald" Writing Bureau, 1919.

———. *The Nigerian Who's Who for 1921*. Lagos: Literary Bureau, 1920.

———. *Yoruba Titles and Their Meanings*. Lagos: Jehovah Shaloni Printing Press, 1921.

Eisenstadt, S. N. "Review Article: Some New Looks at the Problems of Relations between Traditional Societies and Modernization," *Economic Development and Cultural Change*, 16 (April 1958), 436–450.

Elias, T. O. "Makers of Nigerian Law," *West Africa*, June 9, 1956.

Epstein, A. L. "Urban Communities in Africa." In Max Gluckman, ed., *Closed Systems and Open Minds*, pp. 52–82. London: Oliver and Boyd, 1964.

Fisher, Humphrey J. "The Ahmadiyya Movement in Nigeria." In Kenneth Kirkwook, ed. *African Affairs One*, pp. 60–88. London: Chatto and Windus, 1961.

Form, William H. and Warren L. Sauer. *Community Influentials in a Middle-Sized City*. East Lansing: Michigan State University, 1960.

Fowler, Wilfred. *Your Town Council: The Principles and Practice of English Municipal Government Have Been a Guide in the Development of Local Government in Lagos*. Zaria: Gaskiya Corp., 1951.

Furnivall, J. S. "The Political Economy of the Tropical Far East," *Journal of the Royal Central Asiatic Society*, 29 (1942), 195–210.

———. "Some Problems of Tropical Economy." In Rita Hinder, ed., *Fabian Colonial Essays*, pp. 161–184. London: Allen and Unwin, 1945.

Geary, W. N. M. "The Development of Laogs in 50 years—from Head Town of 'Slave Coast' to be 'The Liverpool of West Africa,'" *West Africa*, August 16–October 4, 1924.

*General Manifesto on the Disabilities of the Citizens of Lagos*. Lagos: Lagos Press, n. d.

Gusfield, Joseph R. "Tradition and Modernity: Misplaced Polarities in the Study of Social Change," *American Journal of Sociology*, 72 (January 1967), 351–362.

Gutkind, P. C. W. "African Urban Family Life: Comment and Analysis of Some Rural-Urban Differences," *Cahiers d'Études Africaines*, 3 (1962), 149–217.

———. "African Urbanism, Mobility and the Social Network," *International Journal of Comparative Sociology*, 6 (March 1965), 48–60.

———. "The African Urban Milieu: A Force in Rapid Social Change." In Peter J. M. McEwan and Robert B. Sutcliffe, eds. *Modern Africa*, pp. 332–347. New York: Thomas Y. Crowell, 1965.

———. "The Energy of Despair: Social Organization of the Unemployed in Two African Cities, Lagos and Nairobi," *Civilisations*, 17, nos. 3 and 4 (1967). Reprinted by Centre for Developing-Area Studies, McGill University, Montreal, Canada.

———. "Orientation and Research Methods in African Urban Studies." In D. G. Jongmans and P. Gutkind, eds. *Anthropologists in the Felds*, pp. 133–169. Assen, Netherlands: Van Gorcum, 1967.

———. "The Poor in Urban Africa: A Prologue to Modernization, Conflict, and the Unfinished Revolution." In *Power, Poverty and Urban Policy*, II, *Urban Affairs Annual Reviews*, 355–396. Hollywood: Sage Publications, 1968.

Gwam, L. C. *Great Nigerians*. Published by the Daily Times, 1967.

Hanna, William John, and Judith Lynne Hanna. "The Cross-Cultural Study of Local Politics," *Civilisations*, 16, no. 1 (1968), 81–96.

———. "The Integrative Role of Urban Africa's Middle-Places and Middlemen," *Civilisations*, 15, no. 1 (1967), 12–29.

———. "The Political Structure of Urban-Centered African Communities." In Horace Miner, ed. *The City in Modern Africa*, pp. 151–184. New York: Praeger, 1967.

Hill, Polly. "Notes on Traditional Market Authority and Market Productivity in West Africa," *Journal of African History*, 7, no. 2 (1966), 295–311.

Hodder, B. W. "The Markets of Ibadan." In P. C. Lloyd, A. Mabogunje, and B. Awe, eds. *The City of Ibadan*, pp. 173–190. London: Cambridge University Press, 1967.

Jakande, Lateef. *The Case for a Lagos State*. Lagos: John West Publications, 1966.

Jenkins, George. "An Informal Political Economy." In Jeffrey Butler and A. A. Castagno, eds. *Boston University Papers on Africa*, pp. 166–194. New York: Praeger, 1967.

Kuper, Leo. "Some Aspects of Urban Plural Societies in Africa." In Robert A. Lystad, ed. *The African World: A Survey of Social Research*. London: Pall Mall Press, 1965.

Laotan, A. B. "Brazilian Influence on Lagos," *Nigeria*, 69 (August 1961), 157–165.

Lelard, L. C. "Lagos in Portugal and Lagos in Nigeria," *Nigeria*, 39 (1952), 257–260.

Lewis, William H. "Urban Crucible: Parallels and Divergences, *Africa Report*, 14, nos. 5 and 6, 62–64.

*Local Government in Africa*. Summer conference at King's College, Cambridge, August 28–September 9, 1961. London: Cambridge University Overseas Studies Commission, 1961.

Lofchie, Michael F. "Political Theory and African Politics," *Journal of Modern African Studies*, 6, no. 1 (1968), 3–15.

Lucas, J. Olumide. "Traditional Kingship in Lagos," *Nigeria*, 69 (August 1961), 122–127.

Mabogunje, Akin L. "The Evolution and Analysis of the Retail Structure of Lagos, Nigeria," *Economic Geography*, 40 (October 1964), 304–323.

———. *Yoruba Towns*. Ibadan: Ibadan University Press, 1962.

Macaulay, Herbert. *Henry Carr Must Go*. Kirsten Hall, January 24, 1924.

———. *Justitia Fiat: The Moral Obligation of the British Government to the House of King Docemo of Lagos*. London: St. Clement's Press, 1921.

*Manpower and Employment Research in Africa*. Newsletter published by Centre for Developing-Area Studies, McGill University, Montreal, Canada.

Marris, Peter. "African City Life." In *Nkanga*, no. 1. Kampala: Transition Books, 1968.

Marshall, A. H. "The Adaptation of English Local Government Principles to Colonial Territories," *Journal of African Administration*, 2 (October 1950), 34–38.

Miller, N. S. "The Beginnings of Modern Lagos," *Nigeria*, 69 (August 1961), 107–121.

Miner, Horace. "The City and Modernization: An Introduction." In Horace Miner, ed. *The City in Modern Africa*, pp. 1–20. New York, Praeger, 1967.

Mitchell, J. Clyde. "Theoretical Orientations in African Urban Studies." In Michael Banton, ed. *The Social Anthropology of Complex Societies*, pp. 37–68. Edinburgh: Tavistock Publications, 1966.

Moore, Kofoworola Aina (Lady Ademola). "The Story of Kofoworola Aina Moore of the Yoruba Tribe, Nigeria." In Margery Perham, ed. *Ten Africans.* London: Faber and Faber, n. d.

NCNC. *Gedegbe L'eko Wa.* Yaba: Zik Enterprises, 1953.

Ogundara, Babafemi. "Lagos: Nigeria's Premier Port," *Nigerian Geographical Journal,* 4 (December 1961), 26–40.

Ohadike, Patrick O. "Urbanization: Growth, Transition, and Problems of a Premier West African City (Lagos, Nigeria)," *Urban Affairs Quarterly,* 3 (June 1968), 69–90.

Olusanya G. O. "The Origin of the Lagos Town Council," *Lagos Notes and Records,* 2 (June 1968), 51–58.

Payne, John A. *Payne's Lagos and West Arfican Almanack and Diary for 1884.* London, 1884.

Payne, John Augustus Otunba. *Table of Principal Events in Yoruba History.* Lagos: Andrew H. Thomas, 1893.

Rabinowitz, Francine. "Sound and Fury Signifying Nothing," *Urban Affairs Quarterly,* 3 (March 1968), 111–122.

Reissman, Leonard. "Urbanism and Urbanization." In Julius Gould, ed. *Penguin Survey of the Social Sciences,* pp. 36–55. London: Penguin Books, 1965.

Rowat, Donald C. "The Problems of Governing Federal Capitals," *Canadian Journal of Political Science,* 1 (September 1968), 345–356.

Rudolph, L. I., and S. H. Rudolph. "The Political Role of India's Caste Associations," *Pacific Affairs,* 28, no. 3 (1955), 235–253.

Schulze, Robert O. "The Role of Economic Dominants in Community Power Structure," *American Sociological Review,* 23 (February 1958), 3–9.

Sjoberg, Gideon. "The Rise and Fall of Cities: A Theoretical Perspective," *International Journal of Comparative Sociology,* 4 (1963), 107–120.

———. "Urban Community Theory and Research: A Partial Evaluation," *American Journal of Economics and Sociology,* 14 (January 1955), 199–206.

Sklar, Richard L. "Political Science and National Integration—A Radical Approach," *Journal of Modern African Studies,* 5, no. 1 (1967), 1–11.

Sobande, Obadia Adegboyega. *Notes and Comments on the Life of Mr. H. Macaulay.* Lagos, n. d.

Trimingham, J. S. "Islam and Christianity among the Yoruba," *East and West Review,* 19 (October 1953), 109–111.

Wallerstein, Immanuel. "Ethnicity and National Integration in West Africa," *Cahiers d'Études Africaines* no. 3 (October 1960), 129–138.

Wirth, Louis. "Urbanism as a Way of Life," *American Journal of Sociology,* 44 (July 1938), 1–24.

Wood, Rev. J. B. *Historical Notes of Lagos, West Africa.* Lagos: Church Missionary Society, 1933.

PUBLIC DOCUMENTS, GOVERNMENT REPORTS, AND OFFICIAL PUBLICATIONS OF NIGERIAN POLITICAL PARTIES

*Action Group of Nigeria Programme of Organization (Lagos Branch),* 1964.

*Annual Colonial Reports: Lagos,* 1887–1905.

*Annual Colonial Reports: Nigeria,* 1914–1932.

*Annual Colonial Reports: Southern Nigeria,* 1896–1913.

*Annual Reports of the Lagos Town Council,* 1950–1966.

*Blue Books of Southern Nigeria,* 1906–1913.

*Blue Books of the Lagos Colony,* 1894–1905.

"Constitution and Rules for Egbe Omo Ibile Eko." Mimeographed. London, n. d.

*Constitution of the Action Group of Nigeria.* Lagos: Amalgamated Press, 1962.

"Constitution of the Nigerian National Democratic Party." N. d.

# Bibliography

*Constitution, Rules and Regulations of the National Council of Nigeria and the Cameroons.* Lagos, 1955.

"Despatch by the Secretary of State for the Colonies to the Governors of the African Territories," February 25, 1947. In *The Principles of Native Administration in Nigeria: Selected Documents,* ed. with introd. by A. H. M. Kirk-Greene, pp. 234–248. London: Oxford University Press, 1965.

Fowler, W. *A Report on the Lands of the Colony District.* Lagos, 1949.

Jones, G. C., and Keith B. Lucas. *Report on the Administration of Lagos Town Council.* Lagos, 1963.

*Lagos Executive Development Board Tribunal of Inquiry Proceedings.* 1967.

"Memorandum on Lagos by the Lagos Committee on the Review of the Constitution of the Federal Republic of Nigeria." Mimeographed. Lagos, n. d.

*Memoranda Submitted by the Delegations to the Ad Hoc Conference on Constitutional Proposals for Nigeria.* Lagos: Nigerian National Press, 1967.

Nigeria. *The Dosunmu-Stapleton Commission of Inquiry Report.* Lagos, 1958.

————. *Industrial Directory.* 3d ed. Lagos: Ministry of Industries, 1963.

————. *Legislative Council Debates,* 1923–1951.

————. *Parliamentary Debates,* House of Representatives, 1957–1965.

————. *Population Census of Lagos, 1931.* Lagos: Federal Office of Statistics, 1931.

————. *Population Census of Lagos, 1950.* Lagos: Federal Office of Statistics, 1950.

————. *Population Census of Lagos, 1963.* Lagos: Federal Office of Statistics, 1963.

————. *Population Census of the Western Region of Nigeria, 1952.* Lagos: Government Statistician, 1953–54.

————. *Report by Sir John Imrie, C.B.E., into the Relationship between the Federal Government and the Lagos Town Council.* Lagos: Government Printer, 1959.

————. *Report of a Commission of Inquiry Regarding the House of Docemo.* Lagos: Government Printer, 1933.

————. *Report of an Inquiry by Mr. R. N. Rapson, M.V.O., into Alleged Irregularities by the Lagos Town Council in Connection with the Collection of Money and the Issue of Permits and the Allocation of Market Stalls in Respect of Proposed Temporary Markets at Ereko and Oko-Awo.* Lagos: Government Printer, 1959.

————. *Report of the Commission of Inquiry into the Administration of the Lagos Town Council.* Lagos: Ministry of Information, 1952.

————. *Report of the Lagos Town Planning Commission with Recommendations on the Planning and Development of Greater Lagos.* Lagos: Government Printer, 1946.

————. *Report of the Native Courts (Colony) Commission of Inquiry, 1949.* Lagos: Government Printer, 1952.

————. *Report of the Tribunal of Inquiry into the Affairs of the Lagos City Council for the Period October 15, 1962 to April 18, 1966.* Lagos: Government Printer, 1966.

————. *Report of the Tribunal of Inquiry into the Affairs of the Lagos Executive Development Board for the Period 1st October 1960 to 31st December 1965.* Lagos: Government Printer, 1968.

————. *Report of the Tribunal of Inquiry into the Purchase of Scania-Metropol Buses from Sweden.* Lagos: Lagos State of Nigeria, 1970.

————. *Report of the Tribunal of Inquiry into the Reorganization of Local Government Councils in the Lagos State.* Lagos: Lagos State of Nigeria, 1970.

————. *Report of the Working Party on Statutory Corporations and State-owned Companies.* Pts. I and II. Lagos: Ministry of Information, 1966.

————. *Report on Educational Development in Lagos.* Lagos: Government Printer, 1957.

————. *Report on Lagos Housing Enquiry.* Lagos: Federal Office of Statistics, 1961.

————. *Statistics of Education in Nigeria, 1964.* No. 1, vol. 4. Lagos: Ministry of Education, 1964.

————. *Urban Consumer Surveys in Nigeria: Lagos 1959–1960.* Lagos: Chief Statis-

tician, 1963.
*Nigeria Blue Books,* 1914–1938.
Simpson, S. R. *A Report on the Registration of Title to Land in the Federal Territory of Lagos.* Lagos, 1957.
Skalnikova, O. "Ethnographic Research into the Present Changes in the Mode of Life of Urban Population in Africa." In *Proceedings of the First International Congress of Africanists,* trans. from French by C. L. Patterson, pp. 186–197. London: Longmans, 1964.
Tew, Mervin. *Report on Title to Land in Lagos.* Lagos: Government Printer, 1939.
UNESCO. *Social Implications of Industrialization and Urbanization in Africa South of the Sahara.* Paris, 1956.
United Kingdom. "Nigeria: A Preliminary Report on the Administrative Reorganization of the Colony Districts of Nigeria" (1939), in Colonial Office Library, London.
———. *Nigeria: Report of the Commission Appointed to Enquire into the Fears of Minorities and the Means of Allaying Them.* London: H.M.S.O., 1958.
———. *Report on the Amalgamation of Southern and Northern Nigeria and Administration, 1912 to 1919.* Cmd. 468. London: H.M.S.O., 1920.
UN Technical Assistance Program. *Metropolitan Lagos.* Report prepared for Ministry of Lagos Affairs, 1964.
UN Workshop on Urbanization in Africa. *Symposium on the Social Aspects of Urbanization,* April 25–May 6, 1962, Addis Ababa. Part I Report, "Introduction to the Problems of Urbanization in Tropical Africa," prepared by ECA Secretariat, March 7, 1962.
*Urbanization and African Social Change.* Proceedings of inaugural seminar held at Centre of African Studies, University of Edinburgh, January 1963.
*Who's Who in Nigeria.* Lagos: Nigerian Printing and Publishing Co., 1956.


UNPUBLISHED MATERIAL

Brown, Spencer H. "A History of the People of Lagos, 1852–1886." Ph.D. dissertation, Northwestern University, 1964.
Ejiogu, C. N. "Survey of African Migration to the Main Migrant Areas of the Federal Territory of Lagos." Paper read at First African Population Conference, University of Ibadan, Nigeria, January 1966.
Hodder, B. W. "The Markets of Yorubaland." Ph.D. dissertation, University of London, 1963.
Mabogunje, A. L. "Lagos: A Study in Urban Geography." Ph.D. dissertation, University of London, 1961.
Melson, Robert, and Howard Wolpe. "Modernization and the Politics of Communalism. Paper read at annual meeting of American Political Science Association, New York, September 1969.
Ohadike, P. O. "A Demographic Note on Marriage, Family, and Family Growth in Lagos, Nigeria." Paper read at First African Population Conference, University of Ibadan, Nigeria, January 1966.
Orewa, G. O. "The Development of Local Government Service in Nigeria and the Problem of the Local Civil Servant." Paper read at Nigerian Institute of Public Administration Conference, Lagos, July 7, 1967.
Physical Planning Research Programme, Interim Report no. 2. "Lagos State: Population Models for National and Regional Planning, 1952–1967." Nigerian Institute of Social and Economic Research, Ibadan, May 1969.
Sklar, Richard L. "A Note on the Study of Community Power in Nigeria." Paper read at annual conference of African Studies Association, Washington, D.C., October 13, 1962.

# Bibliography

Colonial Office Library, London:

1. (P)  12782 Adeniji-Jones, C. C. "Political and Administrative Problems of Nigeria," *West Africa*, September 1, 1928. In *Nigeria Pamphlet no. 35*. 1927 Folio.
2. (P)  10940 Cameron, D. "Note on the Report of the Commission of Inquiry regarding the House of Docemo." In *West African Pamphlet no. 213*. 1933 Folio.
3. (P)  10940 Cameron, D. "Note regarding the Head of the House of Docemo." In *West African Pamphlet no. 214*. 1933 Folio.
4. (P)  12782 Geary, W. N. M. "The Development of Lagos in Fifty Years." In *Nigeria Pamphlet no. 13*. 1924 Folio.
5. (P)  10940 Lagos Native Advisory Board Rules, 1899. Folio *West African Pamphlet no. 21*.
6. (P)  10398 Memorial of the Inhabitants of Lagos, 1889. *Nigeria Pamphlet no. 2*.
7. (P)  20172 Rossiter, H. V. The Henry Carr Library. 1946 Folio.

Correspondence and papers of local officials of major political parties in Lagos.
Election manifestos and policy papers of major political parties in Lagos.
"House of Docemo." Address delivered by Herbert Macaulay at Iga Idungaran, Lagos, November 7, 1942, on the celebration of the tenth anniversary of the installation of Oba Falolu of Lagos as head of the House of Docemo.
Interviews with selected community leaders, elected councilors, and municipal officials.
Lagos City Council Files (listed as indexed by the Council):

| | | |
|---|---|---|
| 001547 | 22/8/58 | Annual Reports for "Nigeria" |
| 001568 | 13/1/59 | Annual Reports General |
| 001576 | 27/2/59 | Iga Idungaran |
| 001583 | 7/4/59 | Sir John Imrie's Report |
| 001586 | (n.d.) | Appointment of Senators for Lagos |
| 001596 | 26/6/59 | Division of functions between LTC and the Federal Government |
| 001597 | 1/7/59 | Press Reports of Council Meetings |
| 001599 | 26/6/59 | Scholarships for Lagos Indigenes |
| 001600 | 26/6/59 | Registration of Traditional Chiefs in the LTC |
| 001600B | (n.d.) | Appointment of Oba of Lagos |
| 001627 | (n.d.) | Press Releases |
| 001645 | 13/2/60 | LTC and LEDB Consultative Committee |
| 001647 | 1/3/60 | Chairman's Remuneration |
| 001671 | 28/9/60 | Symposium on the Social Aspects of Urbanization |
| 001695 | 5/6/61 | Transfer of Council's Assets and Funds |
| 001722 | 2/1/62 | Judicial Decisions concerning and of interest to the LTC |
| 001729 | 13/2/62 | Liaison between LTC and Voluntary Organizations |
| 001757 | 7/9/62 | Industry |
| 001808 | (n.d.) | Improvement of Market Administration |
| 001823A | 5/5/66 | Villages within the Federal Territory of Lagos |
| 001848 | 7/9/66 | Administration of Lagos |
| 001849 | (n.d.) | Municipal Courts |
| 00575 | (n.d.) | Municipal Election Procedure |
| 00587 | 22/8/44 | Lagos Town Council Questions |
| 00288 | (n.d.) | 165/1938 Motion |
| 00590 | 4/9/44 | Township Ordinance, cap. 57 and Amendments |
| 630A | (n.d.) | Residence of non-Europeans in European Residential Areas of Ikoyi, Apapa, Plan of |

| | | |
|---|---|---|
| 00736 | (n.d.) | Legislative Council Election 1947 |
| 00841 | 15/1/48 | Ratepayers' Association "C" Ward Correspondence |
| 00869A | 28/4/65 | Assignment of responsibilities to Ministers and Ministries |
| 00874 | 4/6/48 | Elections Ordinance |
| 00882 | 10/7/48 | Constitution 1950 |
| 00957 | 15/8/49 | Lagos Township Census 1950 |
| 00980 | 13/5/50 | Lagos Town Local Government Ordinance 1950, Preparation of Voters' List |
| 001004 | (n.d.) | LTC 1950, Constitution of |
| 001011 | 11/11/50 | Communications from the Mayor |
| 001025 | 31/1/51 | Bye-election 1951 B Ward (Resignation of Oba Adele II) |
| 001036 | 21/3/51 | Presiding Officers' Reports on Municipal Elections |
| 001047 | 22/5/51 | Western House of Assembly Election |
| 001065 | 5/11/51 | Annual Meeting of the LTC |
| 001070 | 15/11/51 | Chairman's (Mayor's) Correspondence, Town Clerk |
| 001072 | 26/11/51 | Presiding Officers' Reports on Western House of Assembly |
| 001097 | 8/4/52 | Questions by Councillors |
| 001099 | 15/4/52 | Council of Ministers Western House of Assembly |
| 001124 | 7/8/52 | Constitutional Position of the Council of Ministers |
| 001128 | 18/8/52 | Lagos Local Government Ordinance—Reform of LTC (Local Law) |
| 001137 | 21/10/52 | Questions—LTC and the Parliament (2/12/60) |
| 001157 | 6/2/53 | Committee of Management |
| 001206 | 17/8/53 | Municipal Election. Determination of the Town of Lagos into Wards |
| 001401 | (n.d.) | London Constitutional Conference |
| 001504/A | (n.d.) | Minutes of Council to Supreme Headquarters State House |
| 001008K | (n.d.) | Lagos Local Government Ordinance—Resignation of Traditional Members and Councilors |
| 198/1934 | 5/12/34 | Re-Organization of the LTC |
| 00279 | (n.d.) | LTC Election—1935 |
| 00587 | (n.d.) | Questions to the LTC by the Hon. Dr. C. C. Adeniji-Jones |
| 126/1935 | 20/1934 | Claims to Lands in Lagos |
| 78/1937 | 25/5/37 | Representation from Jam'at Muslim Community of the Central Mosque reappointment of their General Secretary |
| 145/1937 | (n.d.) | Returns of non-Lagosian Officers of the LTC, Notification re 600a of the General Orders |
| 13/1938 | (n.d.) | Northern Communities now resident in Lagos |
| 44/1938 | (n.d.) | Relationship of Council and LEDB |
| MP 00278 | (n.d.) | Town Council Election 1938 |
| 69/1938 | (n.d.) | Financial Arrangements of the LTC |
| 145/1938 | (n.d.) | Legislative Council—1938 Election of Members |
| 0071 | (n.d.) | Clubs in Lagos, Water Supply to |
| 00124 | (n.d.) | Hausa Compound—Yaba Estate |
| 00125 | (n.d.) | Town Planning Lagos Island |
| 00212 | (n.d.) | Legislative Council Election 1940–1941 |
| Vol. 2 | | Legislative Council Election—1943 |
| Vol. 3 | | Legislative Council Election—1945 |
| 00270 | (n.d.) | LTC Official and Nominated Members, Appointment of |
| 00271 | (n.d.) | LTC Election Wards and Elective Representation |
| 00278 | (n.d.) | LTC Election 1938 |
| 00279 | (n.d.) | LTC Election 1935 |
| 00280 | (n.d.) | LTC Election 1932 |
| 00281 | (n.d.) | LTC Election 1929 |
| 00282 | (n.d.) | LTC Election 1926 |
| 00283 | (n.d.) | LTC Election 1923 |

## Bibliography

| | | |
|---|---|---|
| 00284 | (n.d.) | LTC Election 1920 |
| 00285 | (n.d.) | LTC Election 1919 |
| 00290 | (n.d.) | Legislative Council Election 1926 |
| 00291 | (n.d.) | Legislative Council Election 1928 |
| 00292 | (n.d.) | Legislative Council Election 1933 |
| 00293 | (n.d.) | Legislative Council Election 1923 |
| 00312 | (n.d.) | LTC Elections 1941–1942 |
| 551 | (n.d.) | Unemployed Persons in Lagos |
| 00130 | 15/5/51 | Vol. 12 *Annual Reports* 1950–1951 |
| 00130 | (n.d.) | Vol. 13 *Annual Reports* 1951–1952 |
| 00130 | 21/5/53 | Vol. 14 *Annual Reports* 1952–1953 |
| 00130 | 16/6/54 | Vol. 15 *Annual Reports* 1953–1954 |
| 00130 | 4/3/55 | Vol. 16 *Annual Reports* 1954–1955 |
| 00130 | 12/4/56 | Vol. 17 *Annual Reports* 1955–1956 |
| 00130 | 14/6/58 | Vol. 18 *Annual Reports* 1956–1957 |
| 00130 | 20/6/58 | Vol. 19 *Annual Reports* 1957–1958 |
| 00130 | 5/8/59 | Vol. 20 *Annual Reports* 1958–1959 |
| 00130 | 14/3/60 | Vol. 21 *Annual Reports* 1959–1960 |

Minutes of monthly council meetings
Minutes of meetings of council subcommittees

National Archives of Nigeria, Ibadan:

Gwam, L. C. "Dr. The Hon. Obadiah Johnson, 1849–1920," *Sunday Times,* November 8, 1964.

———. "Dr. Nathaniel Thomas King, 1847–1884," *Sunday Times,* November 15, 1964.

———. "Seamanship—The Hon. Capt. James Pinson Labulo Davies, 1828–1906," *Sunday Times,* January 1, 1965.

———. "Dr. Mojola Agbebi, Hon. 1860–1917," *Sunday Times,* November 1, 1964.

———. "The Rt. Rev. Bishop Isaac Oluwole, 1852–1932," *Sunday Times,* December 6, 1964.

———. "Dr. H. Carr, 1863–1945," *Sunday Times,* October 18, 1964.

———. "The Hon. Christopher Alexander Sapara Williams, 1855–1915," *Sunday Times,* October 25, 1964.

———. "Dr. Hon. John Augustus Otonba Payne, 1839–1906," *Sunday Times,* November 29, 1964.

The Commission of Colony Office, Lagos (Reference no.: Comcol. I):

| Serial no. | File no. | Subject | Date |
|---|---|---|---|
| 98 | 50 | Jam'at Party of Muslims | 1935/1954 |
| 514 | 248/3 | Lagos Native Council | 1938 |
| 515 | 248/4 | Nigerian Youth Political Movement | 1938 |
| 530 | 248/24 | Faji Market Women Vendors' Guild | 1939 |
| 592 | 248/96 | Islamic Society of Nigeria | 1942/43 |
| 4203 | 3045/S.7./Vol. I | Local Government Reforms | 1949/50 |
| 4217 | 3045/S.22 | Transfer of Lagos from West | 1954 |
| 4827 | 3500 | Lagos Area Council | 1950 |
| 608 | 248/121 | Lagos Market Women's Union | 1943 |
| 735 | 375 | Lagos Town Council Elections | 1924/47 |
| 745 | 387/Vol. II | Markets in Lagos Township | 1941/57 |
| 906 | 587/Vol. II | Ahmadiya Movement in Islam | 1941/51 |
| 1049 | 636 | Lagos Minor Political Matters re Eleko | 1928/29 |

| 1053 | 644/Vol. 1 | Chief Obanikoro, Misc. | 1928/33 |
| 2199 | 1349 | Lagos Muslim Community, Central Mosque Judgments | 1919/39 |
| 2263 | 1420 | Hausas in Lagos | 1932–56 |
| 2283 | 1447/Vol. I | Family of Docemo | 1933–53 |
| 2284 | 1447/Vol. II | Family of Docemo | 1953–55 |
| 2293 | 1465 | People's Union | 1932–33 |
| 2304 | 1491 | Ilorin Community in Lagos | 1932–53 |
| 2628 | 1741 | Northern Communities in Lagos | 1922–49 |
| 2629 | 1741/1 | Beriberi Community in Lagos | 1944–46 |
| 2630 | 1741/S.2 | Heads of Northern Communities in Lagos | 1945–50 |
| 5448 | 3844 | Balogunship of Lagos Muslims | 1954 |

Nomination papers of candidates for Lagos Town Council elections, 1932–1965

Private papers of Herbert Macaulay.

Reports and memoranda distributed to members of local branches of major political parties in Lagos.

Yesufu, T. M. "Labour in the Nigerian Economy." Lecture delivered on Nigerian Broadcasting Corporation program, October 1967. Mimeographed. Ministry of Information, Lagos.

———. "Manpower and Educational Objectives for Nigeria's Reconstruction and Development." Paper read at Conference on National Reconstruction and Development, University of Ibadan, March 1969.

NIGERIAN NEWSPAPERS

*Daily Comet*
*Daily Express*
*Daily Service*
*Daily Sketch*
*Daily Telegraph*
*Daily Times*
*Lagos Daily News*
*Lagos Weekend*
*Lagos Weekly Record*

*Morning Post*
*New Nigerian*
*Nigerian Outlook*
*Nigerian Pioneer*
*Nigerian Tribune*
*Sunday Post*
*Sunday Times*
*West African Pilot*

# Index

Abagbon chiefs (warriors), 140, 203, 345 n. 3

Abakaliki, 225

Abayomi, Sir Kofo, 185–186, 308, 326 n. 63, 330 nn. 6, 9, 335 n. 31, 343 nn. 52, 53

Abayomi, Lady Olayinka, 235, 332 n. 16, 335 n. 31

Abeokuta: return of liberated slaves to, 21; refugees from, 22, 30, 159, 325 n. 58; and immigration, 36, 64; councilors from, 68. *See also* Egba people

Abijo, Pa, 336 n. 51

Abiodun, Chief Yesufu, the Oniru of Lagos, 327 n. 69

Aborigines of Lagos and Colony Provinces, 260

Aburi, Ghana, 265

Action Group: party finances, 88; and land, 98; as a political vehicle of indigenes, 111, 274, 279; strategy against Azikiwe, 121–122; launched in Lagos, 123–124; NCNC assessment of, 138; and Area Councils, 141, 215; internal structure of, 142–148; ward breakdown of support for, 157–162; and constitutional status of Lagos, 170, 250, 252–254, 255, 260, 261, 263, 266–267; position regarding council representation of chiefs, 175–176; and appointment of town clerk, 179; and market women, 236–240; and *Rapson Report*, 236–238; and local government reforms, 238–249; ward leaders of, 337 n. 59; mentioned, 58, 67, 72, 117, 186, 217, 218, 308, 330 n. 7, 332 nn. 19, 22, 23, 333 n. 25, 334 nn. 29, 30, 335 nn. 31, 32, 337 nn. 61, 66, 349 nn. 21, 25, 350 n. 15, 352 n. 37

Adebola, H. P., 121, 137, 296, 298, 301, 329 n. 90, 332 n. 19

Adedoyin, Adeleke, 121–123, 169, 178, 214, 287, 289, 332 n. 19

Adelabu, Adegoke, 88, 322 n. 28, 334 n. 30

Adele I, oba of Lagos, 213 fig. 2, 347 n. 26

Adele II, Adeniji, oba of Lagos: and Area Councils, 60, 118–119, 120, 121, 140–141; and Ahmadiya sect, 106; supported AG, 124; withdrew support from AG, 126; opposed within traditional community, 128; and succession dispute, 214–218; and market women, 235; mentioned, 58, 111, 192, 213 fig. 2, 219, 221, 235, 236, 243, 248, 261, 288, 308, 331 n. 11, 332 n. 23, 347 nn. 26, 29

Adeniji-Jones, Dr. C. C.: political profile of, 57–58; ally of Macaulay, 90; refused to support NCNC, 91; mentioned 56, 286, 323 n. 39, 324 n. 42

Adeniji-Jones, Dr. O., 191, 344 n. 59

Adeyemo, J. A., 342 n. 33

Ado, oba of Lagos , 203

Afolabi, Chief, 336 n. 51

African cities: study of, 1–6; prevailing views of and communalism, 282–284. *See also* Urbanization

African Continental Bank, 136, 139

*African Morning Post*, 331 n. 10

AG. *See* Action Group

AG Women's Wing, 142

AG Youth Association, 142, 146, 254

Agbebi, George D., 50, 286

Agbebi, Majola, 50

Agbon-Magbe Bank, 146

Agege, 31

Agege market, 227, 348 nn. 8, 9

Agger, Robert E., 314 n. 23

371

# Index

Aguiyi-Ironsi, J. T. U., 241, 262, 333 n. 25, 349 nn. 30, 32

Agusto, Alhaji L. B.: and Muslim education, 77; and Ahmadiya sect, 106–107

Ahmadiya congregation, 106–107, 109, 111, 124, 128, 141, 145, 216, 259

Ahmadiya Movement in Islam. *See* Ahmadiya congregation; Sadr Anjuman Ahmadiya

Ahmed, Mirza Ghulam, 106

Ajao, J. A., 145

Ajasa, Sir Kitoyi, 56, 78, 91, 108, 164

Ajaye (wife of the Olofin), 18

Ajayi, J. F. Ade, 345 n. 1, 346 nn. 6, 9

Ajegunle, 31, 317 n. 30, 321 n. 20

Ajose, K. R., 107

Ajose, Professor Oladele, 217, 267

Akarigbere chiefs (kingmakers), 140, 203, 345 n. 3

Akinbiyi, D. M. O., 122, 179–180, 342 n. 28, 349 n. 21

Akinola, R. A., 316 n. 24, 317 n. 39

Akinsanya, Samuel, 330 n. 9

Akinshemoyin, oba of Lagos, 204, 213 fig. 2, 346 n. 4

Akintan, E. A., 323 n. 34

Akintola, S. L., 129, 330 n. 6, 333 n. 25, 335 n. 31

Akinwumi, S. O., 337 n. 59

Akinyede, Chief Gilbert B. A., 186, 337 n. 59

Akitoye, oba of Lagos: and the slave trade, 19–20; and British rule, 26; granted Ologbo district to Saros, 26, 95; and succession dispute, 205–208; mentioned, 213 fig. 2, 307, 323 n. 34, 351 n. 32

Akus, 21

Alaga, Madam Sinotu, 239

Alagas (market chairmen), 230–231

Alakija, Lady, 332 n. 16

Alakija, Sir Adeyemo, 78, 91, 92, 108, 215, 324 n. 42, 332 n. 16

Alakija, O., 115, 286

Alakoro, 140

Alayabiagba market, 234, 321 n. 22

Ali, Mohammed, 320 n. 8

Al-Koranic congregation, 105–109. *See also* Koranic, congregation Al-; Shakiti people

All-Nigerian Muslim Council, 107

Almond, Gabriel A., 313 n. 8, 338 n. 1

Amaros: origin of, 22, 27–29; status in

Lagos, 30; tax imposed on by Oba Kosoko, 206; mentioned, 66

Amos, Ladipo, 335 n. 31

Anber, Paul, 321 n. 19, 353 n. 3

Ani, Michael, 180, 181

Anibaba, Alhaji, 349 n. 29

Animashaun, Adam Idris, 128, 327 n. 75

Ansar-ud-Deen Society, 109–110, 111, 259, 328 n. 80

Anti-Slavery and Aborigines Protection Society, 115

Anton, Thomas J., 314 n. 25

Anyiam, Chief Fred, 125, 139, 289, 305, 336 n. 45

Apapa: functional zone, 35–36; residence patterns in, 44; voting patterns of, 158–159; mentioned, 97, 153

Apapa land case, 96–97, 108, 325 n. 54. *See also* Oluwa, Chief

Apapa market, 227, 232, 348 n. 9

Araromi, 44

Area Councils: formation of, 118–119, 120–121; internal structure of, 140–141; mentioned, 59–60, 123, 142, 215, 235, 308, 331 nn. 11, 16, 334 n. 29

Aroloya, 105, 107

Aromire, Chief, 97

Ashipa (originator of Lagos dynasties), 18, 203

Association of Central Lagos Residents, 327 n. 69

Association of House Owners and Tenants, 326 n. 69

Association of Land Owners and Residents of Central Lagos, 186

Association of LCC Senior Service Officers, 181

Association of the Descendants of Lagos Chiefs. *See* Egbe Omo Oba

Atini, 213 fig. 2, 347 n. 26

Atlanta, Georgia, 7

Awa, Eme O., 332 n. 18

A Ward Ratepayers' Association, *See* A Ward Voters' Association

A Ward Voters' Association, 120, 331 n. 16

Awe, B., 347 n. 1

Awolowo, Chief Obafemi: opinion of press, 79; and Macaulay, 92; and local government reforms, 123; and electoral success of AG, 126; threatened secession of the Western Region, 253–254; life of, 332 n. 25; criticism of Azikiwe, 334 n. 28; mentioned, 129,

# Index

Gabaro, oba of Lagos, 203, 213 fig. 2
Gaiser Ltd., G. L., 131
Gbadamosi, Alhaji S. O., 335 n. 31
Geary, W. N. M., 316 nn. 19, 20, 322 n. 32, 346 nn. 9, 12, 13, 14, 15, 19
*Gedegbe L'eko Wa* (Lagos is Free), 254, 350 n. 20
General Sanitary Board, 164
Gilbert, C. W., 314 n. 23
Giwa, W. A., 336 n. 46
Glover, Sir John: attitude toward Oba Docemo, 25–26; opinion of Saros, 26; and Lagos development, 30; and settlement of Abeokuta refugees, 30, 326 n. 58
Gold Coast Colony, 23
Goldrich, Daniel, 314 n. 23
Goodluck, Wahab, 129, 329 n. 90. *See also* Labor
Gould, Julius, 314 n. 19
Government Offices Sitting Committee, 168
Gowan, Yakubu, 263, 333 n. 25
Gusfield, Joseph R., 354 n. 4
Gutkind, P. C. W., 1, 313 n. 3, 321 n. 17, 329 n. 89

Hailey, Lord, 91, 316 n. 4, 323 n. 37
Hakim, F, R., 107
Hanna, Judith Lyne, 314 n. 24, 315 nn. 28, 30, 34
Hanna, William John, 314 n. 24, 315 nn. 28, 30, 34
Hausa people: population of, 39; residence patterns of, 44; introduced Islam in Lagos, 105–106; mentioned, 112, 129, 159, 256, 317 n. 42, 335 n. 38, 347 n. 26
Hauser, Phillip M., 314 n. 18
Herberg, Will, 328 n. 83
Hodder, B. W., 347 n. 1
Hodgkin, Thomas, 329 n. 87, 335 n. 42, 336 n. 43
*Hoskyns-Abrahall Report*, 183, 309, 327 n. 71, 339 n. 10, 342 n. 42
Hunponu-Wusu, Chief S. T., 129
Hunter, Floyd, 315 nn. 26, 29
Huntington, Samuel P., 314 n. 12

Ibadan: rival of Lagos, 4; councilors from, 68; headquarters of AG, 123; mentioned, 88, 314 n. 17, 334 n. 30, 347 n. 1
Ibibio people, 45, 317 n. 42

Ibn-Nalla, Ligali, 108. *See also* Nalla, Ligali ibn-
Ibo National Progress and Welfare Association, 335 n. 34
Ibo people: in Lagos, 38; and religion, 39–40; residence patterns of, 44; urban influence of, 83–87; ethnic solidarity of, 112; and NCNC success, 121; and NCNC leadership, 125–126; NNDP (new) strategy against, 130–131; and party identification, 137, 139; and ward voting patterns, 157–162; mentioned, 59–60, 64, 81, 92, 138, 160, 228, 254, 256, 273, 274, 317 n. 30, 318 n. 20, 321 nn. 17, 18, 19, 20, 21, 22, 24, 329 n. 85, 334 n. 28, 335 n. 34, 353 n. 3
Ibo State Union, 83, 125, 137
Iddo: functional zone, 36; voting patterns in, 159–160; mentioned, 17, 97
Iddo market, 233, 234, 321 n. 22
Idejo chiefs, 17, 90, 94–97, 108, 140, 346 n. 3. *See also* White Cap chiefs
Idera market, 225
Idewu-Ojulari, oba of Lagos, 203, 213 fig. 2
Idumagbo. *See* Isale Eko; Lagos Island; Slum clearance
Idumagbo market, 224–225
Idunmota, 17
Ife, Madam, 349 n. 29
Ifedirah, Madam M., 349 n. 29
Iganmu, 158–159
Ijaw people, 39, 112
Ijebu: people, 11, 204, 225; immigrants in Lagos, 17, 36, 64; allied with Oba Kosoko, 19; councilors from, 68; property owners, 87
Ijora, 97, 158–159
Ikeja, 31, 131, 246, 259, 308, 339 n. 7
Ikeja Area Planning Authority, 172
Ikoli, Ernest, 78, 79, 330 nn. 6, 9
Ikorodu, 138
Ikoyi: residence patterns in, 29, 44; functional zone, 35; voting patterns in, 160; mentioned, 30, 101, 153
Ile-Ife, 17
Ilorin, 69, 105, 109
Ilu Committee, 140, 203, 204
Immigration. *See* Urbanization
Imoudu, Michael, 129, 329 n. 90. *See also* Labor
Imrie, Sir John, 181
*Imrie Report*, 196, 309, 342 nn. 36, 39.

376

# Index

Muslim religion

Municipal and Local Authorities Workers' Union, 181

Mushin, 31, 317 n. 30, 321 n. 20

Mushin market, 227, 348 n. 8

Muslim religion: and descendants of liberated slaves, 21; strength of, 39–40; social significance of among indigenes, 45, 111; representation of on council, 52, 67, 68–73, 70 fig. 1; and educational deprivation, 76–77; and Jam'at congregation, 89; urban growth of, 105–110; and ward voting patterns, 157–162; and market women, 228, 243, 273; and polygamy, 327 n. 74, mentioned, 59, 124, 282, 322 nn. 29, 33, 327 nn. 75, 78, 331 n. 10, 337 n. 57

Muslim Welfare Association, 128

Nabale, Uganda, 9

Nalla, Ligali ibn-. *See* Ibn-Nalla, Ligali

National Bank of Nigeria, 58, 146

National Congress of British West Africa, 115

National Convention of Nigerian Citizens: and the nationalist elite, 56–59; Macaulay president of, 92; allied with NNDP (old), 117–118, 120–121; lack of appeal among indigenes, 118; split with NNDP (old), 121–123; decline of, 124–128; affiliated with NEPU, 129; internal structure of, 135–140; compared with AG, 148; ward breakdown of support for, 157–162; argued for federalization of Lagos, 252, 254; supported statehood, 259; mentioned, 59–60, 67, 83, 170, 175–176, 178, 179, 186, 215, 216, 218, 221, 235, 238, 239, 248, 249, 250, 252, 261, 274, 308, 324 nn. 40, 42, 330 nn. 7, 8, 332 nn. 16, 19, 23, 334 n. 29, 335 nn. 32, 33, 34, 36, 336 nn. 44, 45, 46, 47, 48, 51, 337 nn. 57, 63, 341 n. 25, 349 nn. 21, 25, 29, 352 n. 37

National Council of Nigeria and the Cameroons. *See* National Convention of Nigerian Citizens

National Council of Women's Societies, 348 n. 14

National Emergency Committee, 58, 59, 119, 318 n. 16

Native foreigners: referred to as Oyinbos, 15, 22; and community power structure, 49–55; defined, 51, 317 n. 1; sources of elite status, 75–80; mentioned, 150, 272, 280, 318 n. 5. *See also* Elites; Emigrants; Saros

Nayyar, Abd-ur-Rahman, 106, 107

NCNC. *See* National Convention of Nigerian Citizens

NCNC Elements' Shomolu Union, 335 n. 35

NCNC Market Women's Association, 128, 236, 239. *See also* NCNC Women's Association

NCNC Market Women's Wing. *See* NCNC Market Women's Association

NCNC Women's Association, 136, 137, 239

NCNC Youth Association, 136, 137

NEPU. *See* Northern Elements' Progressive Union

New Dehli, India, 349 n. 3

New Haven, Conn., 10, 276

*New Nigerian*, 80

Nigerian Building Society, 194, 344 n. 68

Nigerian Civil War, 38

Nigerian Federation of Labour, 329 n. 90

Nigerian Labour Congress, 59, 120, 235

Nigerian Labour Party, 129

Nigerian Legislative Council: African members of, 51; NNDP monopoly of elective seats on, 116; and NYM electoral victory, 117; voting regulations for, 149; mentioned, 57, 78, 118–119, 165, 185, 248, 272, 308, 323 n. 39, 330 nn. 2, 4, 331 n. 15, 339 n. 7

Nigerian Motor Drivers' Union, 181

Nigerian Muslim Council, 107

Nigerian National Alliance, 127

Nigerian National Democratic Party (new): establishment of, 129–133; and market women, 239, 241; mentioned, 333 n. 25, 352 n. 37

Nigerian National Democratic Party (old): allied with NCNC, 57; and 1950 council election, 59–60; and the *Daily Times*, 78; and Herbert Macaulay, 90–91; origin of, 116–118, 120; split with NCNC, 122–123; internal structure of, 133–135; dominated Lagos elections, 149; and market women, 235; mentioned, 108, 137, 214, 221, 308, 323 n. 39, 325 n. 54, 330 nn.

# Index

Oluwa, Chief, 90, 97, 134, 322 nn. 32, 34, 325 n. 55. *See also* Tijani, Amodu

Onikoyi, C. B., 336 n. 45

Onikoyi, Chief, 97

Onipede, Dr. F. O., 267

Oniru, Chief, 97

Onisiwo, Chief, 97

Onitiri, S. A., 337 n. 59

Oparah, G., 125, 296, 298, 302, 305, 340 n. 19

Orewa, G. O., 341 n. 26

Orlu, 138

Oshodi, Abiola A., 336 nn. 45, 46

Oshodi, Adisa, 236–238 *passim*

Otegbeye, Dr. Tunji, 129

Ottun, Muhammad Raji Bakrin, 128

Ouidah (Whydah), Dahomey, 19

Owerri, 38

Oyekan I, oba of Lagos, 210, 213 fig. 2, 351 n. 32

Oyekan II, Adeyinka, oba of Lagos: as NCNC candidate, 120; and succession dispute, 214–218; fought for a Lagos state, 262–265; mentioned, 213 fig. 2, 220, 235, 264, 308, 327 n. 69, 332 n. 16, 345 n. 1, 347 nn. 25, 26, 31

Oyingbo market, 227, 232, 233

Oyo: empire, 18; ally of Oba Kosoko, 19; and immigration, 36; councilors from, 68; mentioned, 204, 225, 323 n. 34

Palma, 20, 207, 209, 307

Parkin, David, 313 n. 7

Payne, John A., 316 nn. 8, 22

Pearse, Elizabeth, 57

Pearse, James, 57

Pearse, S. H., 90, 115, 144, 164, 165

Pelewura, Madam Alimotu, 90, 134, 234

Peoples' Union, 115

Perham, Margery, 317 n. 4, 323 n. 34, 344 n. 61

Plunkett, George Washington, 93, 325 n. 46

Polsby, Nelson W., 314 n. 23

Popo Aguda (Brazilian Quarter), 28. *See also* Amaros

Port of Lagos, 32–34, 245. *See also* Nigerian Ports Authority

Porto Novo, Dahomey, 204

Portuguese: exploration of Lagos, 17; and the slave trade, 18; expelled by the British, 19; supported Oba Ko-soko, 19; and Amaro culture, 27; area of Lagos, 27–29; mentioned, 204, 208, 346 n. 4

Post, Ken, 334 n. 29

Powdermaker, Hortense, 313 n. 7

Prest, Arthur, 335 n. 31

Presthus, Robert, 314 n. 23, 315 n. 29

*Price Report*, 309, 346 n. 23

Public Health Department, 171–172, 177, 190–191, 233

Rabinowitz, Francine, 314 n. 24

Randle, Dr. John, 108, 115

*Rapson Report*, 236–239 *passim*; 309, 335 n. 37, 348 n. 21, 349 n. 22

Reform Club, 115

Reis, Mrs. A., 349 n. 29

Reissman, Leonard, 314 n. 19

Residence patterns: and class structure, 43–45; correlated with voting behavior, 154–156

Rewane, Alfred, 335 n. 31

Ribadu, Alhaji Mohammadu, 131, 308, 351 n. 27. *See also* Ministry of Lagos Affairs

Riordon, William L., 325 n. 46

Rocha, C. J. da. *See* Da Rocha, C. J.

Rocha, Dr. Moses da. *See* Da Rocha, Dr. Moses

Roman Catholic Mission, 189. *See also* Catholicism; Christianity

Rowat, Donald, 349 n. 1

Rudolph, L. I., 354 n. 4

Rudolph, S. H., 354 n. 4

Sadipe, Bola, 336 n. 45

Sadr Anjuman Ahmadiya, 107. *See also* Ahmadiya Movement in Islam

*Sagoe Tribunal Report*, 186, 309, 322 n. 24, 326 n. 62, 343 nn. 51, 54

Salami, B. B., 336 n. 48

Sardauna of Sokoto. *See* Bello, Alhaji Ahmadu, Sardauna of Sokoto

Saros: established community, 24, 26; acquired land, 26, 95; compared with Amaros, 27–28; cultural duality of, 27; and Oba Kosoko, 206; mentioned, 21, 28, 30, 66, 330 n. 6

Saro Town, 26–27. *See also* Olowogbowo

Sauer, Warren L., 315 n. 28

Savage, Dr. Akinwande, 115

Savage, "Daddy" William Akilade, 26, 50

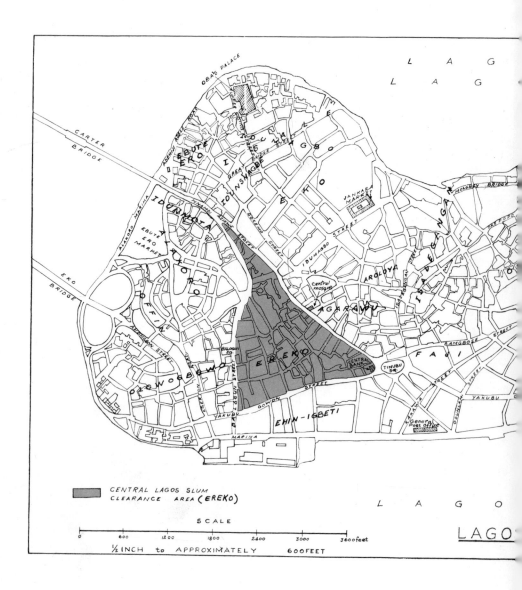

CENTRAL LAGOS SLUM
CLEARANCE AREA (EREKO)

SCALE

0    600    1200    1800    2400    3000    3600 FEET

½ INCH to APPROXIMATELY 600 FEET